FIRST
TO THE
RHINE

FIRST
TO THE
RHINE

THE 6TH ARMY GROUP
IN WORLD WAR II

HARRY YEIDE
AND
MARK STOUT

ZENITH PRESS

To those Americans and Frenchmen who fought then, including Riley Mayhall, who was at Crailsheim with the 10th Armored Division, and to those Americans and Frenchmen who today risk their lives side by side in Afghanistan in the cause of freedom.

First published in 2007 by Zenith Press, an imprint of MBI Publishing Company LLC, Galtier Plaza, Suite 200, 380 Jackson Street, St. Paul, MN 55101 USA

Zenith Press titles are also available at discounts in bulk quantity for industrial or sales-promotional use. For details write to Special Sales Manager at MBI Publishing Company, Galtier Plaza, Suite 200, 380 Jackson Street, St. Paul, MN 55101 USA.

To find out more about our books, join us online at www.zenithpress.com.

Editor: Scott Pearson
Designer: Jennifer Maass

Printed in the United States of America

Library of Congress Cataloging-in-Publication Data

Yeide, Harry.
  First to the Rhine : the 6th Army Group in World War II / by Harry Yeide and Mark Stout.
    p. cm.
  ISBN-13: 978-0-7603-3146-0 (hardbound w/ jacket)
  1. United States. Army. Army Group, 6th—History. 2. World War, 1939–1945—Campaigns—France, Southern. 3. World War, 1939–1945—Regimental histories—United States. I. Stout, Mark, 1964– II. Title.
D769.255.Y45 2007
940.54'1273—dc22

                    2007010125

On the front cover:
Riflemen from the 3d Infantry Division enter Zweibrücken. *NARA, Signal Corps photo*

On the back cover:
American and British comrades rest beside a farmhouse in southern France. *NARA, Signal Corps photo*

CONTENTS

ACKNOWLEDGMENTS

We would like to thank our benevolent spouses, Nancy and Pam, for their loving patience during the time we worked on this book. Thanks to Andrew Rawson for sharing material he has collected on American general officers. We would also like to thank the cheerful and efficient public servants at the National Archives and Records Administration's document, microfilm, and still photo reading rooms in College Park, Maryland. The taxpayer is getting a good deal.

INTRODUCTION

British historian Charles Whiting termed the U.S. Seventh Army "America's forgotten army." The Franco-American 6th Army Group, of which it was a part, has languished in even deeper obscurity. The war in southern France is often rather dismissively recalled as the "champagne campaign." The fighting in the Vosges hides in a historical mist as baffling as the one that often blanketed those mountains. The shorthand description of the war generally runs "after the Battle of the Bulge, the Allies overran Germany"; and the French receive hardly any attention at all in American texts. The truth is that the landings near St. Tropez in August 1944 were more vigorously contested than those in North Africa or at Anzio. Fierce and costly battles raged in the coastal ports and at Montélimar. The Allies first smashed the Germans west of the Rhine in the 6th Army Group's zone; the battles in Alsace in January 1945 nearly destroyed two American armored divisions; the last month of fighting inside Germany cost Seventh Army as many casualties as it suffered during the German *Nordwind* offensive; and the French, for all their problems, carried off many of the dashing successes in southern France and bled just as profusely as their American allies.

Writing history entails innumerable big and little decisions about what to include and what to exclude. We intend this work to be the story of the U.S. Seventh and French First armies and the men who fought in their ranks. As such, it focuses on the Allied side of the conflict and does not attempt to provide equal treatment to the German perspective. The details of the nearly static fighting in the Vosges during October 1944 do not lend themselves to extensive division-by-division discussion in a work such as this. The main actors were often at the battalion and company levels. Readers who wish to explore a more detailed account of the bloody fighting during the period can turn to works such as Franz Steidl's *Lost*

Battalions (Presidio Press, 1997) and Keith Bonn's *When the Odds Were Even* (Presidio Press, 1994). For similar reasons, we have also chosen not to dwell on the lengthy period of French pressure on the Colmar Pocket before the final offensive that crushed it, and various other smaller incidents.

It may not be apparent to the casual reader, but it is difficult to tell exactly what happened so many years ago. Indeed, historians sometimes say that the past is gone, never to be recovered, and a "history" is merely a story we tell about that vanished past. This book exemplifies that principle. Contemporary reports written by separate participants in any given incident are likely to differ, sometimes substantially. This is true in any field of human endeavor, but it is particularly true in the intrinsically confusing domain of warfare. On top of this, later accounts introduce additional flaws of memory or self-justification.

The reader may note that we have relied on substantially different source bases to relate the American and French parts of the story. American military records on the period are fulsome, whereas those of the French available to us—essentially the material reported up the chain of command, such as a few G-3 (operations staff) reports and a virtually complete set of G-2 (intelligence staff) reports—generally are lacking in detail. We have relied more heavily on personal accounts, including those of key commanders, as the basis for the French actions described. Likewise, German military records for key commands are not available to the authors (the collection of captured records at the National Archives is excellent for some formations and completely lacking for others). We have relied heavily on post-war accounts written by German commanders for the U.S. Army's historical division.

We have elected to use acronyms to identify French divisions and regiments (for example, 2d DB for 2d *Division Blindée*, or Armored Division), a practice followed by American forces at the time. We hope that this approach makes it easier for readers to keep track of formations that, because of the large number of colonial troops involved, often bear unusual designators to the eye of the English speaker accustomed to simple American and German formulations such as "1st Infantry Division." A glossary at the end of the book will help readers refresh their memory on the meaning of French acronyms. We have also adopted the U.S.

Army's Center of Military History practice of italicizing German formation designators to improve clarity for the reader.

One note on photographs: Seventh Army was badly served by its Signal Corps photographers. Unfortunately, the moving pictures division at the National Archives refused to convert key Signal Corps film to video, so we could not fill in the pictorial record with frame captures.

We have taken small liberties with texts drawn from the military records and personal accounts to correct grammatical errors and spelling mistakes, and to introduce consistency in references to unit designators, equipment, dates, and so on. Translations from French and German are our own, and we alone are responsible for any errors that may have crept into the text as a result of this process.

We recognize that British forces reached the Rhine delta at Arnheim, which sits above the Nederrijn in Holland below the point where the Rhine gives way to multiple smaller streams, during Operation Market-Garden in September 1944. We are discussing the real thing.

Harry Yeide and Mark Stout
September 2005

CHAPTER 1

AN UNEASY ALLIANCE

The French position in the war was, of course, not an easy one. . . . [T]heir Army as well as their pride had been shattered in the great debacle of 1940. . . .

—Dwight Eisenhower, *Crusade in Europe*

On 6 August 1944, lead bombardiers in a formation of thirty B-26 medium bombers from the 42d Bombardment Wing, Mediterranean Allied Tactical Air Force (MATAF), eyed a five-span, steel-truss railroad bridge across the Rhône River at Arles, France. Weather had scrubbed almost all missions the day before, the first day after MATAF had issued its directive on air support for Operation Dragoon, the Allied invasion of southern France. Today, however, conditions were more than adequate, and 120 thousand-pound bombs whistled downward on cue. Bridges were notoriously difficult to destroy from the air, but luck was with the Americans on this day, and a terrific explosion tore loose much of the eastern-most pier. The second pier crumbled to within fifteen feet of the water, and the third was obliterated to within five feet. The span crashed into the river, and the B-26s winged away, having lost not a single aircraft to German flak.[1]

When B-25s from the 57th Bombardment Wing struck the railroad bridges at Avignon two days later, the flak was thick. One aircraft pulled up and away from the formation, a wing trailing a plume of bright flames. Three parachutes billowed open before the plane nosed downward into a death spiral. The bombardier was lucky enough to get out; he landed in a field, where he was found by the French Resistance, or maquis, before the

Germans could arrive. Dressed as a civilian, he was carefully shepherded into Italy and back to Allied lines.[2]

Shortly thereafter, on 12 August, a team of fifteen American commandos placed plastic explosives on two high-tension electricity towers some ten miles southeast of the German air base at Chabeuil and blew them both. The men had parachuted in five days earlier and joined forces with the Drôme Department maquis elements commanded by Jean-Pierre de Lassus.[3]

Henri Faure listened intently to his illegal radio, monitoring the BBC broadcasts on 13 and 14 August. He heard two phrases that meant a great deal to him: "Nancy has a stiff neck. . . . The war is running." As a member of the Resistance, Faure knew what the phrases meant: full-fledged guerrilla warfare, cutting rail lines and communications. His particular mission was to sever the underground trunk line from Marseille to Paris. Dressed as workers for the government telephone and telegraph service, Faure and a friend set out for the southern outskirts of Valence, on the Rhône River, to carry out their mission. In broad daylight they dug down to the cable as German convoys rolled by a few meters away. After dark, they came back, placed explosives at two points on the cable, and hooked wires to the detonators. Moments later an explosion neatly cut the cable and rendered the line unusable.[4]

* * *

Other Allied aircraft and irregular ground forces were hitting similar targets the length and breadth of southern France. Despite the occasional hiccup, the plan concocted by Allied Forces Headquarters (AFHQ)—the supreme combined command for operations in the Mediterranean—to paralyze German forces in the region was proceeding nicely.

To *Generaloberst* Johannes Blaskowitz, commanding *Army Group G* in southern France, these were "infallible warnings" that an Allied invasion force was on its way. He knew that a rumor was circulating among the French populace that the landings would occur at Fréjus, the same place that Napoleon had reentered France in 1815, and have the same initial goal of reaching Digne and Grenoble.[5]

DECISIONS AND PREPARATIONS

Allied military planners first discussed an invasion of southern France in connection with the Trident summit meeting in Williamsburg,

Virginia, in May 1943, but they dropped the idea as impractical. The American Joint Chiefs of Staff (JCS) in August that year decided to support landings in the Riviera under the initial code name "Operation Anvil" as an adjunct to the planned cross-Channel invasion of Normandy. The JCS proposed that once Italy had been eliminated from the war, Rome captured, and Corsica and Sardinia secured as support bases, Allied forces would land in the Toulon-Marseille area, turn those ports into major supply points, and advance northward up the Rhône River valley.[6] This set the stage for a debate between the British and Americans that lasted until shortly before the landings occurred.

While nuts-and-bolts questions such as the availability of shipping and landing craft offered fertile ground for spirited disagreements, the more basic split was over strategic vision. British prime minister Winston Churchill, who was already considering post-war realities and was deeply distrustful of Soviet dictator Josef Stalin, wanted to retain as many American divisions in Italy as possible to take part in a drive through the Alps to Vienna or into the Balkans. Chief of the Imperial General Staff Gen. Alan Brooke thought the Vienna scheme unworkable, but he also offered sound military arguments against an early Operation Anvil. Winding down fighting in Italy to free divisions, he assessed, would allow the Germans to shift troops to Normandy or the eastern front. The enemy, moreover, could easily move reserves to contain and possibly destroy a beachhead in southern France if it preceded Operation Overlord.[7]

President Franklin Roosevelt and the American chiefs had no interest in pursuing Churchill's Balkan dreams and had long lacked enthusiasm for the Italian campaign. General Dwight "Ike" Eisenhower, supreme commander of Allied forces in the European theater, seemed to waffle a bit between the views of the American and British chiefs, but once his troops were ashore in northwestern France, he offered his own military arguments as to why Anvil should proceed. Ike was intensely interested in the logistic demands posed by his goal of destroying the German armed forces in the west, particularly after the Allied breakout from Normandy in late July. Allied forces had captured only one substantial port in usable condition—Cherbourg—and he badly wanted Marseille and the route up the Rhône valley to accelerate the delivery of divisions and supplies. More than forty divisions were in the pipeline, but they could not be brought to the front through the Normandy logistic bottleneck. The landings would also free Eisenhower's forces advancing across northern France from having to worry about their right flank. Moreover, the American government had gone to considerable expense to train and equip French divisions in North Africa, and the only practical way to get them quickly into battle was through southern France.[8]

The operation was an on-again, off-again affair until 11 June 1944, when the Combined Chiefs of Staff reached the final and necessary agreement to stop the offensive in Italy at the Pisa-Rimini line and to launch Operation Anvil. Although Churchill continued to badger Roosevelt to cancel the landings until a week before they took place, General Brooke made his reluctant peace with the plan once it fit into, as he later wrote, "its right strategic position." Brooke urged Churchill to adopt the attitude, "All right, if you insist on being damned fools, sooner than falling out with you, which would be fatal, we shall be damned fools with you, and we shall see that we perform the role of damned fools damned well!" [9]

* * *

The operation was code-named "Anvil" for most of its developmental history, but on 1 August, on orders from the Combined Chiefs of Staff, the name was changed to Dragoon, because the Allies feared that the original code name had been compromised.[10] Field Order 1 for Operation Dragoon, issued on 5 August, instructed Seventh Army, supported by Western Naval Task Force and XII Tactical Air Command (TAC), plus MATAF assets as requested, to land in southern France east of Toulon, then capture that city.

In broad outline, the Anvil/Dragoon plan called for a reinforced three-division assault under the control of Maj. Gen. Lucian Truscott's VI Corps, which was in turn subordinated to Lt. Gen. Alexander "Sandy" Patch's Seventh Army, which reported directly to AFHQ. Truscott's troops were to seize a forty-five-mile section of the Côte d'Azur east of Toulon that stretched from Cavalaire-sur-Mer northeastward to Agay. French II

Corps, commanded by General of the Army (*General*) Jean-Marie de Lattre de Tassigny, which was temporarily subordinated to Seventh Army, was to land in the secured beachhead and strike westward to capture Toulon and Marseille while VI Corps protected the right flank. Another French corps was to come ashore as transportation from North Africa allowed. Planners assessed that Toulon could handle sufficient cargo to supply the consolidation of a bridgehead and that the capture of Marseille was necessary to support an exploitation northward.

The command setup was a bit odd; it took into account political factors involving the French, but only so late in the game as to all but guarantee tensions down the road. The Americans and British had made most of the key Anvil decisions without even consulting the French, who were expected to provide more than half the divisions for the operation. British Field Marshal Henry Maitland "Jumbo" Wilson, Supreme Allied Commander in the Mediterranean, first briefed the French commander in chief, Gen. Henri Giraud, on 7 March 1944. Giraud fruitlessly objected to the idea that an American was to command; he assured Wilson that, despite France's defeat in 1940, the performance of French troops in Italy had proved that there were still some competent French generals.

Allied Forces Headquarters planners and American commanders rejected subsequent proposals by Gen. Charles de Gaulle, president of the French Committee of National Liberation, that a French general serve as senior ground commander or at least hold the deputy-commander job. De Gaulle badly wanted to recover French military prestige, but he had few cards to play in negotiations. A compromise gradually emerged under which de Lattre, heretofore commanding French Army B, was to temporarily command French II Corps under Seventh Army control. On D+6, French Army B was to be nominally activated above II Corps but still be subordinate to Seventh Army, even once a second French corps entered the line. At some point to be determined by Wilson and Eisenhower, 6th Army Group, under the command of Lt. Gen. Jacob "Jake" Devers, heretofore deputy supreme commander in the Mediterranean, was to step in above the two armies, and de Lattre's command would become the French First Army.[11]

Allied Forces and Plans

The Allied force that was assigned the landings when the operation was formally given the green light on 14 June was formidable indeed.[12]

6th Army Group

The 6th Army Group Headquarters, commanded by Devers, was activated on 1 August 1944 in the small port of Bastia, on Corsica.[13] At its creation, the army group commanded no field forces; it was established with an eye toward the future.

Jake Devers was a field artilleryman, born in York, Pennsylvania, in 1887. An athletic, trim officer with a cleft all-American chin, Devers was a West Point graduate and classmate of George Patton Jr. Devers served at various field posts and taught at his alma mater, and he had been greatly disappointed to miss combat duty in World War I. United States Army Chief of Staff Gen. George Marshall tapped Devers for promotion to brigadier general in early 1940 after meeting him in Panama. Devers joined Marshall's staff at the War Department shortly thereafter; he had his second star before the end of the year. Marshall in August 1941 named Devers chief of the Armored Force, and he guided its rapid expansion to a war footing. In May 1943, Marshall sent Devers, by then a lieutenant general, to London as commanding general of the European Theater of Operations (ETO), an assignment that developed in him a distaste for the politicking behind coalition warfare. When Eisenhower was appointed supreme commander of the Allied Expeditionary Force for the invasion of France, Devers moved to the Mediterranean theater, where he arrived in early January 1944, as deputy Allied commander under Field Marshal Wilson.[14]

The 6th Army Group staff was an all-American operation rather than a joint command. American commanders reasoned that the French did not understand American staff organization, procedures, or supply and evacuation systems, and there was no time to teach them. American officers who had helped rearm the French, by contrast, understood their system well enough. The French also lacked experienced officers and were to prove unable to ever fully staff even their large liaison operation at 6th Army Group headquarters. Devers wherever practicable compensated by selecting for his own staff officers who had worked with the French before.[15] He named former senator Henry Cabot Lodge Jr., a Francophile with good political instincts, as his liaison officer to the French army.

Seventh Army

Lieutenant General Alexander "Sandy" Patch, who commanded Seventh Army, was new to the Mediterranean theater. He had earned his senior command spurs leading the American Division, then XIV Corps on Guadalcanal in the Pacific. Born in 1889, the infantry officer had been a West Point classmate of Devers and fought with Gen. John Pershing in Mexico. Thin, wiry, and forthright, Patch spoke quickly and wielded a dry sense of humor.[16]

VI Corps

Major General Lucian Truscott, commanding VI Corps, was a cavalry officer who attributed to that background his deep belief in the value of speed in military operations. He had served on the Mexican border, had experience in the 1st Armored Division, and had helped plan the landings in North Africa; he commanded an infantry regiment during the actual assault. He had also served as commanding general of the 3d Infantry Division during the fighting in North Africa, become VI Corps deputy commander in January 1944, and been promoted to corps command a month later in the midst of the Anzio beachhead fighting. Given the freedom of senior rank, Truscott adopted eccentric dress: a shiny enameled helmet, a weather-stained jacket, a white scarf, and faded cavalry breeches. His corps was deeply engaged in battle until mid-June, leaving the staff little time to prepare for the new venture.

Truscott was allowed to choose the divisions he would take into France. He first selected the 3d ("Rock of the Marne," or "Blue and White Devils") and the 45th ("Thunderbird") Infantry divisions, because they were the most experienced in Italy and had already conducted amphibious assaults. Truscott next tapped the 36th ("T-Patch") Infantry Division because of its excellent performance after the breakout from the Anzio beachhead in early June, a success that he hoped had chased away the mental ghosts caused by bloody setbacks at the Salerno beachhead and the Rapido River crossing.[17]

Truscott's former assistant division commander, Maj. Gen. John "Iron Mike" O'Daniel, a former enlisted man in the National Guard who as an infantry officer had been wounded in World War I, led the 3d Infantry Division. Truscott described O'Daniel as "a rugged, gruff-voiced Irishman, who thoroughly enjoyed fighting and had no equal in bulldog tenacity or as a fighting infantry division commander."[18] Addressing his men before the landings, O'Daniel yelled out, "You can take it from me, boys—hate the Germans! Hate the bastards! Cut your initials in their goddamned faces!"[19] This forthright attitude and hostility to the Germans soon made O'Daniel a favorite of the French commanders with whom he dealt. The division, which had earned the appellation "Rock of the Marne" during the Great War, had first fought in this war in North Africa and—after Morocco, Sicily, and Anzio—considered beach assaults old hat.[20]

Major General John Dahlquist, an infantry officer who lacked combat experience in this war, had recently taken charge of the 36th Infantry Division. Dahlquist nevertheless had, as a young lieutenant, fought in the Vosges Mountains, in eastern France, in the Great War. He had served as deputy chief of staff at the European theater headquarters in London in 1942 and subsequently commanded the 70th Infantry Division during its activation before taking charge of the T-Patch division after its Rapido River crossing fiasco.[21] Dahlquist was personally unpleasant, often dour and rude, and was not well liked by his own men.[22] The 36th Division, a federalized National Guard outfit, had participated in the landings at Salerno and had immense experience with mountain fighting, although losses in Italy had been high, and many of the riflemen were replacements.

Major General William Eagles, another infantry officer who had previously served under Truscott, commanded the 45th Infantry Division. Truscott considered Eagles to be intelligent, well trained, professionally competent, and liked by his subordinates, but he did not view him to be an outstanding battle leader.[23] The division, also federalized from the National Guard, traced its roots back to the Indian wars on the American frontier; its shoulder patch for many years was a three-armed swastika—an Indian good-luck symbol—which it abandoned for a thunderbird when Hitler established the Third Reich. The division experienced its baptism of fire during the landings on Sicily, and it formed one of the assault units again during the Salerno landings. After clawing its way nearly halfway up the Italian peninsula, the 45th Division had been transferred to the Anzio beachhead in January 1944 and entered Rome on 3 June.[24]

Each division had attached to it a separate tank battalion, a self-propelled tank destroyer battalion, three battalions of corps artillery, and miscellaneous support units to keep it running after leaving the beaches.[25] With the attached armor, the truck-rich American infantry divisions were the rough equivalent of full-strength German panzergrenadier divisions.[26] After the three selected divisions withdrew from the line in Italy, their men quickly developed a sense of world-weary common purpose during training around Naples, where they drank together in the bars, sweating in wool combat uniforms, and disparaged or fought the rear-area types, who were instantly identifiable by their comfortable cotton attire. "There is an indescribable feeling of camaraderie that exists in the infantry among men who have fought in the mud, sweated out the 88s and the burp guns together, and eaten K-rations day in and day out up at the front," recalled one regimental history.[27]

Truscott had no American armored division despite his mission to mount a mobile offensive deep into enemy territory. The 1st Armored Division in Italy had to stay there, so for Operation Dragoon, Combat Command 1—generally referred to as CC1, or CC Sudre after its commander, Brig. Gen. Aimé Sudre—from the French 1st Armored Division (1st *Division Blindée*, 1st DB) was attached to VI Corps. Truscott contemplated using Sudre's command to drive up the Route Napoleon from the coast, but a testy exchange in late July with General de Lattre over how long he could keep the tanks convinced Truscott that he would be unable to rely on the French armor.[28]

Truscott decided instead to improvise a combat command, and on 1 August he created a provisional armored group led by his assistant corps commander, Brig. Gen. Frederic Butler. Born in 1896, Butler was an engineer who had previously served as assistant commander of the 34th Infantry Division. The formation, generally referred to as Butler Task Force, consisted of an infantry battalion, a cavalry reconnaissance squadron, two companies of medium tanks and one of tank destroyers, a field artillery battalion, and assorted other units. Butler Task Force in strength closely approximated an American combat command, which was usually built around a battalion each of tanks and armored infantry. The command would form at Le Muy on order once VI Corps was established ashore. Butler and his hastily gathered staff set to work planning for various contingencies, including an advance up the Route Napoleon toward Grenoble to block roads east of the Rhône River near Montélimar.[29]

Special Operations

A Special Projects Operations Center (SPOC) in Algiers controlled most Allied commando activities—some thirty teams in all—in southern France. The SPOC included British, American, and French personnel. Although not subordinated to any of the commands that would land in Operation Dragoon, the SPOC accepted directives from Supreme Headquarters Allied Expeditionary Force (SHAEF), AFHQ, and Seventh Army. In late June, a spinoff—Number 4 Special Forces Group—consisting of sixty-six French-speaking British and American personnel was created and attached to Seventh Army's headquarters to oversee French Resistance and related commando support for the ground troops.[30]

From 6 through 30 June, seven "Jedburgh teams" (named after a castle where they trained) parachuted into southern France, as did two American Office of Strategic Services (OSS) operational groups. Jedburgh teams, originally conceived and organized by the British, were small military liaison and operational staffs consisting of a commander, a second in command, and a noncommissioned radio operator; their job was to advise the maquis or to direct guerrilla operations when necessary. Teams were typically multinational but often had officers who were British, American, or French. The OSS teams were usually fifteen-man combat groups that consisted of French-speaking soldiers who either worked beside the maquis or executed independent attacks on targets such as railroads or small German headquarters.[31]

The Canadian-American First Special Service Force, remembered in history by the nickname "the Devil's Brigade," earned from the Germans for its exploits in Italy, joined the assault force in July. Colonel Edwin Walker commanded 2,060 ranger-trained men.[32]

Two French commando teams were attached to the invasion force as well. The *Commandos d'Afrique*, or African Commando Group, commanded by Lt. Col. Georges-Regis Bouvet, consisted of seven hundred handpicked men. The Naval Assault Group, commanded by Commander (*Capitaine de Fregate*) Seriot, was a small, sixty-seven-man detachment.[33]

The First Airborne Task Force
The War Department declined a request to supply an airborne division for Dragoon, so AFHQ had to make do. By early July, plans for the airborne operation firmed up, and Brig. Gen. Robert Frederick, formerly commander of the First Special Service Force, was given charge of what was dubbed a provisional airborne division. When the unsuspecting Frederick first reported to Devers and was told he would command the airborne operation, he was momentarily taken aback, because he had never led an airborne unit.

"How long will we have to get ready for the mission?" Frederick finally asked.

"Five weeks," replied Devers.

"Well, where are my airborne troops?"

"So far, you are the only one we have."[34]

Like the ground divisions tagged for the operation, most of the trained airborne strength in the Mediterranean was committed to the line in Italy, the British 2d Independent Parachute Brigade with the Eighth Army, and the American 509th Parachute Battalion (plus two batteries of the 463d Parachute Field Artillery Battalion) with the Fifth Army. The seasoned "Five-O-Nine" had been the first American airborne unit to see combat, as part of the invasion of North Africa on 8 November 1942. Dragoon would be the battalion's fifth combat jump. These units were extricated in May and underwent intensive training with the 51st Troop Carrier Wing.

Fresh outfits arrived from the States, including the 1st Battalion, 551st Parachute Regiment; the 550th Glider Infantry Battalion; and the 517th Parachute Regimental Combat Team (RCT). The first two formations deployed to an airborne training center in Sicily, and the 517th

Parachute RCT was attached to Fifth Army to gain ten days of battle experience. To encourage some level of cohesion among these disparate units, all were transferred along with their transport aircraft to the Rome area in June for further preparations.

Several odds and ends were added to his force and given glider training, including a Japanese-American antitank company from the 442d Infantry Regiment (outfitted with British airborne 6-pounders that fit into Waco gliders), the 602d Pack Field Artillery Battalion, and two companies of chemical mortars (4.2-inch). The War Department also supplied a division staff drawn mainly from the 13th Airborne Division.[35]

Ten English-speaking French paratroopers from the Shock Battalion (*Battalion de Choc*, a special forces unit of the Gaullist intelligence service, *Bureau Central de Renseignements et d'Action*, or BCRA), based in Cuttoli, Italy, were ordered to join the provisional airborne division to act as guides and scouts. Sergeant Schevenels was assigned to Frederick's headquarters, where he learned that he would accompany the commanding general during the drop.[36]

The French Army
Just as Henry Ford's assembly lines produced an endless number of identical automobiles, so, too, the U.S. Army produced an endless number of companies, battalions, regiments, and divisions, all identical, with only the rare Japanese-American or African-American segregated battalion to break the monotony.

The French army was quite different. It had a strong regimental tradition, and these regiments were drawn from all over the empire. Thus, there were great variations among them. Furthermore, the divisions, although largely restructured and re-equipped on the American model, all had their own character, because they had been put together from whatever units and manpower could be scrounged from the wreckage of 1940.

De Lattre's divisions and supporting units represented about 250,000 soldiers of almost every background imaginable. Some of the soldiers were veterans of the Free French forces who had been fighting since 1940. By mid-1944, twenty thousand individual Frenchmen had escaped

France, crossed the Pyrenees into Spain, and joined whatever parts of the French army they could find. In November 1942, the Army of Africa had also joined the cause. Africans were heavily represented in the ranks in a way that they were not in the defeated army of metropolitan France.[37]

North Africans made up ninety-five thousand of de Lattre's troops, and another fifteen thousand were from sub-Saharan Africa. The proportion of Africans in the armored divisions was about one-quarter, whereas in the colonial infantry divisions it was about two-thirds. About 70 percent of the manpower in the infantry regiments overall was made up of Africans. Only about 2 percent of the officers, however, were "indigenous"–in the terminology of the day–and the biggest number of them was Moroccans.[38]

Some of these Africans, particularly the Moroccans, had joined the French army out of genuine respect and admiration for French officers they knew or of the French administration. This loyalty in part resulted from the fact that most Moroccans saw the French army's *Régiments de Tirailleurs Marocains* (Moroccan Sharpshooter Regiments, or RTMs) as the Sultan's former army, belonging ultimately to him but temporarily entrusted to the French government. The fact that there were some Moroccan officers in the RTMs also helped. Sometimes Moroccan loyalty resulted from an interesting blend of religious belief and personal respect for their French officers. Some Africans wanted to escape their social surroundings and make something better of their lives, see the world, or prove their worth as warriors.[39]

Others, however, were reluctant warriors at best. The Senegalese tirailleurs were an interesting product of French colonial policy. The term "Senegalese" could be highly misleading. Some were, in fact, from Senegal, but others were from as far away as Madagascar. Moreover, being a tirailleur was a sign of colonial subservience.

Even among those African troops who liked and respected the French, there was a widespread desire for independence or at least increased autonomy for their homelands. Moreover, a goodly number of African soldiers had no love at all for the French. In fact, some future leaders of postwar nationalist movements in North Africa fought in the French army. De Gaulle was acutely aware of the existence of these feelings in the army. The day before the Dragoon landings, he wrote about this very problem to a senior French officer, "[I]t is a matter of keeping North Africa from slipping through our fingers while we liberate France."[40]

* * *

De Lattre's forces included some of the best mountain troops in all the Allied armies, six thousand Berber warriors, called *goumiers*, from Morocco. Bearded and wearing the djellaba, their traditional cloak, which most of their French officers wore as well, and often carrying vicious-looking knives, these warriors had developed a fearsome reputation in Italy, where they had been part of the French Expeditionary Corps. Formed into company-sized *goums*, battalion-sized *tabors* (made up of goums), and regiment-sized *groupements de tabors Marocains* (GTMs), and leading their sturdy mules, the goumiers had shown an uncanny ability to infiltrate through some of the worst terrain that Italy had to offer, showing up where they were least expected and sowing violence and death among the enemy.[41]

Nonetheless, when de Lattre told the American and British planners that he intended to bring the goumiers with him to France, the planners were not impressed; nor was Lieutenant General Patch. De Lattre stood firm: It was his army liberating his country, and he had delivered his professional judgment of what the task required. Eventually he won out, and the planners agreed that an unspecified number of goumiers could be used. Making artful use of this ambiguity in the invasion plan, de Lattre told his staff, "We speak of 1,000, we think of 2,000, and we embark 6,000."[42]

In July, the Pope became involved. Unfortunately, it was not just among the Germans that the goumiers had developed a fearsome reputation. During the advance on Rome, there had been a breakdown in discipline among a few goumiers, who went on a rampage of rape and looting. The guilty were quickly punished, but the goumiers' reputation was in tatters. Pope Pius XII himself objected to the use of "savage Africans" on the European continent.[43]

General Jean de Lattre de Tassigny was a man with excellent military judgment and the willingness to do whatever was necessary to carry out his judgment. Though some of his officers loathed him, thinking him more interested in glory than in the serious matters of warfare, this was a minority view.[44] In fact, he was respected by nearly everyone who knew him. Devers described him as "a very capable and dramatic individual, as well as a fighting soldier."[45] Certainly, de Lattre was not always pleasant to be around, but he had a good heart and was passionately devoted to the liberty of France. Paul Paillole, a French intelligence officer who worked with de Lattre, described him as "all at once charming and absolutely odious, demanding and generous, but always enthralling and passionately involved."[46]

An American liaison officer who had occasion to observe de Lattre up close recounts a story that illustrates well all the characteristics that Paillole mentioned. De Lattre, a night owl, liked to hold meetings with his corps and division commanders after dinner. When the meeting was over, he would often say to his weary subordinates, "Let's see how things are going on the front!" and lead them on a tour of frontline units. De Lattre's car would often drive with its headlights on. Although this never caused him problems, his generals following behind in their own cars sometimes came under fire from the by now alerted enemy.

"On one of these late night expeditions," the American recalled, "General de Lattre passed a French antitank gun position without being challenged; in fact, the two men were probably asleep. 'Have those men report to my headquarters tonight!' the general snapped to an aide. As the staff was assembling for dinner, the two men, scared out of their wits, arrived. The general chewed them out. 'What have you done for France?' he roared. One of them gulped and managed to say, 'We did get one Tiger tank, sir.' 'Soldiers of France!' General de Lattre exclaimed, kissing each on either cheek. He then went to the sideboard in the dining room, picked up two bottles of wine, and gave one to each, then a fat roast chicken apiece. 'Go get another tank!' he told them. The staff watched their dinner walk out of the door with the men."[47]

Commissioned from St. Cyr in 1913 as a second lieutenant of cavalry, de Lattre found himself in the Great War. In its first month, he was wounded in the chest by a German lance during a cavalry skirmish. De Lattre had the best of the engagement, however, personally killing three Germans with his sword, a weapon his grandfather had carried during the Napoleonic Wars. In 1915, he became an infantryman and rose to battalion command. Wounded four times, he ended the war as a captain. The year 1921 found him in Morocco, where again he managed to get himself wounded. A few years later he was sent to the *Ecole de Guerre*, where he graduated at the top of his class. In 1939, he became the youngest general in the French army. Early the following year, he took command of the 14th Infantry Division, which acquitted itself well when the German invasion came. With a Franco-German armistice looming, he unsuccessfully urged the High Command to dispatch the division either to England or North Africa.

De Lattre was soon appointed a military district commander in the small Vichy army. However, he set to work so vigorously training his troops and so effectively inculcating patriotic spirit in them that the Vichy government decided in the fall of 1941 that it should send him away to Tunisia. He became commanding general of French forces in Tunisia under an old mentor, Gen. Maxime Weygand, the overall commander of French forces in North Africa. De Lattre and Weygand agreed that if Axis forces were ever to enter Tunisia, they would resist. Soon they were both relieved. De Lattre was sent back to France as a military district commander once more. In November 1942, when the Allies came ashore in North Africa, the Germans occupied the nominally independent Vichy France. De Lattre, who had been back up to his old tricks of encouraging French patriotism in the Vichy army, urged his subordinate division commanders to resist to the best of their ability. As de Lattre's units started moving into position, the French Ministry of War, having been tipped off by de Lattre's second in command, intervened. They countermanded de Lattre's orders, replaced de Lattre with his duplicitous deputy, then ordered that officer to arrest him. De Lattre was sentenced to ten years in prison. But before long he was able to saw the bars of his windows and scale down the prison walls. A few weeks later, he managed to reach London. After a short stay there, he left for North Africa, where he placed himself at the disposal of General de Gaulle. De Gaulle had him promoted to general of the army and made him commander of all French forces in the Mediterranean. It was in this capacity that de Lattre commanded the first French army to return to French soil.[48]

In January 1944, the French Committee of National Liberation and the Allied High Command drafted a plan for French rearmament. Largely using American money and equipment, they would put together the various pieces of the French army that then existed and form from them five infantry divisions and three armored divisions, plus a variety of smaller combat units and an array of support units. The 2d *Division Blindée* (2d DB), under Gen. Jacques Leclerc, was to represent France in the Normandy operations. The other seven divisions would make up de Lattre's *Armée B*, later the French First Army. The first four divisions to come ashore in southern France were to be the 1st *Division Francaise Libre* (the 1st Free French Division, an infantry outfit also known as the 1st DMI, or *Division de Marche d'Infanterie*), hereafter the 1st DFL; the 1st DB; the 3d Algerian Infantry Division (3d DIA); and the 9th Colonial Infantry Division (9th DIC).[49]

* * *

The French Forces of the Interior (FFI) had organized with considerable British assistance following the fall of France in 1940, and the FFI were by now formally subordinated to de Gaulle's French Provisional Government acting in concert with SHAEF. De Gaulle in July appointed Gen. Gabriel Cochet the commanding general, FFI, southern zone, to complement Gen. Marie-Pierre Koenig in London, who commanded the maquis in northern France.

The movement was an uneasy alliance of groups ranging from the Gaullists of the *Armée Secrète* to the Communists in the *Francs-Tireurs et Partisans* (FTP). As of early June 1944, the Allies estimated that they were supplying 85,500 guerrillas in southern France. In April and May, those maquis received nearly 15,000 small arms, 140 mortars, and some 16 tons of high explosives from North African supply points alone.[50]

The Dragoon Plan Up Close

The Allies planned that their commandos would land the first blows and further isolate the battlefield. Shortly after midnight, the Canadian-American First Special Service Force was to seize the islands of Port-Cros and Levant to knock out coastal guns that had been detected by aerial reconnaissance.

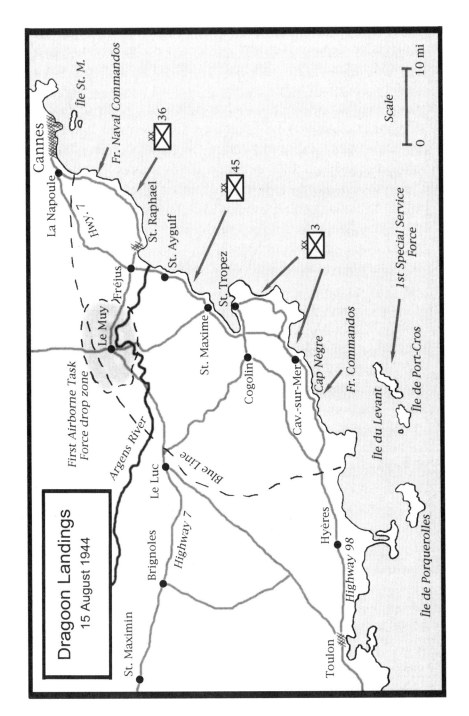

Dragoon Landings
15 August 1944

Bouvet's African Commando Group was to destroy a battery atop the towering rocky height of Cap Nègre, west of Cavalaire Bay, then block the coastal road to prevent German reinforcements from approaching from Toulon. The small French naval demolition party was to block the coastal road from Cannes, on the northeastern flank of the landing zone.[51]

Airborne drops were to follow near the inland road hub of Le Muy, set in the Argens River valley and surrounded by wooded hills that were cultivated on the lower slopes. Pathfinders were scheduled to jump at 0323 hours, followed by the main jump at 0412 hours.[52] Truscott expected the airborne force to assist the landings by attacking the German defenders in Fréjus from the rear in addition to blocking German reinforcements from reaching the beaches.[53]

The Argens River, which reaches the sea south of Fréjus, and the Gulf of St. Tropez divided the amphibious landing area into three roughly equal zones. Sandy beaches were scattered along a rugged and rocky coastline so beautiful that it had attracted wealthy sunbathers for many years.

Patch had assumed that Truscott would assign his most experienced division, the 3d Infantry Division, to his right wing, where resistance was expected to be the strongest, but Truscott chose the Texas National Guardsmen of the 36th Infantry Division for that task. Truscott viewed Fréjus as critical for several reasons. The best road inland, the Route Napoleon, followed the Argens River valley to Le Muy, then ran on to Grenoble. Moreover, the only airfield in the area was located there, and the nearby beach would be essential to landing supplies until the French captured the major ports. A direct assault would be exposed to enfilading fire and risked high casualties, so Truscott decided to first put the 141st Regimental Combat Team (RCT) on the beach at Agay to clear resistance and protect the right flank. The 143d RCT was to follow immediately, take St. Raphael, then attack Fréjus from the south and east. Only six hours after the initial landings was the 142d RCT to hit the beach at Fréjus after a massive air and naval bombardment.

The 45th Infantry Division was to land in the center, east of Ste. Maxime, with the 180th RCT (using two battalions) and the 157th RCT (one battalion) abreast. After clearing the beach, the division was to take the high ground of the Chaines de Mar—which rose to a height of two thousand feet and paralleled the coast—drive to the "Blue Line" established as the corps' initial beachhead perimeter, and make contact with the airborne force. Other elements would assist the 36th Infantry Division in clearing the beach south of Fréjus.

The 3d Infantry Division was to land on the left with the 15th RCT (two battalions) and the 7th RCT (two battalions) abreast. The Blue and White Devils were to clear the beach, seize St. Tropez, strike inland to the Blue Line, and link up with French commandos protecting the left flank.[54]

To provide immediate armored support to the assault wave, roughly one company of medium tanks from each division's attached tank battalion was equipped with British-designed duplex drive (DD) conversion kits. These transformed the M4 Shermans into amphibious vehicles able to hit the beach with the first GIs.

The Other Side of the Hill

Army Group G was responsible for southern France, which was divided between *Nineteenth Army* along the Mediterranean coast and *First Army* along the Atlantic. *Generaloberst* Johannes Blaskowitz, who had last seen battle in Poland in 1939, commanded *Army Group G*. *General der Infanterie* Friedrich Wiese, a highly decorated eastern front veteran and reputed Nazi fanatic, took charge of *Nineteenth Army* in July.

Operation Overlord's success and the manpower-consuming fighting to bottle up the Allied beachhead led to a steady stripping of combat formations from the south. *Nineteenth Army* lost a panzer and three infantry divisions and in exchange gained the *11th Panzer Division* from *First Army*, the battered *198th Infantry Division* from the eastern front, and the badly mauled *716th Infantry Division* from the Normandy front.

As of 15 August, German forces defended nearly 350 miles of French Mediterranean coast. To the west, *General der Flieger* Erich Petersen's *IV Luftwaffe Field Corps* controlled the *716th Infantry, 198th Infantry*, and *189th Reserve division*s. *Generalleutnant* Baptist Kniess' *LXXXV Corps* held the Rhône valley and most of the landing area. It consisted of the *338th, 244th*, and *242d Infantry divisions*. The *148th Reserve Division*, which was subordinated to *General der Infanterie* Ferdinand Neuling's

LXII Reserve Corps, manned the line just west of the Italian border. To the rear, the *11th Panzer Division* was near Bordeaux, and the *157th Reserve Division* was in the Grenoble area.

Some of these divisions were far from peak condition. Though it would soon cause the Allies much consternation, the *11th Panzer Division* had arrived near Bordeaux in June to reconstitute after nearly being destroyed on the eastern front. It had sent one of its two tank battalions to Normandy, also the destination for four infantry battalions from the *338th Infantry Division*. The Germans were lucky to have the *11th Panzer Division*; on 11 August Hitler himself had countermanded an order that would have sent the division far to the north to Chartres and out of the Dragoon fight. The *157th Reserve Division* was scattered around the mountains fighting the maquis, and the *716th Infantry Division* had lost so many men that it was incapable of offensive operations. The third regiment of the *148th Reserve Division* was just organizing and had a cadre strength of only about two hundred men. Excluding the *338th Infantry Division* (50 percent strength), the divisions had on average about 80 percent of their authorized manpower.[55] They lacked assault gun battalions, which were often attached elsewhere, and 37mm antiaircraft and mobile mortar companies, typically fielded on other fronts. Many troops were ethnic Germans from occupied areas who were considered on average less reliable, and many of the commanders were older men no longer fit for duty on the eastern front.[56]

By July 1944, the German military was already suffering a manpower shortage.[57] A sizable proportion of the troops in France consisted of peoples of the Soviet Union and Eastern Europe, often referred to as the *Osttruppen* (east troops). After the Battle of Kursk, Hitler, at *Reichsführer SS* Heinrich Himmler's instigation, became concerned about the loyalty of the approximately eight hundred thousand *Osttruppen* fighting on the eastern front, and he ordered most of them to the west and the Balkans. Often these men had been prisoners who had decided to fight alongside their captors, or even Soviet citizens who had willingly joined the Germans out of a desire to free their land from Bolshevism but now found themselves opposing the western Allies.[58]

Frequently these troops were more trouble than they were worth. In March 1944, even before the Allied landings, the FFI in the Lyon area had found that Ukrainians, Poles, and Serbs were often willing to fire a stray shot or two in order to disclose the presence of their unit when it was about to spring a trap upon the Resistance. The Poles, moreover, made a practice of emptying the gas tanks on German trucks.[59]

The German ground formations had access to ammunition supplies sufficient for a protracted battle, but fuel was in short supply. *Nineteenth Army* had adopted stringent conservation measures to build up small reserves. Scattered and well-camouflaged supply dumps survived Allied air attacks during the spring and summer with little damage, and once supply vehicles were limited to moving during the night beginning 20 May, losses fell to negligible proportions.[60]

* * *

German shore defenses were much weaker than they had been in the portion of the "Atlantic Wall" running through Normandy. German field commanders had for months judged that they could not prevent an Allied landing. They urged preparation to fight a battle inland from the beaches to exploit the defensively advantageous terrain, but Hitler demanded that his troops stop any invasion at the water's edge. Hitler nonetheless diverted much of the available steel and concrete needed to build beach defenses to a pet scheme to construct a "U-boat strongpoint" at Marseille.[61]

By August, only three hundred pillboxes had been completed along the entire southern coast, and only some eighty of those were armed. Beach defenses, barriers, and minefields were in a similar state, and Wiese assessed that in almost all stretches of coast the defenses amounted to little more than light field emplacements.[62]

* * *

By early August, Blaskowitz was already chafing at his orders to defend the Mediterranean and Atlantic seacoasts at the shoreline, which he blamed on political considerations in Berlin. Allied forces that had broken out of Normandy were racing eastward and threatened his rear, having reached a point only 150 miles from *Army Group G*'s supply line through Dijon. His communications relied mainly on the French telephone and telegraph systems, which the Resistance was close to disrupting completely. Blaskowitz sought permission to withdraw his forces to the Dijon area, where they would be able to offer a concentrated defense, but his proposal was rejected.[63]

Instead, as Wiese characterized his own *Nineteenth Army*'s dispositions, "[the main line of resistance] had in reality become a strong line of outposts, behind which there was almost nothing."[64]

DECEIVING AND SOFTENING UP

British colonel Dudley Clark in March 1941 had established "A" Force, which portrayed itself as the headquarters of the nonexistent 1st Brigade of the Special Air Service, a commando force that also did not (yet) exist. Its mission was to deceive Axis forces about Allied intentions. "A" Force made itself so useful that in late 1943, as preparations were being made for a cross-Channel invasion, it set about convincing *Army Group G* that an invasion of southern France was imminent in order to keep it from sending large reinforcements to Normandy until at least D+25—that is to say until roughly 1 July.[65]

The Allies did not know it, but the Germans were never really convinced by the ruse, which may have been fortunate, because the Allies turned their attention toward preparing for a real invasion of southern France. "A" Force, working with the French intelligence services operating in North Africa that had their own "special means," or double agents, was charged with implementing a complicated new deception plan called Ferdinand.[66] This plan sought to make the Germans believe that the main Allied effort would be in Italy, with twin landings at Genoa and Rimini, on Italy's Adriatic coast, outflanking the Gothic Line. At the same time, Eisenhower supposedly would be in command of an invasion of *western* France in the Bay of Biscay. Meanwhile, two British armies in the eastern Mediterranean would stand ready to invade the Balkans, perhaps moving through Turkey to take advantage of Soviet entry into Bulgaria. In short, the Allies should be expected everywhere except in southern France.

Despite its scattershot nature, Ferdinand was actually quite effective. A key reason for this was that the British had known from signals intelligence as early as June that Hitler himself was worried about a landing at Genoa. This may have been fortunate, because *Fremde Heere West* (*FHW*, or Foreign Armies West, the General Staff intelligence office responsible for watching the western Allies) felt otherwise. In mid-July, *FHW* believed that the most threatened sector in the western Mediterranean was between St. Raphael and Hyères. It was a frighteningly accurate call. However, though German naval intelligence would never be convinced of the threat to northern Italy, by 4 August, *FHW* had flip-flopped and deemed a landing in the area of Genoa more likely.[67]

By late July, the German army judged that a landing somewhere in the Mediterranean was imminent. It was unsure of the Allied target, however, and set the relative odds at 4:5:1 of an operation in southern France, northwestern Italy, or the Adriatic Sea. In anticipation of one of the first two options unfolding, the *Oberkommando der Wehrmacht* (*OKW*, High Command) on 3 August issued instructions that the fortifications along the Franco-Italian border be manned. In light of developments in northern France, *OKW* thought that the probability was increasing that new landings would target the French coast. This view was strengthened by the identification of French units in Corsica and systematic air attacks against batteries east of Marseille, the transportation net in the Rhône valley, and the ports of Marseille, Toulon, and St. Raphael.[68]

Oberbefehlshaber West (*OB West*, Commander in Chief West) *Generalfeldmarschall* Günther von Kluge, however, assessed in his appreciation on 7 August that a second Allied landing was no longer likely, although a subsidiary amphibious operation near the frontline might occur to help open the road to Paris.[69]

* * *

While "A" Force worked on German minds, air and guerrilla units gnawed at the sinews. Mediterranean Allied Tactical Air Force on 12 July adopted its plan to support the landings, the dual mission of which was to soften up the German defenses and paralyze the enemy's ability to move, all without giving away the landing site. Air operations began on 5 August, with phase one targeting German aircraft based in southern France and northern Italy, lines of communication in the same areas, and submarine bases if aerial reconnaissance spotted any U-boats. Phase two (Operation Nutmeg) started on 10 August and pounded coastal defense batteries, troops, and coastal radar. In order to protect the actual landing zone, attacks of equal intensity were launched in the Dragoon area as well as Sète, Marseille/Toulon, and Genoa. Phase three (Operation Yokum), which lasted from 0600 to 0730 hours on D-day and included heavy bombers flying from the United Kingdom, directed intensive air attacks against the actual landing beaches and any artillery that the Germans might be able to bring to bear on the assault force. Phase four (Operation Ducrot) returned to a phase-one-like effort to hit troops and paralyze transportation links in the area east of the Rhône River.[70]

Throughout July and early August, meanwhile, the maquis destroyed bridges, railroads, tunnels, and power and communications lines across southern France. They ambushed small groups of enemy troops on roads, which forced the Germans to move about in large numbers when they moved at all. Resistance groups as large as five thousand men, supplied by Allied aircraft flying out of England and North Africa, seized control over patches of territory.

Although the maquis could not withstand a concerted German attack, the enemy lacked the manpower to do much more than clear critical points. That said, the Germans did secure what they absolutely had to, such as the Rhône valley, and the Resistance never posed an insurmountable obstacle to essential movement.

As the landings neared, Allied commandos in growing numbers—in coordination with Seventh Army's Number 4 Special Forces Group— jumped into southern France to fine-tune resistance activities. The night of 3–4 August, one such Allied mission commanded by a British major parachuted into the Basses-Alpes after winging across the Mediterranean Sea from North Africa. Operating with the maquis, the unit blew up so many targets that the major had to cross German lines on 18 August to ask Seventh Army for more explosives. Other teams identified targets for air strikes by Allied bombers.

Local maquis commanders received orders to place themselves at the disposal of regular Allied force commanders after the landings. American personnel were reminded that when dealing with the irregulars, they should remember that these were members of the recognized armed forces of an Allied nation who had been in contact with the enemy for four years.[71]

* * *

On 13 August, *Army Group G* reported that the Allies had completed destruction of bridges along the Rhône and Var rivers. It noted an accumulation of landing craft sufficient for at least a division and the departure of escort vessels from North African ports. Landings east of the Rhône were expected within days, and *Nineteenth Army* had been placed on alert. Von Kluge rejected a request to halt the withdrawal of the *338th Infantry Division* (he changed his mind on 14 August), but he ordered that the *11th Panzer Division* be moved to the east side of the Rhône—a move that Blaskowitz had fruitlessly requested a week earlier. With the commitment of the reserve regiment of the *244th Infantry Division* to replace the departing *338th Division*, the *11th Panzer Division* was *Nineteenth Army*'s only reserve.[72]

The first panzergrenadiers from the *11th "Ghost" Panzer Division* started eastward that evening, but they faced a two-hundred-mile cross-country march through difficult mountainous terrain before they even reached the Rhône River, where they were to find the bridges already mostly destroyed. The division commanding general, *Generalmajor* Wend von Wietersheim, immediately abandoned plans to move only at night—the normal defense against Allied control of the air—and ordered his vehicles to roll during daylight using freshly cut vegetation as camouflage. Still, Allied fighter-bombers claimed a toll, because movement was restricted to a single main road; the maquis held the countryside, and the guns for the division's antiaircraft battalion had not yet arrived. Heavy tanks and artillery, meanwhile, shuttled eastward on ten trains.[73]

The *242d Infantry Division*'s *765th Grenadier (Infantry) Regiment* was responsible for the entire stretch of coastline destined to serve as the landing area. The regiment, like several others in southern France, had its normal complement of three battalions, plus a fourth *Ostbattalion* made up of Azerbaijanis who manned the defenses between Cap Cavalaire and St. Tropez. The 1st and 2d battalions stretched eastward from St. Tropez, and the 3d Battalion was in local reserve.[74] The division had a single platoon of Mark IV tanks attached to it.[75]

* * *

By 14 August, everything was in place, and de Lattre informed the journalists with him that there would soon be an invasion of the Mediterranean coast. Seeking to manage their expectations, he told them that the tempo of the operation might be slow at first but would soon pick up. "Despite the difficulties of this audacious operation," he wrote, "we have absolute faith in its success because the means used are strong, the general situation is developing favorably, and above all our troops have magnificent morale. . . . The German is still able to achieve local successes, he is able to succeed in limited counterattacks, but he is incapable of retaking the initiative and passing over to a general counteroffensive. Clausewitz wrote: 'In the absolute form of war, there is only one success, the final success.' "

At the bottom of the press release, de Lattre wrote: "Make no allusion to the place, to the date, to the means."[76]

CHAPTER 2

INVASION

I've heard a lot of people say the landings in southern France were soft. That's not true. We had plenty of trouble, and the fighting was tough. . . .

—Audie Murphy, most decorated
American combat soldier of World War II

The African Commando Group had the honor of establishing the first toehold on the coast of France. Plans called for a main landing at Cap Nègre at 0045 hours, supported by two smaller ones at Rayol, two miles to the east, but unanticipated currents and haze resulted in all elements landing west of their intended sites. As a result, a ten-man patrol, assigned to knock out a blockhouse at Rayol, came ashore at the base of Cap Nègre. Its guns were the designated objective for a sixty-man team, to be followed by the main body.

The sergeant in charge, Noel Texier, decided to play the hand he had been dealt, and he led his men up the 350-foot face of the prominence. The Germans had sharpened the stones to prevent scaling, and the commandos were soon bleeding from a host of cuts. As the men neared the top, the quiet was shattered by the explosions of grenades being dropped by the defenders. Texier, mortally wounded, fell to the bottom, and several of his men were also killed or wounded; the remaining commandos held on until silence again descended on the scene.

Farther west, Capt. Paul Ducournau, commanding the group assigned the assault on Cap Nègre, realized that his two landing craft were approaching the wrong place on shore and ordered the skipper of his vessel to turn around and motor farther eastward. The second landing craft pressed ahead and deposited thirty commandos on the beach. German machine-gun fire lashed the Frenchmen as they waded out of the surf just in front of a barbed-wire-protected gun position. The commandos dove for cover and for three hours had the short end of a raging firefight.

Ducournau, meanwhile, landed with the remainder of his command at Cap Nègre about 0100 hours and led the men up the punishing stone face of the prominence. The Germans evidently thought they had driven off a raid during Texier's ascent and had stood down, because the commandos were able to cut their way through the barbed wire at the crest before flares burst and German machine-gun fire sought out the Frenchmen. The commandos charged, shooting and throwing grenades as they went, some pouncing on defenders with their daggers. The rush carried the Frenchmen to two guns, both of which they destroyed. Soon the garrison surrendered; twenty-two Germans lay dead or wounded.

The main body landed on a quiet stretch of coast and, although a mile from its designated beach, made its way to the coast road, where it established the roadblock it had been assigned. Despite mishaps, all key objectives had been achieved.

Meanwhile, the Naval Assault Group, transported on PT boats, landed as planned on the far right of the VI Corps assault zone. The commandos almost immediately stumbled into a minefield, and the explosions alerted the defenders, who opened fire on the immobilized Frenchmen. Only eight men emerged unscathed. They linked up with American troops about 1600 hours and joined the French commandos at the far end of the beachhead. Another seventeen wounded showed up in a civilian hospital at St. Raphael, perhaps guided there by the maquis; the remainder were killed or captured.[1]

A few miles northeastward up the coast road toward Cannes, another group of twenty French commandos—probably belonging to the Special Projects Operations Center in Algiers—jumped into the darkness at 0430 hours. Sometime after dawn, they encountered a large group of German troops, and during the ensuing shootout fifteen of the Frenchmen were wounded. The commandos retreated and remained hidden on a hill above the road until contacted by American forces the next day.[2]

* * *

By comparison to the sharp violence on shore, the pre-landing raids against the nearby islands were anticlimactic. At about 2300 hours on 14 August, First Special Service Force rangers descended into rubber boats from the decks of "four-stacker" World War I destroyers converted for transport use and headed toward their objectives.[3]

The first boats touched shore on Île du Levant about 0030 hours. The thirteen hundred commandos from the 2d and 3d regiments executed a difficult climb up sheer cliffs, only to encounter not German resistance but the incredibly dense, chest-high underbrush that gave the maquis their name. A patrol moved off stealthily through the dark toward the gun positions detected in aerial reconnaissance photographs. There, the keyed-up men discovered ordinary drainpipes disguised to resemble large gun barrels. A two-hundred-man German garrison, which occupied a nearby cave, engaged the attackers, but most of the Germans surrendered about daybreak after being pounded by shells from a British destroyer, bazooka rounds, and small-arms fire.

The 1st Regiment's assault team could find not a single German when it landed on nearby Île de Port-Cros. After daybreak, however, some 110 Germans who were holed up in a thick-walled Napoleonic-era fortress and a chateau opened fire with machine guns. The badly outnumbered but well-protected defenders held out until induced to surrender by 15-inch shells from a British battleship.[4]

* * *

The air was clear and cool near Rome when the Provisional Airborne Division took off after dark on D-1. There was no moon, so the pilots would need clear conditions over the drop zones to pick out landmarks such as large hill masses. The meteorologists reported that a high-pressure system controlled the target area, which precluded storms but raised the possibility of ground fog. Arriving over the Riviera, pilots found haze that cut visibility to a half mile and winds 90 degrees off the direction forecast.

At 0205 hours, six aircraft dropped chaff and rubber parachute dummies with noisy rifle simulators north and west of Toulon to create a large radar signature and the appearance of an airborne landing. Intercepted radio messages indicated that the deception had completely fooled the Germans.

In the actual area of operations, only the British pathfinder team was delivered to the proper landing zone. The pathfinders had their radio beacons up and running by 0430. The main drop went reasonably well considering that the geography forced an atypical drop altitude and the troops had to jump through clouds. The 2d Independent Parachute Brigade's 6th (Royal Welch) Battalion dropped as planned—it reported in at 60 percent strength—but more than half of the 4th and 5th (Scottish) battalions were scattered.

The American pathfinder teams were dropped so far off course that they could not guide in the first wave using Hollophane lights and luminous ground panels. As a result, the C-47 transports delivered half of the 509th Parachute Infantry Battalion Combat Team to its drop zone but unloaded the rest twenty-five miles away near St. Tropez, including an entire stick that jumped to its death in the sea. The 517th Parachute Regimental Combat Team was scattered over an area roughly twenty-three miles by twelve miles in size. The 1st and 2d battalions wound up in the general area of the planned landings, but other elements wound up as far as twenty-five miles away. Most of the 460th Parachute Field Artillery landed as planned, but a battery was misdelivered to Fréjus.

Unbeknownst to *General der Infanterie* Ferdinand Neuling, *LXII Reserve Corps* commander, the scattering of the 517th Parachute Regiment saved him from death or capture that morning. Fifteen of the paratroopers had spent weeks studying intelligence about his residence at Draguignan. The Resistance supplied architectural plans, and a neighbor reported details of his daily activities. The small commando team dropped too far to the east to pay an early-morning visit to Neuling.

* * *

French sergeant Schevenels had taken off with Brig. Gen. Bob Frederick at 0150 hours. After the aircraft crossed the French coast, Frederick issued a few orders, then stood in the doorway of the aircraft. He would be the first man out. At 0445 the green light came on, and the general cried "Go!" and hurled himself out of the plane and into the dark. Schevenels was the sixth man out the door.

Corporal Duff Matson, Frederick's bodyguard, landed hard and injured his leg. He spotted the blue glow of Frederick's flashlight from the vicinity of a nearby parachute and hobbled toward his charge. Matson noticed five or six figures creeping toward the glow from another direction and realized from the dim outline of their helmets that they were Germans. The corporal shouted a warning and opened fire. Two of the shadows fell to the ground, and the others ran.

Frederick looked up at Matson without any apparent worry and returned to studying his map. Matson could barely walk, so Frederick set off alone to find his troops. Moving cautiously through the pre-dawn fog, he spotted what looked to be a German soldier. Frederick stealthily approached, then leapt, intent on silently breaking the man's neck.

The figure cursed with a distinctly British accent, and Frederick relaxed his hold.

"I say, old boy," the para gasped, "you are a bit rough!"

Landing in the dark, Schevenels, meanwhile, realized that he was far away from Frederick, the man he was intended to support. Suddenly he heard voices speaking German. Schevenels froze and waited while the voices faded into the distance, then he began to seek his *General*. At 0800 he succeeded.[5]

* * *

When the pilots pulling the first wave of gliders arrived over the drop zone about 0815, the ground was still socked in by fog. The C-47s turned and headed back to Rome with their cargos undelivered; they returned late in the afternoon for a successful second try. The second wave had better luck, and gliders began to touch down about 0930.[6]

The glider landings built up steam as the day wore on. They generally took place where they were supposed to, and nearly 95 percent of glider troops were available for missions as of 1900 hours on D-day. Antiglider obstacles nonetheless wrecked a large number of aircraft.

* * *

The British 4th Battalion had the crucial mission of taking the road hub at Le Muy but could assemble only 40 percent of its men. The paras seized the high ground northeast of town by 0730 hours. A company then captured Las Serres and, after fending off several small German attacks, a bridge over the Nartuby River. The battalion nevertheless lacked the strength to take the main objective. The 6th Battalion, meanwhile, was able to secure the town of La Motte and link up with the 517th Parachute Infantry Regiment, while the 5th Battalion guarded the drop zone. (Division commanding general Frederick soon ordered the British brigade back to Italy after concluding that it had not captured Le Muy because the commander lacked the will to fight.)

The American paratroopers from the 509th Parachute Infantry Battalion quickly seized control of the high ground and roads that were essential for movement out of the beachhead—or toward it for any German counterattack. Vicious disorganized skirmishes flared throughout the drop zones, including at Le Muy. By 1700 hours, Lt. Col. Bill Yarborough had assembled the "Five-O-Niners" who had landed near Le Muy, ascertained by patrols that the Germans still held the objective, assembled three 75mm howitzers from the 463d Parachute Field Artillery Battalion, and begun to shell the defenders.

At Les Arcs, some five miles southwest of Le Muy, Maj. William "Wild Bill" Boyle was able to assemble fewer than fifty men from the 1st Battalion, 517th Parachute Infantry Regiment, before moving into town. His paratroopers encountered German troops at a railroad bridge, and heavy shooting broke out. Unfortunately, it transpired that the garrison—a full battalion in strength—had left Les Arcs during the night to take up positions in response to the invasion alert. The Germans returned in strength after daybreak and pinned down Boyle and his men. Casualties were mounting, and Boyle realized his situation was hopeless. He ordered his small command to slip away, narrowly escaping a German encirclement.

* * *

Captain Jess Walls and his Company C, 509th Parachute Infantry Battalion, plus a few lost souls from Company B and the 463d Parachute Field Artillery Battalion, found themselves at St. Tropez. Walls realized that he and his men were in the middle of the target zone for the looming air and naval bombardment and had to find a way to signal that fact to his own side without alerting the Germans. Walls had his men display orange panels and spell out "US" with parachutes arranged on open ground, which did the trick.

About 0600, the paratroopers heard loud explosions as the German garrison began to destroy port facilities in St. Tropez. By this time,

Company C had encountered elements of the FFI *Brigade de Maures*, commanded by Marc Rainaud, which had taken up positions nearby a day earlier. Together, they overran St. Tropez by 0900. The German garrison hunkered down in the citadel and nearby pillboxes, which the paratroopers realized they could not capture by charging across open ground against heavy machine-gun fire. Walls and Rainaud, who had been shot in the neck but kept fighting, decided to pull back to better defensive positions outside the town. The German commander evidently interpreted the withdrawal as presaging a heavy naval bombardment and surrendered his garrison. This action later enabled 3d Infantry Division troops to land on the beach nearby without a shot being fired.[7]

* * *

As dawn lightened the eastern sky, Sandy Patch and Lucian Truscott waited off St. Tropez aboard their command ship, *Catoctin*, surrounded by a thousand transports that had loaded the invasion force in Naples and small Italian ports from Pozzuoli to Salerno. Men who had come to this shore aboard those ships had already finished eating steak and fresh eggs, the by-now traditional last meal offered by the quartermaster to invasion troops, and clambered into their landing craft in the last moments of darkness.[8] Not far away, Winston Churchill stalked the decks of the Mediterranean fleet flagship, the destroyer *Kimberly*, having come to watch the landings he had so bitterly opposed. The mountains just behind the coast were still barely visible in the morning haze when the first flights of bombers winged overhead to drop their deadly loads on the defenses. The invasion commanders were able to hear the distant rumblings from the explosions for a short while before the guns on the fleet's battleships, cruisers, and destroyers drowned them out with their own fierce bombardment, which began at 0650 hours. Haze and smoke raised by the bombings forced the warships to conduct unobserved fire in much of the assault area, but the shelling nevertheless was generally effective in neutralizing major beach defenses and underwater obstacles. From his vantage point seven thousand yards offshore, Churchill could detect no German fire coming off the beaches. Perhaps remembering his own military adventures as a young man, Churchill regretted not having arranged to go ashore himself.[9]

The assault divisions were the most experienced outside the Pacific theater, but this landing would nonetheless involve some firsts for Mediterranean theater troops: the first daylight landing, the first against beaches with prepared defenses, and the first in which the element of surprise would involve, at most, the exact time and place.[10]

* * *

The 36th Infantry Division landed on the right wing and, as expected, encountered the stiffest German resistance. The 2d Battalion, *765th Grenadier Regiment, 242d Infantry Division*, defended the St. Raphael–Fréjus area, flanked to the northeast by an *Ostbattalion* of the *148th Reserve Division* and backed by the 3d Battalion, *765th Grenadier Regiment*, in reserve at Fréjus.[11]

An unknown soldier from the 2d Battalion, 141st Infantry Regiment (on the right end of the 36th Infantry Division's landing zone), recorded a typical experience from that morning as his outfit's landing craft headed for the beach at about 0700:

> Now our boats straightened out into a line of Vs made up of five boats each. Suddenly, the motors took on a new deep-throated roar and the square prows rose higher out of the water as we headed into the beach, passing the slower LCMs, rocket-launching craft, amphibious six-by-sixes carrying 105mm howitzers mounted in a firing position, patrol craft, and finally tiny minesweepers. At 4,000 yards we passed the last control boat and heard a young Navy officer on the bridge yell something through a loudspeaker. The skipper of our boat, a Brooklyn lad who had landed troops on Omaha Beach, looked at his watch and muttered, "On 'de nose."
>
> To a GI landing in the assault wave, it is very important to hit the beach with dry feet. The axiom that old invasion troops follow is "get off the beach fast," and it's tough enough trying to move fast when you're loaded down with 90 pounds of equipment without having 100

pounds of water sloshing around in your shoes and pants. We had lots of confidence in this kid from Brooklyn when he said, "I'll put you guys on land wid dry feet if I lose my boat doing it."

Now we were 2,000 yards offshore and the great rocket ships began to send their screeching cargo into the air. The sea was rolling lightly, and the increased speed threw a fine salt spray into our faces. At 1,000 yards the din of thousands of rockets and shells crashing into the beach ahead became a steady roar in which the concussion caused by no single shell could be heard. Now the water became rough, and the boat lurched violently from side to side. The shore disappeared completely behind a heavy curtain of smoke, fog, and spray.

By now, the feeling of anticipation and fear that is in every soldier's heart and mind as he approaches an invasion was gone. Two minutes to eight o'clock. The skipper opened the throttle on the powerful marine motor all the way. . . . Quieter now . . . occasional chatter of a machine gun . . . a small, fast, heavily armed Navy scout craft cut in on our right with its fifty-calibers going wide open at a bulky object through the haze . . . Île d'Or . . . the Navy was still throwing big shells farther inland beyond the beach. Suddenly a rocky coast loomed up ahead of us, and the skipper yelled, "Brace yourself!" as the boat crashed up on the rocky beach. There were machine-gun bullets cracking over the gunwale and splintering the right side of the boat, but we didn't notice anyone getting hit. Within 40 yards of us, two Sherman tanks enclosed in great box-like canvas covers churned up out of the water, instantly dropped the hood like snakes leaving their skins, and rumbled off down the beach with their 75s blasting still belligerent-minded German machine gunners out of existence.[12]

* * *

The 141st Infantry Regiment landed under moderately intense fire—mostly from antiaircraft guns—on what few Americans would even call beaches. An extremely narrow strip of rocky shale separated the water from steep embankments, beyond which the coastal road and a railroad traced the top of the bluff.[13]

For the most part, the GIs were amazed at the slight opposition they encountered at the waterline, and they scrambled up the slopes and seized their initial objectives by 1000 hours. As prisoners were brought in for interrogation, the reason for the weakness of the initial resistance became more apparent: Most of the defenders were Poles and Russians from the *148th Reserve Division*'s *Ostbattalion*. The regiment pushed almost due north; the coastline at this point bent nearly 90 degrees toward La Napoule before turning east again to Cannes and the Île Ste. Marguerite, just offshore. Few emplacements along the shoreline were designed for lateral defense, so the Germans hurriedly converted almost every villa into a strongpoint, which the GIs had to assault and clear. While the 1st Battalion moved up the coast, the 2d Battalion, protected on the left by the 3d Battalion, moved quickly inland, severed Highway 7 between Fréjus and Cannes, and turned eastward to seize the high ground overlooking the latter town.[14]

The 143d Infantry Regiment followed the 141st across Green Beach at 0945 hours, at which point it was some four thousand yards east of St. Raphael, its main objective. The 1st Battalion first seized high ground above the port village, turned over the position to the 3d Battalion, then looped back to threaten the town from the northeast. The 2d Battalion rolled up beach defenses from the flank and assaulted St. Raphael along the coast road.[15]

The 2d Battalion ran into a fortified roadblock manned by German coastal artillery and Luftwaffe personnel. The battalion commander, Lt. Col. Gauldin Watkins, became one of the first casualties when he stepped in front of a German tank to accept the surrender of two soldiers and was struck in the chest by machine-gun fire.[16]

Three companies from the *765th Grenadier Regiment* defended St. Raphael, and matters did not improve much once the roadblock had been dealt with. Prisoners revealed that several tanks supported the infantry.

German fire slowed the advance, and St. Raphael remained in German hands when night fell.[17]

About noon, following some delays, the 142d RCT began its assault on Red Beach, following a remarkably precise strike by nearly a hundred B-24s. The navy, however, halted the landing craft a few thousand yards offshore, much to the annoyance of Truscott, who was observing the operation. Deeming the beach too well protected by undamaged coastal batteries and underwater obstacles, the latter because several radio-controlled floating bombs designed to clear lanes failed to detonate, the navy around 1400 hours decided to put the 142d Infantry ashore across Green Beach, which the 141st Infantry had already secured.[18]

Because of the shift in landing beaches, at about 1530 hours the 142d Infantry Regiment moved inland toward Agay and Fréjus. The latter, its chief objective, lay ten miles distant. The operations order specified that the town had to be taken that night. Minor clashes with the enemy and daytime heat slowed the advance, and darkness fell before the 1st Battalion reached the high ground above Fréjus. The night was black and moonless. The arrival of the 3d Battalion, which had the mission of capturing the town, was slow, and no attack was possible before nearly dawn.

With three regiments using the same beach, which was only 250 yards wide, it became a logistic bottleneck. Truscott arranged for CC Sudre to come ashore across the 45th Infantry Division's beaches; he then landed in France to join his forward command post (CP).[19]

* * *

The 3d Infantry Division hit the beach at about 0800 on the left wing, which was defended by the *Ostbattalion* of the *242d Infantry Division*'s *765th Grenadier Regiment*.[20] Two battalions of the 7th Infantry Regiment went ashore at the extreme left with orders to push westward down the coast, and two battalions of the 15th Infantry landed on the right, less than two miles across a peninsula from its chief objective at St. Tropez. The 30th Infantry Regiment debarked across the beaches secured by the 7th Infantry, ready to exploit inland to the north and northwest.

Lieutenant William Dieleman's "battle patrol," one of four 150-man special teams in the division, landed at the left extreme of the 7th Infantry's beach with the mission of moving two thousand yards westward to the town of Cavalaire-sur-Mer and clearing the peninsula on which it sits. From this commanding terrain feature, the Germans could sweep the beach with direct or observed artillery fire.

Staff Sergeant Herman Nevers, a squad leader, was one of the first ashore. "As we started inland from the water," he related, "I suddenly noticed a wire just above my head. I looked back [and saw] a hanging mine explode and tear the platoon leader into small pieces. The force of the explosion blew S/Sgt. James P. Conner about ten feet and knocked him to the ground."

Conner was wounded but insisted on pressing forward. As the squad neared a bridge, a German soldier jumped up, and Conner shot him. Moments later, a heavy mortar barrage disorganized the platoon, and in the confusion some of the men followed the wrong platoon. Conner rallied the remaining twenty men, only to be shot in the back by a sniper.

Nevers begged Conner to get medical care, but the sergeant refused. "No, they can hit me, but they can't stop me. I'll go until I can't go any farther." Conner told the men, "If there's only one of us left, we've got to get to that point and clean it up so the guys coming in after us can get in safely."

Conner led his men forward again. A German soldier in a foxhole shot him in the leg, and Nevers shot the German as Conner dropped to the ground. Conner refused first aid and urged Nevers onward with the fifteen remaining men. The outfit cleaned out the objective, killing a few enemy troops and capturing forty in the process. For his role in the assault, Conner was awarded the Medal of Honor.[21]

* * *

Staff Sergeant Audie Murphy was one of the men from Company B, 1st Battalion, 15th Infantry Regiment, who landed in the first wave near St. Tropez shortly after 0900. Murphy, who had already been decorated for bravery in fierce fighting after the Anzio landings in Italy, led his rifle platoon inland until they were driven to ground by machine-gun fire from a ridge not far ahead. Murphy ran forty yards back through the whizzing bullets and found an American machine-gun crew. He borrowed their weapon, dashed back through the enemy fire to his men, and told them he was going to crawl ahead to take out the machine-gun nest. His old friend Lattie Tipton volunteered to go with him.

Murphy set up his machine gun, but just as he was ready to fire, the enemy soldiers waved a white flag. Tipton stood to accept the surrender and was cut down by another blast of gunfire. Murphy went berserk and had little memory of what happened next. His Distinguished Service Cross citation offers this account: "In the duel that ensued, Sergeant Murphy silenced the enemy weapon, killed two of the crew, and wounded a third. As he proceeded, two Germans advanced toward him. Quickly destroying both of them, he dashed alone toward the enemy strongpoint, disregarding bullets that glanced off rocks around him and hand grenades that exploded as close as 15 yards away. Closing in, he wounded two Germans with carbine fire, killed two more in a fierce, brief fire fight, and forced the remaining five to surrender."[22]

Technical Sergeant John Shirley commanded a squad not far away in the 3d Battalion's landing area. His men made it safely across the beach but were then ordered to take the high ground just ahead. He later recalled, "It was a little unreal, more like a training exercise. Germans fired rifles at us, and men were hit on both sides of me. A half hour later, we stood on the crest of the hill. . . . My twelve-man squad on the beach was now a seven-man squad."[23]

By and large, the 3d Infantry Division encountered light resistance elsewhere, and by mid-afternoon all regiments were rolling past their initial objectives. The 7th Infantry linked up with the French commandos at Cap Nègre about 1435 hours. After a rough night, the unfortunate French had suffered a strafing by Allied fighters, despite releasing yellow recognition smoke. The regiment's 1st Battalion finally encountered a strongpoint on the coast road at about 2300 hours that brought it to a halt and offered stiff resistance well into the next day.

By 1945 hours, the 2d Battalion, 15th Infantry Regiment, arrived at St. Tropez, where it found the paratroopers and maquis already in control of most of the town. The regiment then assembled and followed the 30th Infantry inland through Cogolin, harassed only by snipers.[24]

* * *

The 45th Infantry Division's 157th and 180th Infantry regiments landed at 0800 hours against negligible opposition from the single infantry battalion defending the coastline. The main problem was mines: All four duplex drive (DD) tanks that landed on Blue Beach hit mines, and another tank was disabled on Yellow Beach.[25]

The 157th Infantry fanned out, raced inland, and seized most of its objectives by 1900 hours. German resistance outside Ste. Maxime delayed the 3d Battalion only briefly. The 180th Infantry pushed northeast up the coast road toward St. Aygulf and the high ground south of the Argens River, and all elements made excellent progress until halting late in the day after running into German defenses around St. Raphael and Fréjus. By 2030, reconnaissance patrols established contact with the 509th Parachute Infantry Battalion near Le Muy.[26]

Truscott arrived at Ste. Maxime shortly thereafter and found Eagles at the division CP nearby. Because the division had already secured its D-day objectives and was nearing the Blue Line, Truscott ordered the 180th Infantry Regiment to push eastward during the night to assist the 36th Infantry Division in securing Red Beach at Fréjus.

* * *

The VI Corps staff estimated that the invasion force had broken the backs of two German infantry divisions. In fact, the landings were going so smoothly that Patch alerted de Lattre to begin debarkation of French II Corps troops the next day, one day ahead of schedule.[27]

Amid the bustle of his CP, Truscott contemplated how he could destroy the rest of the German forces in southern France. In Africa, Sicily, and Italy, he had always tried to strike at the enemy's flank and rear with destruction in mind, but the Germans had always been just as mobile as his own forces and been able to escape such traps. This time, however, Truscott was certain that the Air Corps could bring down every bridge along the Rhône and prevent the Germans from escaping westward. The Seventh Army's plan called for an advance westward with two corps abreast to capture the major ports, with which he was in full accord. But there was a spot some hundred miles northward where high ground east of the Rhône created a narrow bottleneck near the town of Montélimar. The Germans, he expected, would concentrate their forces to stop the Seventh Army push westward, and Truscott saw an opening to send a strike force toward Grenoble and from there to the high ground just upstream from Montélimar. No army plan had foreseen such an early exploitation, but Truscott had. This was exactly why he had created Butler Task Force.[28]

* * *

Generaloberst Blaskowitz had been visiting the *IV Luftwaffe Field Corps* area when he received word that the landings had begun. As of midday, *Army Group G* headquarters had an accurate but general picture of the Allied landings. Now that Blaskowitz knew exactly where the enemy was, he rushed to the corps' headquarters and ordered that troops west of the Rhône River be shifted eastward to be closer to the beachhead.[29]

The first formation able to respond was *Regiment Bründel* (a combat team including elements of the *932d Grenadier Regiment*), from the *244th Infantry Division* at Marseille. The troops were hastily loaded into trucks and, with the *18th "Tyroller" Antiaircraft Regiment*, ordered to attack the airborne invaders at Le Muy. The *148th Reserve Division* received instructions to attack from the east.[30] The *11th Panzer Division*, meanwhile, had reached the west bank of the Rhône only to find all of the bridges down; it had to set about finding ferries and a coal barge sturdy enough to hold forty-five-ton Mark V Panther tanks. *LXIV Corps*, on the Atlantic coast, was also ordered to send all its bridging units to Avignon to help rectify the situation.[31]

By the night of 15 August, Blaskowitz could see the inevitable outcome. He lacked the resources to mount an effective counterattack, and he concluded that all he could accomplish was to buy time until the High Command, perforce, decided to initiate a withdrawal from southern France. Meanwhile, Blaskowitz could only hope that Lt. Gen. George Patton's spearheads, then around Troyes, did not turn southeastward to complete the encirclement of *Army Group G*.[32]

CONSOLIDATION

The problem of Le Muy remained unresolved early on D+1, and Frederick ordered the 550th Glider Infantry Battalion to take the objective by a night attack. The paratroopers jumped off at 0200 hours, but as dawn approached, the Germans held on firmly. The battalion was ordered to withdraw and strike again at 0900. As the Americans pulled back in the dark, two companies engaged each other in a spirited firefight after each mistook the other for Germans. Supported by the 509th Parachute Infantry Battalion's mortars on high ground to the south, the glider troops moved out again at noon, only to be held up by a German strong-point south of town.

About noon, VI Corps assistant commander Brig. Gen. Frederic Butler, whom Truscott thought was one of the most fearless men he had ever met, made his way forward on a personal reconnaissance mission and found Lt. Col. Bill Yarborough and his "Five-O-Niners." Spotting a 45th Infantry Division reconnaissance platoon, Butler attached it to the 509th Parachute Infantry Battalion, further attached the paratroopers to the 45th Division, and made his way to the division CP to arrange for some tank support for the assault on Le Muy. While these decisions were being made, VI Corps lacked any contact whatsoever with Brigadier General Frederick and was unaware that he was also operating against the town.[33]

The cavalry arrived in the form of a platoon of Shermans and three assault guns from the 191st Tank Battalion. They made their way from the beachhead at about 1330 hours. Seventy-fives boomed, and German resistance caved in. "Five-O-Niners" climbed aboard the tanks and entered Le Muy, as did patrols from the 550th Glider Infantry Regiment from the opposite direction. The town was secured by 1500 hours.[34]

The 517th Parachute Regimental Combat Team was cheered by the arrival of its 3d Battalion, which had conducted a twenty-five-mile forced march from its mistaken drop zone at Fayence. The exhausted men were directed to advance on Les Arcs and clear it before daylight. Supported by artillery and mortars, which dropped a thousand rounds on German strongpoints in just twenty minutes, the paratroopers did just that.[35]

* * *

The 551st Parachute Infantry Battalion, meanwhile, reached Draguignan, where the Americans found about one hundred maquis surrounded by four hundred Germans. At 0900, standing at Frederick's side, French ser-geant Schevenels heard the radio speak. "The enemy is still holding out in Draguignan. The town is nearly liberated but the hospital has become a strongpoint and a villa called 'Gladys' where General Neuling had his headquarters is, it seems, a veritable blockhouse."

Frederick ordered the 551st Parachute Regiment to take the town and dispatched Sergeant Schevenels to go there to assist the Company B commander, Captain Evans. Schevenels soon found himself walking point for the company, perhaps because he knew every rock in Provence. Less than a mile from Draguignan, a German machine gun opened up from behind a low stone wall. Schevenels leapt into action, bounding over the low wall, his submachine gun at the ready. Suddenly he saw the German, who seemed to be fumbling with a magazine. With a burst from his weapon, Schevenels cut him down. The Americans continued on.

As the Americans entered Draguignan, Schevenels was back on point. The Germans were resisting fiercely in the town. An American sergeant suddenly went down near Schevenels, hit square in the chest. Two other Americans were down on the ground moaning from wounds as well.

Unexpectedly, Captain Evans turned to Schevenels and said, "See what you can do with the 2d Platoon." Paratroopers seldom lack confidence, and Schevenels was no exception. Swiftly seizing the reins of his unexpected command, the French enlisted man ordered his platoon to flank the German position, which the men did under fire from machine guns and panzerfausts. Quickly, however, the Germans realized that their position was no longer tenable and surrendered.

But these were only a few Germans, and the villa "Gladys" was still holding out, apparently with Neuling inside. Evans and Schevenels under a white flag urged Neuling's representative, a colonel, to surrender, but it was no use; the Germans were unwilling to capitulate without a fight. A few well-placed mortar rounds from Schevenels' platoon satisfied the colonel's honor, and soon thereafter much of the *LXII Reserve Corps* staff filed out of the villa with their hands in the air. Draguignan was in Franco-American hands, but the again lucky Ferdinand Neuling had disappeared.[36]

* * *

Truscott obtained Patch's permission to attack northwestward without waiting for the French divisions to land and organize, so he decided to place CC Sudre in the gap between the 3d and 45th Infantry divisions to help clear the area between the Durance River and the coast. Truscott issued a field order that laid down the general objectives and lines of advance for his divisions. The 3d Infantry Division was to seize positions along the Real Martin River (little more than a creek), hold them until relieved by French II Corps, then push up Highway 7 toward the Rhône delta. The 45th Infantry Division was to advance northwestward from Le Luc. The 36th Infantry Division was to press eastward toward Cannes until the beachhead was secure, then be ready to advance northward up the Route Napoleon. From this point until the American drive inland ground to a halt a month later, Truscott issued most of his orders verbally to his division commanders, who did the same with their own subordinates.[37]

*　*　*

The 3d Infantry Division on D+1 pushed westward along the coast road and Highway 7, which ran parallel to the coast, encountering light resistance mostly from individual strongpoints along the main highways. Truscott wanted the 7th Infantry Regiment to hold a line between Carnoulles and Hyères until relieved by the French while the rest of the division pressed up Highway 7 through Brignoles and St. Maximin to cut the roads out of Toulon to the north.[38]

The 30th Infantry Regiment led the push inland. "Improvisation paid dividends," the division's history recorded. "It was found that an entire infantry battalion could be completely loaded on transportation within a regiment, including tanks, [tank destroyers], jeeps, and other assorted vehicles without having recourse to non-organic vehicles. It was a common sight to see a whole rifle battalion moving down a road—doughboys draped over the 3-inch guns of tank destroyers, clinging to the slippery-sided tanks of the 756th, or loaded sixes-and-sevens to trailer-hauling jeeps."[39]

By nightfall, prisoners revealed that the Blue and White Devils were encountering elements of two battalions from the *917th Grenadier Regiment* that had arrived on foot from reserve positions.

*　*　*

The 45th Division's 180th Infantry Regiment and Company C, 191st Tank Battalion, cleared St. Aygulf and Villepey. At the same time, the German counterattack from the west developed as weak probes by as many as four infantry battalions at Les Arcs and Vidauban during the day. Paratroopers and elements of the 45th Infantry Division readily turned back the Germans, who lost about half their attacking force.[40]

Aware that the Germans were trying to push a column toward Le Muy from the west, Truscott late in the afternoon ordered the 45th Infantry Division to turn the 157th and 179th Infantry regiments westward around Vidauban to head off any further German counterattack. The 157th Infantry's 2d Battalion ran into a determined German defense at Le Luc, which held up the advance until the next day, but the regiment's other two battalions continued to roll forward against only sporadic resistance.

Truscott's maneuver directed the weight of the Thunderbird Division's attack up the Verdon/Durance River valley parallel to the 3d Infantry Division's advance. A few hours later, Truscott instructed the elements of the provisional armored group—soon to be officially labeled Butler Task Force—to assemble at Le Muy by 1600 the following day.[41]

* * *

The 36th Infantry Division, meanwhile, was still trying to take some of its D-day objectives. The 142d Infantry Regiment's 3d Battalion entered Fréjus before daylight. Moving silently through the blackness, a scout squad surprised and captured without a shot two squad-sized roadblocks located only a hundred yards apart. The GIs of Company K cautiously advanced through the silent streets until, at 0500, flares popped suddenly in the sky and a hail of small-arms, machine-gun, and mortar fire caught the men in a crossfire. German troops held many of the buildings around them, as well as a camp on a ridge a hundred yards above the road into Fréjus. As soon as there was enough light for the men to see, the 3d Battalion started the grim business of clearing the defenders house by house, which took on a nail-biting edge when a panzer—well hidden and bypassed during the fighting—opened fire an hour after dawn. After slinging several shells at the Americans, the panzer withdrew unmolested toward friendly lines. The 2d Battalion, meanwhile, assaulted the German position on the ridge and subdued the resistance by 1040 hours.

The 3d Battalion took over the advance and pushed inland from Fréjus through Puget. Just past the town, German antitank and assault guns ambushed and destroyed the three lead tanks. The Americans responded by calling down a massive naval and artillery barrage on the defenders, who destroyed their guns and fled. Company B, 753d Tank Battalion, destroyed two assault guns during the fighting.[42]

The 143d Infantry Regiment, meanwhile, again attacked St. Raphael with its 2d Battalion supported by artillery, tanks, and tank destroyers. The GIs worked their way through mortar fire, barbed wire, mines, and booby traps and captured the village by 0900 hours. The limited resistance reported up the chain strongly suggested that most of the German troops had withdrawn during the night. The remainder of the regiment, meanwhile, cleared Red Beach and established roadblocks astride avenues of approach from the north as far as twenty miles inland.[43]

The first German pressure against VI Corps' right flank emerged at 0900 hours, when the 2d Battalion of the *148th Reserve Division*'s *8th Jäger (Light Infantry) Regiment* counterattacked the 141st Infantry Regiment. Moving westward out of Cannes, the Germans advanced with three companies abreast supported by covering fire from a fourth company on high ground. The Americans dispersed the assault with artillery and small arms, but air reconnaissance detected more German troop movements in the Cannes–La Napoule area. Prisoners, moreover, confirmed the presence of other elements of the *148th Reserve Division*. German resistance built steadily during the day, and fire from assault and self-propelled guns became intense at times. Because the Germans had blown many of the bridges along the coast road, the 36th Infantry Division could not push tanks or tank destroyers forward until the engineers made repairs.[44]

Thus far, the invasion of southern France had cost Seventh Army a remarkably low 95 men killed and 385 wounded.[45]

* * *

Nineteenth Army commanding general Wiese visited the *242d Infantry Division* on 16 August and concluded that he no longer had a continuous front. From his perspective, the battlefield was breaking down into a series of small-group fights.[46] As the Seventh Army history characterized the situation, "For the first three days after the landing, German defensive measures amounted to little more than guerrilla warfare. Terrain opportunities were exploited to achieve a sort of checkerboard system of isolated and uncoordinated defense, with small groups attempting to install and maintain hastily built roadblocks." About the best Wiese could hope to accomplish was to build walls to the west and east of the American bridgehead; he had no large formations with which to fill the vacuum to the north.

The failure of a German counterattack on 8 August hundreds of miles away at Mortain, meanwhile, was about to dramatically influence the fighting in southern France. *Generalfeldmarschall* von Kluge concluded on 11 August that the operation, intended to stem the American breakout from Normandy, had miscarried, and he soon realized that Allied forces were threatening a massive encirclement of his formations west of the Seine. On 15 August, Hitler ordered forces in northwestern France to break out of the rapidly closing Falaise Pocket.

Two days later, he instructed *Army Group G* to disengage from the enemy except for units occupying Marseille and Toulon, to retreat northward to link up with the southern wing of *Army Group B*, and to occupy the line Sens-Dijon–Swiss border. An initial order to withdraw elements not committed to the battle reached *Army Group G* on 17 August, and instructions for a total withdrawal arrived the next day. The *11th Panzer Division* was to protect the Rhône valley and serve as rear guard for the *Nineteenth Army*. A corps headquarters (presumably *LXII Reserve Corps*) with the *148th* and *157th Reserve divisions* was, if pressed by the enemy, to retreat into the French-Italian Alpine positions and was resubordinated to *Generalfeldmarschall* Albert Kesselring's army group in Italy.[47]

Blaskowitz had been urging this decision for some time, but he now faced the question of whether he could carry out the plan. He had no phone or radio contact with his corps defending the Atlantic coastline below the Loire and had to issue orders via road couriers—heavily escorted because of the maquis threat. It is likely that he was also concerned about Allied airpower. Perhaps because of these various problems, the plan he established foresaw passing Avignon only four days after commencing the movement—scarcely a speedy withdrawal. Blaskowitz took direct command over *Nineteenth Army*'s retreat into the Rhône valley and ordered the establishment of temporary lines of resistance each day to shield the movement, which would take place mainly at night. Blaskowitz was alarmed at the order to the *148th Reserve Division*; he realized that the road to Grenoble would be left open should the division depart toward the Alps. Blaskowitz therefore ordered the division to stay where it was until *Nineteenth Army*'s retreat was under way, which was about all he could do about the problem.[48]

Blaskowitz formed two groups: All *Nineteenth Army* elements west of the Rhône were subordinated to *IV Luftwaffe Field Corps* and forbidden to cross to the eastern side until north of Lyon. East of the river, all formations were subordinated to *LXXXV Corps* except for the *11th Panzer Division*, which *Nineteenth Army* retained under its direct control.[49]

* * *

From Seventh Army's perspective, the most logical route into the interior for Allied forces was the Argens River valley, up which Highway 7 runs from Fréjus to Aix-en-Provence (hereafter Aix), and hence to Avignon and up the Rhône valley along the east bank of the river.[50]

On 17 August, the 3d Infantry Division's 7th Infantry Regiment continued to move slowly along the coast road against strongpoint-based resistance that claimed a few lives here, a tank there. Inland on Highway 7, the 30th Infantry Regiment's 2d Battalion reached Brignoles at 1840 hours, where the first determined resistance yet encountered along the route stopped the advance in its tracks. The German defenses consisted of roughly two battalions from the *242d* and *338th Infantry divisions*, which waged a successful delaying action through the following day.[51]

The 45th Infantry Division was still clearing Le Luc, and late in the afternoon it encountered another vigorous delaying action at Barjols. The division's artillery entered the battle in a significant way for the first time at Le Luc and Barjols, but the two thousand rounds expended that day still paled in comparison with the intensity of action in Italy, where expenditures three times higher were typical.[52]

The stepped-up fighting was the result of German efforts to establish at least a temporary defense in the area. A motorized battle group subordinated to the *189th Reserve Division* had crossed to the east bank of the Rhône near Arles and was spotted near Le Luc. A captured document indicated that the battle group, built around the *15th Reserve Regiment*, included elements of the *198th* and *244th Infantry divisions* and amounted to roughly two infantry regiments supported by two artillery battalions, antitank guns, and mortars.[53]

On 17 August, VI Corps instructed the 36th Infantry Division to concentrate at Draguignan and relieve the First Airborne Task Force by nightfall. Two regiments were assembling as ordered by midmorning, but the

141st Infantry—responsible for holding the right flank until relieved in turn by the airborne—was becoming embroiled in a scrap against the most effective German formation to appear to date. The regiment clashed again with the *148th Reserve Division*, when elements of the *239th* and *252d Reserve regiments* were identified. The 141st Infantry Regiment also came under heavy shelling, which it concluded originated from guns on Île Ste. Marguerite, off Cannes, which caused heavy casualties in the 1st Battalion. The division requested naval gunfire to suppress the German batteries and asked for even more when the initial pounding failed to silence the German guns. Two navy destroyers raced boldly into Cannes harbor and largely cured the problem with direct gunnery.[54]

The First Airborne Task Force, meanwhile, received orders to hand over its sector to the 36th Infantry Division and deploy to protect the right flank of VI Corps, where Truscott believed the German offensive threat had dissipated. The paratroopers had suffered relatively light casualties—350 men—in two days of fighting. They would soon be joined in the Cannes area by First Special Service Force (replacing the British 2d Independent Parachute Brigade), a company of tank destroyers, and a heavy artillery battalion with the mission of pushing across the Var River toward Nice.[55] The fighting there into November would be a sideshow to the Allied drive into France, particularly after Eisenhower on 19 October forbade any operations east of the border with Italy. But it was vicious mountain warfare: One "Five-O-Niner" later said, "Someone called the southern France invasion the Champagne Campaign; that might sound like having a good time, but I was twice the sole survivor of my platoon. Does that tell you anything?"[56]

* * *

The VI Corps advance westward along the coast neared its end on 18 August, when Butler Task Force set out toward Grenoble, and Truscott ordered O'Daniel to hold north of Hyères with three battalions and await relief by French forces. "I hope you will be relieved by D+6," Truscott said. "I want you to push on your reconnaissance very aggressively."[57] (The operations of Butler Task Force are covered separately in the next chapter.)

After slowly crawling forward over Highway 7—which was also being used by the 3d Infantry Division, resulting in aggravating traffic snarls—

Combat Command Sudre plunged into its first battle at 0700 when the Frenchmen ran into an antitank strongpoint on the road from Cabesse to Carces. After a sharp engagement, the French captured several antitank guns and 159 prisoners.[58] Truscott encountered a happy Sudre a short while later at the combat command CP, located in a hotel where the proprietor was serving the French officers *petite dejeuner* with wine and liqueurs while citizens celebrated outside. The French had cut the road north out of Brignoles. Truscott told Sudre to keep pressing toward St. Maximin when he finished with the welcoming committee.[59]

* * *

Lieutenant General Devers visited VI Corps' CP the morning of 19 August to get his first look at his future command in battle.[60] The landings had barely dented Seventh Army. As of midnight the preceding night, American losses totaled 1,116 killed or missing and some 2,500 wounded or injured, British losses were 368 killed or missing and 91 wounded or injured, and French losses amounted to 38 killed or missing and 225 wounded or injured. (The number of missing would drop over the next several days as paratroopers rediscovered their units.) The Allies in exchange had eliminated 10,621 enemy troops as prisoners alone.[61]

The day provided an omen of how Franco-American command relations might work now that both parts of the team were on the battlefield. Patch, at de Lattre's request, ordered VI Corps to send CC Sudre twenty miles back the way it had come to release it for French use at Toulon the next day. Truscott objected strongly: Sudre was already on his way to Aubagne, between Toulon and Marseille, from where he could attack in concert with the rest of de Lattre's forces, and sending the tanks back down Highway 7 would delay his corps immeasurably. Truscott had his chief of staff contact Patch, who replied, "It may be necessary to do a little countermarching, but it's something that has to be done." Truscott then drove to see Patch, who told him he had raised Truscott's objections with de Lattre, who remained insistent on having his way. Patch said he had made the decision for "political reasons" to head off any delay in French action against Toulon.

As soon as Sudre had executed his countermarch amid the predicted traffic confusion, de Lattre sent him back up the same road to take the objective that Truscott had given him in the first place. De Lattre had apparently flirted briefly with the notion of sending CC Sudre straight at Toulon as part of the attack on that city. For whatever reason, he changed his mind and decided to send Sudre's unit to Aubagne after all. Obviously, de Lattre did not adequately communicate to the Americans the reasons for his vacillations. It is not clear that in the long run it made a difference. Truscott already did not like him, and his relationship with Patch was to survive much worse trials later.[62]

The Germans had evacuated Brignoles during the night and broken contact along the entire Seventh Army central sector.[63] The 3d Infantry Division surged forward into a vacuum, and from noon on 19 August through noon the following day it advanced nearly thirty miles. Where the division's left wing remained pegged to the coastline, the first French troops arrived to relieve the 7th Infantry Regiment, although the relief dragged on through the following day.[64]

On the corps' right wing, the 36th Division detected that the *148th Reserve Division* had begun disengaging and withdrawing toward Italy.[65] The 45th Infantry Division, in the central sector, finally secured Barjols and rolled farther inland into the vacuum. Motorized columns were ordered to "keep going until stopped by enemy fire." The division crossed the Durance River without any German interference, but elements probing toward Sisteron reestablished contact with Germans in a mood to fight.[66]

CHAPTER 3

BREAKOUT AND THE BATTLE AT MONTÉLIMAR

[My] orders to Butler were to lead to one of the
most gallant exploits of the entire war.

—Lucian Truscott, *Command Missions*

Brigadier General Frederic Butler fumed in the early-morning light of 18
August at the sight before him, and he hounded his men to clear the
obstruction. His task force's bold cavalry sweep around *Nineteenth Army*,
less than an hour old, was stopped completely by a roadblock painstak-
ingly constructed by 36th Infantry Division engineers to protect the first
bridge west of Draguignan. Steel rails and cables, posts, boulders, antitank
mines, and two hundred pounds of explosives blocked the route, despite
Butler's coordination the day before with Dahlquist's staff to permit the
armored group to pass through the lines. Finally, after a half-hour of frenzied labor, one lane was clear and the main column started to move while
a reinforced cavalry troop scouted on the right flank.[1]

All the disparate pieces of the provisional armored group had assembled
as ordered except for the engineer company, which had never seen action
before. The 117th Cavalry Reconnaissance Squadron, a battalion-sized
command around which Butler planned his operation and communications
net, had been split up for the landings, sending one ad hoc section to each
of the infantry divisions. Reunited, the squadron fielded five troops: three
reconnaissance troops, each equipped with jeeps for scouts and a dozen M8
Greyhound armored cars for firepower; a light tank troop outfitted with
seventeen M5A1 Stuarts; and an assault gun troop fielding six M7 Priest

self-propelled howitzers in place of the standard-issue M8 howitzer motor carriages. The Greyhounds and Stuarts were armed with only light 37mm main guns and machine guns, and the M7s added a handful of powerful 105mm howitzers. The (reduced) 753d Tank Battalion provided the main armored punch with its two tank companies—seventeen M4 Sherman medium tanks apiece—and an assault gun section outfitted with 105mm howitzers mounted in Shermans. Company C, 636th Tank Destroyer Battalion, contributed twelve M10s outfitted with 3-inch guns, which were significantly more effective against German armor than the 75mm cannons in the Shermans, but they still could not penetrate the frontal armor of the German Mark V Panther medium tank except at close range and with luck. The some 875 men who filled the ranks of the 2d Battalion, 143d Infantry Regiment, were mounted in deuce-and-a-half trucks, and the 59th Armored Field Artillery Battalion was ready to provide fire support from its eighteen M7 Priests.

Truscott had given Butler oral instructions on 17 August to push off at 0600 with Sisteron, on the Durance River, as his first objective. After some discussion on the subject, Truscott left it to Butler to choose his route. Butler and his staff had carefully studied the maps and concluded that the Route Napoleon, which ran through Digne to Sisteron, cut through such mountainous terrain that a handful of determined men could stop the advance. Butler instead decided to start westward out of Draguignan to Riez, then swing north to Sisteron. Asked by Truscott how long it would take him to reach Sisteron, Butler replied he would certainly make it in three days and possibly two. Furthermore, he told the seemingly incredulous corps commander that he would reach Riez, forty-five miles distant, the first night.

Truscott's plan was the height of audacity. To cut off an entire army with a full armored division would have been aggressive generalship, and to try the same with a true armored division combat command a stroke of daring. Although similar to a combat command in numbers of tanks, men, and artillery, Butler's ersatz combat command would not be able to draw on division resources—such as heavy artillery and well-coordinated tactical air support—that similar components of armored divisions could summon in a moment of need. The 36th Infantry Division, therefore,

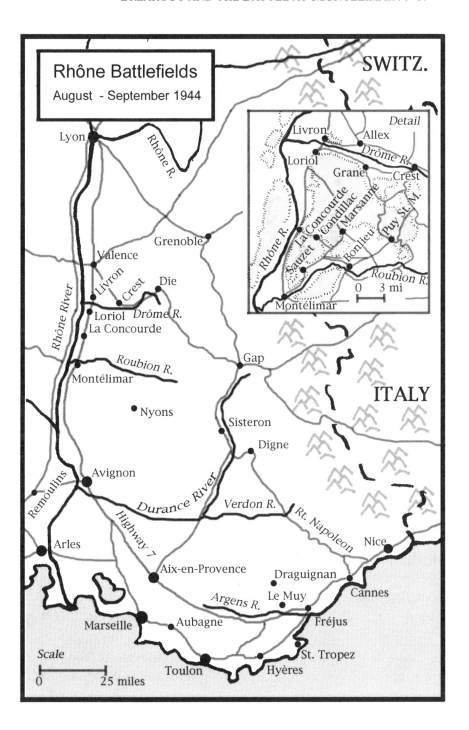

Rhône Battlefields
August - September 1944

almost certainly would have to nearly match the speed of the armored advance if VI Corps were to apply enough muscle to bar *Nineteenth Army*'s escape.

Adding to the challenge, Truscott did not have the element of surprise, at least beyond the tactical. Blaskowitz had anticipated his maneuver and on 16 August had reported to *OB West* von Kluge that he expected the Americans to strike for the middle Rhône valley via Digne once they had solidified their bridgehead.[2] Knowing that the Americans were coming was one thing. Spotting and stopping Butler's command was another thing entirely.

* * *

With cavalry reconnaissance elements in the lead, Butler's main column left Draguignan and hooked northward, fanning out over subsidiary roads toward the day's objective. Troop C, on the right flank, scored the first coup after destroying several antitank guns. The recon men chanced upon *LXII Reserve Corps* commander *Generalleutnant* Neuling, whose luck had finally run out.

The advance was getting into gear. The field artillery battalion's cub spotter plane was aloft and giving real-time reconnaissance information to the point. Soon the artilleryman noticed that a bridge in one village on the route of advance had been blown, and he directed the column along a winding bypass through the hills. The maquis, by and by, reported that a German delaying force had occupied said village, and Butler—who had a Seventh Army maquis liaison officer with him—left the job of ejecting the enemy to the FFI. This was only the first of many such small instances: Butler lacked the manpower to protect his line of communication and relied entirely on the Resistance to secure it for him.

The column rolled onward through Salernes and Montemeyan, meeting nothing but the occasional German motorcycle or staff car. At every halt, vehicles moved under cover as protection against possible German air attack.

One reconnaissance platoon reinforced by tank destroyers scouted southwestward off the main route to the road hub at Barjols. M8 Greyhounds had just rolled into the village when sniper fire rang off the armored sides. The commander and gunner worked in an open-topped turret, so snipers posed a deadly threat. As if that were not enough, two self-propelled guns clanked into view with the clear intention of doing the recon men no good. The little 37mm guns on the M8s barked first, and the rounds penetrated the thin armor on the German guns. Still, the odds looked bad, and the platoon retreated out of town and exchanged fire with the Germans from there. Butler arranged for help from the 45th Infantry Division, and elements of the 179th Infantry Regiment arrived at dusk, just as German infantry were pressing an attack toward the recon men, who were almost out of ammunition. As noted in the preceding chapter, the 179th Infantry fought for two days to secure Barjols.

At Quinson, on the Verdon River, some ten miles short of the day's objective, the maquis again made a crucial contribution. The cub reported that the bridge was out, and the first jeeps to reach the scene had difficulty fording the stream. The maquis pressed the citizenry into service to cover the riverbed with flagstones and help push vehicles to the far bank. There was a certain irony in the situation: Allied bombers had unsuccessfully tried to destroy the bridge, and the maquis, concluding that its removal must be important, had in fact blown up the span. Indeed, Butler would soon learn that bridges knocked down by the Resistance were the greatest impediment to the task force's speedy progress. Butler also contacted the VI Corps air officer to request that he cancel all bridge bombing missions in the Durance valley because they were hindering his advance.

The point reached Riez with four hours of daylight remaining, and Butler decided to halt and refuel when the supply trucks caught up after dark rather than press on. No sooner had the vehicles moved under cover than a flight of German bombers with fighter escorts roared overhead toward the landing beaches, a stroke of fortune for the task force. At this point, only cavalry elements with three attached infantry platoons and a few tanks, tank destroyers, and artillery pieces were in Riez, the rest of the task force being stretched out between ten and forty miles to the rear. That evening, Butler was delighted when an American captain from one of the OSS action teams reported to him with a tough French World War I veteran in full uniform. Butler decided he could make good use of them on the morrow.

Butler Task Force had almost immediately fallen out of contact with corps headquarters because the broken terrain blocked radio communications. Truscott's chief of staff, Brig. Gen. Arthur White, finally reached Butler at 1920 hours to complain that he had received no reports during the day and charged that an observer in a cub light plane had reported the task force advanced guard appearing very slow and cautious. Truscott would follow up the next day with a searing note demanding contact every two hours, but he at least dispatched to Butler the powerful radio gear necessary to do that.

Seventh Army late on 18 August received from the British Ultra codebreaking program the details of the German withdrawal order, so Sandy Patch was aware that Butler Task Force would face no large threat from its east flank.[3] There is no evidence that Patch shared this closely held information with Truscott, who clearly was given tips on other Ultra intelligence having to do with the locations of enemy divisions.

* * *

Butler decided to reach Sisteron on 19 August and ordered Troop B to protect his right by advancing through Digne, Troop A to proceed up the Durance River, and Troop C to protect his left west of the Durance. He placed the local maquis forces under his OSS captain and assigned them and some light tanks and assault guns to reinforce the Digne mission, because several hundred Germans were reported to be stationed there.

Troop B ran into resistance at Mezel, eight miles outside Digne, but the Germans gave way after a two-hour skirmish and fought small rear-guard actions all the way back to Digne. American scouts slipped into town but retreated under fire, so the command commenced pounding Digne with tank fire preparatory to an assault by the maquis infantry, which failed.

The other task force elements rolled ahead with only minor encounters with the enemy, but Butler learned again that tactical air support could be a two-edged sword. Near Oraison, two American fighter-bombers appeared over vehicles strung out on the road because the advance had been slowed by joyous crowds. Butler had an air liaison team with him, and the men on the ground could hear the pilots casually discuss whether to strafe the column. The transmitter was dead, so the troops on the ground popped yellow smoke to indicate that they were friendlies. To their horror, the pilots did not see or did not understand this signal. The planes dropped their belly tanks and attacked, leaving thirteen men dead and three vehicles wrecked. As a result, an aggrieved Butler requested that Seventh Army cancel all armed reconnaissance and bombing missions in the Durance valley area south of Grenoble.

Butler dispatched a patrol from the central column to approach Digne from the west, but it ran into resistance backed by armored cars in Malijai. Butler then sent a second column, including a company each of medium tanks and infantry, to clear up both situations. The Germans folded in Malijai after a few rounds of 75mm gunfire, and the Digne garrison ran up the white flag before the tanks even cut loose.

By nightfall, the bulk of Butler Task Force was at Sisteron. The command had run off the edge of its army-supplied maps and turned to locally acquired Michelin maps. Butler's supply line already stretched 125 miles back to the supply dumps.

* * *

On the morning of 20 August, Truscott instructed Butler to reconnoiter to the north and west to establish whether he could move to Montélimar. Truscott told him to be prepared to move on Grenoble instead and promised definitive word later in the day. In the meantime, he suggested that he would order the 36th Infantry Division to Sisteron by the next day. Indeed, Lieutenant General Patch the preceding day had instructed Truscott to alert one infantry division to move on Grenoble upon Seventh Army orders.[4]

Truscott was already thinking that it was time to turn the rest of his corps northward and give a push to the Germans east of the Rhône and south of Montélimar. When O'Daniel offered that morning to capture Marseille instead of waiting for the French, Truscott refused. A short while later, Truscott told Eagles, "[It] looks like [the Germans] are pulling out in front of us. . . . Looks like we should shift our weight to the north."[5]

Truscott called Patch and got the green light to send Butler to Montélimar and push the entire 36th Infantry Division in behind him.[6] He also met with Eagles, who said he would have two regiments across the Durance River that night—a step that Dragoon planners had not expected to occur until 15 October! Truscott told him to send the 179th Infantry

Regiment north along the river, which would bring it into contact with Butler's and Dahlquist's forces in the area of Sisteron.[7]

Butler during all this time had received none of Truscott's instructions because of the still unreliable communications setup, so he acted on his own in response to reports of German forces moving south from Grenoble. He pushed his outpost line closer to Grenoble and sent a strong patrol supported by assault guns to the road nexus at Gap to protect his right flank. The command picked up some maquis along the way. A small task force of the 2d Battalion, 143d Infantry, arrived separately after getting lost because of a damaged radio, lack of maps, and misleading road signs switched around by the maquis to confuse the Germans.

That evening, Truscott signaled Butler, "You will move at first light 21 August with all possible speed to Montélimar. Block all routes of withdrawal up the Rhône valley in that vicinity. Thirty-sixth Division follows you." (This message did not reach Butler until 0400 hours the next morning, by courier.)[8]

* * *

German defenses along Butler's route of advance were catastrophically disorganized. *Army Group G* exercised no control over the only substantial unit, the *157th Reserve Division*, nor for practical purposes did Kesselring in Italy. Meanwhile, orders were issued to destroy the mountain roads in the area, but local forces could not comply because they had been stripped of their engineers.[9]

Army Group G commanding general Blaskowitz, moreover, as of 20 August was operating in an intelligence vacuum, but he could imagine what the enemy ought to do. He told *Nineteenth Army* to reckon with an American advance through Digne toward Valence, on the Rhône River, or to Grenoble and ordered the dispatch of a mobile group to secure Valence against that eventuality.[10] If Wiese complied, however, it is not apparent in his field orders of 20 or 21 August (captured by VI Corps), which established local defensive phase lines and gave responsibility for operations to the *338th Infantry* and *11th Panzer divisions*.[11]

Generalleutnant von Wietersheim, meanwhile, finally gathered all elements of his *11th Panzer Division*—and enough fuel to enable his tanks to fight—on the east bank of the Rhône. The general had already received orders two days earlier to screen the withdrawal of *Nineteenth Army* up the Rhône (an order soon amended to simultaneously spearheading the withdrawal and securing all entrances to Highway 7 from the east). His first mission was to prevent an American breakthrough toward Avignon at Aix. The first 3d Infantry Division patrols appeared at about dark on Highway 7 at Aix, where they stopped after taking fire from German troops.[12]

* * *

Truscott on 21 August experienced his first hint of worry since the landings. One reason was that he was already having difficulty supplying his forward elements from the beaches, in large part because all units were still at the stripped-down assault scale of transport; planners had expected heavier fighting close to the beaches.[13] The 3d Infantry Division was in the best shape. The outfit had been the first of the assault divisions to board its ships, and it had found time for loading adjustments that increased the number of vehicles actually transported from a scheduled 3,337 to more than 4,500.[14]

Posing a more immediate concern than supplies, tactical reconnaissance the day before had detected heavy artillery moving south from Lyon, which VI Corps supposed signaled the deployment of a division-sized unit, possibly the *11th Panzer Division*. The corps headquarters was also scrambling to track down reports of 150 tanks advancing toward the 3d Infantry Division at Aix and the appearance of the *11th Panzer Division* at Avignon.[15] In point of fact, von Wietersheim had deployed only reconnaissance elements and a few combat groups, including panzers; he held the bulk of his division in reserve to counter any American breakthrough.[16]

At about noon, Truscott ordered the 3d Infantry Division, which that morning had captured Aix, to halt the bulk of the command in place. Rather than defend the city, the *11th Panzer Division* had attacked simultaneously with the Americans. The German attack pinned one battalion of the 30th Infantry Regiment in place, but a second battalion occupied Aix. "There are indications the *11th Panzer Division* is out in front of you, and there is a possibility you might get a counterattack," Truscott told the doubtless unsurprised 3d Infantry Division CP. In the course of the afternoon, Truscott decided to hold the 45th Infantry Division in place, too.[17]

The panzer division's success in pinning two infantry divisions in place without major offensive action may have been due in part to the fact that Seventh Army's G-2—despite being aware of the Ultra intelligence that the Germans were withdrawing wholesale—issued a report on 21 August indicating that *Nineteenth Army* might still opt to fight where it stood.[18] Whether Truscott was yet aware of the Ultra information is unclear, but in any case VI Corps was stretched almost to the breaking point. Truscott later explained, "While I did not believe that [the] Germans were in any position to launch a major counterattack, a sudden thrust against either the 3d or the 45th Infantry Division might be somewhat embarrassing since my only reserve division was now advancing north from Draguignan."[19]

The 3d Infantry Division, which was to supply the push to *Nineteenth Army*'s withdrawal up the east bank of the Rhône, did not swing northward toward Montélimar for another two days.[20] By then, German units were destroying bridges behind them for the first time, which indicated that their delaying mission had been completed.[21]

RACE TO THE CHOKEPOINT

"We were attempting to set the stage," wrote Truscott in his memoirs, "for a classic–a 'Cannae'—in which we would encircle the enemy against an impassable barrier or obstacle and destroy him."[22] The Rhône valley offered several points at which such a maneuver was possible, one of them north of Montélimar. The town sits on the east bank of the Rhône on a ten-mile-long plain, north of which is the narrow Cruas Gorge, known as the "Gate of Montélimar." From this point north, the valley is generally narrow, save for a plain in the area of Valence. Highway 7 runs along the east bank of the Rhône, and Highway 86 matches its course along the west bank; railroads run parallel to both roadways. Two hill masses (designated 294 and 300, after their heights in meters) dominate the valley on the eastern bank just north of Montélimar. Hill 430, northeast of Montélimar, overlooks the small Roubion River, which flows into the Rhône at that point, as well as the roads along the north bank of the Roubion that offered a potential bypass around the chokepoint on the Rhône.[23]

Butler had overextended himself toward Grenoble in the north, and he now had to rapidly shift his command seventy miles westward to reach the Rhône. Fortunately, enough fuel had caught up with the task force that it could make the race, and ammunition was in ample supply. Leaving a holding force backed by medium tanks and tank destroyers at Gap, Butler ordered his point to be on the road by daybreak.

Lieutenant Colonel Joseph Felber, commanding the 753d Tank Battalion and the main column of armor and infantry, received orders at 0600 on 21 August to pass through Die, then, operating behind a reconnaissance screen, take the high ground overlooking the Rhône approximately three miles south of Livron. The lead reconnaissance elements—Troop B, 117th Cavalry Reconnaissance Squadron—reached the high ground by mid-afternoon. Two platoons probed south to the outskirts of Montélimar, and Greyhound armored cars and Stuart light tanks fired on German vehicles moving north along Highway 7 and at aircraft taking off from a nearby airfield.

Troop C, meanwhile, advanced down the Drôme River from Crest, took the high ground east of Loriol, and cut Highway 7 north of the river near Livron. A patrol advanced to within two hundred yards of the highway bridge across the Drôme; then a fifteen-man demolition squad crept to the span and set charges. The first hint that the Germans had of trouble was when the bridge blew under the very wheels of their column. Once the main bridge had been knocked down, the cavalrymen spotted German forces crossing at a ford closer to the Rhône. One platoon charged to the ford, shot up the German column, and blocked the crossing. Another platoon rolled north up the highway and fell upon the tail of another German column; it threaded its way through the vehicles with all guns firing and destroyed fifty trucks.

Truscott had for the moment achieved his bold desire and cut *Nineteenth Army*'s escape route. But only two platoons of light reconnaissance troops held the chokepoint, and the Germans immediately realized their danger. Shortly before dark, German counterattacks pushed Troops B and C back from their advanced positions, which left only one platoon overlooking the highway near Loriol.

Felber Force, meanwhile, rolled toward its objective over steep and winding roads, dropping elements here and there along the route to secure key junctions, and closed on Condillac about 2145 hours. After examining the terrain, Felber concluded that he lacked the manpower to hold all of the high ground and decided to occupy hill masses to the north and south of the road running from Condillac down to La Concourde, where it intersected Highway 7 near the Rhône. Felber had only a rifle company (less one squad), a heavy weapons company, a few antitank guns, a company of fourteen medium tanks, a handful of tank destroyers, an armored field artillery battalion (less one battery), and a company of noncombat engineers. Felber deployed his limited resources on the high ground and at a few strategic roadblocks, positioning four tank destroyers to command the Rhône road by fire. M7 Priests clanked into firing positions while forward observers made themselves comfortable, peering down on the German *Nineteenth Army* snaking northward below them. Felber obtained Butler's permission to outpost several more hills with Troop B, 117th Cavalry Reconnaissance Squadron, and met with the local FFI commander, who supplied two hundred men to assist in manning outposts and roadblocks.

By 2300, Felber Force was in position.[24] Troop A, 117th Cavalry Reconnaissance Squadron, arrived that night from Gap after being relieved by the 36th Infantry Division, but the medium tanks and tank destroyers lagged behind them.

* * *

The 36th Infantry Division during the day rolled north largely unopposed over roads cleared by Butler Task Force, the stage of the advance through southern France that was captured in the catch phrase "champagne campaign." Friendly crowds jammed the roads in towns scattered among picturesque mountains and valleys.[25]

The 142d Infantry Regiment reached Gap and established roadblocks north of town. A battalion from the 143d Infantry was close behind, ready to advance toward Grenoble at first light. Dahlquist's last regiment, Col. John Harmony's 141st Infantry, was still south of Digne. Harmony's troops had turned to commandeering every vehicle they could find to motorize themselves—including, as things turned out, the Spanish consul's car, which was returned upon request. At 1815 Truscott radioed Dahlquist, "Reinforce Butler with one infantry regiment and the bulk of your [155mm] Long Tom and [105mm] M-1 battalions. Blocking the Rhône valley is your primary mission."[26]

Truscott's instructions appear to have overlooked the logistic situation. The VI Corps chief of staff the next day would complain to Seventh Army, "On the gasoline situation, it was very critical last night, and we had to short our divisions, especially so with the 36th Division and the Butler Force. If those people run out of gas, then this whole thing will blow up."[27]

* * *

The sky gradually lightened enough on the morning of 22 August that the tank and tank destroyer gunners of Felber Force could see through their sights, and the men were delighted to observe a target-rich environment of German vehicles below them crawling past hulks destroyed by shelling during the night. Cannons barked, shells flew true, and soon so much additional wreckage clogged the route that it became temporarily blocked.[28] There were many smaller paths parallel to the highway, however, so German movement never ceased entirely.

Slowly the ranks of Butler Task Force were swelled by additional formations—the missing armored field artillery battery, plus another column including a half-dozen more tank destroyers. But, as Butler later observed, "The Germans were building up against me faster than were our own forces building up."[29]

Artillery, tanks, tank destroyers, armored cars, and even the infantry's 57mm antitank guns rained death on Highway 7 during the long daylight hours. The 59th Armored Field Artillery Battalion smashed several trains, which blocked the rail line on the east bank of the river. Two trains carrying munitions put on an impressive display of pyrotechnics as they burned.

Butler's main concern that day turned out not to be the Rhône highway but rather German efforts to advance from Montélimar along the north bank of the Roubion River and thence northeastward across his rear, which Felber now protected with a small reserve force. Five Panthers supported by panzergrenadiers smashed a roadblock at Cleon, temporarily cut off Troop A of the 117th Cavalry Reconnaissance Squadron, and rolled toward Puy St. Martin, where Felber had his command post. Felber had only a few tank destroyers at hand, which engaged the Germans, but the Shermans and tank destroyers on the road from Gap that were to form the core of his reserve had not yet arrived. A cub artillery plane was dispatched to drop a message of dire need to the column. Butler described what happened next: "[O]ur rescue column arrived for a movie finish. The German tanks that had crossed the Roubion were destroyed, the infantry were driven back, and on the south bank several fires burned merrily where our guns had found trucks and light vehicles. It was a good honest fight. The reserves had arrived in the nick of time."

The arrival of Panthers and panzergrenadiers was a sure sign that the *11th Panzer Division* was joining the battle. Butler signaled Dahlquist, "French [maquis] infantry support absolutely unsatisfactory repeat absolutely unsatisfactory. Request one infantry battalion by motor without delay." Receiving word that infantry was on the way, Butler assured Felber that he would soon have help for his overextended reserve. But after the day's slugfest, Butler Task Force was down to twenty-five rounds of artillery ammunition per tube, half of Butler's desired minimum. Fire ceased until supplies arrived after dark.[30]

* * *

Dahlquist had selected the 141st Infantry Regiment for the critical job of reinforcing Butler and ordered the regiment to send its 2d Battalion to Livron, because the other two battalions were still strung out along the route back to Digne. Regimental commander Col. John Harmony, who accompanied the 2d Battalion, ordered his 1st Battalion to follow, but a shortage of gasoline grounded the outfit. In a handwritten note to Truscott, Dahlquist explained that he had less than five thousand gallons of gasoline on hand. "Be assured that I realize [the] situation, and I am dispatching forces to Butler to the *maximum* extent allowable by transport."[31]

Truscott, for his part, in late morning flew to the 36th Infantry Division CP, where he found Dahlquist gone to Gap. Truscott was angry when he learned that the 141st Infantry Regiment and corps heavy artillery battalion, which should have been on their way to Montélimar, were still in bivouac, pending clarification of (false) reports that a strong German force was approaching Gap. Truscott soon had everyone moving where he wanted them to go.

Truscott followed up with a letter to Dahlquist in which he made clear that he expected the 36th Infantry Division would need all of its resources at Montélimar, where it not only had to block Highway 7 along the river but any bypass routes to the east. Truscott wanted no more than blocking forces around Gap and to the east. He told Dahlquist that he was sending Eagles' 179th Infantry Regiment northward for attachment and that Dahlquist should employ the formation around Grenoble, where the remainder of the 45th Infantry Division would follow as soon as possible.[32]

A still angry Truscott got Dahlquist on the phone late in the evening. He wanted the 143d Infantry Regiment, which had entered Grenoble at midday only to find the Germans gone, to strengthen the chokehold at Montélimar. The 45th Infantry Division's 179th Infantry Regiment was well positioned to carry out the mission, Dahlquist pointed out, instead of having to double the 143d Infantry back. Truscott agreed to swap the missions of the 179th and 143d Infantry regiments, but he snapped, "I want you to do what I told you the first day. Your primary mission is to block the Rhône valley, and I expect you to do it. . . . When the 179th reports to you, you send them over to the Rhône valley, and you will go over there yourself and assume command. . . . And when you run out of gas, you park your trucks and move on foot." (The VI Corps G-3 journal records a confused phone conversation the next morning involving the corps and division chiefs of staff and the 45th Infantry Division deputy commander that resulted in the 179th Infantry being sent to Grenoble after all to replace the 143d Infantry, though none of the participants were at all certain whether Truscott or Dahlquist had changed his mind on the subject.)

Dahlquist, meanwhile, had spoken with Butler, who planned to attack Montélimar that afternoon if he could organize the maquis and the next morning if he could not. Indeed, Butler was optimistic that he could capture the town quickly.

As for the rest of VI Corps south of *Nineteenth Army*, as O'Daniel told Truscott, "We're in contact with nothing." O'Daniel's 3d Infantry Division—still held on a leash by Truscott, who was trying to arrange for the French to fill in and free the division to push north—began a cautiously paced advance by phase lines. The Germans had largely broken contact with the 45th Infantry Division as well. As he had indicated to Dahlquist, Truscott ordered the Thunderbird Division to swing around the 36th Division and take position at Grenoble, less the 179th Infantry

Regiment, which he had ordered to join Dahlquist. "I think I am going to have a battle up where Butler is," Truscott explained to Eagles.[33]

* * *

Nineteenth Army finally overcame its information blackout on 22 August, when the *11th Panzer Division* hit Butler Task Force's lines north of Montélimar, and road reconnaissance detected the 36th Infantry Division on the move east of the retreat route.[34] Army commanding general Wiese ordered *LXXXV Corps* to move the *198th Infantry Division* north to reinforce the panzer division.[35]

Army Group G's headquarters, meanwhile, evacuated Avignon on 22 August and moved to Lyon. There, Blaskowitz took command over all military elements in the vicinity to organize the reception of his retreating forces. The administrative army headquarters for southern France, dubbed *Oberkommando Dehner*, scraped up every available security unit and *Ostbattalion* to secure the area around Lyon and Dijon. Blaskowitz, denied communication and even road reconnaissance, now found himself completely cut off from the battle, as "in pre-technical days," he later wrote.[36]

The Battle of Montélimar

Truscott appears to have been still agitated when he again called Dahlquist's CP at 0200 hours on 23 August, only to find the 36th Division commanding general already gone to track down Butler. "I want to get word to Butler or to General Dahlquist, if he is over there, to interrupt by demolitions that main road. Do you understand? In the Rhône valley. I don't want a single vehicle to get up that road!"[37]

Butler Task Force troops were doing their best to block the Rhône highway with direct and artillery fire, which added steadily to the wreckage along the roadway. But Butler still faced a sticky situation to his rear early on 23 August. Another crucial roadblock had collapsed at Sauzet on the road that passed east of Butler's main positions after the maquis had mistakenly allowed panzers and grenadiers into town, thinking they were Americans. In the early dawn light, the panzer crews spotted a Sherman tank outposting the hill just north of town and little more than a mile from the American CP. Long-barreled 75mm cannons roared and smashed the

M4. Just as things looked rather dire, the first trucks bearing the 2d Battalion, 141st Infantry Regiment, arrived. Backed by several Shermans, the reinforcements attacked Sauzet and restored the situation.[38]

Other German probes followed, and tanks and tank destroyers engaged panzers at several points east of Condillac. Butler Task Force radioed to Seventh Army at 0845 that enemy columns were moving north along the road east of its CP and requested that any fighter-bombers in range be put on call for strike missions. Seventh Army replied that none were available, though in extreme emergencies Spitfires could strafe ground targets.[39]

Butler Task Force dissolved as of 0900, although Butler for the time being continued to direct the action, and the 36th Infantry Division took command of all its elements.[40] The 36th Division's gasoline shortages, at least, had been momentarily resolved by the morning hours, in part by using ten thousand gallons taken from the 45th Infantry Division's meager reserves and in part by dipping into captured German stocks.[41] Colonel Harmony established his regimental CP at Condillac, and at about 0930 the 1st Battalion staff arrived. In response to instructions from Butler, Harmony ordered battalion CO (commanding officer) Lt. Col. William Bird to attack Hill 300, which was three and a half miles north of Montélimar and extended along a ridge to La Concourde, where he was to establish a roadblock. Harmony told Lt. Col. James Critchfield, commanding the 2d Battalion, to attack Montélimar with the support of some tanks and tank destroyers.[42]

By noon, the 1st Battalion had one company on the north slopes of Hill 300. Company C, however, which had been instructed to enter La Concourde and cut Highway 7, ground to a halt east of town under heavy artillery, mortar, and small-arms fire. An hour later, Maj. Robert Osborne arrived with his 3d Battalion, and Harmony ordered him to occupy the high ground four miles south of Livron and to block the north-south roads through that area.[43]

The T-Patch Division had established its first, tenuous presence at the chokepoint, having traveled 250 miles since the first boots touched shore eight days earlier.[44] At 1530, Felber turned over command of his sector to Colonel Harmony.[45] The sole supply route for the 141st Infantry

Regiment—the road from Marsanne to Condillac—was still subject to almost constant harassing fire.[46]

The 2d Battalion attack on Montélimar at 1630 hours appeared doomed from the start, despite support from newly arrived 155mm Long Tom guns. The tanks and tank destroyers failed to appear on time, and a group of maquis who were to have supported the operation dispersed when they were hit by a German counterattack.[47] Butler, who observed the operation, thought the Germans were having the better of it and obtained Dahlquist's permission to stop the attack and withdraw the cavalry screen—which had been bypassed by the enemy assault elements—through the friendly infantry line. The battalion dug in on high ground roughly two thousand yards northeast of Montélimar.[48]

At the same time that the Germans hit the 2d Battalion, another force estimated to be one company of infantry supported by armor tried to throw the rifle company off Hill 300. The 141st Infantry Regiment after-action report (AAR) asserts that the tank destroyers withdrew and had to be tracked down to get them back in the battle, but the S-3 journal indicates only that two vehicles had to move because German half-tracks had approached their positions. In any case, the description of the attacking force indicates that it came from the *11th Panzer Division.*

When direct assault failed, the Germans infiltrated through and around the 1st and 2d battalions using a maze of roads and trails that the Americans lacked the manpower to block. The fact that there were no significant clashes suggests that these Germans were escaping rather than trying to cut off the battalion.

Harmony changed the 2d Battalion's orders at about 2140 hours to seize the high ground north of the road leading east out of Montélimar, and he withdrew the 3d Battalion to the area of his CP. Meanwhile, along the Drôme, American forces had withdrawn four miles east of the Rhône, where cavalry reinforced by the 141st Infantry Regiment's antitank and cannon companies manned a roadblock north of the river.[49]

* * *

As reports from reconnaissance units arrived at the *11th Panzer Division* CP confirming the American bid to cut off the *Nineteenth Army's* retreat, the Germans threw the division's armored reconnaissance battalion, strengthened by some panzers and an artillery battery, forward toward Loriol and Crest. The battalion's mission was to prevent at all costs any renewed American push westward down the Drôme River to the Rhône. Von Wietersheim also raced his noncombat elements north past the bottleneck into the area of Valence.[50] He now had orders to extricate his delaying forces from the south and send them forward as well.[51]

* * *

At 1930 hours, Dahlquist's chief of staff ordered Harmony to reestablish the roadblock on the Rhône road, but he was told that the job was impossible. The Germans were shelling the area incessantly, and the regiment's own supply of artillery ammunition was low and had to be conserved.[52]

Consulting with Dahlquist and Butler late in the day, Truscott judged that mistakes had been made but suggested that they were water under the bridge. He told Dahlquist to secure the ridge overlooking Highway 7. Dahlquist was so sure he could do so with the resources in place that he asked to divert the 143d Infantry Regiment to Valence. Truscott agreed as long as the town could be taken without a fight, but he still wanted the regiment to march to Montélimar. Truscott directed that Butler Task Force be reconstituted to provide a mobile strike force.[53]

Pressure on the Germans from the south remained minimal, as reflected in the 3d Infantry Division's morning intelligence summary, which reported the situation "generally quiet with little enemy contact."[54] Von Wietersheim took advantage of this situation to redeploy his screening forces in the south to the Montélimar area.[55]

24 August: Grappling and Maneuvering

"Then came Montélimar!" recorded the history of the 141st Infantry Regiment, which had experienced some of the worst fighting in Italy. "A name that was to take its place along with Salerno, the Rapido, San Pietro, and Cassino, a place where battle reached its highest crescendo. . . . For us, Montélimar and the week from 24 to 30 August was one of the fullest 168-hour weeks of the war."[56]

Early on 24 August, *11th Panzer Division* reconnaissance elements in the Drôme valley reported that they had made contact with unidentified

American forces. Wiese realized he was going to have to fight his way through the chokepoint at Montélimar and, if possible, open a parallel escape route via Bonlieu-Grane-Allex. He ordered the *198th Infantry Division*—which he subordinated to von Wietersheim—and the *18th "Tyroller" Antiaircraft Regiment* forward to Espeluche, southeast of Montélimar, by forced march. Ominously, American pressure in the Drôme valley had increased during the day.

Not far to the south, Company C, 1st Battalion, 141st Infantry Regiment, launched its second attempt to cut Highway 7 at La Concourde after a brief artillery preparation. Tanks, tank destroyers, mortars, and Company A on Hill 300 laid down supporting fire, and the GIs fought their way into La Concourde by 1430 hours. After clearing the buildings, the company—which by now had suffered heavy casualties—advanced again until encountering German troops dug in at a bridge on the main road.

After pounding Company C with artillery, a large German force supported by tanks counterattacked from the south. The GIs fell back to the original line of departure under direct high-velocity tank fire. German attacks also hit battalion positions on the high ground and by day's end had driven the American rifle company off the top of Hill 300 to its lower northern slopes. Regimental CO Colonel Harmony ordered the battalion to withdraw a thousand yards to the east, where a parallel ridge would still permit direct fire against targets on Highway 7. Nevertheless, Truscott's tentative grip on the chokepoint had slipped again.[57]

* * *

East of Montélimar, probable *11th Panzer Division* elements were spotted at about 0730 hours infiltrating around the 2d Battalion, 141st Infantry Regiment, a problem that soon engaged the outfit so thoroughly that it could not execute the movement orders received the night before. (The battalion commanding officer, Lt. Col. James Critchfield, stated in a post-war account that some of his men did manage to briefly cut Highway 7 about dawn before the Germans struck his lines.) The GIs first spotted a small group of the enemy approaching the battalion's right flank, and a rifle platoon backed by three tanks assaulted the Germans and took fifty-two prisoners. About the same time, another group of Germans appeared on the battalion's supply route back to Sauzet. Company F attacked, supported by 81mm mortars, and dispersed the Germans.

The Germans had clearly decided to remove the obstruction by 1300 hours, when enemy troops appeared to the front and on both flanks of the 2d Battalion. Three probable Mark Vs on the south bank of the Roubion picked off the supporting American tanks and tank destroyers one by one; then panzers clanked into position and pounded the GIs in their foxholes from close range. Tank-infantry attacks from all three directions followed and again cut the battalion's supply route. As casualties mounted, the GIs hung on grimly, thanks to the supporting fire of three artillery battalions, which were directed personally by Critchfield after his artillery observer and some of his battalion staff had been hit. Division ordered the outfit to withdraw under cover of darkness.[58]

The regimental history recorded, "For us in the 2d Battalion, Montélimar means a barren hill with German tanks and infantry surrounding us for six unforgettable hours; thousands of rounds of our own artillery thudding into waves of Germans that were flung at our position from every side; Mark V tanks so close you could feel the heat from the motor; a withdrawal at night from a hill covered with burning, exploding tanks, knocked out guns, and dead men. We will never forget the eerie sight of a [now turretless tank destroyer] pulling a knocked-out ton-and-a-half and a 57mm AT [antitank] gun loaded down with fifty men swathed in blood-soaked bandages and a handful of medics with their white and red helmets gleaming in the moonlight."[59]

The 2d Battalion fought its way back to Sauzet, where it reorganized while the 3d Battalion slipped in on its left to hold the flank.

* * *

Wiese visited von Wietersheim at the *11th Panzer Division* CP, which had just moved to a spot east of Montélimar, to deliver an order to attack at 1100 hours on 25 August. Von Wietersheim showed Wiese a captured order for American operations north of Montélimar that convinced Wiese he had only hours to act; he could not even give the just-arriving and fatigued *198th Infantry Division* a moment's rest. The route of advance was to be up the roads parallel to the main road along the bank of the Rhône, through Cleon to Grane.[60]

* * *

Indeed, Dahlquist had instructed the 142d Infantry Regiment to consolidate his line northeast of Montélimar by swinging into positions along the small Roubion River in the vicinity of Cleon. It was this order that had fallen into German hands when a courier drove his jeep into a German roadblock. The regiment moved under cover of darkness, deployed two battalions along the shallow stream, and placed a thin screen of combat engineers on the right to tie into the 3d Battalion, 141st Infantry Regiment. The two regiments now held a line that ran nearly due east from the Rhône above Montélimar and faced to the south. A company of maquis settled into position on high ground on the open left flank.

The ground along the Roubion was flat and open—excellent tank country. The regiment set mines, blew the bridges across the river, placed its only two available tank destroyers in reserve, and emplaced its artillery on a ridgeline to the rear.[61]

* * *

The 143d Infantry Regiment had in the meantime been relieved at Grenoble by elements of the 179th Infantry and was engaged in a peculiar evolution, marching southward and westward back in the direction of Montélimar parallel to and east of the *Nineteenth Army*'s flight northward along the Rhône. At Valence, the regiment nearly cut off not only the forces east of the river but also parts of the *IV Luftwaffe Field Corps* that were crossing from the west side at that point.

At 1900 hours Dahlquist ordered the 143d Infantry to seize Valence immediately, and the 1st Battalion moved out toward the town after coordinating a plan for a three-pronged attack with Commandant Le Giand, of the local maquis. The main force consisted of a rifle company mounted on some tanks and the M10s of two platoons from Company B, 636th Tank Destroyer Battalion. After rolling through one German roadblock, the force encountered heavy fire east of Valence.

Dusk was deepening when the German fire lashed the column, and GIs scrambled off the decks and into the roadside ditches. The armor could not maneuver off the road for fear of crushing its own men; nor could it fire at dimly seen targets for fear of shooting friendlies by mistake. A tree crashed down across the road in front of one M10, doubtless loosed by planted explosives, and a high-velocity gun wrecked the tank destroyer. Bazooka and rifle grenades sought other armored vehicles, silhouetted by small lights that lit up every twenty yards along the road. The German ambush knocked out two tanks, and the American force sustained some fifty casualties before drawing back.

A maquis force failed to show up on the right flank for the second attack, which cost Company B another M10 to direct fire. The third prong, on the left, also halted in the face of heavy resistance from the town.[62]

The 143d Infantry Regiment broke off the Valence attack and, on new orders from Dahlquist, concentrated its forces at Crest that night before moving over darkened roads lit by the flash of a heavy artillery bombardment to Puy St. Martin.[63] The regiment (less two infantry battalions and the antitank company) now made up part of the reconstituted Butler Task Force, which had set up its headquarters at Le Bois during the day. The other elements of Butler's command were the 117th Cavalry Reconnaissance Squadron (less Troop A), the 753d Tank Battalion (less one light and two medium tank companies), a company of the 636th Tank Destroyer Battalion (less six tank destroyers), the 93d Field Artillery Battalion, and Company F from the 344th Engineer Regiment (reinforced).[64]

* * *

Dahlquist phoned Truscott late that evening to report the failed German attempt to punch through his line east of Montélimar and asked—despite the approach of his own 143d Infantry—that a regiment from the 45th Infantry Division be shifted to Crest to support him the next day. Truscott replied, "You can expect no assistance tomorrow. You must hold the pass with the forces at your command. You can expect a full-scale attack tomorrow. I realize that. Good luck, and I have full confidence in your ability to do it." Truscott evidently relented somewhat; just after midnight his chief of staff called the 45th Infantry Division headquarters to urge the outfit to rush its tanks north to reinforce Dahlquist.

Truscott's formal directive to Dahlquist for the next day said, "Troops of your command must physically occupy the road on the east bank of the Rhône River between Montélimar and Livron at some point." As soon as Dahlquist read the message sometime after midnight, he (erroneously) replied that fighting was ongoing in Valence on the east bank of the Rhône and the road was already interdicted.[65]

To the south, a disorganized relief of 3d Infantry Division elements by the French had reached critical mass. The division's G-3 reported to VI Corps, "At present, there are various and sundry groups of Frenchmen now passing through various and sundry elements of ours, none of whom quite know what their mission is or where they are going, but our orders have been issued that when any Frenchman gets west of any American, the American is automatically relieved." The 15th and 30th Infantry regiments were expected to concentrate in staging areas by the middle of the next day, and the division had new orders: Prepare to advance toward Montélimar.[66]

25–26 August: Truscott Nearly Gets His Chokehold

The *11th Panzer Division*'s attack (including the subordinated elements of the *198th Infantry Division*), aimed at opening a second escape route behind the American forces overlooking the Rhône valley, hit the morning of 25 August. The *198th Infantry Division*'s artillery had not yet come up, which allowed for only piecemeal supporting fire.[67] With the American operational order in hand, von Wietersheim aimed the attack at the weak link between the 141st and 142d Infantry regiments near Bonlieu and along the Rhône road.[68]

The *326th Grenadier Regiment* overran the 36th Infantry Division's 111th Combat Engineer Battalion, which was holding a three-thousand-yard front at Bonlieu. Covered by direct fire from panzers, German riflemen crossed the shallow river and pushed back the engineers several hundred yards. A second battalion-sized assault supported by six panzers—so skillfully camouflaged that American artillery observers on the ridgeline to the north had trouble spotting them—then shattered the engineers and pushed on toward Marsanne. The Americans responded with a crushing artillery barrage, which broke up the attack. By the time the 1st Battalion, 143d Infantry Regiment, which had been attached to the 142d Infantry as its reserve force, arrived to seal the breach, the GIs found the Germans already falling back and easily restored the Roubion River line by nightfall.[69]

* * *

Truscott was still grasping at air on Highway 7. Various records indicate that VI Corps headquarters falsely believed that the reconstituted Butler Task Force had cut the road some three thousand yards south of Loriol early on 25 August but that by 1020 the force had withdrawn under enemy pressure. The task force records and Butler's post-war account reflect no such series of events.[70] The 141st Infantry Regiment's 1st Battalion did possess the forward slope of a hill mass facing the highway, and by late morning the regiment was planning an attack to cut the road again.[71]

* * *

The *11th Panzer Division* had taken advantage of the open road, and its reconnaissance battalion and a few panzers probed farther to the north and east. Soon, VI Corps received reports that a column of a hundred German vehicles preceded by tanks was moving eastward south of the Drôme, and the 36th Infantry Division took it under artillery fire that von Wietersheim would later describe as "heavier than we had imagined [possible]."[72, 73]

Dahlquist told Butler to move his armor to Grane to block the German advance, and by 1230 the 753d Tank Battalion had orders to engage and destroy the enemy panzers. Lieutenant Colonel Felber led a column consisting of his own Company C (less one platoon) and four M10s from the 636th Tank Destroyer Battalion over winding roads to Grane. Reports from an attached artillery observer suggested that the German column might already be turning back westward, and the American command encountered only small-arms and mortar fire when it tested the defenses in town. Although Felber requested permission to pursue the enemy westward, he was ordered to hold at Grane.[74]

German armored reconnaissance elements north of the Drôme had a clear road, and by about 1700 hours they had advanced through Allex and nearly reached Crest, through which ran the 36th Infantry Division's only supply route. The 143d Infantry Regiment—which now consisted of little more than its 3d Battalion, because it had to transfer the 1st Battalion to strengthen the 142d Infantry—established roadblocks around Crest to thwart the Germans. After being relieved by some engineers, the reduced battalion moved to the area of Marsanne.[75]

Dahlquist told Truscott that he was short of armor, and Truscott ordered Eagles to send his tanks to Nyon and to motorize a battalion or even a company of infantry to go along if possible. This force was then to approach Montélimar from the southeast. Orders reached the 191st Tank Battalion by 1430, and the armor moved to Nyon, only to find it still occupied by Germans. T-Patch officers directed the tanks along a detour to Roynac, where the battalion went into 36th Infantry Division reserve along with the 3d Battalion, 157th Infantry Regiment.

Meanwhile, VI Corps called for air attacks against German concentrations southeast of Montélimar and in mid-afternoon demanded to know why it was getting no response. Upon being informed that the targets were within the bomb safety line, Truscott said he would take personal responsibility for the attacks. Soon, air strikes, reinforced by artillery fire, were under way south and southeast of Montélimar.[76]

Air strikes and artillery fire also destroyed the railroad bridges across the Drôme in the vicinity of Loriol. Maquis reports indicated that German troops nevertheless were fording the river at four spots with little hindrance.[77]

* * *

With the failure of the attack toward Crest, the Germans were in a perilous situation. Troops were bunching up in Montélimar, and American armor was sporadically interdicting the Rhône road. Alarming intelligence reached Wiese that American troops held Crest, had arrived at Valence, and now held Bourg, northeast of Valence (which was not true). The *11th Panzer Division* appeared to be the only hope of dealing with those problems, and Wiese ordered the *Ghost Division* to hand over much of its sector to the infantry and concentrate to hold the heights commanding the critical stretch of road between Condillac and Livron. The only bright spot was that American pressure from the south was still so weak that Wiese could redeploy the *338th Infantry Division* to relieve von Wietersheim and leave only a small blocking force to the south.

Wiese's problems were just then worsening further.

* * *

Early that morning, Dahlquist had instructed the 141st Infantry Regiment's commander Colonel Harmony to cut Highway 7 "at all costs."

The regiment's 1st and 2d battalions had lost so many men in the recent fighting that Harmony doubted he could organize a force strong enough to establish and hold a roadblock, but he set to work.

At 1500 hours, two rifle companies from the 141st and 143d Infantry regiments launched coordinated attacks that recaptured the key features on Hill 300 and opened the door to another shot at La Concourde. The 1st Battalion, 141st Infantry, then sent two rifle companies down the road from Condillac supported by the eight surviving M10s from Company B, 636th Tank Destroyer Battalion, and three Shermans from the 753d Tank Battalion. Within an hour, the small force had severed the German escape route against only scattered resistance.

The infantry commander decided to establish his roadblock in a depression measuring some 250 yards north to south and 100 yards east to west, and he grouped the entire force there to ensure close support for the riflemen. The tank destroyer commander fruitlessly objected that his vehicles were placed so that they had poor fields of fire.

By 2040 hours, German infantry arrived by truck and took up positions only eight hundred yards from the roadblock, and soon more were arriving from north and south. Colonel Harmony doubted his men could hold the position and asked Division for permission to blow a bridge near La Concourde and pull back to the high ground, but Dahlquist responded that the block had to be physically manned. Observed artillery fire kept the Germans at bay while there was still light to see, but the night came inevitably.[78]

In Montélimar, the sounds of battle told von Wietersheim that the Americans held Highway 7 at La Concourde, and he resolved to personally lead an attack to break through. About 0100 hours on 26 August, the *11th Panzer Division* struck the roadblock from several directions after an intense artillery barrage. Sgt. Wayman Davis, a tank destroyer commander, recalled, "Infantry came down the road and over the knolls and milled down into the depression. There were at least a hundred of them. Some were shouting in good English, 'Come on, you bastards, give up!'"

A German panzer company commander who had advanced with the panzergrenadiers then fired flares that illuminated the armor for his tanks standing off in the dark. One panzer fired at Davis' M10 from near point-blank range, and he could not rotate his turret to return fire because trees blocked the gun barrel. Davis' tank destroyer burst into flames, and the closest M10 to his position was taken out of the fight when another panzer rammed its barrel in the confusion and stripped the traversing mechanism.

Five M10s and all of the tanks were quickly knocked out, and a sixth tank destroyer was damaged. Following a two-hour exchange of fire, the Americans became disorganized and retreated to the main line of resistance 1,500 yards to the rear. The Germans had also lost heavily among the panzergrenadiers.[79]

The *11th Panzer Division* pushed on to take Hill 300 and restored control over the heights above La Concourde. Dahlquist's chief of staff asked Harmony whether he could attack again but was told no. At 0445, Division told the 141st Infantry Regiment that Butler Task Force would reestablish the roadblock later in the day.[80]

* * *

Combat flared along the east shoulder of the German escape route on 26 August. Before dawn, Dahlquist ordered Task Force Butler's 143d Infantry Regiment, which was still at battalion strength because of detachments, to attack through the Condillac pass toward La Concourde at 1300 hours to reestablish the roadblock on the Rhône River road. The 3d Battalion pushed off nearly as scheduled but by 1800 was still fighting to establish itself along the ridgeline overlooking the highway. Because of these difficulties, the 3d Battalion of the 45th Infantry Division's 157th Infantry Regiment was brought forward to the vicinity of Condillac to press the attack the next morning.

In the meantime, 36th Infantry Division artillery pounded the Germans along the river, the level of devastation inflicted at this point limited primarily by the availability of shells. Supply trucks were making a roundtrip of 150 miles, and each battery had to retain a seven-hundred-round reserve in anticipation of German counterattacks.[81]

* * *

A battalion of German infantry from the *305th Grenadier Regiment* supported by four panzers struck again at the seam between the 141st and 142d Infantry regiments and forced a crossing of the Roubion River, again at Bonlieu. At the same time, a German column evidently trying to envelop the 142d Infantry's line to the east was spotted. Fortunately for the Americans, the 1st Battalion, 142d Infantry, only two hours earlier had shifted into the vicinity of the latter column and, reinforced by the two reserve tank destroyers, drove back the Germans, with a loss of two panzers and heavy casualties. The attached battalion from the 143d Infantry, meanwhile, once again restored the Roubion River line.[82]

* * *

Truscott decided to take another stab at closing the Rhône farther north and sent the 157th Infantry Regiment (less a battalion) through Crest to attack westward down the Drôme along the north bank. With his reconnaissance troops falling back, von Wietersheim committed his reserve in the valley to a counterattack at Allex, where his men ran into the 2d Battalion of the 157th Infantry. Shermans from Company B, 191st Tank Battalion, exchanged fire with six panzers. The American gunners claimed one victim, but return fire struck two M4s, one of which burned. At dark, the Germans backed off westward.[83]

Truscott was already thinking about his next possible Cannae. He visited Butler's headquarters during the evening and ordered the task force to take Loriol, swing back through Crest to the north, "highball [it] to Lyon," and cut off German troops exiting the Rhône valley.[84] The day's tough fight along the Drôme, however, suggested that Truscott might be getting ahead of himself.

27–28 August

Wiese instructed *LXXXV Corps* to break through via the Condillac road on 27 August using the *198th* and *338th Infantry division*s supported by some tanks. American artillery fire along the main highway that day was so deadly that traffic was barred from using it and shifted to alternate routes on small parallel byways.[85]

Butler Task Force's Lt. Col. Joseph Felber had the misfortune to have received orders to reestablish a roadblock at La Concourde by attacking down the very same road that Wiese planned to use. Felber was given Company A, 191st Tank Battalion; the light tank troop from the 117th Cavalry Reconnaissance Squadron; and the 3d Battalion, 157th Infantry Regiment to do the job. Felber had been lightly wounded a day earlier while searching on foot for a German tank or SP gun that had gotten behind American lines in the high ground near Condillac and was causing some mayhem, eluding bazooka teams sent to hunt it down. The bowl-shaped depression outside La Concourde, in which the 1st Battalion, 141st Infantry, had set up its defenses two days earlier, posed problems for an attacker from this direction. Panzers and antitank guns in the village, on ground west of the highway, and to the north had perfect fields of fire.[86]

The infantry jumped off before daylight supported by medium tanks and four tank destroyers. Sniper rounds gave way to machine-gun fire from some houses that straddled the road eight hundred yards east of the objective. When the assault company went to ground, a platoon of Shermans rolled forward and blasted the defenders out, although a covering tank destroyer hit a mine and was disabled. When the infantry rose to advance once again, the gun behind American lines opened fire on them from the rear.

At about this time, three Panthers and some German infantry appeared on the north flank, where the slope of the rise blocked American artillery fire. The GIs had no bazookas, because the truck carrying them had been wrecked the night before. A Sherman platoon maneuvered to a small ridge, and gunners opened fire at eight hundred yards only to watch their shells bounce off the thick, well-sloped German armor. A tank destroyer crept to the Germans' right flank and managed to knock out one of the Mark Vs but was dispatched almost immediately in return. The Germans nevertheless pulled back after scattering Company K.

The attack got moving again at 0930, but when the infantry emerged from the housing cluster, heavy fire drove the Americans back to shelter almost immediately. The panzers attacked again while alternate routes of advance were being reconnoitered, and in this engagement the Shermans knocked a track off one Panther, then pounded the tank with fourteen rounds at six hundred yards, which finally set the vehicle alight.

Felber set the next attack for 1815 hours and jumped into his jeep to visit Butler's CP. On his return trip in the company of Col. John Harmony, the 141st Infantry Regiment commander, Felber's jeep was hit by the hidden German gun, which killed his driver and wounded both officers. Harmony's wound was serious enough to require evacuation to Italy.

The attack jumped off on schedule and again halted in the face of withering fire. Six American fighters wheeling overhead chose this moment to pounce and strafed Felber's command for fifteen minutes, ignoring yellow recognition smoke grenades and scattering infantry and tanks. The tank company commander was wounded, and two Shermans caught fire, provoking frenzied firefighting efforts by the other crews to douse the flames before they ignited leaking fuel from the remaining tanks.

Felber tried one last attack before giving up at 2015 hours.[87] Butler Task Force was ordered to disengage and move to the Drôme valley to attack Loriol.[88]

* * *

Farther south, the day passed so quietly on the heretofore hotly contested Roubion River line that American commanders began to speculate that the bulk of the enemy forces might have escaped to the north. Strong combat patrols from the 142d Infantry Regiment encountered no opposition when they probed southward to find the 3d Infantry Division, which was just pushing up Highway 7, but fierce enemy fire greeted patrols pushing northwestward toward the Rhône.[89]

* * *

Almost all remaining elements of the *11th Panzer Division* shifted to the north bank of the Drôme on 28 August, and von Wietersheim sent his armored reconnaissance battalion to probe to the east and north and to screen Valence. The battalion reported no substantial contact with American forces; the *Ghost Division* had reached safe ground.[90]

The *11th Panzer Division*'s rear guard tangled with Felber Force again, this time near Loriol, where Panthers firing from hull-down positions claimed three Shermans and two tank destroyers.[91] Butler Task Force nevertheless by late afternoon pushed into the outskirts of Loriol and cut Highway 7 with two roadblocks. Just before midnight, German infantry supported by panzers launched a vigorous attack that drove the Americans reeling back out of town.[92]

* * *

On the night of 28–29 August, Wiese faced a desperate situation: Much of *LXXXV Corps* still faced encirclement. Wiese summoned Kniess to the *11th Panzer Division* CP northeast of Livron and reviewed the situation. It was time for a desperate gamble: Wiese ordered his troops to break into small combat groups and exfiltrate during the night toward Valence. There, Kniess would rally those who had already made it through and establish a new defensive line with the help of the *11th Panzer Division*.[93]

That same night, Dahlquist swung his 142d Infantry Regiment northward in a bid to cut the escape route again, but he was too late. The GIs entered Livron against only scattered resistance, but the *11th Panzer Division* waged an effective rear-guard action against American efforts to follow up much beyond the Drôme River. The 142d Infantry Regiment turned to mopping up—still a profitable enterprise as its artillery laid waste to yet more escaping German vehicles, and the infantry rolled up another 650 prisoners.[94]

Confused and at times sharp engagements continued elsewhere south of the Drôme as the last German combat units tried to slip away. Butler Task Force pushed its way back into Loriol against vigorous resistance that collapsed when the GIs entered town, where a company from the *757th Grenadier Regiment* surrendered.[95]

Along the high ground from La Concourde northward, close-quarters fighting between elements of the 143d Infantry Regiment and German infantry backed by panzers and antiaircraft guns endangered the 3d Battalion command post and scattered or forced back much of the 2d Battalion. At one point, Lt. Col. Theodore Andrews, the 3d Battalion's commander, had to call down an artillery barrage on his own position because the Germans were overrunning his lines; a company commander in Andrews' command post was killed by the friendly fire. Still, the Americans by now had the upper hand and continued their spree of destruction. The day's prisoner take included *Generalmajor* Otto Richter, commanding general of the *198th Infantry Division*.[96]

By 1100 hours, almost no Germans were visible along the Rhône highway. As sniper fire continued to be a problem, the 3d Battalion of the 143d Infantry sent out a patrol to warn a group of twelve GIs spotted moving northward along the road. The men turned out to be from the 3d Infantry Division's 7th Infantry Regiment. The division's 15th Infantry Regiment was at that moment clearing the few remaining Germans from the buildings of Montélimar.[97] The battle of Montélimar was history except for the mopping up.

* * *

The 36th Infantry Division during the battle at Montélimar had fired seventy-five thousand artillery rounds at the Germans, most of them concentrated in a narrow strip along the Rhône River. The T-Patchers estimated German casualties to have been eleven thousand and claimed to have destroyed 2,100 vehicles, 1,500 horses, and numerous artillery pieces.[98]

The men at Montélimar nonetheless were not pouring any champagne. Where the Germans had chosen to fight, this operation had been just as tough as anywhere else that the Wehrmacht meant business. The 143d Infantry Regiment, for example, had during August suffered the loss of more than five hundred men killed, wounded, or missing in action. The 191st Tank Battalion had lost twenty-four tanks and fifty-four men killed, wounded, or missing.[99]

* * *

The situation was still perilous from the German perspective. Reconnaissance indicated that the American spearhead was now east of Lyon, and the *11th Panzer Division* was sent off to try to prevent another near debacle.[100] Nonetheless, Wiese could only marvel at what seemed to be a miracle: Despite its heavy losses, the bulk of *LXXXV Corps* had slipped by the Americans and reached Lyon. At Lyon, *Nineteenth Army* headquarters reestablished contact with the *IV Luftwaffe Field Corps*, which was just arriving relatively unmolested and was able to deploy to screen the onward movement of the weary *LXXXV Corps*.[101]

Army Group G would report on 22 September that 209,000 men had left southern and southwestern France and only 130,000 of them had escaped. Even though the manpower of the *148th* and *157th Reserve divisions* in the Alps represented part of the difference, the losses had been enormous.[102] *Nineteenth Army* had lost 1,316 of its 1,480 guns.[103] The last two divisions to slip free were badly mauled: The *198th Infantry Division* was reduced to 350 to 400 men per regiment but had escaped with much of its heavy equipment. The *338th Infantry Division* had escaped with a total strength of only 1,100 combatants and ten artillery pieces.[104]

Nonetheless, the withdrawal had been well executed—in contrast to the collapse in northern France—and *Nineteenth Army* had successfully rescued so much materiel that it would be remarkably well supplied during the next stage of fighting before the Vosges Mountains.[105]

CHAPTER 4

BATTLE FOR THE PORTS

General de Lattre interrogated me: "What do you have for troops?" I answered him, "My regiment is behind me!" And the general said to me then: "Toulon is waiting for you!"

—Colonel Raoul Salan,
Mémoires: Fin d'Un Empire

Corsica. 17 August. A stocky, rather jovial-looking French general watched with satisfaction as his Moroccan goumiers boarded the American LSTs that would take them to France to get their piece of the action that was already under way there. Augustin Guillaume had fought in the French army in World War I. Taken prisoner by the Germans, he was held in a camp that contained many Russian officers who had surrendered at the Battle of Tannenberg. Being a man of rare intellect, Guillaume used his incarceration as an opportunity to begin his lifelong study of the Russian language, an endeavor that after the present war would take him to Moscow as military attaché.

But Russian was not enough. Still in captivity, he also took advantage of the presence of prisoners from North Africa in order to learn some Arabic. Between the wars he served in both operational and intelligence positions in the Army of the Rhine, in France, Yugoslavia, and North Africa. In North Africa, he was exposed to these remarkable goumiers whom he now watched as they led their mules aboard the ships.[1]

Guillaume was far from alone among French army in his dedication to the goumiers. Until World War II upset the tradition, as it did many others, recruitment had been managed by the individual goumiers themselves, who brought in their younger brothers, cousins, and friends. The new recruits did not sign a contract with the army; rather they chose a particular French officer they respected and said to him, "*Je vais avec toi*" (I go with you). Inevitably, this built a bond between officers and men. During the period between the fall of France and the liberation of North Africa, the French, and General Guillaume himself, had gone to great lengths to keep the goums as a force off the books and under the noses of the unsuspecting Germans. This devotion was not just a matter of respecting the goumiers' skill as warriors. It was tradition. After all, these men and their ancestors had served France for a century.[2]

Suddenly Guillaume's reflections were interrupted. It was the American base commander, a General Ratay. Ratay had noticed that there were more goumiers than his documents indicated there should be. De Lattre's plan, "we speak of 1,000, we think of 2,000, and we embark 6,000," had reached its culminating point. Confronted with this fact, Guillaume told Ratay that although it was true that there were more goumiers here than there should be, his men preferred being crowded into the ships to missing the party. Ratay persisted, raising the question of the mules, warning that if the seas were high and the ships overcrowded, it would be very dangerous to overload the vessels. Guillaume responded that if necessary they would throw the mules overboard and they would swim behind the ships to France. Ratay admitted defeat and agreed to close his eyes to these French irregularities.

That night Guillaume stepped on board the American Landing Ship, Tank (LST) that would take him home, but also into the hell of battle. So it was that a microcosm of the Franco-American alliance—General Guillaume and his French officers, their Moroccan soldiers, and what seemed to Guillaume like an astonishingly young crew of Americans under the command of a man who was notary public in civilian life—set out across the Mediterranean to do battle with the Nazis. The liberation of France was already under way. There was work to be done.[3]

* * *

During the planning for Anvil/Dragoon, Lieutenant General Patch had given de Lattre's forces the mission of capturing Toulon, then Marseille. De Lattre had seemed taken aback, responding, "General Patch, you are giving me a tremendous task. Do you expect my army to accomplish both of these missions?" Patch replied, "Well, General, I feel that since Toulon and Marseille both are French ports and French cities of such great importance, the honor of their capture obviously should go to the French army."[4]

De Lattre, very concerned about French honor, buckled down to planning. He considered the army at his disposal. The first two divisions ashore, the bulk of his forces while capturing the ports, would be two incomplete infantry divisions, the 1st DFL, under General Diego Brosset, and the 3d DIA, under Gen. Goislard de Monsabert. Also coming ashore in the first wave would be Combat Command 2 of the 1st DB and Guillaume's goums.

The 1st DFL's Brosset was a down-to-earth officer who had left a comfortable job as a professor of strategy and tactics at the war college in Bogotá, Colombia, in order to join de Gaulle in June 1940. This act earned him a death sentence in absentia from a Vichy military tribunal, but Brosset did not care. He put to good use his long years of inter-war experience in North Africa while fighting for de Gaulle in Chad, Egypt, Somalia, Abyssinia, and Kenya before being given command of the 1st DFL in 1943 and leading it in the Italian campaign. Perhaps because he had spent the first five years of his career as an enlisted man, Brosset was not a self-important senior officer. He once wrote of himself, "I will never be a real general because a real general is always a general, even in pajamas." Brosset was built like an athlete and always seemed to be wearing short pants. He liked to command his division as if it were a company, jumping on moving tanks, yelling at soldiers to exhort them to greater efforts, and directing obscenities in the direction of the enemy. "I will never be a real general," he said, "but my division is a real division."[5]

General Goislard de Monsabert, commanding the 3d DIA, was a short and stocky man and, unlike the informal Brosset, was, in the words of de Lattre, as "rigidly faithful to the uniform of a French general, [with] all the bearing of a 17th-century Gascony cadet." With those comments, he evoked the recollection of Alexandre Dumas' d'Artagnan, the famous (albeit fictional) seventeenth-century Gascon Musketeer. Certainly

Monsabert, like d'Artagnan, enjoyed a fight. He had assumed command of the division after its previous commander had fallen in battle in Tunisia. He had also led it in Italy, breaking through the Gustav line at Castelforte and through the Hitler line at San Oliva.[6]

De Lattre had a great deal of confidence in Brosset and Monsabert and their battle-tested divisions. He also had deep respect for the skills and bravery of the goumiers. Thus, he was confident that with these forces he could liberate Toulon and Marseille. However, he knew that it would not be easy. Looking at the problem in mid-July, De Lattre guessed that by D+5 or D+6 the Germans could oppose him with coastal defense forces as well as two divisions, of which one, the *11th Panzer*, would be armored. This left his two incomplete divisions, albeit reinforced by other units, with little if any margin of superiority. The only available course of action, then, was to attack Toulon as quickly as possible with whatever forces were available and hope to be able to build up forces more quickly than the Germans.[7]

There was another reason to want to capture Toulon and Marseille as quickly as possible, and that was to prevent the destruction of the ports at the hands of the German forces. "Counter scorch" teams consisting of French naval personnel had infiltrated Toulon and Marseille during June and July to keep the Germans from destroying the docks or blocking the channels. The teams did heroic work. The team in Marseille, for example, managed to pour concrete into the primer ducts leading to preset charges, thereby preventing the destruction of several quays. However, there was only so much that small teams could do.[8]

These were the issues in play when, starting at 1700 hours on 16 August, the 1st DFL landed at the Sylvabelle beach, on Cavalaire Bay, and the 3d DIA, de Lattre's corps headquarters, and CC2 of the 1st DB, landed at the La Foux beach, at the far end of St. Tropez Bay. Despite the fact that a German plane penetrated the Allied antiaircraft defenses and dropped bombs that killed or wounded eighty men, the French landing continued with only scant interruption. At about 2300, de Lattre managed with some difficulty to get past the zealous MPs guarding Patch's headquarters to get the bigger picture. Patch told him that the three bridgeheads had merged and his forces had already reached or even passed the Blue Line.

The invasion was going well. De Lattre turned his attention to getting his forces ashore and organized.[9]

That task took up de Lattre's attention for two full days. By late on 18 August, with the Americans already vigorously exploiting outward from their bridgehead, de Lattre was beginning to think about the task ahead. The landings had gone far better than expected, but Toulon remained the key, and he feared that it would be a tough fight. Even in his first report to de Gaulle after the landing, de Lattre had his mind on that city. "My impression is that the enemy will concentrate all his efforts on the strongpoint of Toulon," he wrote, still concerned about the balance of forces between his army and the Germans. Toulon was surrounded by two continuous rings of defenses, some newly built by the Germans, others old French fortresses, and an inner city that had been fortified by Vauban, the famous military architect of the seventeenth century.[10]

Given the American successes thus far, de Lattre faced the question of whether to stick with the original plan for taking Toulon. During planning, de Lattre had set two conditions for starting the operation against Toulon. The first was that French forces should be in contact with the city's outer fortifications. By the end of 18 August, this condition had been met, and the news there was good: Those defenses seemed less coherent than had been foreseen.[11] The other condition, however, was that the first two echelons of the French force should be present. At this point, de Lattre had only sixteen thousand men, along with thirty tanks and eighty medium guns, merely a portion of his first echelon. His preconditions for the assault would not, his staff told him, be met for eight to ten days.

De Lattre agonized, but by the end of the day he had decided to be bold. He summoned his division commanders, Brosset and Monsabert, to discuss the plan. He told them they were going to take Toulon, then move on Marseille. In Toulon, he meant to take the enemy by the throat, attacking from the east and fixing the enemy, then drive a dagger into the German flank by coming out of the mountains to the north of Toulon and completing the encirclement to the west of the city.[12]

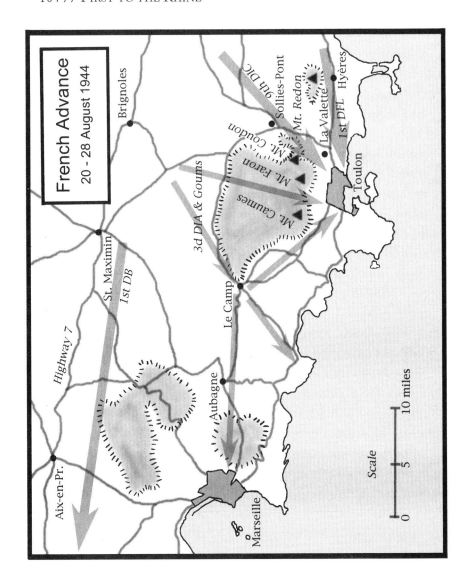

As they left the beaches and marched under the hot summer sun toward the frontlines and possible death, the thirsty soldiers of the 1st DFL had been greeted by deliriously happy civilians who poured out of their houses to cheer them on and plied them with wine.[13] Brosset and his probably tired and hung-over division were to "take the enemy by the throat"; they got the task of marching along the coastal road right into the teeth of the German defenses. Monsabert was to be on Brosset's right, farther inland, with the available elements of his 3d DIA. Monsabert expected to face weaker defenses, but his flanking movement would have to push through some exceedingly rough terrain before swooping down upon the Germans.

Truscott's VI Corps was to protect the French right flank on the north. General du Vigier, commander of the 1st DB, was to help in this effort with CC2, such as it was at this point in the landings, while pushing westward in the direction of Aix and Marseille, all along staying ready to intervene if the 3d DIA ran into trouble. To help in this effort, du Vigier also had at his disposal another colonial regiment from the African army: the 2d Regiment of Algerian Reconnaissance Spahis (RSAR).[14]

Spahis—the word is a cognate of the Anglo-Indian word *sepoy*—came from Algeria and from Morocco. They had existed since the 1830s and in their day had been among the world's most dashing cavalry units. In fact, it was as horse cavalry that they fought the Germans in 1940. The 1st Brigade of Spahis, consisting of the 6th Algerian and the 4th Moroccan regiments, won the title of "the only unconquered unit of the debacle" after its vigorous fighting withdrawal that took it all the way from Luxembourg to the Rhône. In the later rearmament it was decided that the spahis would be re-equipped as motorized reconnaissance units.[15] The 2d RSAR consisted of about 60 percent ethnic Frenchmen from Algeria, 28 percent ethnic Frenchmen from metropolitan France and elsewhere, and about 12 percent Algerian Muslims, riding M3 or M5 Stuart light tanks and M8 armored cars.[16]

De Lattre instructed Brosset to kick off the attack with a flanking movement around the German positions at Hyères; this was the outermost bastion of the Toulon fortress. To help secure Brosset's movement, de Lattre gave him Bouvet's African Commando Group to seize a large fortified rock, Mont Coudon, which rose 2,300 feet above the surrounding plain, providing the Germans with an excellent observation point.

De Lattre had just made these arrangements when word came that his second echelon would arrive ahead of schedule. In fact, General Magnan, commander of the 9th DIC, who was in charge of the second echelon, presented himself at de Lattre's headquarters at Cogolin and offered a battalion of infantry—part of Colonel Salan's 6th RTS—and twelve artillery pieces. Magnan had been commander of the Free Corps of Africa in Tunisia, and his division, which was now forming, consisted largely of natives of West Africa under French officers. It had had a warm-up, liberating Elba in June, but even before getting into combat, the division had taken substantial casualties. One of its battalions had gone to the bottom, torpedoed by the Germans while in transit from West Africa to North Africa. The division had also lost a company when its barracks had been bombed in Algiers. Already this division had a score to settle with the Germans.[17]

This was a welcome addition to de Lattre's available forces. Despite the coercion that brought many of them into the service, the Senegalese tirailleurs acquitted themselves well in the 1940 campaign, and the Germans respected their fortitude. One German newspaper, reporting on the experiences of a Pomeranian unit that fought against the Senegalese in 1940, described the impressions of one soldier: "The French fought tenaciously; the blacks especially used every resource to the bitter end, defending every house. To break them, we had to use flame throwers and, to overcome the last Senegalese, we had to kill them one by one." Many of the Senegalese troops came out of the 1940 campaign feeling that many of the ethnic French units had given a poor account of themselves, having succumbed to defeatism and become demoralized while they themselves had fought to their utmost.[18] They maintained this level of performance throughout the war. For their part, the French soldiers looked on the Senegalese tirailleurs with a mixture of racist-tinged paternalism and genuine respect.[19]

De Lattre ordered Magnan to position himself between Brosset and Monsabert, facing west. He would thus be approaching Toulon from the northeast with his division, which largely consisted of Senegalese tirailleurs, forming as it went, augmented only by a few tanks.[20]

At 2200 hours on 18 August, de Lattre received a visit from a member of the Resistance who had exfiltrated Toulon with orders to find the French commander and report on the German defenses in the city. This new information confirmed the importance of moving quickly. De Lattre learned that German forces were moving eastward to meet his fixing force but also that they were busily reoccupying and rearming the northern defenses of the city and generally preparing positions throughout the city. Moreover, the Germans expected reinforcements to arrive from Marseille.

Having so audaciously reworked the plan, however, de Lattre had to seek American authorization to act. At dawn on 19 August, Devers visited de Lattre's headquarters and heard what de Lattre intended. Devers was (by French accounts) shocked but promised to support de Lattre's proposals with Patch, who therefore naturally assented.[21]

De Lattre returned to his headquarters at Cogolin.[22] Waiting for him was an intelligence assessment that suggested that he had made the right decision because the ports were in grave danger. An assessment by French intelligence on 19 August was quite worrying: "The Germans have decided on the large scale destruction of all the quays and piers of Marseille." The canal from the Rhône to Marseille, the channel from l'Estaque, and another channel had been blocked with sunken ships. Moreover, the north entrance of the port of Marseille was completely blocked by six sunken ships, and the northwest entrance was partially blocked. The Germans were preparing to destroy the port's cranes, and other preparations were under way. As for the port of Toulon, the FFI were telling de Lattre's headquarters at about this time that as of 2 August, the sole way of avoiding the destruction of the port of Toulon was by a surprise attack by the FFI and that the quays were mined every five meters.[23]

De Lattre made one last-minute change, adding Sudre's combat command—which the Americans had returned to French control—to the far outside of his forces to provide security for the movement around to Toulon's rear and the onward movement to Marseille. Then he ordered the attack to begin on the morning of 20 August.[24]

The Germans, for their part, were worried not just by de Lattre's II Corps but by the FFI. On 19 August, a German noncommissioned officer in a pioneer (engineer) battalion serving near Toulon wrote home: "The situation is, in general, very serious, and we can expect anything. If there weren't these damned terrorists, things wouldn't be half so bad. . . . I am now in the Toulon region, which we will defend as much as we can with our feeble forces. The enemy is greatly superior in numbers and is constantly landing new forces. On our side, however, the supply lines are cut by the terrorists who come out of the mountains and execute one *coup de main* after another."[25]

Hyères

In order to get to Toulon, the 1st DFL had to go through or around Hyères, a sizable town that lay squarely astride the westward axis of advance toward the port and was the forward-most part of Toulon's defenses. As the French troops approached Hyères, they were brought up short by fire from antitank guns of the *242d Infantry Division* within the town and by artillery fire from large-caliber guns in the Maurette Mountains, a large mass of hills north of Hyères, which was dominated by the strongly defended Mont Redon. Brosset sent one regimental combat team northward to infiltrate and encircle the German positions there while he approached Hyères frontally.[26]

The task of taking Mont Redon fell to the 5th Battalion, which included the *Bataillon d'Infanterie de Marine et du Pacifique* (BIMP). The BIMP had been formed through the amalgamation of an infantry unit composed largely of Bretons that had suffered such serious casualties that it was merged with the *Bataillon du Pacificique*, many of whose members were Tahitians. This ûnit took the Mont Redon position on 20 August despite several German counterattacks.[27] By the end of the day, Hyères was cut off from the north and east.[28]

To complete the isolation of Hyères, the 9th DIC, operating farther north of the 1st DFL, attacked to drive the Germans off the line running from Solliès-Pont to La Farlède, thus slipping in behind Hyères. The very incomplete 9th DIC was still forming up, marching directly from the landing beaches, when on 20 August its 6th Regiment of Senegalese Tirailleurs (6th RTS, or light infantry) pushed through difficult terrain with excellent support from armor and engineer units and attacked Solliès-Pont. The German defenders brought this attack to a halt on the northern edge of Solliès-Pont, however. The next morning, a determined attack allowed the Senegalese to wrest control of the town away from the Germans, and the regiment's 3d Battalion was likewise able to seize the nearby hilltops, which it held against numerous German counterattacks supported by artillery. Another battalion cleared out the ferocious-looking barbed-wire defensive positions that cut across the road south of Solliès-Pont; the Germans were covering these positions with machine-gun nests emplaced every hundred yards.[29] That task completed, the tanks rushed through the breach and headed south. A sign at the side of the road read, "Toulon, 14 kms."

Not far down the road at La Farlède, the tanks ran into an ambush. The lead tank was destroyed and blocked the passage of the tanks behind. The Germans cut down two trees behind the rear tank, then picked off eight French tanks one by one before further French forces arrived to save the situation.[30]

With the Farlède disaster behind them, the mad dash continued to La Valette, spearheaded by light tanks and the few remaining medium tanks under Captain de Pazzis. At 1915 hours on 21 August, de Pazzis radioed that he was in La Valette, far to the rear of Hyères. His radio promptly died, out of power. The captain's small tank force was now out of communication and far ahead of the Senegalese infantry marching in his direction, fighting their way through the Germans who had closed up their lines behind the French armor. Little did de Pazzis know that he was cut off in the very same small town that Admiral Ruhfus, the overall German commander for the Toulon area, was using as his headquarters.

The Germans also put up a fight at Solliès-Pont on 20 August, but the 9th DIC outflanked the town through the woods, supporting the move with tanks and artillery. After a sharp clash, the Germans were driven out. This action completed, Hyères was now cut off also from the northwest and was effectively isolated.[31]

* * *

The enemy forces defending in the Hyères area and behind the Gapeau River were a motley crew. They included an Armenian battalion that was beginning to show signs of disloyalty—the result of diligent work by the Resistance, which had approached them through intermediaries in the Armenian community in Marseille—and a company of troops put together from the crews of a submarine flotilla based in Toulon.[32] Nevertheless, they were in well-prepared positions. As Army B's daily G-2 report put it, "[T]he length of the coast in the direction of Hyères and Toulon, pillboxes and artillery fire were troubling our progress."[33] Nonetheless, the 1st DFL, though it had not succeeded in ejecting the Germans from Hyères, was pounding away. A frontal assault against the town by Colonel Raynal's 4th Brigade, attacking across the Gapeau River, was stopped short after scant progress by heavy fire near the Golf Hotel. It was clear that this hotel was the key to Hyères.[34]

The Golf Hotel, an immense concrete building protected by barbed wire, was northeast of Hyères. The Germans had dug tunnels connecting various parts of the grounds so they could move forces with relative impunity to threatened locations. Worst of all, in front of the hotel was approximately half a mile of completely open ground: the golf course. Manning this site, the Germans had infantry as well as two antitank guns and three antiaircraft guns. Twice Colonel Raynal's brigade attacked, and twice it was repelled.[35]

Raynal decided to let his artillery do the work, so the infantry pulled back and two battalions of French 105mm artillery and one battalion of 155s worked over the target from essentially point-blank range of half a mile. They fired a thousand rounds, of which some hundred hit the building. At the same time, Allied warships cruising offshore dropped more than two hundred shells into the unfortunate town of Hyères, softening it up against the French arrival.[36]

The 4th Brigade still could not take the hotel and move on past. Finally, at 1600 hours on 21 August, a frustrated Colonel Raynal sent an order to Captain Magendie, commander of the BIMP, which was on Mont Redon: Take the Golf Hotel by 1730. The Pacific marines did have one advantage that the 4th Brigade's other attackers had not had: A member of the unit knew this concrete building from the inside. Nonetheless, the marines, showing more audacity and bravado than smarts, attempted to rush the hotel in their jeeps and scout cars; they took heavy casualties for their trouble. Somewhat vexed, the marines called down still more artillery fire on the hotel. Five hundred more shells rained down on the building, damaging it heavily, but the Germans inside showed no signs of capitulating.

The marines were forced once again to assault the building. Captain Magendie assembled a hundred volunteers and took personal command of the effort. The men dashed forward, crossed the barbed wire, and made their way into the hotel through the windows and the various holes that had been blown into the walls. As troops outside watched the upper floors of the building, Lieutenant Sauvat and his Tahitians attacked the dining room and cleared the first floor, and small groups under sublieutenants cleared out the second and third floors.

Now came the difficult business of cleaning out the belowground areas: the cellars and the tunnel to the garden, which had several entrances within the cellars. As Lieutenant Malettes and his men blocked access to the cellars from within the building, Captain Magendie found one entrance to the tunnel; he killed some Germans at the entrance and took others prisoner. From this spot, he was able to hear the muffled cries of Germans in one branch of the tunnel that had apparently collapsed under the artillery barrage.

In all, 137 prisoners were taken at the Golf Hotel. Tank destroyers of the 8th *Regiment de Chasseurs d'Afrique* (8th African Chasseurs, or 8th RCA—one of several such ethnic French cavalry units from the Army of Africa now equipped with armor—were already moving past the hotel, and the French assembled their prisoners on the golf course. At this point, General Brosset drove up. Even before praising his own marines, Brosset turned to the Germans and congratulated them on their fine defense.[37]

The French advance now continued. The 21st and 24th battalions entered and drove through Hyères, supported by the 8th RCA's tank destroyers and reconnaissance vehicles of the 1st *Régiment de Fusiliers Marin* (naval infantry, marines). It was decided that one motorized battalion would be left behind to help the FFI mop up any stray Germans. A foreign legion battalion slipped by the town to the south and took the Mont des Oiseaux, on the coast. The rest of the division moved on toward La Valette. The battle for Toulon was about to begin in earnest.[38]

TOULON

The hills above Toulon surrounded the city in an arc, with three significant high points: Caumes, Faron, and Mont Coudon. The Germans had turned all of them into strongpoints. Moreover, the St. Mandrier Peninsula, south of the city, was bristling with heavy artillery.

Inside these formidable defenses, the Germans had prepared well. All the approaches to the city were blocked with antitank obstacles, pillboxes, and minefields. Firing trenches and blockhouses were well placed and protected with wire and mines. The Germans had prepared bridges and viaducts for demolition. German engineers had even prepared to induce landslides to create additional barriers when needed. Moreover, the Allies knew that at least four fortresses within the city were heavily fortified.

On 20 August, even before the capture of Hyères, the French had broadly surrounded Toulon.[39] Now some of those troublesome German strongpoints had to be dealt with. The first order of business was depriving the Germans of those commanding heights. On 20 August there was an illustration of the reason why, when the Germans on Mont Coudon brought elements of the 9th DIC under fire near La Farlède. The 9th DIC turned to the African Commando Group, sitting in the massif between Valaury and Le Revest, to clear the hill. The commandos set out for Mont Coudon during the night; despite getting lost for a time, by 0800 on 21 August they were in place and ready for their attack.

The commandos started up the hill. Almost immediately the Germans opened small-arms fire on them, but by noon the French had overrun one emplacement. Unfortunately, on the eastern peak there were still four more gun positions and a fort to deal with. In stifling heat, Colonel Bouvet gave his final instructions. Captain Ducourneau would lead the assault at the head of the 1st and 3d commandos. After dealing with some outlying German positions, the commandos were facing the walls of the fort itself. Fortunately, the Germans were not particularly vigilant, and Ducourneau and his men were particularly brave. The captain decided that he would personally scale the fortress walls. He removed his shoes and, taking a rope with him, climbed up a corner on protruding stones. Upon reaching the top, he lowered the rope, and some troops climbed up behind him. Others infiltrated into the fort, having found a collapsed section of the wall. There was further luck. The 3d Commandos found a ladder on location and with it penetrated from the fort's south side. Coming from three directions, they surprised the enemy, whose first clue that the French were inside the walls was when they opened fire. Soon there was hand-to-hand combat in the first enclosure; then the French cleared out the subterranean chambers with the use of hand grenades.

At 1530, the German commander realized that the fort was lost. In an act of self-sacrificing desperation, he called in German artillery fire on his own position. By the time it was all over, only 6 of the 120 original

German defenders emerged unharmed. French casualties were also high, but at least the fortress was in their hands. They soon brought up a heavy mortar and from their commanding heights they quickly took out two German 100mm guns hidden in an orchard below.[40]

In the meantime, General Monsabert, whose 3d DIA was swinging around Toulon north of the city to drive the dagger into its back, had divided his still understrength division into three tactical groups, each of approximately two battalions plus reconnaissance elements. The groups were named after their commanders: Linarès, Bonjour, and Chappuis. These groups turned toward the enemy between the Meounes-Le Camp axis and the sea.

The Linarès group, on de Lattre's far right flank, facing generally west, had turned south and infiltrated through the Morieres Mountains to reach the small village of Le Revest-les-Eaux. At this village was an entrance to a deep gorge, the ravine of the Dardennes, which runs into the heart of Toulon. The route was well covered by the dominating heights of Mt. Caumes and Mt. Faron, which lay hard on Toulon. On 21 August, Linarès also sent his 3d RTA (Regiment of Algerian Tirailleurs) against Mt. Caumes, which the troops succeeded in taking.[41]

* * *

As the French were seizing the three heights around Toulon, the 3d DIA minus Linarès' group continued moving west, north of Toulon. On 20 August they reached Le Camp, a crossroads town roughly halfway between Toulon and Marseille. Here they found a German roadblock, which Bonjour's men swept aside. Bonjour's group, by this time reinforced with tank destroyers, now turned left, to the southwest, and fell back upon Toulon. The encirclement was complete when reconnaissance troops belonging to Bonjour placed tank destroyers astride the Toulon-Marseille coast road. (Chappuis' group of the 3d DIA would soon push west through Le Camp and play a central role in the battle for Marseille.)[42]

In sum, by the end of 21 August, de Lattre's forces had completed the encirclement of Toulon, breached its outermost defenses, and seized two of the three key hilltop fortresses. The luckless German forces inside were blocked from escaping westward out of Toulon toward Marseille. The 3d RTA even thrust some infantry and two tank destroyers into the outskirts of Toulon on the west. The Germans counterattacked violently and ejected the French forces, but the encirclement remained total.[43]

Monsabert now ordered Linarès to increase the pressure on Toulon by reducing the Faron heights. Linarès gave the job to the Shock Battalion, which was attached to him for the purpose, and the elite unit stormed the prominence on 22 August, capturing the German garrison. The French had now captured the forts on all three of the critical heights around Toulon: Caumes, Faron, and Mont Coudon. Moreover, the French had drawn very close to Toulon in the north and held high ground overlooking the city.[44]

* * *

The French nonetheless had their problems. Certainly these problems were smaller than those of the Germans, but they were alarming. Captain de Pazzis and his handful of tanks were still cut off and under severe pressure in La Valette. On the morning of 22 August, Salan's subgroup of the still-forming 9th DIC was pushing forward through German artillery fire to effect a rescue. To get to La Valette, however, they had to go through some difficult terrain. Then the 3d Battalion of the 6th RTS received the arduous task of taking the Baudouin height, which overlooked the route to La Valette. Salan's subgroup also had to force its way through Les Minimes, a ravine that provided the Germans with an extremely strong defensive position. Nevertheless, a section of French light tanks was able to sprint through and make its way to La Valette.

As the tanks approached the town, a rain of high-caliber artillery shells fell around them. The lead vehicle, nicknamed *Bretagne,* was blown on its side by the shock of one particularly close explosion. The driver and one other crew member were horribly burned by boiling oil, but they managed to scramble out. They were immediately captured by German infantry. Arguably this cruel fate was a blessing by comparison with what awaited the two crew members still in the tank. The commander was in the turret with his gunner, who was dazed from the shells that had come loose from their racks and fallen on him. The commander was being crushed by his gunner but could not wriggle loose because his fingers were caught in the turret hatch. The commander ordered the gunner to use his knife to cut off his fingers to allow them both to escape. The gunner may have been dazed, but he comprehended the situation enough to refuse this terrible order. Left with no alternative, the commander, with his one free hand, pulled out his knife, opened it with his teeth, and, in an act of superhuman will, cut off his own fingers.

The light tanks' move forward was not a total disaster, this grim event notwithstanding. Two of the tanks were able to penetrate German lines and join the beleaguered Frenchmen in La Valette. However, no infantry had been able to follow, and the breach closed behind them, leaving the force in La Valette still too weak to break out.

Meanwhile, the main body of the 1st DFL was continuing its advance along the coast, having pushed on through Hyères. It moved rapidly to La Garde, taking control of the town at 2100 hours on 22 August. It had just dispatched elements of the 2d Brigade to silence the German artillery that was menacing the division's right flank from the Touar heights, as well as elements of the 4th Brigade to deal with German artillery off the French left flank at Le Pradet.

The 1st DFL was in a clinch with the enemy and getting the best of the infighting. Brosset decided to concentrate his forces in order to break through the second line of German defenses on 23 August. The 2d Brigade had a sharp fight to seize the Touar Massif, which it did by 1500 on 23 August. The division moved inexorably forward. With the BIMP as the sharp end of the spear, it fought through a determined German force defending behind barbed wire and ditches, and by nightfall it had broken through. The road to Toulon was wide open. General Brosset came to the scene. After driving through the breach in his jeep, he rushed into the city, entered it, and soon came back to exhort his men, "Come on, I have already kissed at least two hundred girls!" A few elements of the 1st DFL were able to follow and reach the big city.

Artillery duels raged during the night of 22–23 August. Early the next morning, things were still stalled at Les Minimes. At La Valette, however, Salan had gathered all available tanks, including light tanks from the Moroccan Colonial Infantry Regiment (RICM), to support an attack by the 2d Battalion of the 6th RTS. The Senegalese infantry had to fight its way across and around a seemingly endless number of ditches, fences, hedgerows, and reservoirs, all apparently defended by snipers. The RICM was not unscathed either; one lieutenant had his eye torn out by a German bullet, but he nonetheless commanded his tank until he was dragged out of the turret and taken away for medical help. The Senegalese showed great bravery, and around midday they burst into La Valette and relieved de Pazzi's tanks, which had been dug in for forty hours.[45]

Also on 23 August, Colonel Bouvet of the African Commando Group sent the 2d and 3d commandos from Mont Coudon to mop up the area between the heights of Le Coudon and Mt. Faron, where the Shock Battalion held positions. As they made their way down the slopes of Mont Coudon, they heard gunfire behind them at the crest of the hill. Germans were trying to infiltrate back onto the hill and recapture the fortifications from the 1st Commando, which had been left behind. Bouvet quickly sent back the 2d Commando to strengthen the French grip on this critical height, and the German efforts were soon thwarted. The 3d Commando alone proceeded on the original mopping up mission. This was tough work that entailed driving the Germans out of several rock quarries west of Mont Coudon through the liberal use of mortar fire and flamethrowers. The German defenders fled in the direction of La Valette, where they surrendered to the Senegalese.[46]

* * *

German admiral Ruhfus was headquartered at La Valette. As the Senegalese and the armor approached, Ruhfus crossed Toulon harbor in a fishing smack to St. Mandrier, a town on a peninsula to the south of Toulon. De Pazzis had not put Ruhfus out of the fight, but this action essentially did; the German garrison now chose to regard him as a "*Flüchtling*" who had fled his post.[47]

With the Germans in disarray, one company of Senegalese passed through La Valette and pushed into the eastern suburbs of Toulon. Seven light tanks of the RICM went with them and carried on even farther, penetrating to the vicinity of the Arsenal Maritime, where they linked up briefly with units of the 3d DIA. Then they all retreated back to St. Jean de Var, bringing thirty prisoners with them.

A squadron of M10s belonging to Colonel Charles' Colonial *Régiment de Chasseurs de Chars* (tank destroyers), usually known as the RCCC, participated in the capture of the Chateau de Fontpre, where they captured 6 artillery pieces, 3 antitank guns, and 120 prisoners. The Senegalese then passed Beaulieu and surged forward to Fort Ste. Catherine.

Weighing the situation, the RCCC's reconnaissance section determined that there was no time like the present and that the German defenses were weak and could not stop a lightning thrust into central Toulon. At 1930 hours, the section took off and penetrated all the way to the heart of Toulon, to the Place de la Liberté, though they were unable to stay long.

Monsabert's men were not about to let Magnan's 9th DIC and Brosset's 1st DFL be the only ones to enter the city. On the morning of 22 August, two columns of the Shock Battalion under Captain Lefort began infiltrating Toulon. Meeting with a battalion of Algerians, one column seized the Place du Colonel Bonnier, the starting point of the main road to Marseille. The other column flowed like water through the weak spots in the German defenses, sometimes even moving as individuals. Aided by enthusiastic members of the FFI, they were able to reach many key points in the eastern part of the city. It was a light infantry fight against German pillboxes and snipers. In the face of this, the Germans started withdrawing into their main strongholds, abandoning their smaller positions and emerging from them only for brief counterattacks.

Lefort regrouped his men at two locations, not wanting them to spend the night thinly scattered across the city. Only one group continued to fight a guerrilla-type action alongside the FFI. Another, which had been unable to disengage, holed itself up opposite the Palais de Justice for a tense night, made all the more stressful by the fact that they were holding fifty-three German prisoners.[48]

The next morning, 23 August, troops of Linarès' subgroup from the 3d DIA filtered into Toulon through the Dardennes Ravine. The Germans were surprised, but they immediately assembled their forces near the Poudrière (powder magazines) on the old waterfront and launched violent counterattacks.[49]

This was not the only German effort to take back the initiative. At 0600 the Germans at the Arsenal Maritime attacked one of the Shock Battalion's strongpoints, driving in the direction of the Pont-du-Las (Las Bridge). They managed to push the two platoons of Frenchmen back to the Place du Colonel Bonnier. One squad took refuge in a house for a last stand. Out of ammunition, the men were surrounded and forced to surrender. As they walked out of the house, the Germans shot them down with machine-gun fire. Despite this atrocity, the French held at the Place du Colonel Bonnier with the help of the armor of the 7th RCA and the 3d Algerian Spahis, and the Germans fell back, their sortie having failed.

At noon, Colonel Linarès held a meeting with several of his officers to decide how they would officially take possession of the town. They decided that they must fly the Tricolor over the Place de la Liberté, in the heart of Toulon. An American observer advised the assemblage that a rolling artillery barrage was absolutely necessary if they were to avoid heavy losses in this endeavor. This was too much for one spahi officer. "*Et merde!*" he burst out. "We are at home!" The spahi's family lived not far from the Pont-du-Las. Linarès decided that all his units should share in the glory of formally reclaiming Toulon. So it was that a company of the Shock Battalion, a section of the 3d RTA, four tank destroyers of the 7th RCA, two light tanks and two scout cars of the 3d RSAR, and an ensign from the French ship *Wassilief* set out. This diverse group advanced by stages toward the Place, supported along the way by the FFI. It was a hazardous job, because the Germans were sending enfilading fire through the principal thoroughfares, but before too long thirty infantrymen, a light tank, and a tank destroyer reached the Place. Upon arriving, the sailor and a pretty young woman pressed into service for the occasion shared the honor of raising the Tricolor as the others presented arms. Moments later, elements of 9th DIC and separately some troops from Brosset's 1st DFL, with Major Viktor Mirkin at their head, rushed into the square. These latecomers were disappointed to have missed out on the great occasion, but at least liaison had been made among their units in the very heart of the city.[50]

* * *

That afternoon de Lattre visited the northern area of Toulon, where he found morale among both soldiers and civilians to be high. Further tasks remained. First, the Germans still blocked Highway 8 to Marseille. The French dealt with this obstruction that afternoon. Second, of course, the final reduction of Toulon remained.[51]

In fact, the French grip on the city was tenuous, and the German defenders in Toulon were continuing to resist, having received orders to fight to the last man. Through liaison officers, the French could call in Allied naval gunfire, and they were very willing to flash this ace in the hole. Major Mirkin took two tanks to the Arsenal Militaire in the Mourillon section of the city. Entering the arsenal, he told the German commander to choose between immediate surrender and naval gunfire. The commander capitulated, and seventeen officers and eight hundred enlisted men marched into captivity.[52]

There was still resistance elsewhere in the city on 24 August, particularly in the area of the docks. The French stepped up the urgency of their operations when a radio intercept indicated that the Germans had received orders to destroy what remained of the port facilities.[53] Much damage had already been done, in fact: the 9th DIC reported on 24 August that the port was "entirely destroyed."[54] The Germans still clung to the four main bastions of Ste. Catherine, Artigues, de Malbousquet, and Lamague, from whence they laid down well-aimed artillery and mortar fire against the attackers.[55] De Lattre gave the 9th DIC the mission of conquering these objectives and thereby effectively completing the liberation of Toulon. Meanwhile, de Lattre told Monsabert to start moving toward Marseille.

Fort Ste. Catherine, with its high walls and a drawbridge, was defended by sixty-five Germans. On 24 August, Major Gauvin, commanding the 2d Battalion, 6th RTS, undertook to negotiate with them, his Alsatian chauffeur serving as his interpreter. Gauvin's interlocutor was a senior officer of the Luftwaffe. The German started by saying that he would never surrender to the "terrorists," by which he meant the maquis, who were eager to get into the fight alongside Gauvin's forces. Once assured that they would surrender to the French army, the Germans gave up.[56]

The capitulations continued, with surrender terms discussed and accepted at many fortifications in and around Toulon. Other fortifications were simply stormed. On the morning of 24 August, other enemy forts and strongpoints began to surrender one after another. The two hundred troops at the Arsenal Maritime gave up at 0900. At 1300, the garrison at Fort St. Louis spiked its guns. Other forts followed suit that afternoon. By dark, organized resistance had ceased in the eastern part of the city.[57]

The Fort d'Artigues was perhaps the hardest nut for the 9th DIC to crack. On the morning of 24 August, Major Gauvin arrived to demand surrender. The defenders refused, feeling that the position was still defensible and a valuable spot from which to direct Germany artillery fire. They also objected to the fact that, in approaching the fort, Gauvin had made use of a captured German officer, who had ordered the defenders around the fortress to leave their positions. One group had obeyed this order, and French troops had moved in. This left the Germans at a disadvantage as soon as combat resumed. Gauvin recognized the soundness of the objections and agreed to a one-hour truce in order to restore the status quo ante.

Combat raged at the fort throughout that day, though the French had an advantage: They had found plans for Fort d'Artigues in Fort Ste. Catherine and were thus able to target its weak points. The French attackers included FFI forces; 105mm artillery of the 3d Battalion, RACM (Colonial Artillery Regiment of Morocco); and the 155mm guns of the 11th RACAOF (Colonial Artillery Regiment of French West Africa). Engineers led by Resistance forces attempted to destroy the blockhouse that guarded the entrance to the fort, losing a lieutenant in the process. Progress was slow in the attack, and Gauvin was wounded and had to pass his command to his deputy.

The next day, 25 August, the French, growing exasperated, decided to telephone the Germans to demand their surrender. Colonel Salan, now on the scene, delivered an ultimatum. "At 1900, my Senegalese will receive the order to massacre you all!" This did not produce an immediate surrender, but the Germans did agree to negotiate. Salan sent Gauvin, who was now somewhat recovered. Gauvin allowed five gravely wounded Germans to be immediately evacuated. The Germans remaining inside were a gloomy lot. Nonetheless, the German officers demonstrated exemplary military courtesy.[58] The surrender became effective on 26 August at 0800 hours. Five hundred Germans paraded past Colonel Salan on their way to the prisoner-of-war camp.[59]

* * *

Throughout the battle, the French had made good use of their artillery—six battalions of 155mm and a comparable number of 105mm—outside the city. Observation posts on the heights above Toulon allowed the

French artillery to fire accurately and greatly to the detriment of the defenders. Nonetheless, the two thousand German sailors on the St. Mandrier Peninsula had engaged in artillery duels with the French all around the city, despite six days of pounding by the XII Tactical Air Command and Allied ships cruising offshore. On 26 August at 0600, the commander of the Six-Fours Fort blew up his ammunition depots and surrendered five hundred prisoners.

By noon all resistance in and around Toulon had ended, but still the German naval gunners on St. Mandrier held out. The Allies decided it was time to get serious. Approaching within five miles of the fortress, the Allied naval forces unleashed salvo after salvo; the barrage was punishing and unremitting. Soon explosions and fires were observed. On 27 August the ships returned, and a light bombardment provoked no return fire. The German naval gunners were defeated. At 1745, General Magnan, commander of the 9th DIC, ordered a cessation of artillery fire on St. Mandrier, and negotiations began. Shortly before midnight, Admiral Ruhfus and the last defenders agreed to capitulate effective at 0600 on 28 August.[60]

At 1000 on 28 August, General de Lattre triumphantly rode into town.[61] In eight days of combat for Toulon, 2,700 Frenchmen had been killed or wounded. The Germans had lost thousands dead and seventeen thousand prisoners. Critically for follow-on operations, work could now begin to repair the port facilities.[62] De Lattre and his Army B had just won their first victory in the liberation of France. The second victory was only hours away.

MARSEILLE

Marseille was a sprawling city with extensive suburbs and a two-ringed defensive system. The Germans had strongpoints on each of the four main roads leading into the city, and they made good use of the available terrain. That said, Marseille's natural defenses were not as formidable as those of Toulon. Thus, the German outer defenses were not a continuous line but rather a series of breakwaters that would allow bypassing penetrations. Because Marseille did not have a system of well-integrated hilltop fortresses, as Toulon did, the Germans placed a greater emphasis on

122 // First to the Rhine

defending the suburbs, intending thereby to prevent attackers from reaching the heart of the city. They made extensive use of roadblocks and mines in doing this.[63]

Within the city, things were somewhat different. In the center of Marseille was a series of blocks and casemates around two last-ditch redoubts—the port installations at the north, and the well-fortified and -manned hill of Notre Dame de la Garde to the south. Artillery and mortars covered all approaches to the port area. Two islands in the bay had forts that guarded the sea-lanes. The Germans had positioned ships at key points in the harbor, ready to be sunk on short notice to hamper use of the port.[64]

* * *

Defending Marseille was a large number of *Kriegsmarine* troops, the majority of the *244th Infantry Division*, and pieces of four other divisions. The *244th Infantry Division*, under *Generalmajor* Schaefer, consisted largely of ethnic Germans "who came from the east," but it had no *Ostbattalions*. Schaefer felt that the division was not united because its troops came from all over greater Germany. Nonetheless, their morale was good, and they were willing to fight hard, although many of the troops were older and had already been wounded on the eastern front. On the plus side, the combat experience of these troops somewhat compensated for their physical defects. The Germans had 150 to 200 artillery pieces, as well.[65]

Despite the fact that he had capable forces at his disposal, Schaefer realized that they were in a grim position. The *242d Infantry Division* was bottled up in Toulon, leaving the *244th Division*'s northern flank exposed. Thus, the French could fall upon Marseille from the northeast or the north. Alternative possibilities were from the east, which Schaefer deemed unlikely, or even from the sea. Because of the many possible directions for the Allied advance, and because he lacked spotter planes, he could not hope to divine the direction of the enemy blow before it fell. Moreover, his units had strictly limited mobility, so they would be largely unable to mass at a threatened point or to counterattack in any great strength. In other words, the French blow would come out of the blue and would, necessarily, have great local numerical superiority.[66]

* * *

On the evening of 19 August, de Lattre, not far from where Schaefer was having these gloomy thoughts, was buoyed with optimism. In fact, he reconsidered his plans for Marseille, which he had originally intended to attack after Toulon. Bonjour's spahis had already approached the cross-roads at Le Camp, which was midway between the two cities. (An outpost in Le Camp belonging to Schaefer was already under intense pressure from Resistance forces that, ironically, were impeding the ability of the Germans to pull back toward Marseille.[67]) For de Lattre, this seemed to be "more than an opportunity; it was a temptation." General Monsabert urged de Lattre to yield to the temptation and allow his division to fall upon Marseille. But de Lattre resisted, and Bonjour's troops, after capturing Le Camp at dawn on 20 August, turned to the southeast and finished the envelopment of Toulon.[68] Nevertheless, de Lattre also allowed them to send elements to Aubagne, which he deemed the key to the outer defenses of Marseille. He also gave to Monsabert Sudre's CC1, which by now had been released back to the French by the U.S. VI Corps.[69]

The 1st and 3d GTMs, meanwhile, were walking from the landing beaches to Marseille (their natural gait was inconsistent with marching, according to one historian).[70] They were strung back practically to the landing beaches along a route now aptly called the Road of the Moors. De Lattre described the "uninterrupted column of goumiers, trotting along in single file together with their mules, barefooted, their hob-nailed boots hanging about their necks or slung at their belts with their tin helmets. The endless striped *rezza*s and djellabas [cloaks] gave the landscape an African appearance."[71] The appearance of the goumiers varied from goum to goum. Some wore thin beards. Others were clean-shaven with a little pigtail with brown wool woven into it hanging down from the back of an otherwise nearly shaved head. Many carried vicious-looking knives.[72]

* * *

Sudre's CC1 arrived at Le Camp in the late morning of 21 August. He was ordered to advance on Marseille, outflank it to the north, and push past it in the direction of Aix. He was also to seize and hold the Aubagne-Gemenos-Couin highway triangle. Sudre set off followed by the 2d

Regimental Combat Team of the 3d DIA, Chappuis' 7th Algerian Tirailleurs, and the rest of Guillaume's goumiers. Executing this order brought them to German roadblocks at Aubagne. The 2d GTM, under Colonel de Latour, was normally a straight-leg infantry outfit that marched where it had to go. Somehow, it had glommed onto fifty trucks, thereby substantially increasing its mobility. So when the lead armor elements reached the outskirts of Aubagne before nightfall, de Latour's goumiers were available and ready for action.[73]

The presence of French regular forces in the mountains at Le Camp made Schaefer realize that the enemy, contrary to his initial expectation, might come from the east after all. Thus, it was no surprise to him when the French fell upon Aubagne.[74] The French forces attacked the town in the early morning of 21 August led by the tanks (cavalry) of the 2d *Régiment de Cuirassiers* (2d Cuirassiers) and the infantry of the 3d Zouaves, another ethnic French unit from the Army of Africa. They met stiff resistance from three German battalions supported by 88s and 105s, all behind minefields. The battlefield was crisscrossed with walls and hedges, which caused much of the action to be fought at close quarters, an infantry fight in which Sudre's armor was of little use but de Latour's goumiers were able to shine.

The 2d GTM—which the Germans took for members of the Resistance—bore much of the brunt of the fighting. Two of three captains in its 1st *Tabor* were killed. A German counterattack reached the command post of the 15th *Tabor* and was driven back by a brave band of secretaries, stretcher-bearers, and signalers wielding hand grenades. Despite this flirtation with disaster, the 15th Tabor was able to enter the town early that evening by means of a flanking movement to the north; it seized nineteen German artillery pieces. The 1st Tabor entered the town from the south.[75]

Able to receive only spotty messages from Aubagne, Schaefer had great difficulty making out what was really happening there. He could not determine whether any French regular infantry had been present, how civilians could have destroyed his artillery, and how French tanks could have been so successful in the face of such stiff antiarmor defenses. What he did know was that Aubagne was lost. Indeed, by the next morning, the town was in French hands and the armor and tirailleurs could move forward again. "This, our first encounter with the enemy . . . ," Schaefer wrote, "was more than unsatisfactory and a bad omen for what was still to come."[76]

After taking Aubagne, the 2d GTM was oriented generally south and west. Continuing to move forward, it fell upon the Trois Ponts tunnel, blocked its exits, and compelled the surrender of 1,200 Germans who were sheltered inside. Among them was General Boïe, *Feldkommandant* (field commander) of Marseille and commander of the city's southern defense sector, which was now smashed.[77]

Meanwhile, the rest of CC1 pushed on to La Pomme, a small crossroads town northeast of Marseille. Attempting to turn southwest onto Highway 8, which led straight into Marseille, the armor was blocked at Cadolive and Peypin, two towns on higher ground. On 22 August, Monsabert, leaving armored elements at Peypin to tie down the Germans, sent two infantry battalions of the 7th RTA off the road, around the flanks of the German obstruction, and up into the Etoile Mountains. The 3d Battalion went to the south and right of the obstruction, and the 2d Battalion pushed on farther east.[78]

* * *

The French infantry filtered through the Etoile Mountains and entered Marseille. Advance troops of the 2d Battalion, 7th RTA, after scrambling for nine hours over difficult terrain without sighting the enemy, reached the north suburbs. Meanwhile, the 1st GTM, under Colonel Leblanc, moved farther north through the mountains before swinging west to cut the city's communications on the northern flank. Captain Lefort's Berbers captured an entire battalion of German infantry along the way, then cut the road linking Marseille to Aix at a town called Septèmes. Here the GTM got into difficult combat with the Germans, who were dug into prepared positions blocking this route into Marseille between the hills. The 1st GTM flowed farther to the east, eventually making its way through and over the hills and reaching the sea, thereby completely cutting off and encircling Marseille.[79]

In the course of these fights, Colonel Leblanc's forces seized the field hospital belonging to the German forces defending the northern sector.

Deprived of everything other than rudimentary medical resources, the German commander of the sector, *Oberst* von Hanstein, a highly experienced officer, was soon forced to ask Leblanc for a temporary truce so as to evacuate his wounded. Schaefer later acknowledged this action as being chivalrous, though he noted that Leblanc seized the opportunity to urge surrender on his German counterpart.

The next day, 27 August, saw extremely violent combat. Von Hanstein's troops refused to surrender and died where they stood. Several were literally still fighting when they were crushed under the treads of the tanks that the French had been able to bring up. Others climbed trees or onto roofs waiting for a point-blank panzerfaust shot at tanks, despite the fact that the explosions were often at such close range that the shooter himself would be wounded. At nightfall, von Hanstein was obliged to ask once again for a truce to evacuate his wounded. This time, however, Leblanc refused, pointing out that von Hanstein's wounded would be increasing in number over time, but Leblanc's ability to deal with them would not be increasing. Soon von Hanstein and Leblanc started negotiating the surrender of German forces north of Marseille. Von Hanstein's superiors in the city surrendered before those negotiations could be completed.[80]

Inside Marseille

As all this was going on, an insurrection stoked by the Resistance had developed in Marseille and throughout the surrounding area. *Generalmajor* Schaefer had anticipated a widespread revolt as the Allies advanced, and he was correct. Schaefer estimated that there were as many as eighty thousand rebels. By 18 August, "the mob did as it pleased after darkness had fallen," Schaefer later wrote. He found that the numerous incoming and typically incomplete reports of clashes gave no clear, understandable picture of the situation.

To the German commander, all this was a serious threat to his rear, doubly so because the German troops who had been assigned expressly to suppress rebellion in Marseille had already begun streaming north as part of the withdrawal from southern France.[81] The German consul general, *Freiherr* von Spiegel, tried to evacuate Marseille along with his staff, but their motorcade came under such heavy fire from the FFI that they were forced to turn back. And it was not just German diplomats who were inconvenienced by the insurrection. Schaefer found that many of his units were hindered in completing or were even unable to complete the movements they had been ordered to do. It soon became impossible for German officers to leave their command posts without strong escorts. Schaefer himself was meeting with the commander of the army coastal artillery at the latter's command post when FFI attacked it. The maquis were soon chased off, but when Schaefer left they tried to gun him down. He survived thanks only to the machine-gun fire laid down by his escort car. The commander of Schaefer's engineer troops was also attacked and his driver killed. The officer himself survived and was helped by a Frenchman who hid him, provided him with civilian clothes, and the next day took him back to German positions.

On the afternoon of 20 August, Schaefer received a telephone call from the consul general, who was insistent that Schaefer refrain from executing the destruction of the port area, which was scheduled to begin that evening. Schaefer thought he detected something wrong in his colleague's voice. Later he learned that the diplomat had been dragged from his home by the FFI and taken to the town hall, where the maquis had formed a provisional government. It was from this location that he had been forced to make this telephone call. Schaefer did delay the beginning of the destruction operations and ordered that parts of the plan not be executed. Nevertheless, in the days that remained for the Germans' occupation of Marseille, they managed to wreak horrible destruction on the port's valuable infrastructure.[82]

These intense FFI operations had shaped the urban battlefield on which de Lattre's army would soon have to fight very much to the French advantage. The Germans' defenses, though still capable of mounting counterattacks, had generally "crystallized into precise points," in the words of de Lattre.[83]

* * *

The picture was certainly grim for the Germans, but de Lattre had his own troubles. The FFI formations that were beleaguering Schaefer were trying to force de Lattre's hand. On the night of 21–22 August, a delegation of FFI came to General Monsabert's headquarters and reported that the patriotic insurrection in Marseille required urgent support from the 3d DIA. This posed a dilemma for Monsabert. Should he respond to the FFI request and send forces directly into Marseille from Aubagne, or should he support the two battalions of the 7th RTA that he had just sent plunging into the mountains? The southernmost of these two battalions had met up with a unit of maquis near Allauch, but they had promptly come under German attack and were invested in the hamlet of Les Olives, not far outside Marseille. Worse yet, there was no word at all of the other battalion, farther to the north, which was supposed to be pushing eastward.

Monsabert decided to support the FFI in Marseille. He sent the 1st Battalion of the 7th RTA and Sudre's CC1. Accompanying them was a British officer wearing a Scottish scarf and flying the insignia of the 7th RTA on his radio car. He stood ready to call in naval gunfire from the Allied ships offshore. The main road along the Huveaume River turned out to be defended and mined, but a parallel secondary road along the north side of the river was completely open, and no naval gunfire was needed. This combined force drove directly into Marseille, where it was greeted by a delirious crowd controlled with difficulty by FFI troops on motorcycles.

De Lattre had urged boldness upon his subordinates, but in his view Monsabert's move bordered on rashness. If Monsabert ran into trouble, de Lattre had no forces available to pull his fat out of the fire—the battle for Toulon was in full swing at this time—and no assistance was likely to be forthcoming from the Americans either. The *11th Panzer Division* had appeared to the west of Aix and was preoccupying the nearby U.S. 3d Infantry Division. In fact, Lieutenant General Patch had just directed de Lattre to expand his area of action to cover the 3d Infantry Division's flank and even take over some areas where the American division had been operating.

To bring matters back under control, de Lattre held a conference with his commanders on 22 August at General Sudre's command post, a stylish hostelry. De Lattre was surprised and annoyed to see chic young men and their scantily clad female companions sipping cool drinks, seemingly oblivious to the fact that a war was going on a few miles away. Shaking off his exasperation at the callous attitude of these young people—not the first time that French civilians would cause him annoyance—de Lattre laid down the law: His commanders would not enter Marseille until sufficient forces were available to win. He drew a line on the map, roughly corresponding to the boundary between Marseille and its suburbs, and announced that the offensive into the city would not kick off until the encirclement had contracted down to that line. In part, de Lattre hoped to draw out the Germans to the less dense suburbs to minimize both the destruction and the risk attendant upon street fighting in a big city.

To pick up the territory that the Americans had suddenly left to him and to ensure that French forces would reach the Rhône as soon as possible in association with the Americans, de Lattre reassigned most of CC1 back to du Vigier's 1st DB effective the next day. He ordered du Vigier to immediately secure the aqueduct near Aix that supplied the water to Marseille. He allowed only two squadrons (companies) of Shermans to be committed to the fight in the city.[84]

As the 1st and 3d GTMs became available near Marseille, General Guillaume split them into two groups, the left and right wing of the French force. The 3d GTM was to try to reach Marseille from the south, into an area that de Latour would reach when he pushed through Aubagne, while the 1st GTM was to try to reach the city from due north.[85] This brought the 1st GTM, under Colonel Leblanc, to Peypin, which a German battalion was tenaciously holding against all comers.

Not long after the arrival of the 1st GTM, the German *244th Infantry Division* monitored the following message on its battalion's network: "Assemble with remaining forces for our last counterattack." There was no more contact with the battalion after that, and Schaefer never learned the fate of the unit. In fact, his force had just lost eight hundred men as prisoners to the French. The arrival of the goumiers had done the trick.[86]

The night after the 22 August commanders' conference, de Lattre learned of this victory by the 1st GTM and CC1. He then ordered du Vigier to take up position on 24 August to the northeast of Marseille, where he could either jump in and join the operations of the 3d DIA against the city or exert himself toward the Rhône and Avignon.

In the afternoon of 22 August, just as de Lattre's orders—which limited French action to the suburbs for the time being—were being prepared, the French troops that had passed through Aubagne reached the outskirts of Marseille. Hundreds of civilians streamed out of the city to meet them. At daybreak on 23 August, Colonel Chappuis, commander of the 7th RTA, who was in the advance guard with the 1st Battalion of the regiment and a squadron from the 2d Cuirassiers, allowed the spirit of the moment to take him, and he led his forces straight into the city, passing the line that de Lattre had ordered not be crossed. No Germans were to be seen, and Chappuis felt that he was acting in a manner consistent with de Lattre's earlier instructions that no favorable opportunities should be missed. Monsabert later justified this action by writing that "if the chief [de Lattre] had been in this situation, he would have condemned inactivity."

So Chappuis pressed on. At 1000 hours he was descending toward the Old Port. Suddenly, the Germans attacked violently. Chappuis' infantry and tanks were in need of relief. Unfortunately for them, the other two battalions of the 7th RTA had met serious resistance on their way into the city, and the rescue force was not available. Informed of this emergency, de Lattre reacted quickly, ordering the rest of Sudre's combat command into Marseille. He further ordered the 9th DIC to take over the battle for Toulon, relieving the 3d DIA to concentrate on Marseille.[87]

General Monsabert decided that he would be as far forward as possible, namely with Colonel Chappuis right in the city. Accordingly, on 23 August he set up his headquarters in the headquarters of the 15th Military Region, next to the Prefecture, which on 21 August had been seized by an FFI force consisting largely of sailors, firemen, and policemen. Because of the FFI's shaping operations, Monsabert was able to protect his division headquarters with only a few half-tracks and some Lewis guns set up outside on the pavement.

Nonetheless, the French were in an extremely precarious position. It was true that the German positions in the eastern part of greater Marseille were cut in two. However, separating these two halves was only a thin thread of French forces running from Aubagne to the Old Port area. "In truth," de Lattre recalled, "we did not really know who was encircled, the enemy or ourselves." However, the German commanders seemed shocked by the suddenness of the French thrust.[88]

On 23 August, Colonel Chappuis telephoned the German consul general and asked him to arrange a meeting with *Generalmajor* Schaefer to discuss how the population of Marseille could be protected. The meeting was set for 1500 but it had to be postponed until 1630 to allow General Monsabert to attend, at his request. Monsabert had an even more ambitious agenda for the meeting. He apparently intended to capitalize on the shock and confusion that seemed to prevail among the Germans. Through an interpreter, he asked Schaefer to surrender. Schaefer was surprised and angered. He did not respond to that request and instead complained about the behavior of the maquis, saying that he did not recognize them as a military force and that their behavior compelled him to declare the city a combat zone and shell it. The French incursion into the city only made the situation worse, he said. The parlay ended abruptly, and fighting began again at 1915 hours. Schaefer's forces continued bringing artillery fire down upon the French troops that were entering the city from all sides, guided by FFI scouts who knew every pillbox and minefield, having done a detailed study of the city.[89]

Among those entering Marseille was General Guillaume, who wanted to confer with his boss, Monsabert. A member of the FFI guided Guillaume through the streets as shots bounced off the pavement all around them. The situation was confused, and engagements were happening everywhere. Upon reaching Monsabert's office, Guillaume, clearly impressed by the chaos, stated his opinion that it was all "crazy." Monsabert replied, "Yes, and the craziest one is me." Guillaume did not contradict him. Monsabert was little interested in the feats of the tabors, who had neutralized large German forces in the course of forcing their way from three directions through the city's outer defensive lines. Instead, Monsabert was fixated on the hill on which the cathedral of Notre Dame de la Garde was perched. The hill was not far from his headquarters, and Monsabert told Guillaume that it needed to be taken at all costs. From there the valuable docks just to the north could be controlled, though the Germans also held strong positions right along the water's edge from which they were vigorously counterattacking.[90]

* * *

On 25 August, elements of the 3d DIA that had been freed up from fighting in Toulon arrived and reinforced the 3d GTM, battling outside

Marseille. Together they moved along the La Ciotat road and into southern Marseille, where they attacked in the direction of Notre Dame de la Garde, but the Germans held fast.[91]

The goumiers continued to rip the German forces asunder. On 26 August, the 2d GTM seized the Parc Borely, taking then the Corniche and its surroundings, after which they proceeded to Fort Saint-Nicolas and participated in its surrender.[92]

All this time, the focus had been on the hilltop cathedral, a tough defensive position. The hill was steep and the streets were narrow with hairpin turns. This was perfect terrain for infantry ambushes, but it put a chill down the spine of tankers, who prefer to be able to maneuver and to keep infantry as far away from their tanks as possible. The French, however, had morale on their side. They were winning the fight for the city, and they were going to liberate this hill and the cathedral that stood at its top.[93]

Two battalions of the 7th RTA supported by two squadrons of tanks of the 2d Cuirassiers were to mount the decisive attack on 25 August. The 2d Squadron of the 2d Cuirassiers, commanded by Captain Fougère, was to support the Martel Battalion of the 7th RTA in taking the Notre Dame de la Garde hill. Major Martel and Fougère's forces were to attack generally from the north. Meanwhile, Major Valentin's battalion of the 7th RTA, supported by Captain Ardisson's 4th Tank Squadron, was to attack from the south side of the hill.[94]

Martel's Algerians, with some sappers and numerous FFI volunteers, started fighting their way up the hill through the narrow streets, but they soon found themselves bogged down. His battalion brought to a halt by withering fire, Martel called in Fougère's squadron to salvage the situation. Fougère decided that Lieutenant Moine's platoon of Sherman tanks would support the infantry to the left advancing along the Rue Breteuil. Lieutenant Laporte's platoon would go west and attempt to outflank the Germans.

With treads clattering, Laporte's tanks moved up the Boulevard de la Corderie. The local civilians peered through windows and popped their heads out of doors to watch them, cheering them on, oblivious to the danger that would soon erupt as the tanks used their main guns to destroy a German antitank gun.

Soon Laporte's platoon reached the Boulevard Tellene, where they were supposed to turn left and climb the hill toward Notre Dame. But they could not; the hill was too steep and the turns were too tight on the old city street. Seeing that the flanking movement he had been ordered to undertake was impossible, Laporte decided that he had only one real option: a frontal attack up the Boulevard Gazzino. Here, too, the slope was steep, but it looked doable. The first tank moved forward up the hill, began to slow, then ground to a halt. It hung there for a moment, then began to roll backward out of control, finally crashing through a storefront before coming to rest out of the action for the time being.

The other four tanks, however, were able to negotiate the hill and moved forward, soon coming under a hail of fire from German defenders with small arms and antitank guns. The tanks returned fire and kept moving forward. At the end of the Boulevard Gazzino was a courtyard and beyond that the basilica. The two lead tanks, including the *Jeanne d'Arc* and *Jourdan*, under Laporte's deputy—a man named Loiliot— pushed on through and took up positions near the basilica. Two other French tanks, including the *Joffre*, with Lieutenant Laporte in it, stayed in the courtyard. Loiliot quickly came under brutal fire from the defenders all around, who had flamethrowers, grenades, and panzerfausts. Loiliot desperately needed support, but behind Laporte there were Germans as well, threatening the tanks. It was a precarious position made all the worse by the fact that Martel's infantry had been unable to follow; they were still far down the hill.

At that moment, Captain Fougère appeared on the scene in his tank, the *Duguesclin*. He quickly sized up the situation and realized that they needed to open up their fields of fire to improve their mutual support. The *Duguesclin* and the *Joffre* working together smashed the wall of the bishop's garden to improve their tactical position.

Before Fougère and Laporte could take advantage of the expanded fields of fire, however, the *Jeanne d'Arc* erupted into an enormous ball of flames. A flamethrower and an antitank shell had simultaneously struck the Sherman, reducing it immediately to a flaming hulk and killing its entire crew. The *Jourdan* immediately moved to take up the *Jeanne d'Arc*'s position near the basilica. As it advanced, there was another explosion:

The *Jourdan* had hit a mine. The crew was alive, and the tank's weapons still worked, but the tank itself was immobilized. To make things worse, the equipment carried on the outside of the tank was in flames. Loiliot leapt from the *Jourdan*, axe in hand, and cut away the burning gear, then scrambled back inside the protection of the tank's armor.

Things were looking grim for the French. Enemy mortar fire began to fall all around, and the tanks, which were running out of ammunition, began to fire back less and less frequently. Captain Fougère had already urgently ordered Moine's platoon of tanks to come rescue the endangered French armor on the hill. Without infantry, however, there was little prospect of real success. In the *Jourdan*, Loiliot realized that it was only a matter of time before he and his crew were killed inside their immobile tank. He ordered the crew to flee one by one. Soon he was alone in the crippled tank.

For a moment there was a slackening of German fire. Acting on impulse, Loiliot threw himself out of the turret, ripped the Tricolor from its mounting on the hull, and carried it in a mad dash into the basilica. An FFI soldier, appearing out of nowhere, followed him. A hail of bullets splattered around Loiliot; he was wounded but kept going. Moments later, the French flag was flying from the railing of the basilica. This reckless act of bravado stunned the Germans defending the site and seemed to turn the tide of the battle.[95]

Meanwhile, Martel's battalion of the 7th RTA was still fighting its way up the hill under automatic-weapons fire. Making liberal use of grenades, the tirailleurs cleared each defended building in turn on their way up to the basilica. The Germans were surrendering now. At 1600 hours, the French raised the Tricolor above the dome.[96]

With the infantry and Moine's tanks all starting to arrive, the Germans gave up. Later that day, a French army chaplain celebrated a mass in the newly liberated Notre Dame de la Garde.[97] The next day, the French mopped up the areas surrounding the cathedral and also around Fort Saint-Nicholas. The fort itself, now under constant artillery fire, surrendered.

There were still pockets of German resistance in various areas of the city, and sporadic firefights continued through 26 and 27 August, including engagements along the waterfront. Really, however, it was all over but the shouting. On the evening of 27 August, *Generalmajor* Schaefer sent a letter to General Monsabert requesting a meeting to discuss the terms of surrender. At 0700 the next day, Schaefer came to Monsabert's headquarters and the deal was done. This was the same day that Toulon fell. It was a remarkable achievement by the French.[98]

That day de Lattre wrote to Charles de Gaulle, "On D+13, after seven days of operations, there no longer remains in the Army B sector a German who is not dead or captive." The news was not all good, however. The Germans had wreaked immense damage on the port, though less than they might have if not for the efforts of the Marseille "counter scorch team." The Germans had sunk 75 ships in the channels, mined the port, and sabotaged 257 cranes. Immediately, Allied engineers went to work. An all-out effort allowed the first Liberty ship to unload alongside a quay in Marseille a mere three weeks after the battle was over.[99]

On 29 August, a parade of the 3d DIA and the 1st DB, the goumiers, and the FFI took place in the Old Port area amid delirious enthusiasm from the newly liberated locals. The 3d DIA's band played, and "La Marseillaise" was heard once again in a free Marseille. A mass was celebrated at the Notre Dame de la Garde. But already de Lattre was looking north.[100]

CHAPTER 5

FRENCH PURSUIT UP THE RHÔNE

> The Air Force dropped bombs ahead of us.
> Then we would go forward and liberate—save a
> village. There were French and American
> troops with us, too. When we liberated a village
> they would gather all the children together—
> get a soldier to guard them and then feed them.
> Then we would move on.
>
> —Yeo Kouhona, Senegalese tirailleur[1]

Intelligence was providing information to de Lattre's army about the German retreat northward, and on 26 August an eyewitness appeared. A young French lady had left Lyon on 19 August traveling south and come to Avignon two days later. She told the French army that in the entire length of the Rhône valley, down which she had just traveled, there was a continuous stream of German troops heading north. On 27 August, French intelligence reported that the German units heading north through Avignon were intermixed and in disorder and had taken with them only the equipment they could carry. German soldiers were fleeing on bicycles, cars, horses, or whatever they could find to carry them.[2]

De Lattre meant to put his forces between these retreating Germans and the Reich and to sow among them what death, destruction, and confusion he could. However, there was essentially no plan for doing this. The Allies had drawn up detailed plans for the operations against Toulon—plans that de Lattre had promptly trashed—but they had done little planning for any exploitation northward. The Anvil outline said only that all Allied forces would exploit the victory in Provence, pushing in the general direction of Lyon and Vichy. This was all very well, but even though some French forces were already at Avignon, most were generally strung out along the southern French coast, and the Americans were to their north.

Only the U.S. 3d Infantry Division had stayed in the coastal areas, protecting the French northern flank. The French forces were in a benign trap.

De Lattre realized that he would have to maneuver not only against the Germans but also against his American allies. This was grossly unsatisfactory to the Frenchman, who later wrote, "[I was] determined to extricate myself as rapidly as possible, resuming the march upon the enemy, not behind our friends, but at least beside them." He thought the logic of his desire to be given room to run was only strengthened by the fact that he had the only Allied armored division in southern France, General du Vigiers' 1st DB.

The Rhône River, one of France's five great *fleuves*, loomed large in de Lattre's thinking. The Rhône runs roughly north-south to Lyon, where the Saône joins it from the north and the Rhône itself turns sharply east. If de Lattre's forces at Avignon could get across the Rhône there, they could advance rapidly northward into the central regions of the country.

De Lattre also had his eye on Grenoble, a psychologically and militarily important objective. In the planning conferences, the Americans had suggested that de Lattre set his sights on that city. He was open to the idea, but he was wary. Grenoble was perilously close to the Alps, where he felt he might get roped into unglamorous defensive operations that would not help reestablish France's pride and confidence in its military. Accordingly, in his mind he set the Route Napoleon up to Grenoble as the far eastern limit of his zone. In order to double his chances of breaking out of the American "trap," de Lattre decided to split his forces. Some would cross the Rhône and drive north in the direction of Lyon, and others would move through Grenoble, which the Americans had already liberated.[3]

On 25 August, however, a fly landed in the ointment. Even as the battles of Toulon and Marseille were still raging, de Lattre received Patch's instructions for the pursuit of the retreating German forces. Army B was to complete the conquest of Toulon and Marseille, maintain garrisons there, and make ready to move toward the *east* to relieve the American forces there so they could move north. This was bad news for de Lattre; his greatest fear was that he would be stuck behind the Americans conducting defensive operations in the Alps while U.S. VI Corps drove north and reached the Rhine.[4]

Nevertheless, there was still hope. Patch also directed Army B to take possession of the Rhône crossings at Arles, south of Avignon. Elements of the 1st DB were already at Arles. The French were also to reconnoiter in force toward Nimes-Remoulins, not far west of Avignon, then east and northward along the west bank of the Rhône. "Reconnoitering in force . . .": Those orders provided a loophole that de Lattre could drive two divisions through. He immediately decided that this reconnoitering to the north would not be a matter merely for spahis but for the entire 1st DB and the 1st DFL.[5]

* * *

Hardly had those divisions started moving when on 28 August Patch issued Field Order 4. The implicit goal was the linkup of all Allied forces that had landed in France—the Anglo-American forces from Overlord and the Franco-American forces of Dragoon. This union was entrusted to the U.S. VI Corps, which was to move north, seize Lyon, then advance toward Dijon.

Field Order 4, moreover, contained some troubling information from de Lattre's point of view. Aside from the "reconnaissance group" moving northward, de Lattre's army was to move east, over to Truscott's right, and relieve the Allied forces, including the First Airborne Task Force, in the Alps, then guard the American right flank along the Swiss border.[6]

In drafting this order, Patch had not consulted de Lattre, who immediately appealed to the Americans and to the overall Allied commander in the Mediterranean, Field Marshal Wilson. De Lattre wangled from them three changes and clarifications. First, he got agreement that his forces that were already moving north would play an integral part in the liberation of Lyon. Second, those French forces, once Lyon had fallen, would move to the right and rejoin the rest of the French army, and the whole would then have its own sector and push in the direction of Bourg, Besancon, Belfort, and Alsace. Finally, de Lattre absolutely insisted, and it was eventually agreed, that the French would not have to relieve the First Airborne Task Force in the Alps, though he would pick up some defensive tasks along the mountainous frontier.[7]

Patch's orders to de Lattre forced the latter to consider the organization of Army B. In his General Operational Order No. 24 of 29 August, he laid out the organization as follows: On the far right covering the Alps would be a group composed of elements of General Dody's 2d Moroccan Infantry Division (DIM), which was now coming ashore. On its left was a second group, made up of the 3d DIA and later to be followed by the 9th DIC, which was to race with Truscott's VI Corps—already in possession of Grenoble—and "to push up behind [the Americans] until the opportunity occurred to slip to their right and advance upon Ambérieu and Franch-Comté." On the far left, beyond the Rhône, was du Vigier's group, which de Lattre had already ordered to exploit northward.[8]

Catching the Americans East of the Rhône

On 30 August, de Lattre put under Colonel Bonjour the 3d DIA's 3d Regimental Combat Team, which was built around the 4th Regiment of Tunisian Tirailleurs (RTT, a Tunisian regiment, despite the titular Algerian nature of the division), only just off the ships from Italy, with the addition of a reconnaissance unit, the 3d RSAR. All told, these were some six thousand men, largely mounted on trucks. De Lattre sent them north with the general guidance to proceed to the region of Grenoble and be ready to continue through Morestal and Lagniue toward Ambérieu northeast of Lyon if the U.S. 3d and 45th Infantry divisions did not obstruct the route.

Colonel Bonjour and his men went north and found that a hole had opened up on the American right flank. Bonjour seized the opportunity and established himself at Belley, Lagniue, and Ambérieu. On 1 September, the 45th Infantry Division, which was on Bonjour's left, ran into the *11th Panzer Division* (covered in the next chapter), and the 4th RTT occupied Nantua, farther north and slightly east from Ambérieu. The 45th Division tried to move around the *11th Panzer Division's* flank to the right a few days later at Bourg and spilled into territory that Bonjour thought should have been his in which to operate. Not to be deterred, the French, squeezed from the west, simply picked up speed and spurted north.[9]

With the French forces widely separated and most of them moving rapidly northward, it became clear to de Lattre that he would have difficulty controlling them all. Accordingly, he summoned General Emil Béthouart, a former *Chasseur Alpin* from Italy. In the early-morning hours of 1 September, de Lattre gave Béthouart command of the two French groups on the right as I Corps. Simultaneously he gave General Monsabert the forces west of the Rhône as II Corps.[10]

General Béthouart was a veteran of Narvik and a man of no small initiative. When the Americans came ashore at Casablanca in 1942, Béthouart commanded the French division there; it was responsible for defending most of the Moroccan coast. The Americans brought him into the secret of the coming invasion at a late stage, and he shared the secret with a few of his most trusted officers. Late at night just before the invasion, he and these officers mounted an unsuccessful coup against the local Vichy authorities in a bid to help the American effort. Béthouart and his followers were arrested. Béthouart himself was court-martialed and spent several days in jail before the rapid change in political circumstances in Morocco led to his release.[11]

French Blitzkrieg West of the Rhône

On de Lattre's left, the action began on 26 August with a serious logistical problem: how to get the 1st DFL and 1st DB across the Rhône River, which was some 250 yards wide with a strong current and with not a single surviving bridge. The French found themselves paying a price for their dramatic success in Toulon and Marseille; because the planners had expected that there would be no need for river-crossing equipment for many weeks, no such equipment was available. To make matters worse, the French engineer units were substantially below half strength, because they, too, had not been a high priority for landing. Nonetheless, de Lattre turned to his chief of engineers, General Dromard, and told him, "Do the impossible."

Dromard's men found three suitable crossing points: Avignon, Arles, and Vallabrègues. At Avignon, there had been an army pontoneers school. Of course, the Germans had destroyed most of its equipment, but along with some wood they found a small barge and some tugs, all of them riddled with holes. Thanks to local carpenters and boatmen, the 2d Algerian spahis were the first across, followed by tank destroyers and an artillery battery. They crossed on a gaggle of rafts, barges, and ferries—whatever could be cobbled together. They were scarcely singing "*Sur le Pont d'Avignon*," but they were crossing, and more forces were following with feverish haste. But the engineers were still at work. On 30 August, the 101st Engineers proudly announced the completion of a real bridge just outside Avignon; it was able to hold vehicles weighing up to nine tons.

Over the next two days, 3,500 vehicles from the 1st DB and the 1st DFL rolled across the new bridge.

Meanwhile, crossings came into service at Arles and Vallabrègues on 28 August. The arrival at Arles on 1 September of eight American landing craft, material (LCMs), which had sailed up from the mouth of the Rhône, was a big help. Soon a company of "ducks"—DUKW amphibious trucks—also arrived, allowing a crossing site to be opened at Aramon.[12]

The Capture of Lyon

Lyon was the next important military prize. Not only was it France's third-largest city, with a population of some half a million, it was also a major transportation hub and thus could play an important role in cutting off the German retreat. This led Allied intelligence to assess that the Germans would defend the city if for no other reasons than to cover the withdrawal of the fleeing Wehrmacht.[13] After a meeting on 29 August between du Vigier and Truscott, in which they discussed how to approach the city, the French launched northward in three columns, with du Vigier's armored division in the lead.[14]

Riding on a wave of enthusiasm, the FFI felt that it could contribute decisively to the liberation of Lyon. The FFI's strength around Lyon steadily increased as the Allies approached until it had some four thousand fighters in the area. The maquis advancing with Monsabert's corps outside Lyon were eager to come to the aid of their comrades inside the city and actually wanted the liberation of the city left entirely to the Resistance. De Gaulle's military representative cautioned against "premature action," however. The regular army may also have learned its lesson from the way in which the FFI had forced their hand at Marseille. In any event, on 30 August, the maquis were ordered to be ready to make contact with the approaching Allied columns that were bearing down on the city. The Resistance would attack only in cooperation with the French and American armies.

On 1 September, the Allies captured documents indicating that the Germans actually intended to evacuate the city and even abandon the defense of the Lyon-Dijon-Besancon triangle.[15] This assessment seemed to be borne out when Truscott's VI Corps, approaching from the east and southeast, met virtually no resistance that would have prevented it from entering Lyon.

Lieutenant General Patch had told Truscott that it would be politically advantageous if French troops were to enter Lyon first, so the VI Corps commander instructed Major General Dahlquist, commanding the 36th Infantry Division, to stay out of the city. Nevertheless, at the request of the maquis, Truscott sent a token patrol—reconnaissance troops from the 636th Tank Destroyer Battalion—into Lyon, where the men found the southern section in the hands of the Resistance and all the bridges blown.[16] The patrol was put at the disposal of the mayor to help keep order, and, operating with the FFI, it neutralized a small German pocket in northeastern Lyon.

On 2 September, French reconnaissance elements reached the outskirts of the city without contacting the enemy. On 3 September, the 1st DFL was the first division to enter the city in force; the troops were met by a deliriously happy populace. They quickly deployed along the western edge of Lyon to block German withdrawals. Finding little actual need for this, the division began to regroup at the end of the day to ensure law and order; but this also proved unnecessary, for, as the Seventh Army operations report recorded, "All was calm."[17]

This was actually untrue. The Lyonnais were raising an enormous ruckus while celebrating their liberation. De Lattre recorded "indescribable enthusiasm." A second lieutenant of the 8th African Chasseurs recalled: "On 5 September, there was a parade under arms in Lyon. The flag, the colonel, and the 1st Squadron took part in it and paraded before General de Lattre de Tassigny. We had often said and repeated that the Lyonnais were cold people and scarcely expansive . . . , a deceptive appearance, [as] it was an unheard of overflowing of enthusiasm. We were feted, acclaimed, applauded, surrounded, bumped into, kissed. Never, for my part, have I been kissed by so many beautiful girls in a single afternoon. . . . It's an unbeatable record."[18]

What little action there was took place north of Lyon. At Villefranche, the French took 2,400 prisoners.[19]

* * *

The French II Corps was now pursuing the retreating enemy along its Lyon-Dijon-Nancy escape route. In so doing, it was protecting Seventh

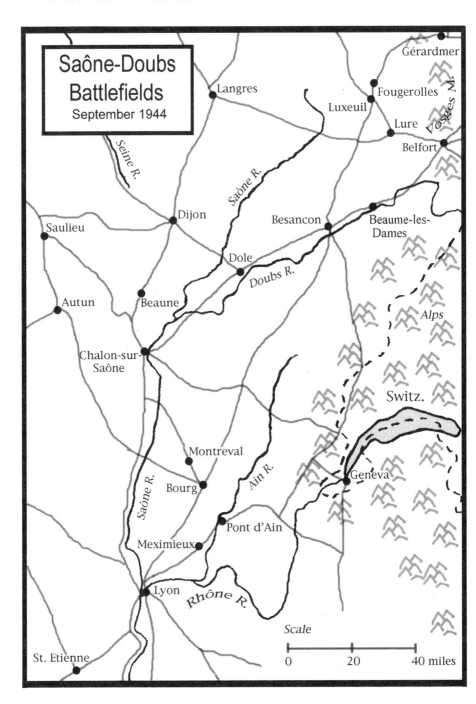

Saône-Doubs
Battlefields
September 1944

Army's flank and was also in a position to link up with Patton's Third Army, which was moving southeast from Paris. On 3 September, Lieutenant General Patch informed the deputy chief of staff of the French army that a task force composed of French troops was to shortly advance toward the northwest and effect a junction with the Overlord forces.

This potential junction of the armies of de Lattre and Patton was a serious concern to the Germans. Allied intelligence indicated that some hundred thousand men, mostly communication and service troops but also including the *First Army*, were attempting to pass through the ever-shrinking corridor between the Dragoon and Overlord forces. A captured document revealed to the Americans that the *716th Infantry Division*, together with elements of the *First Army*'s *16th Reserve* and *159th Infantry divisions*, had the mission of delaying the Allied advance west of the Saône. In particular, three German battle groups from the *716th Infantry Division* were to hold open the escape route through Chalon and Chagny.[20]

* * *

The dawn of 5 September found the French pushing north in hot pursuit of the Germans. That day, the 1st DB came up against the three German battle groups that du Vigier assessed as four battalions. They had taken up positions along the line Charrecey–Chalon–course of the Saône River–Verdun. The French tankers broke the German line on the night of 5 September, destroying two battalions completely, then pressed on. French artillery pounded the retreating Germans who were moving north toward Beaune and Dijon.[21]

Monsabert received a memo from Brigadier General White, the Seventh Army chief of staff, telling him that the VI Corps was still duking it out with the *11th Panzer Division*, but it appeared that the majority of the *Nineteenth Army* was directly in front of Monsabert. "I trust," White wrote, "you will have no difficulty in driving this force northward to its final extermination."[22]

As it moved north, the II Corps was, indeed, driving all before it, needing no encouragement from White. At noon on 6 September, Major Vallin's 2d Cuirassiers—of Sudre's CC1 in the 1st DB—moved out from Chalon in response to an order to get to Beaune as soon as possible. The enemy was fighting hard to protect the railway that connected Montceau-les-Mines with Beaune, then ran to Dijon. Down this railway were moving large German forces, evacuating central France and moving toward the Belfort Gap and the Reich.[23]

Fighting their way through Demigny, the 2d Cuirassiers found themselves in Burgundy wine country. As the 2d Squadron surged on through Ebaty and Corcelles, they were never sure when they would run into "*le Boche,*" as the French called the Germans. It would have been more prudent to move off-road rather than stay on the highway. Moving on the road, of course, meant that they were assuming increased risk, because they would have to deploy from their column into battle order should there be a German attack. However, the cuirassiers did not want to harm these world-famous vineyards, so they stayed on the narrow ribbon of asphalt.

The Sherman tank *Duguay-Trouin* was moving east of Meursault when combat suddenly broke out all around. It seemed that tanks everywhere were firing, except the *Duguay-Trouin.* The driver yelled in alarm to his crewmates, "Why aren't you firing?" He did not know that the first shot in this fight had been taken by a German 88. It had pierced the turret of the *Duguay-Trouin* and instantly killed the tank commander, the gunner, and the loader.

Nonetheless, the French pressed on. By nightfall, the 2d Cuirassiers were near Beaune. They would attack the next day.

* * *

The men of the 3d Squadron, commanded by Captain de Boisredon, spent the night in the small town of Bligny-sous-Beaune. The men were exhausted after the long pursuit from Marseille, and despite the fact that it was raining, they fell asleep straightaway on the ground next to their tanks. The officers gathered for a meal around a small table. Lieutenant Avenati was so tired that he fell asleep three times with his fork in his hand. The squadron commander felt obliged to issue a friendly order that the lieutenant at least *try* to swallow something.

The next morning, 7 September, the 3d Squadron started to move forward into battle with some Zouaves supporting them. Ardisson's squadron was to their left, and a squadron of the 5th RCA was to their right. They also had the support of some French artillery farther to the rear. Beaune was a mere two miles away across the vineyards, and already reconnaissance forces had discovered German antitank positions blocking the way to the town and had taken losses. From his tank *Marengo*, parked in the center of Bligny-sous-Beaune and with Major Vallin and his jeep alongside him, Captain de Boisredon sent this information to his men. De Boisredon ordered Avenati's platoon to advance to destroy the antitank position blocking the way to Beaune.

Avenati's tanks moved off through the streets. De Boisredon and other 2d Cuirassier officers clustered around the *Marengo* listening to the excited chatter on its radio. Soon they heard the voices on the radio start speaking a little louder, in a little higher pitch. The stress of combat showed itself in the tankers' voices. Gunfire could be heard. The officers could not help but share the stress that they heard coming over the airwaves, but they knew that Avenati was a good leader with an excellent, flexible platoon. After what seemed like a long time, Avenati's voice came over the radio reporting that the German antitank position was destroyed.

Now it was the turn of 2d Lieutenant Barral and his platoon of the 3d Squadron. It was to move to the edge of Beaune with a section of Zouaves, then support the infantry as it moved forward. Barral and the Zouave commander conferred briefly over the squadron's one map of the area. Then the column moved out, tanks buttoned up. After emerging from Bligny, the Zouaves moved forward in the ditches to the right and left of the tanks.

Enemy machine guns opened up on the French forces, firing from a wooded area ahead and to the right that abutted Beaune. The tanks stopped and opened fire on the German shooters. Then the French artillery opened up. The infantry moved forward and reached the bridge over the railway line. There was some brief concern that the bridge might be mined, but this fear was soon allayed, and the infantry crossed, closely followed by the tanks.

Beaune, a jumbled mass of houses, was now only a mile ahead, across the fields and hedges in front of Lieutenant Barral's tanks and the Zouaves. But now mortar shells started falling all around the French. The tanks fired back, into the woods to the right, into the fields on a hillside to the left, at another bridge across the railway line.

Barral was busily consulting with a Zouave who was sitting on his tank, *Orleans II*, regulating fire on a German mortar position. At this point, Captain de Boisredon, in the *Marengo*, and Major Vallin, in his jeep, arrived on the scene leading Marechal de Logis Bourguignon's platoon of tanks. De Boisredon told Barral to deploy his platoon to the left of the road to Beaune and ordered Bourguignon to the right of the road.

"Forward!"

Barral took his microphone in his hand, but before he could speak into it a French soldier climbed onto his tank. "Lieutenant! Lieutenant!" the man cried out, "the *Saint-Odile* has broken down!" This was the lead tank of Barral's platoon.

"Broken down? How?"

"We don't know. It won't move anymore. It doesn't want to move. . . ."

"No matter," Barral replied. "We are going to attack. We will bypass you." Barral pulled a submachine gun and some ammunition from his tank and handed them to the soldier from the *Ste.-Odile*, who was unarmed. Then the *Orleans II* moved to the left off the road, followed by the *Ouessant*. Though he had a disabled tank, Barral was not particularly concerned. The information available before the battle, sent to the French army by the inhabitants of Beaune, had indicated that the German defenses were weak on the axis on which Barral's platoon was now advancing.

The platoon moved forward, the Zouaves following behind the shelter of the tanks. German bullets bounced off the armor, but the tanks kept moving. Behind them all came Captain de Boisredon, who was keeping the operations synchronized with a steady chatter over the radio.

"*Thérèse, Thérèse*," he radioed to Bourguignon, "Speed up! You are falling behind *Suzanne*!"

"*Suzanne*! [this was Barral] Why is the *Saint-Odile* not advancing? Is it broken down?"

"*Thérèse*! *Thérèse*! Watch those woods ahead on the right."

Behind these two platoons, Lieutenant Avenati followed, ready to reinforce Barral or Bourguignon as required.

"*Joseph* [de Boisredon] to all his children. Everybody prepare a smoke round!"

Across the fields and hedges the French advanced, the deafening sounds of combat all around them. De Boisredon ordered Barral to divert around a bad bit of ground. Barral circled around the area in question, followed by his Zouaves. He passed the *Oléron*, whose tank commander gestured vigorously at him indicating that there was something wrong with his tank. The *Orleans II* kept moving forward. It fired at a target moving on the outskirts of Beaune. Suddenly the *Poitiers* went up in flames a mere three hundred meters from the town; a German 88 had hit its fuel tank. As the tank burned, its crew members bailed out, their uniforms on fire. They rolled on the ground, desperately trying to put out the flames.

Captain de Boisredon immediately perceived that the intelligence reports about this being the easy approach to Beaune were wrong. He picked up his microphone, "Attention! I think we fell into a trap! Be careful! Move away from the road! Get off the road!" But it was too late. The Germans had put a battery of no less than eight antitank guns on this side of the town. A shell from one of them ripped through the *Orleans II*, and it too burned. Lieutenant Barral shot out of the tank and rolled on the ground desperately trying to put out any smoldering bits of his own uniform. Then he returned to the stricken tank and dragged a horribly burned crew member named Sempéré away from the tank, which was now a veritable inferno. Finding a little bit of cover, Barral and Sempéré waited. It was clear to Barral that the slightest movement would draw German fire. Sempéré, the only other survivor from what moments ago had been a crew of five, was in desperate need of medical attention, but there was nothing to do but wait while the Zouaves and the surviving tanks, all scurrying across the battlefield, took the fight to the Germans. Horrible noises emerged from the burning *Orleans II*. Suddenly it exploded.

An hour went by. The sound of battle faded a bit, but still Barral and Sempéré waited. At one point, a German machine gunner passed not far away from them, but fortunately he did not see them; the smoke from some artillery rounds shielded them from view at the just right instant. Eventually an opportunity presented itself to the trapped men. Barral and Sempéré left the hedge, reached a corn field, and made it back to French lines.

The losses to the 2d Cuirassiers were grave at this point. Two tanks were destroyed. Another had been hit and was able to move only very slowly. The *Oléron* had been hit and immobilized, with one member of its crew gravely wounded. The *Turenn*'s main gun was out of action, but it was using its machine guns to cover the retreat of some still-ambulatory members of the *Oléron*'s crew.

A despondent Captain de Boisredon realized his duty and ordered a retreat. It would be the only time in the entire campaign when he gave such an order.

The French forces fell back and organized themselves along the rail line. Zouaves and tanks took up positions there supported by a company of FFI that had mysteriously appeared out of nowhere. The French artillery began dropping smoke shells between Beaune and the rail line, providing precious obscuration for the horribly mangled French soldiers—mostly naked because their uniforms had been burned off their bodies—who were slowly, excruciatingly, crawling back to their starting points.

* * *

Only the prospect of a massive artillery barrage held out any hope of allowing further progress. Sudre, intervening in the fight, was unwilling to do that to the French town, and he ordered a halt. Sudre now hoped that Colonel Kientz' CC2 would save his bacon through maneuver. Combat Command 2 was heavily engaged, however, and unable to advance on Beaune.[24]

Nonetheless, there was no German counterattack, and during the night the Germans slipped away. At first light the next morning, Major Vallin's group was able to enter Beaune, where they were greeted as victorious liberators by the happy townsfolk. The 1st DB pushed on, mopping up; four hundred German prisoners were taken around Beaune. The division also sent reconnaissance elements to the area south and southwest of Dijon.[25]

The II Corps' lead elements were only twenty-five miles from Dijon, where it could cut the enemy's escape route and outflank the German positions on the Doubs River. Furthermore, it was closing with the U.S. XV Corps from Patton's Third Army. On 9 September, French armored forces reached a point on Highway 74 midway between Beaune and Dijon. Here the Germans attempted to stop them by means of an attack into their flank, but the attempt failed, and three hundred Germans were killed and many others captured."[26]

On 7 September, General Monsabert ordered Lieutenant Colonel Demetz, commanding the 2d Dragoons augmented by a detachment from the 1st DFL, toward Autun. To the 1st DB under du Vigier, Monsabert reiterated an earlier order to get to Dijon as soon as possible.[27]

Approaching Autun from the south, Demetz' column reached Paray-le-Monial at 2100 hours, and he found the FFI waiting in force to join him. It was a diverse group from the Pyrenees, the Haute-Garonne, Tarn, Lot, Correze, Languedoc, Limousin, and the Massif Central. All had freed their home provinces of Germans without any help from de Lattre's army. Then they had pursued the Germans northward on foot, in requisitioned and salvaged vehicles, even by train. In short, they were spoiling for more chances to take it to *le Boche.*[28]

These FFI found themselves near Autun, numbering twenty-five thousand and armed mostly with weapons taken from the fleeing Germans. This was a real asset for Demetz. Among this gaggle of Resistance units were such as the *Corps Franc Pommiès* (CFP), named after the man who organized them in southwest France in late 1942, André Pommiès. In September 1944, the CFP formed an infantry brigade, 4,800 strong in nine battalions. They were equipped with small arms but had few mortars, antitank weapons, artillery, or anti-aircraft guns.[29]

Demetz knew that the retreating Germans had little choice but to go through Autun, so he believed that he could best damage the German cause by taking the city straightaway. With his gigantic FFI force, he approached the city on 8 September with two large columns. One moved west around the city to cut the roads to the north and west, though some Germans were able to escape, fighting their way through the weak French blocking force north of the city. The other column moved around to the east. One tiny element of the western wing of the French force took the crossroads at the small town of Dracy St. Loup, north of Autun. At the crossroads a French armored car got cut off and was in grave danger. The commander of the armored car dispatched a runner to summon help, but the runner was promptly killed. A second runner was dispatched: General de Lattre's sixteen-year-old son, Bernard, who had required special permission from Charles de Gaulle personally in order to enlist. Bernard fell seriously wounded. A third runner, however, managed to get through, and soon help arrived.

That morning, a group of Franc-Tireurs et Partisan (FTP), the Communist-controlled portion of the Resistance, displaying more initiative than Demetz probably desired, tried to take Autun by surprise, breaking into the town from the south. There was sharp fighting, and the partisans were expelled, having lost forty men killed and thirty-five taken prisoner. Shortly thereafter, the Germans executed these prisoners.

By mid-afternoon, Demetz' forces had completely surrounded Autun, and he was in a position to retaliate for this atrocity. Pushing into the city from two directions with armor and infantry, mostly provided by the FFI, the French penetrated all the way to the town center. The Germans, however, still held out in the northern part of the town. At 2200 hours, a large German force supported by antitank guns and armored cars attempted a breakout to the north. Some made it through, only to be chased down and wiped out the next day.

* * *

Southwest of the city, at the town of Fontaine-la-Mère, a small force consisting of a section of tank destroyers, the engineers of the 2d Dragoons, a squadron from the 8th Dragoons, and an FFI unit were helping to hold the perimeter around Autun. In command of this detachment was Major Robert de Neuchèze. In 1940, Neuchèze as a captain had been attached to the 2d Regiment of Dragoons in the Army of the Armistice. When that regiment was dissolved in late 1942, he became the chief of the armed forces of the Resistance in the Department of Gers, which meant that he worked hard helping establish the CFP. By late the next spring, however, his cover was blown, and he had to flee the country. He was caught trying to cross the Spanish border, but he soon escaped from custody. He went to Toulouse, where he was given the task of reestablishing the 2d Dragoons in Africa. With the regiment's standard wrapped around his body, he was taken away to Algiers by submarine. Now it was 1944, and he was back with the 2d Dragoons fighting alongside his CFP.[30]

During the night, Neuchèze and his troops had to turn to face an element of Blaskowitz's army, *Kampfgruppe Bauer*, four thousand men strong, which was driving toward Autun. Bauer's *kampfgruppe* slammed into the small French force southwest of Autun during the night. Lieutenant Teyssot, a former aide-de-camp to de Lattre, was standing atop his tank destroyer, *Notre Dame de Paris*, directing its fire when he took a bullet in the chest and fell, mortally wounded.

Despite this loss, the French bravely held off three attacks by *Kampfgruppe Bauer*, which used the dark to infiltrate all around the French positions. However, at about 0400, the Frenchmen, who by this time were running out of ammunition, moved out of Bauer's way, westward to Étang. Though in the end they had been pushed aside, Teyssott and his comrades had fulfilled their duty. The Germans were held back from Autun, where they would have fallen upon the French rear just as the battle raged to subdue the last pockets of German resistance in the city.

At 0700, large FFI reinforcements arrived from three directions, and two hours later the city was completely in the hands of the French. Colonel Demetz turned his attention briefly to the threat posed by Bauer in the south, sending legionnaires and maquis to deal with it. Then he resumed the movement of his force to the north, policing up some of the Germans who had fled Autun, but otherwise moving forward unimpeded. The detachment that had held out so heroically at Fontaine-la-Mère was ordered to Autun. This meant fighting its way through Fontaine-la-Mère again. Neuchèze mounted the tank destroyer that so recently had belonged to Lieutenant Teyssot. Near Fontaine-la-Mère, the commander of the tank destroyer on which Neuchèze was riding was killed. Neuchèze immediately moved to take his place, and moments later he, too, was killed. The remainder of the detachment was able to reach Autun.

At 0800, *Kampfgruppe Bauer* reached the defensive positions on the western outskirts of Autun, and combat broke out. A sharp struggle ensued as *Kampfgruppe Bauer* fought for its life and for the life of other German units behind it farther south. Though Demetz was blithely continuing north with the bulk of his force, General Monsabert, benefiting from aerial reconnaissance, realized the importance of the issue at hand. He sent some 155mm artillery to Demetz and ordered him to halt his movement northward, turn around, and fight Bauer with everything at his disposal.

Having just received Monsabert's order, Demetz turned his force around on the morning of 10 September, dispelling any immediate hope of an advance on Bauer's part. Most decisive, however, was the French artillery. Making excellent use of a Piper Cub spotter plane, the 155mm artillery ravaged Bauer's rear line, costing the Germans some 500 men in short order. The Germans were demoralized, and at 0200 hours Bauer surrendered his 3,200 remaining able-bodied men. The FFI eagerly scavenged among the gear abandoned by Bauer's soldiers.

* * *

With Bauer's surrender, the last hope vanished for the *First Army* troops trying to hike out of far southwestern France. A major axis of German retreat was blocked, and no more Germans would make it to the Belfort Gap or to the Reich.[31] Having heard the news of Bauer, and being pressed on all sides by the FFI, *Generalmajor* Botho Elster, the leader of the ad hoc "Foot March Group South," contacted the Americans, and on 11 September he surrendered himself and more than nineteen thousand troops to the U.S. 83d Infantry Division, near Orleans. With Elster's surrender, the threat to the western flank of the French II Corps vanished.

As of the late evening of 9 September, however, those Germans still represented a potential threat. French II Corps intelligence assessed that the German forces were falling back from the west and southwest of France along the axes Moulins-Autun ("which has been denied to him") and Nevers-Dijon. French Forces of the Interior leaders were reporting that forty to fifty thousand Germans were moving along those two axes. General Monsabert renewed his resolve, therefore, to seize Dijon and deny the Germans one of these routes of retreat.

The 1st DB was to move on Dijon, outflanking it to the east with armored units and to the west with infantry. If there was strong resistance at Dijon, Monsabert ordered his armor to keep pushing out to the flank, out to the east as far as possible while still keeping contact and to await the commitment of infantry units being held in reserve for this operation. The 1st DFL was to stand ready to help out at Dijon if needed or to counterattack toward Autun or Bligny.[32]

With Beaune now in the hands of CC1, and with CC2 deployed to the left of that, General du Vigier, commanding the 1st DB, held a council in the town with his subordinates to lay out the plan for freeing Dijon. Though the division faced a lack of fuel, the plan entailed attacking the city from the east and west. First, du Vigier sent out reconnaissance forces consisting of the 2d Spahis, the Shock Battalion, and a section each of tank destroyers and engineers to probe the enemy's positions for weaknesses.

The reconnaissance force faced difficulties. The commander of the 4th Shock Company stepped on a mine and was gravely wounded, along with ten of his men. On another occasion, French tank destroyers hit two German ammunition trucks obstructing a constricted roadway. The French forces were not able to maneuver around these, because the surrounding ground was controlled by the fire from a German strongpoint. On still another occasion, Captain Baudouin and his 4th Squadron of the 2d RSAR found themselves with a thousand Germans at their backs, between them and their jumping-off point, as they moved toward Dijon. They met this foe with audacity in the form of a lieutenant with three armored cars, a tank destroyer, and a half-track. The French at the other side sent out five armed jeeps, and the Germans fled into the woods.

The reconnaissance force thought it wise not to push into Dijon and be swallowed up in that large city. However, the Germans could well imagine the developing French attack of which this reconnaissance force was the harbinger, and they decided to withdraw rather than risk being encircled. When patrols from the 3d African Chasseurs entered the city at dawn on 11 September, they found no Germans; they had pulled out overnight. Dijon, the capital of Burgundy, was free.[33]

That same day, French II Corps armored forces continued to push northeastward toward Langres and the next day reached that town, where they discovered that the Germans were occupying only the fortified citadel. The citadel resisted stubbornly, and the French also had to deal with numerous mines and booby traps throughout the town. Langres was not fully cleared until the night of 13 September.[34] Late on 11 September, the 2d Dragoons encountered a patrol from the U.S. 6th Armored Division twenty-five miles north of Autun; it marked the first physical contact between the Dragoon and Overlord forces.[35]

* * *

As of 12 September, General Monsabert assessed that the situation for the Germans in front of him was grim. He estimated that ten thousand or more Germans were there, but they were of only mediocre military value and lightly armed, being troops from the coast guard, fixed artillery positions, service troops, and so on. They were reduced to retreating on foot because the larger German units had taken their vehicles. These troops seemed ready to surrender whenever a French unit appeared and made the offer.[36]

De Lattre's forces were not going any farther north, though. More of the forwardmost Allied units coming up from the Mediterranean were bumping into Lt. Gen. George Patton's forces advancing from Normandy. On 12 September, elements of the 1st Regiment of Fusiliers Marin from the 1st DFL, which had been sent to Montbard, witnessed the arrival of a section of Moroccan spahis from General Jacques Leclerc's 2d DB, which some three weeks earlier had spearheaded the liberation of Paris and was part of Patton's rampaging Third Army. Lieutenant Ève Curie, one of de Lattre's staff officers, who had been escorting a war correspondent, formally made the contact with the 2d DB.

Farther west, on the Dijon-Troyes road, a half-track belonging to Chadian troops of Leclerc's division was parked in front of the presbytery at Aisey-sur-Seine when a staff car from de Lattre's army drove past. Shortly thereafter, the half-track resumed its journey southward when it met a French jeep, which stopped. General Brosset, the commander of the 1st DFL, was driving it himself. He had taken a break from the fight to visit his family home, which was nearby. That same afternoon, the 2d Dragoons between Saulieu and Clamecy and the Americans at Autun met up with elements of Patton's Third Army.[37]

There was now a continuous Allied front linking the Dragoon and Overlord forces; it was tenuous but would grow stronger every day. The linkup spelled doom for the German forces behind the Allied armies. Elements of the 6th Army Group would, however, mop up pockets of Germans on the Atlantic coast, even on the islands off France, for some time to come.[38]

CHAPTER 6

END OF THE RACE

> The month of September brought a complete reversal in tactics of the Germans facing the Seventh Army. At the beginning they were retreating. . . . At the end they were defending, stubbornly and on the whole effectively, as their hastily reformed units turned to stand with their backs to the Vosges.
>
> —G-2 History, Seventh Army

By the beginning of September, Seventh Army had captured more than fifty thousand Germans (most of them taken by the French at Marseille and Toulon) and killed or wounded an unknown but substantial number of the enemy. The Allies had lost only 2,733 men killed, captured, or missing since D-day.[1] Nonetheless, noted Truscott's operations staff, "As September opened, enemy units opposite VI Corps were withdrawing to the north and northeast, [but] not in disorder."[2]

At Seventh Army headquarters, Sandy Patch saw one more opportunity to destroy *Nineteenth Army* before it could escape through the Belfort Gap. On 28 August, he had issued a field order that instructed French II Corps and VI Corps to converge at Lyon, then continue northward to Dijon and Beaune. He expected the bulk of German forces to turn eastward at Lyon, and he hoped to link up at Dijon with U.S. Third Army elements pushing southeast from Normandy (as discussed in the preceding chapter).

East of the Rhône, Patch sent U.S. VI Corps, on the left, and the French divisions that would soon be grouped in French I Corps, on the right, along parallel tracks northward to cut the German route to Belfort. As events unfolded, the commanders of both corps became convinced that his troops could—and should—take Belfort on the fly, and another source of mutual resentment was born. The initial axes of advance directed the Americans toward Dijon and the French toward Bourg and Besancon.[3]

Truscott, in turn, ordered the 117th Cavalry Reconnaissance Squadron to act as a screening force and maintain contact with the enemy. The 45th Infantry Division was to advance northwestward from Grenoble and cut the routes connecting Lyon and the Swiss border. The 36th Infantry Division was to advance directly on Lyon, while the 3d Infantry Division mopped up around Montélimar.

Major General Eagles' 179th Infantry Regiment constituted the main American maneuver element of Seventh Army at this point, and by 31 August it had reached Pont d'Ain, midway between Lyon and the Swiss border.[4] The first French unit to operate east of the Rhône, the 3d DIA, was just heading toward the battle area via Grenoble.[5]

Prospects for inflicting a rapid and decisive defeat on the Germans looked bright. Nonetheless, Patch was again just a bit too late.

* * *

Indeed, the first day of September produced the first good news that *Generaloberst* Blaskowitz had received in a long time: A liaison officer from *First Army*'s *LXIV Corps*, which had been retreating from the Atlantic coast in a complete communications blackout, worked his way through maquis territory to Dijon to report that his corps was on the way behind him. Blaskowitz learned that the corps had grown to a group of some hundred thousand men by scooping up all Wehrmacht and other German elements, many of them noncombatant, that it encountered along the way. Blaskowitz took two gambles: First, he ordered *Nineteenth Army* to halt its onward movement to take in *LXIV Corps*, which risked a crisis at the wide-open Doubs River near Besancon, where Seventh Army troops might appear at any time. Second, Blaskowitz told *LXIV Corps*, which he subordinated to *Nineteenth Army*, to rush all mobile units ahead to Dijon, despite the danger this posed to slow-moving military and civilian columns left behind.

Blaskowitz had managed to reestablish sporadic contact with *OB West*, and he had received orders to hold onto a bridgehead-like position on the line Plateau de Langres-Dijon-Swiss border, with his right wing anchored on the Moselle River, to cover a planned attack against Patton's flank by the

Fifth Panzer Army. The High Command on 2 September assigned the *XLVII Panzer Corps* to the army group to help it establish a firm northern flank against Patton, but for Wiese and *Nineteenth Army*, only a single division, the *159th Infantry Division*, part of *LXIV Corps*, could be spared. A dozen tanks already in the area, most of them Panthers belonging to the SS, were transferred to the *11th Panzer Division* to cover some of its losses.[6]

Army Group G was going to stand and fight for the first time since the Dragoon landings. But could it hold? That question was of great strategic consequence to Berlin. During the fighting in Normandy and southern France and the retreat toward the German border, German losses in the west had amounted to more than six hundred thousand men and untold amounts of equipment. Of the fifty-five infantry divisions on the western front as of early September (including nine in rehabilitation and four bottled up in coastal fortresses), only thirteen were rated fully combat effective. Similarly, only three of the fourteen panzer divisions were still in top fighting form.[7] If *Army Group G* could not stem the 6th Army Group tide, there was almost nothing between it and the Reich that could.

DISRUPTING THE AMERICAN PLAN

As of dawn on 1 September, the 45th Infantry Division, the northernmost Allied formation, was concentrating its forces east of Lyon in the areas of Meximieux, Chalamont, Pont d'Ain, and Ambérieu preparatory to attacking northwestward. Contact with the enemy had been light the previous day, limited to a firefight at Chalamont. Truscott had intelligence that the *11th Panzer Division* was in the vicinity, and he thought that although something might develop during the day, the Germans probably had little strength. At 0900, the 117th Cavalry Reconnaissance Squadron reported that enemy tracked vehicles had been heard.[8]

Just after 1000 hours, the Germans struck all along the 179th Infantry Regiment's front. The *11th Panzer Division* attacked without its *110th Panzergrenadier Regiment*, which had already departed northward. This time, von Wietersheim's task was merely to give the retreating infantry formations a little more breathing space.[9]

At Meximieux, in the center of the 179th Infantry's zone, two reserve companies of the 1st Battalion and some maquis guarded the town, supported by artillery and a platoon from Company A, 645th Tank Destroyer Battalion. The first German attack, from the northeast at about 0900 hours, was repulsed by observed artillery fire, but it may have been no more than a diversion, for a series of furious assaults from the south followed.

Shortly before noon, a platoon of panzergrenadiers backed by two 75mm assault guns probed the defenses, but they had the misfortune to run into the 1st Battalion's antitank platoon and a platoon of riflemen reinforced by motor pool and headquarters personnel. The Germans withdrew, but they pounded the town with fire from self-propelled artillery as large as 170mm.

Lieutenant Joseph Dixon was just moving two of his M10s into the village when the Germans attacked again about 1430. The two tank destroyers took up positions near the town center, with the first about a hundred yards ahead of the second. The commanders, Sgt. Robert Fitts and Sgt. Wayne Menear, positioned their vehicles so that they were partially concealed by buildings.

Two platoons of panzergrenadiers and five Panther tanks, supported by two 75mm assault guns, advanced again from the south but pulled back after the infantry became pinned down by antitank and small-arms fire. They quickly moved to outflank the American positions and broke toward town from the west, grenadiers riding the panzers.

The Panthers raced up the wide main street into Meximieux, firing their machine guns and crushing everything in their path. Fitts' gunner, Cpl. William McAuliffe, waited until the lead Mark V was only seventy-five yards away before he fired his 3-inch gun. The round penetrated the right front hull of the Panther, which burst into flames. McAuliffe nailed the next tank seconds later at a hundred yards. This panzer also caught fire and drove into a building, setting the neighboring houses ablaze. The other three tanks flew by Fitts.

Menear's gunner, Pvt. James Waldron, hit the third Panther at a range of only twenty-five yards. For some reason, he used a high-explosive (HE) round. The shell did not penetrate the armor, but it shattered the driver's periscope, and the Panther plowed into another building between the American M10s. GIs killed or captured the crewmen as they bailed out.

One of the last two Panthers stopped about fifty yards beyond Menear's M10 and turned around. Waldron immobilized the Mark V with a shot to the right track. The infantry opened up on the panzergrenadiers while a lone bazooka man crawled close to the Panther and disabled its main gun. At this setback, the crew bailed out and ran to a nearby house, which the Americans plastered with 81mm mortar and small-arms fire.

The last Panther crew fired on everyone who moved with its machine guns, and the GIs decided to call down artillery fire despite their proximity to the panzer. Under the shelling, the Panther broke for the woods, but American machine guns killed or wounded all of the panzergrenadiers clinging to the deck before it made good its escape.

The Americans beat off further *11th Panzer Division* probes until dark. One German group succeeded in reaching the eastern part of town, where it destroyed the Ain River crossing. Nonetheless, by day's end the defenders had killed or captured nearly 130 Germans and destroyed eight medium tanks, four light tanks, three assault guns, and seven other vehicles. American losses totaled about 30 men killed or wounded (and 185 presumed captured) as well as two tank destroyers and about twenty-five other vehicles destroyed or damaged.[10]

At nearby Pont d'Ain, the *11th Panzer Division* captured the town, and the 3d Battalion, 179th Infantry, and the 117th Cavalry Reconnaissance Squadron fought a sharp engagement to hold the railroad station west of the village. The 180th Infantry Regiment counterattacked and retook Pont d'Ain before dark.

The Germans broke through a 117th Cavalry Reconnaissance Squadron roadblock at Dagneux, on the road running northeastward out of Lyon, but the Americans refused to give any more ground beyond that. Stiff fighting raged at Loyettes, and elements of the 179th Infantry Regiment and the 117th Cavalry Reconnaissance Squadron held firm.[11]

For all the German effort, the bridge at Poncin, just north of Pont d'Ain, remained unmolested, and elements of the 180th Infantry Regiment and Troop B, 117th Cavalry Reconnaissance Squadron, slipped across and advanced virtually unopposed north and east of Bourg— where the *11th Panzer Division* CP was just setting up shop while camouflaged armored vehicles clattered into positions nearby.[12]

* * *

On 2 September, Truscott ordered the 3d Infantry Division, which had arrived after a ninety-mile march, to attack through the 45th Division's bridgehead across the Ain River. Major General O'Daniel assembled his regiments during the day and sent his first patrols northward after dark, but they encountered almost no enemy presence.[13] Meanwhile, as related in the preceding chapter, the 36th Infantry Division arrived at Lyon.[14]

Truscott was keen to push the lead elements of the 117th Cavalry Reconnaissance Squadron north of Bourg to cut key escape routes, but Troop B had ground to a halt under heavy artillery fire. Truscott applied heat to Major General Eagles to take Bourg with his 45th Infantry Division: "Put the steam on and barge right in there. You haven't anything in front of you except scattered elements of the *11th Panzer Division*, and I think you chewed most of them up yesterday."

"We got fourteen tanks yesterday," Eagles demurred.

"That's about half of what they had left. Knock off that many tomorrow and we can forget about them."[15]

The next morning, Troop B, 117th Cavalry Reconnaissance Squadron, attacked Montreval and by noon had cut all roads to the north, but the destruction of two Mark IVs and two SP guns during the engagement confirmed that VI Corps was about to have another run-in with the *11th Panzer Division*. Troop A arrived by noon, but the advance had unknowingly put the small command in a sensitive position ten miles behind the German line.

The *11th Panzer Division*'s armored reconnaissance battalion, supported by six Panthers, artillery, and engineers, struck back from Bourg and the southwest. The attack isolated Montreval and evolved into a pitched battle. The Germans overran nearly all of Troop B and all but one platoon of Troop A. Troops C and F, plus a battalion from the 179th Infantry Regiment, rushed to the scene, but the enemy's grip on Montreval was firm.

* * *

The 45th Infantry Division, meanwhile, encountered fierce resistance in the vicinity of Bourg itself. The division's history recorded, "The advance on Bourg [was] marked by widespread use of small-arms, machine-gun, and antitank-gun fire by the enemy, plus the fire of self-propelled guns and tanks. A sudden increase in the amount of artillery fire apparently meant that the enemy was making an attempt to establish some form of organized defense at that point." Rather than try to bore straight through the resistance, Eagles maneuvered to capture a series of towns (arguably located in the French zone of advance), which enabled him to outflank the Germans. The *11th Panzer Division* in any event was only trying to delay the 45th Division's advance, and GIs from the 180th Infantry Regiment entered Bourg early on 4 September and found that the enemy had abandoned the city.[16]

* * *

Truscott, in a stroke of perfect timing, had already urgently proposed a change in plan to Patch. With his permission scarcely arrived from Seventh Army, on 3 September Truscott adjusted the VI Corps' axis of attack to the northeast, parallel to the German withdrawal route in the direction of Belfort. Truscott had argued that he would lose contact with the fleeing enemy if he crossed the Saône River, as foreseen by Patch's late-August order, and recommended that he turn his corps to advance directly on Belfort via Besancon. Truscott asserted that he was confident that he could overcome supply difficulties sufficiently to seize the Belfort Gap. Round-trip hauls of four hundred miles for gasoline, ammunition, and rations were now common, but the French railroad was intact north of Sisteron, which allowed the corps to concentrate its trucks to move supplies from the beach to Sisteron. The only change that Patch had made to Truscott's proposal was to order him to destroy the troublesome *11th Panzer Division* for good while he was at it. Patch reassigned the objective of Dijon to French Army B and shifted the axis of advance of the French divisions on his right farther to the east. Truscott later indicated in his memoirs that because of a poor telephone connection, he did not hear Patch's decisions regarding the French, only the all-important go-ahead for his own plan.

By 0200 hours, the 3d Infantry Division had verbal orders to mount trucks and swing across the 45th Infantry Division's rear to Besancon, on the Doubs River. Maj. Gen. John "Iron Mike" O'Daniel's men were soon racing toward Belfort, meeting no resistance from the Germans, who were headed the same way on roads farther north. The rest of the corps, meanwhile, tidied up around Lyon and Bourg. After occupying Bourg, the 45th Infantry Division continued northward, but progress was slow because of blown bridges and long supply lines.[17]

Smashing the *11th Panzer Division* was not as easy as Patch evidently thought, because VI Corps lost nearly all contact with the enemy on 3 September. Prisoners reported that von Wietersheim had just slipped away toward Besancon, leaving a small rear guard at Bourg. His division had again achieved the remarkable: The main body of *Nineteenth Army* had been screened from contact with the enemy for six days.[18] Although the *Ghost Division*'s losses on this date are not known, the *11th Panzer Division* as of 15 September had suffered some 1,500 casualties and the loss of about thirty tanks since the Allied landings, or perhaps half its combat strength.[19]

The French Take Charge of the East Flank

Early on 1 September, Seventh Army notified VI Corps that French forces in the vicinity of Grenoble belonging to Béthouart's I Corps would relieve American troops along the Swiss frontier north of Briancon as soon as possible.[20] Bonjour, the lead element of General Guillaume's 3d DIA, had arrived.

With Bonjour's troops moving rapidly north, late on the night of 1–2 September de Lattre and his deputy chief of staff realized that they might be able to get to the Belfort Gap before the remnants of the *Nineteenth Army*. De Lattre drafted a directive to that effect, envisioning that both of his corps would end up side by side facing east between Switzerland to the south and the Saône to the north. He even envisioned dropping the 1st *Régiment du Chasseurs Parachutistes* (1st RCP), which de Gaulle was retaining as a reserve, on the eastern end of the Belfort Gap.[21]

In his endeavor to get between the Germans and their exit to the Reich, de Lattre could count on help from the special services, and also from the FFI in cooperation with an unexpected ally. A two-hundred-man FFI unit was operating in the Confracourt Woods, at the northern end of the gap and near a critical junction where roads from Paris, Dijon, and Besancon came together. In addition, on 27 August, eighty-two members of the French Special Air Service (SAS) commando dropped into the area and linked up with the Resistance. The American OSS also ordered its agents in the area between Strasbourg and Dijon to do what they could to harass withdrawing German forces. Not to be left out of the act, British SAS units also went in.[22]

Among the units that Blaskowitz sent to guard the Belfort Gap was the *30th SS Grenadier Division*, which was to hold the western end of the gap and conduct antipartisan operations. This was a particularly problematic "Russian" unit made up of former Soviet prisoners of war. It had been formed earlier in 1944, and the division's German officers looked with contempt upon their Slavic troops, many of whom were unenthused about fighting the western Allies, and abused them regularly.

The Ukrainian officers who were nominally in command of two of the division's Ukrainian battalions decided that they would go over to the Allies. They contacted the FFI, and, on the night of 26 August, one of the Ukrainian battalions surrounded the barracks of its German officers and noncommissioned officers (NCOs) and machined-gunned all twenty-five of them, at the cost of no serious Ukrainian casualties. At 1000 hours the next day, while the other battalion was on the move, its senior Ukrainian launched a flare into the sky. An hour later the ninety-five German officers and NCOs had been slaughtered.[23]

After the mutiny, the High Command pulled back the *30th SS Grenadier Division* from this sensitive position.[24] The Ukrainians joined up with the maquis of Confracourt, who referred to them as their "*force de surprise.*" [25]

* * *

On 2 September, the 3d DIA command post was in Grenoble, and Bonjour's group was as far north as Lons-le-Saulnier, Champagnole, and Morez, some forty miles ahead of the American right flank. The 3d DIA's 1st RCT (centered on the 3d RTA and the 7th RCA, a tank regiment), under Colonel Linarès, came into action. It boarded trucks far south near the coast, and on 3 September it leapt northward, covering eighty-five miles, and ended the day to the east of Bonjour's spahis and tirailleurs. With the help of the FFI, Linarès' men also took up positions along the

Swiss border to block the escape of German soldiers trying to cross the border to Switzerland.[26]

Béthouart's troops were well positioned now to drive to the Belfort Gap. Béthouart and de Lattre could practically taste it. However, they did not know that late on the afternoon of 2 September, Truscott had dispatched a messenger to Patch urging that VI Corps move along the Besancon–Belfort axis, right where Béthouart and de Lattre were trying to go. Truscott's memo admitted that the pursuit would be a logical one for the French but asserted they could not be in position to kick off for several days. When Truscott dispatched this memo, he probably did not know that French combat power in striking distance of Belfort was within a day of doubling. Nor, probably, did he know about de Lattre's hope to drop airborne forces into the gap. Even had he known, however, it probably would have made no difference: Truscott's respect for the French was modest, and his sympathy for de Lattre was minimal.[27]

Patch's new order arrived at de Lattre's headquarters during the day on 3 September. The French were now to operate along the axis of Mâcon–Chalon-sur-Saône–Dijon–Épinal–Strasbourg. That route was to the west and north, essentially in Monsabert's II Corps territory. Béthouart's corps could squeeze itself into the tight space between VI Corps and the Swiss border, but VI Corps would do the real work. De Lattre was furious; he and Béthouart were both convinced that they could have gotten to Belfort and plugged the gap. But by the time de Lattre heard of the orders, Truscott's forces had already started moving in their new direction, shouldering the French aside. War is full of "what ifs," but Béthouart was convinced ever after that until 10 September, when German reinforcements started coming from the east, his forces could have gotten to the gap. A post-war discussion with *Generalmajor* von Wietersheim, former commander of the *11th Panzer Division*, only reinforced Béthouart's view.[28]

Béthouart's troops still were able to make some small advances, and the Resistance helped out substantially. On 4 September, the 3d Battalion of the 4th RTT—the lead element of the 3d DIA—helped by a group of FTP utterly destroyed a German *kampfgruppe* at Mouthe. The ferocity of the combat only grew as the French became aware of atrocities committed against local civilians by the mixed group of German soldiers and customs officers and *Ostruppen*, or "Mongols," as Béthouart referred to them.[29] On 5 September, the French army reached Pontarlier, where, with the help of the 2d Ukrainian Battalion, which had recently switched sides, it took the town from a force of Germans and Russian "volunteers."[30]

* * *

Blaskowitz on 4 September issued orders implementing Hitler's instructions that *Army Group G* was to link up with *Army Group B* to the north, hold the area west of the Vosges Mountains to Dijon as a staging area for a counterattack against Patton's Third Army, and protect the routes to the Belfort Gap, to the south. To accomplish the last mission, Blaskowitz ordered that a delaying line be held roughly along the Doubs River, right in the path of VI Corps and French I Corps.[31]

On 5 September, Blaskowitz turned over command of the battle in the Dijon area to Wiese and *Nineteenth Army* and moved his headquarters to Gérardmer, at the edge of the Vosges Mountains. His task was to oversee preparation of a defensive line exploiting the high ground. Construction of the line had begun on 1 September. Blaskowitz had spent time in those hills all the way back to the days before World War I and knew them intimately. Here, he thought, one might stop even a modern mechanized army.

Blaskowitz knew there were two weak points, both opening onto routes leading straight to the Rhine. The first was in the north at Saverne (Zabern in German) Gap or pass, outside his area of influence; the second was the historical path for population movements, the Belfort Gap. Blaskowitz soon had members of the Todt Organization, and even zealous if untrained Hitler Youth, building defensive positions for his troops.[32]

ANOTHER CHOKEHOLD SLIPS

The closest route to the Belfort Gap and relative safety available to the retreating Germans was the Doubs River valley, where the main road ran from Dole through Besancon and Beaume-les-Dames toward Montbéliard and the gap. Once they were past Besancon, the Alps would offer good defensive terrain on the Germans' southern flank.[33]

After trucking seventy-five miles unimpeded by German fire, the 3d Infantry Division's 7th Infantry Regiment reached the area of Besancon at about 0100 hours on 5 September. The 2d Battalion dismounted to attack the city at 0500. The rest of VI Corps was following, the 36th Infantry Division slanting to protect the left flank around Dole, and the 45th Infantry Division angling toward Beaume-les-Dames, farther up the road to Belfort.

Inside Besancon, where the *11th Panzer Division* had arrived a day earlier, von Wietersheim had been shocked to receive the first reports that the Americans were approaching Beaume-les-Dames from the south. The amount of artillery that would soon be falling on his positions told him that this was no reconnaissance probe. By noon, the lead elements of the 15th Infantry Regiment, 3d Infantry Division, joined the 7th Infantry's assault, and the rifle companies of both regiments were soon embroiled in stiff fighting along an arc south of the city.[34] Besancon was the first city in which modern American arms pitted themselves against fortifications built by Vauban, and it would go better than most. The citadel dominated the high ground above the city, and four smaller forts were tied together in a mutually supporting defensive system.

The arrival of the 3d Infantry Division near Besancon unhinged German plans to defend the Doubs River line. *Nineteenth Army* over the next two days threw the *338th* and *198th Infantry divisions* and the just-arrived *159th Infantry Division* into the breach to relieve the *11th Panzer Division*.[35]

German hopes of throwing back the 3d Infantry Division were stillborn. O'Daniel brought all of his regiments into the line on 6 September to attack Besancon from three sides, a task made somewhat easier by the German abandonment of positions south of town during the night. O'Daniel invested the city and captured the smaller forts one by one until, on 7 September, the 1st Battalion, 15th Infantry Regiment, stormed the citadel.

A report compiled on the basis of interviews with participants described the assault on Fort Tousey, one of the auxiliary fortifications flanking the citadel:

> The final attack on Fort Tousey was an envelopment and principally an infantry and . . . heavy

weapons attack. In the late morning, Companies B and C began their final attack on the fort, firing 60mm mortars, light machine guns, attached heavy machine guns, and rifle grenades at their objective.

Individual acts of outstanding heroism contributed materially to the fall of the fort. A buttoned-up medium tank commanded by S/Sgt. Donald Freeman of Company C, 756th Tank Battalion, and led by a Company C [infantry] squad leader, S/Sgt. Robert Smith, who rode on the side of the tank, aggressively moved up the steep slope through steady enemy machine-gun fire from Fort Tousey and the citadel, bullets bouncing off the turret and sides like hail, to within 25 feet of the entrance way. The tank then began firing, under the initial direction of [Smith], directly into the fort entrance. After [the tank fired] thirty-three rounds . . . inflicting casualties [and] damaging the fort's OP tower, . . . a German bazooka team scaled the wall, crossed the ditch surrounding the fort, and, firing at point-blank range at the big target, scored two hits, the first striking the tank turret. This hit, although injuring crewmembers, did not stop the [crew or their commander], who ordered more 75mm rounds to be fired into the fort. The second bazooka round hit the ammunition bank at the rear of the tank, killing the cannoneer, setting the tank afire, and forcing its abandonment. . . .

[A] squad of Company C [moved] up near the tank and began throwing hand grenades into the fort entrance. . . .[A]fter ten hours of steady fighting, . . . infantrymen of Companies B and C closed in for the kill. The white flag was raised from the fort. . . .[36]

The attack on the citadel itself resembled even more closely some medieval assault. Captain Christopher Chaney, commanding the 1st Battalion, put in motion a second envelopment using Companies A and C. While troops moved into position, Chaney, dodging machine-gun fire, guided a tank destroyer to a position five hundred yards from the main gate, which it battered with twenty-five rounds before the gate was sprung. Chaney next ordered the tank destroyer to breach the wall while he set about organizing scaling parties using ladders obtained from local farmers. When the gunfire failed to scratch the mammoth stone walls, Chaney obtained a 155mm self-propelled howitzer, which blasted the fort over open sights from a distance of 1,800 yards. The larger shells also did little harm to the walls, so Chaney shifted the fire to buildings within the fort, adding searching and traversing fire by the battalion's 60mm and 81mm mortars. As secondary explosions rocked the citadel and the scaling party approached the walls, a white flag was run up by the defenders.[37]

After the two-hundred-man garrison surrendered, the Americans determined that although the 155s had barely chipped the old fortifications, the noise of the explosions had unnerved the defenders. Besancon had fallen to direct assault. *Generalmajor* Max Schmidt, who had just arrived to take command of the *159th Infantry Division*, lay among the German dead in the city.[38]

* * *

Meanwhile, on 6 September near Beaume-les-Dames, the 45th Infantry Division established contact with the 3d DIA, which had just captured Maiche, near the Swiss border. The next day, the Americans crossed the Doubs but failed to capture Beaume-les-Dames, where the Germans held out for two days before pulling back toward Belfort. Heavy fire from panzers and tracked "flakwagens" gave the GIs yet another calling card from the *11th Panzer Division*. The 36th Infantry Division in the meantime had crossed the Doubs at Dole and captured a fuel dump containing 177,500 gallons of gasoline, a godsend for the supply-starved VI Corps.[39]

Wiese concluded that after the fall of Besancon, a concerted attack by the Allies could have reached the Belfort Gap.[40] Sandy Patch evidently agreed in substance, because he told 6th Army Group commanding general Devers that his rate of advance was more limited by difficulty of supply than by any determined and effective enemy resistance.[41] The VI Corps on 9 September had captured a German situation map that confirmed Truscott's suspicion that the defenses in the Belfort Gap were still relatively weak, and he could take them with the forces at his disposal.[42]

The Americans, however, did not turn eastward down the road to the Belfort Gap; they instead continued northeastward into hilly wooded terrain that gave the enemy every defensive advantage. By this time, Truscott was aware that French I Corps would be operating on his right between the Doubs and the Swiss border, but he still expected to be able to wheel right, north of the river, and capture the gap before the Germans could strengthen their defenses.[43] The 45th Infantry Division advanced from Beaume-les-Dames to Villersexel, the 3d Infantry Division moved from Besancon to Vesoul, and the 36th Infantry Division moved along a parallel course on the corps' left flank. The Seventh Army history recorded, "The rolling foothills of the Vosges were admirably suited for delaying actions. Rain had softened the roads, and fog reduced possible air support. In the towns of Villersexel, Vesoul, Lure, and Luxeuil, the Germans made determined stands. Their line of communications west of the Vosges was to be held open as long as possible in order to gain time to prepare [the defenses]." Indeed, by 12 September, VI Corps faced strong opposition across almost its entire front. The pursuit phase was most definitely over.

* * *

On 7 September, two platoons of the 3d squadron, 3d RSAR, approached Glainans, not far from Clerval in the Department of Doubs, where they spotted Panther tanks at the edge of the village. The squadron commander, Captain Quenetain, decided to call on the 4th RTT and attack with some of these brave Tunisians, beside whom the Algerians had fought their way from the beaches of Provence. The mixed force of infantry, tanks, and tank destroyers set out that afternoon to drive the Germans from the town.[44]

Lieutenant Capdaspe and his platoon were the trailing force and in a good position to watch the unfolding events. Capdaspe was watching as all hell broke loose. The Germans fired a volley of shells at the attacking force, and tirailleurs dove for whatever cover they could find.

All of a sudden a shell, probably from a Panther, hit Capdaspe's tank and killed the driver, who had stuck his head out of the vehicle to survey the situation. At the same moment, a shell blew through the turret, flying between Capdaspe and his gunner. Both men evacuated the tank immediately, miraculously only slightly wounded. Immediately they came under machine-gun fire. Capdaspe found himself running for cover alongside a young officer of the tirailleurs. Both men were hugging the ground tightly as the machine-gun fire played all around them. Realizing that their position provided insufficient cover, Capdaspe sprinted away when there was a pause in the fire. The tirailleur did not follow. With a quick glance over his shoulder, Capdaspe saw that the man was dead.

The platoon of spahis led by Officer Candidate Clévenot fared no better. His platoon came under withering fire from the very beginning of the attack. From his observation position in his scout car, Clévenot ordered his men to stop and seek cover. Preparing to move out, his driver discovered that the car would not start and got out to crank it. Clévenot was just getting out of the scout car when the engine sprang to life. At that moment a shell went off in the tree below which the car was idling. There was a burst of flame and smoke. When it dispersed, Clévenot was dead in the road, having fallen without a sound. Three other spahis were crying out in pain.

The attack was broken. Three French soldiers were dead and twenty-four wounded. The Germans still held Glainans.

* * *

Despite de Lattre's hopes of getting to the Rhine, everything was grinding to a halt. The 3d DIA was tangling with the *11th Panzer Division* at Valdahon and Beaume-les-Dames, and the corps was running into Mark IVs and Panthers. The 3d DIA was low on supplies, even being reduced to begging them from Truscott. The 9th DIC, newly subordinated to Béthouart, was stopped while it lent its trucks to perform army-level tasks. The 2d DIM was still holding down the Alps, along with the goums. The never-sleeping *11th Panzer Division* on 8 September counterattacked the I Corps where it had reached the Doubs before Montbéliard and drove back the Frenchmen. "We had to resign ourselves; the pursuit was over," Béthouart remembered. "Progressively, the front was stabilizing."[45]

* * *

Army Group G had gathered *Fifth Panzer Army* at Remiremont beginning on 11 September to stage a counterattack against Patton's rapid advance in Lorraine, which Hitler hoped would stop Third Army's spearheads. The attack led to a series of tank battles later in the month that chewed up much of the German tank reserve in the south.[46]

German accounts do not shed light on the question of what role the Allied approach to the German frontier played in inspiring their more determined resistance at this point. A German map of the Reich in 1944 incorporated Alsace and Lorraine, ethnically mixed regions that had belonged to Germany from 1871 to 1918, and Hitler had annexed again in 1940 after the French defeat. The frontier followed the crest of the Vosges Mountains from the Swiss border to a point just southwest of Sarrebourg, then tracked northwestward to the area west of Metz before turning due north to Luxembourg. It is reasonable to assume that Hitler's orders to defend every inch of German soil applied to *Elsass-Lothringen*, as the region was known in Berlin. A special order from Hitler on 17 September read in part, "The battle in the West has largely moved onto German soil; German cities and villages will be battlegrounds. This fact must make our fighting more fanatical and harden every available man in the battle zone to turn every bunker, every apartment block in a German city, every German village into a fortress. . . ."[47]

* * *

On 14 September, VI Corps received a new plan from Seventh Army that directed it to advance through the Vosges Mountains in the direction of Strasbourg and gave responsibility for capturing the Belfort Gap back to the French. Truscott, who doubted the French could mount any serious attack before October, was livid.[48] Patch's new orders meant salvation for a *Nineteenth Army* that was on the brink of disaster. Wiese's command south and west of Épinal was in danger of complete destruction on 14 September, a situation that *Army Group G* recognized. Blaskowitz on 15 September authorized Wiese to fall back on a new line running roughly Charmes-Épinal–west of Belfort.[49]

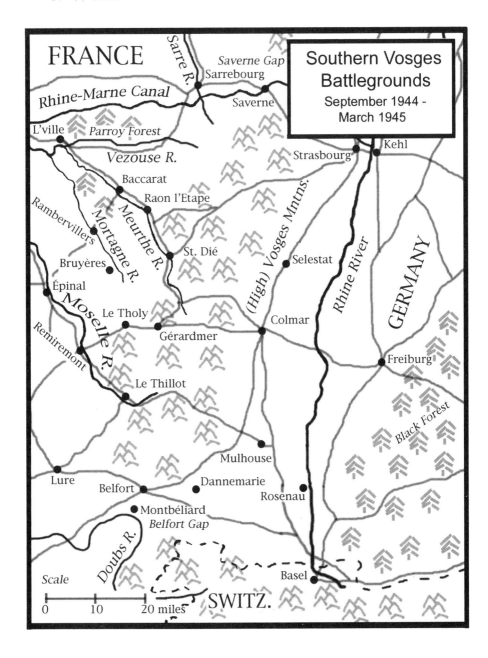

FRANCE

Sarre R.

Saverne Gap

Sarrebourg

Rhine-Marne Canal

Saverne

Southern Vosges Battlegrounds
September 1944 -
March 1945

L'ville — Parroy Forest

Vezouse R.

Strasbourg

Kehl

Baccarat

Raon l'Etape

GERMANY

Rambervillers

Mortagne R.

Meurthe R.

St. Dié

(High) Vosges Mntns.

Selestat

Rhine River

Bruyères

Épinal

Le Tholy

Gérardmer

Colmar

Freiburg

Moselle R.

Remiremont

Le Thillot

Black Forest

Mulhouse

Lure

Belfort

Dannemarie

Rosenau

Montbéliard

Belfort Gap

Doubs R.

Basel

Scale

0   10   20 miles

SWITZ.

REGROUPING

At this time, Patch was forced to correct the problem inherent in Franco-American dispositions. Although he had anticipated as early as 2 September that after the capture of Lyon, the French army would take up a position on his right wing and advance along the Bourg-Belfort axis, he had been putting off making his move with the full approval of Field Marshal Wilson. He anticipated shifting VI Corps to the west of the Rhône to continue driving northward until linking up with Third Army near Dijon.[50] Patch's main concern had been to cut off as many German forces as possible, and because VI Corps had gained quite a lead while the French reduced the defenses at Marseille and Toulon, he had sensibly plunged ahead with little regard for boundaries. Eisenhower forced the matter on 9 September, when he promised to transfer a three-division corps from Third Army to Seventh Army but insisted that there be no intermingling of American and French units. This meant that VI Corps would have to move to the left wing of 6th Army Group from its position sandwiched between two French corps. French II Corps was still pushing almost due northward west of the Rhône and would have to stop and shift nearly fifty miles to the east.

A pause for regrouping became necessary from 14 to 20 September. Perhaps the commanders believed that the Germans were so licked that they could not offer serious resistance again along the southern axis of Allied advance—a dream that many held at that time regarding the northern axis. These hopes were just about to be dashed amid the mud and blood of the Siegfried Line fighting around Aachen. The 6th Army Group history rationalized the missed opportunity: "Actually, the regrouping operation did not cause substantial delay because any considerable advance in strength was forced to wait for the establishment of adequate lines of communications."[51]

Truscott knew that excuse to be nonsense. He fired off a private letter to Patch on 15 September in which he reiterated that he could supply a force adequate to capture the Belfort Gap. He argued that VI Corps' strength would be frittered away in the easily defended Vosges without making a contribution to the strategic effort and suggested that his corps be withdrawn and used for an attack on Genoa, Italy, as a better alternative to the current plan. Patch phoned Truscott to express his lack of appreciation for such advice and proceeded with his plans.[52] So on 17 September, Truscott ordered a halt to offensive operations until French II Corps could relieve the 3d and 45th Infantry divisions.[53]

For the French, it was a difficult pill to swallow when the order from Patch arrived on 14 September establishing the general direction of VI Corps operations as Gérardmer—Strasbourg. Nevertheless, the French II Corps wheeled to the east and aimed itself at the Belfort Gap.[54] Béthouart's I Corps, previously pushed off the side of the road, was allowed to line up squarely facing the gap, which by 19 September was well defended.[55] I Corps was to the south and II Corps to the north in the new French zone. North of II Corps was the U.S. VI Corps.[56]

The French army facing the Germans at the Belfort Gap still controlled only four divisions plus a few other units. A fifth division, the 2d Moroccan Infantry Division (2d DIM), was occupied in the Alps, clearing the valleys and pushing the Germans into the frontier passes. Another division, the 4th Moroccan Mountain Division (4th DMM), had only barely started landing, and one more, the 5th DB, was behind it on the list.[57]

* * *

Despite Truscott's confidence, supplies—and not just of fuel—were a growing concern. On 1 September, the 191st Tank Battalion expressed concern that long road marches and shortages of spares were forcing the battalion to continue using worn-out tank tracks.[58] The 753d Tank Battalion also reported near-critical shortages of tracks, support rollers, bogey wheels, and tank engines. On 6 September, the battalion commander warned Major General Dahlquist that his tanks would not be operational after two more days of movement unless parts could be obtained, and at mid-month Company C had only three tanks that would run.[59] Similarly, at one point almost half of the M10s in the 645th Tank Destroyer Battalion were deadlined, most because of worn-out tracks.[60]

Devers Takes Charge

The structure of Allied forces in France was simultaneously undergoing a thorough restructuring. The 6th Army Group headquarters had moved to St. Tropez on 31 August. On orders from Field Marshal Wilson, Devers on

3 September flew to Eisenhower's headquarters to discuss SHAEF's assumption from the Mediterranean theater headquarters of operational control over Dragoon forces, which Wilson judged should happen fairly soon. Ike decided that SHAEF would take control on 15 September, at which time 6th Army Group would enter the command chain, and that IX Air Force would assume operational control over XII Tactical Air Command. Devers on 7 September flew to Patch's headquarters, by then in Grenoble, to inform him of Eisenhower's views and also ordered his own headquarters to move to Lyon.

The command changes took place as planned at 0001 hours on 15 September, resulting in the somewhat odd situation that Devers was for some time simultaneously one of Eisenhower's army group commanders and Wilson's deputy commander. Seventh Army was relieved of responsibility for operational control over French forces as of 19 September but was charged with continuing maintenance and logistic support until further notice. When de Lattre's Army B passed from control of Seventh Army to that of 6th Army Group on 19 September, it was redesignated French First Army. Wilson and AFHQ retained responsibility for administration, logistic support, maintenance of Dragoon forces, and civil administration in southern France for the time being.

The contact between Seventh and Third Army troops raised the question of the border between their respective 6th and 12th Army groups. Already, Devers' staff saw a dilemma. One proposed line running from Langres to Strasbourg would leave 6th Army Group facing the maze of the Black Forest in Germany with no favorable route toward an important objective inside the Third Reich. A second proposed line running from Langres to Hockenheim resolved the maneuver problem but would spread out 6th Army Group to a worrisome extent, even with an extra corps. SHAEF on 17 September chose the second option.

Allied commanders received some excellent news on the logistic front on 18 September when Liberty ships began unloading at ten dock berths in Marseille; civilian supplies were being brought in through Toulon. The amount of rolling stock in southern France had far exceeded pre-invasion estimates, and Devers' staff estimated that by 1 October the railhead at Dijon would be capable of fully supporting ten divisions. Military railway service was already substantially supporting ten divisions plus corps, army, and army group units but could not move sufficient ammunition or fuel for sustained combat operations. Four hundred miles of pipe had been unloaded for the construction of a gasoline pipeline from the coast to the front to help resolve that problem.[61]

Amalgamating the French Army and the FFI

During this time, de Lattre was not only fighting the Germans and maneuvering against the Americans, he was also struggling to keep the morale of his troops up and to forge a new French army. This army would bring together the sharply divided bodies of men (and some women) who bore arms for France, and be a unifying symbol for a new France.

In September, General Molle, whom de Lattre had put in charge of the First Army's "FFI Office," wrote him an alarming memo. Molle noted that for two years the weight of the war had fallen on the colonial troops, and everyone knew it. They had fought their way to glory in Italy, Toulon, and Marseille. The tirailleurs, the spahis, and the other colonials, as well as their French officers, all believed that it was time that the Frenchmen of France shouldered their burden in the liberation of the country. Molle warned that if they did not take this step, and rapidly, they should expect a bloody wakeup call later that could have been avoided. Moreover, the morale of the Moroccans was not good and that of the Algerians was simply bad. Bitterness, he warned, was turning into a deceitful anger.[62]

De Lattre became persuaded that France's North African colonies had reached the extreme limit of their capabilities, and it was morally necessary for the French youth to pick up the burden. The Anglo-Americans and the colonials could not and should not be solely responsible for the liberation of metropolitan France.[63] De Gaulle held similar views; writing on 7 October, he ordered the amalgamation of the FFI and the French First Army.[64]

The French leadership also believed, as did some of the colonials themselves, that "the black troops [were] unsuited to the winter climate of the east of France," which was indeed suffering a particularly soggy fall that would soon give way to a bitter winter. Tafolotien Soro, a tirailleur in the 13th RTS, was one of those who suffered greatly. "It was very cold," he remembered. "It broke our feet."[65] Exacerbating these problems was the fact that much of de Lattre's army was still wearing its summer uniforms; the cold weather uniforms were still on the beaches of Provence. This made the September rains particularly hard to bear, and there were cases of frostbite before the month was out.[66]

So it was not just cold hard politics but also cold weather that led de Lattre's army to embark on the "whitening," or *blanchiment*, process. In the 9th DIC, the French decided that 9,200 Senegalese should be sent to southern France, where it was thought they would be better able to handle the climate. Similarly, the 1st DFL had five infantry battalions to send south, including battalions from the Cameroons, French Equatorial Africa, and Djibouti, as well as other miscellaneous personnel, totaling more than six thousand men. Over time other units would go through similar processes.

This "whitening" of the 9th DIC and 1st DFL was completed by the end of October. One result of it was that the 4th, 6th, and 13th Senegalese tirailleurs, because they no longer contained any "Senegalese," were renamed the 21st, 6th, and 23d regiments of Colonial Infantry (RIC), respectively. Often, of course, the Africans switched places with their French replacements in rear areas, but sometimes the turnover actually happened on the frontlines. On certain days, observant German soldiers might have seen young French soldiers in trenches just a few hundred yards away receiving overcoats, helmets, and rifles from Africans who then departed for the rear.[67]

The replacement of colonial troops with ethnic Frenchmen dragged on, and *blanchiment* never was completely finished before the war ended. As late as spring 1945, a Somali regiment still fought in the 1st DFL, and in June 1945 the Sultan of Morocco came to inspect his victorious troops in Germany.[68]

So, as fall came on, de Lattre, who was short of forces anyway, was actually losing to *blanchiment*, the weather, and the Germans. Given this burning need for forces, and the political necessity of bringing together the two completely different French armies, the regular army and the FFI, the amalgamation of the two began in earnest when the French First Army reached the Vosges.[69]

* * *

Long ago, de Lattre had begun planning for this day. As early as 1 March 1944, he had set up a school near his headquarters not far from Algiers to which his officers, NCOs, and men came "for initiation in new methods and to make the contacts that cemented the community spirit." What de Lattre had specifically in mind was the future amalgamation of his French army with the maquis. To this end, members of the Resistance who had recently escaped from France were regular speakers at the school, where they told of their suffering, struggles, and hopes.[70]

Later in the year, when the time came, de Lattre found the problem of the amalgamation to be complex and delicate. In Lyon, the day after its liberation, de Lattre addressed this question in an interview with a journalist from the *Patriote*, in which he laid out the key principles for the amalgamation, as he saw them. "We will never effect an absorption, pure and simple, of the FFI. . . . It is indispensable to retain their name, their mystique and their group pride. . . . Given the actual circumstances of our army at war, its structures must not be changed. . . . When conditions permit, a synthesis will be effected between what they represent and what we represent, with the most generous understanding between both of them. . . . To all the merits and all the fighting qualities they have acquired in the life of the maquis, we ask them to add order and discipline, so that the country may recognize in them already a reconstituted part of tomorrow's army."[71]

* * *

De Lattre's army was a justifiably proud organization with a strong sense of hierarchy, duty, and respect. As a rule, promotion in it had been earned, and the rewards had been infrequent. By contrast, the FFI was made up of ad hoc units that had been clandestinely raised and had operated in the shadows. Where duty and hierarchy were the organizational glue that held together the army, personality played a central role among the maquis. One result was that each Resistance unit was different. Where traditional military virtues flourished in the army, de Lattre observed that the "revolutionary military virtues" flourished in the maquis. "Their common trait was audacity allied to the spirit of independence."

Many members of the army were troubled by the uneven nature of the FFI's organization (a battalion might contain 300 or 1,200 men), the inadequate nature of their equipment, their distinctly unmilitary approach toward discipline, and the high rank that many of their officers had reached with so little military experience. Their political stance, which for many FFI was distinctly left-leaning, was also profoundly troubling to many Frenchman in de Lattre's army. For their part, the FFI had largely mirror-image perceptions of the regular army and its personnel. One of the most prominent maquis leaders thought that the FFI alone "must give birth to the [new] French army" in the words of his "Provisional Instruction on the General Organization of the FFI," promulgated just as the French First Army was approaching Dijon.[72]

Despite these difficulties, de Lattre on 23 September ordered that all maquis joining the army must join for the duration of the war.[73]

There were bumps in this road, of course. General Molle warned de Lattre that there was a gulf between the Frenchmen in the Army of Africa and the nation at large. Many people in France, knowing nothing of the Army of Africa, believed it to be an army of mercenaries. Their slogan was that the FFI should not be merged into the army, but the army should be merged into the FFI. The Resistance members attached to Molle's division received an anonymous flyer that described de Lattre's army as colonials led by Vichyite officers.

"Two days ago," Molle wrote, "I received a highly cultured FFI officer, who, after eight days spent in the companies of the first echelon of my division, enthusiastically shared the guts, the ambiance of this Army. He admitted, however, that it would be difficult to convince his comrades because . . . the Army of Africa was considered an army of 'fascists.' " Molle was astonished and asked how this colonel's associates could possibly believe this. The colonel explained that de Lattre's army was the descendant of Weygand's army, "that is to say, of that army which in the Levant in 1940 was preparing operations against Russia." Molle observed, "From distrust to animosity is only one step."[74]

On 7 October, de Gaulle wrote to de Lattre with new orders concerning the FFI: "It is essential that we participate in the future battles of 1945 with the maximum of forces. Nothing is more important for the moment than to form new large units." Accordingly, he ordered de Lattre to give each of his divisions the equivalent of a regiment of FFI and take the best FFI of de Lattre's zone and form from them a new division.[75]

The amalgamation picked up speed, and soon the regular units of the First Army found themselves extremely busy as large numbers of FFI applied to join. In the end, 137,000 maquis would join the pre-existing army of some 250,000.[76] They came from all corners of France. Some were Spanish Communists in exile who dreamed of defeating the German fascists, even if they could not defeat Franco. Although having foreigners in the French army was problematic on its own terms, it did reduce their numbers on the Spanish border, from whence the French government feared some of them might mount raids into Spain.[77]

De Lattre ordered that First Army–style battalions be formed from the FFI units. At least initially, FFI companies would be kept together and retain their own officers, but pre-existing battalions would be broken up, a measure largely aimed at the Communist FTP. The Ministry of War felt that surrounding FTP companies with other non-Communist companies would reduce the odds that the larger units would be, in the words of one French general, "receptive to certain political forces."[78]

The amalgamation of FFI into the armored units, notably the 5th DB, was particularly successful. The armored units were short on infantry, and the FFI took well to the armored style of rapid-paced operations and raiding. Infantry units, however, generally did not warm to the newcomers, and the attached battalions never felt as though they received equal treatment except in the various commando units—the African Commando Group, the French commandos, and the Shock Battalion.[79]

In fact, the incorporation of FFI into infantry units caused much resentment. General Brosset, commanding the 1st DFL, for example, wrote to de Lattre in early November that his regular troops resented the extra latitude that their new FFI colleagues received—or took in some cases. Maquis commanders issued their own propaganda newspapers without clearance from higher authority, and FFI soldiers did not show proper respect to regular officers. Some FFI units had even given leave to as many as half of their men. All of this was troublesome, of course, but furthermore, regular officers resented the rank inflation that had taken hold in the Resistance forces. Beyond that, senior French officers were concerned that there was a lack of zeal for fighting among the French population generally. Brosset noted that postal censors had intercepted many letters to FFI troops from their friends urging them not to fight when they could be safe in the rear, letters from mothers urging their sons to come home, and other such appeals.[80]

As the process wore on, de Lattre took the FFI battalions that had been rejected by regular army regiments, and he formed from them new regiments composed almost entirely of FFI soldiers. In this manner he was able to make himself fifteen infantry regiments and several artillery units.[81]

There was no end of headaches. De Lattre recalls in his memoirs that the process engendered a great deal of hostility and drove some of his senior officers nearly to distraction. In some cases, the issues were tragicomic. Colonel Salan's newly renamed 6th RIC received the grandiosely named "Paris Brigade," under the command of Colonel "Fabien," the nom de guerre of a young, vigorous veteran of the Spanish Civil War, an up-and-coming member of the underground Communist party. "Fabien" was a natural soldier and a born leader, but he had one critical weakness: a personal interest in ordnance disposal. His office in the town hall of Habsheim was often littered with German mines and explosives. Salan was unable to persuade the young officer to give up this hobby. Predictably, in late December, "Fabien" accidentally blew up the town hall, killing himself and his senior staff in the process.[82]

Other times, the issues cut straight to the heart of army morale. In early October, de Lattre found himself facing the issue of a very young FFI colonel who was on the fast track for promotion to general. De Lattre had to ask his superiors to name simultaneously to the rank of general de Lattre's deputy chief of staff, Linarès, who was from the regular army, in order not to create dissension and further morale problems in the ranks of the First Army.[83] De Lattre wrote in his memoirs that some people criticized him for spending long evenings with twenty-eight-year-old FFI colonels while making regular officers wait. However, the army commander felt that this was a price that needed to be paid. The amalgamation of the First Army and the FFI may have been de Lattre's greatest victory.[84]

CHAPTER 7

INTO THE VOSGES

The peaks of the mountains in [the] High
Vosges afford outstanding long-range fields of
observation and fire in all directions. In clear
weather, visibility from the geographical crests
of the ridges and hills is limited only by the cur-
vature of the earth. . . .

—Keith E. Bonn, *When the Odds Were Even*

Truscott got VI Corps moving again on 19–20 September even though
the relief of 3d and 45th Infantry division troops by the French was still
wrapping up. The 117th Cavalry Reconnaissance Squadron, at the left
end of the corps line, probed toward Épinal until it encountered strong
roadblocks just short of the objective. The local maquis reported that
German forces were crossing to the east bank of the Moselle River at
Épinal and destroying the bridges behind them. The 45th Infantry
Division re-positioned from the corps' right to its left and prepared to
follow the 117th Cavalry Squadron to Épinal, while the 36th Infantry
Division (now in the center) moved into positions from which to establish
bridgeheads across the Moselle River. The 3d Infantry Division still had
nearly ten miles to go before it reached the west bank of the Moselle.

"I am assuming the enemy is defending the river," speculated Major
General Dahlquist.

"It looks like they may be," replied Truscott.

The VI Corps was now oriented eastward along a twelve-mile front,
but once the river was crossed, it was to advance northeastward again.
Two main routes through the Vosges led eastward from Épinal, one
through St. Dié and the other through Gérardmer. Truscott assigned the
key objectives of Baccarat and St. Dié to the 45th and 36th Infantry

185

divisions, respectively, while the 3d Infantry Division was to take Gérardmer and maintain contact with the French on the right. The corps was then to push through the Saverne Gap.[1]

* * *

Wiese's *Nineteenth Army* had two weak corps opposite Truscott. *Generalleutnant* Lasch, who had taken command of *LXIV Corps* on 3 September, held the line from Épinal south to Remiremont, the initial objectives of the 45th and 36th Infantry divisions, respectively. He had available on his right the *716th Infantry Division* and some weak battle groups and on his left the depleted *189th Reserve Division* (soon redesignated the *189th Infantry Division*). The *716th Division* had some 2,500 combat effectives, and the *189th Division* about 1,500 drawn from division cadres, stragglers, and a Luftwaffe training unit. The *IV Luftwaffe Field Corps* defended the line south of Remiremont with the battle-weary *338th Infantry Division* on the right and the again relatively fit *198th Infantry Division* on the left, plus a hodgepodge of combat groups.[2]

* * *

The Moselle in this area roughly marked the beginning of the foothills to the High Vosges Mountains, and the terrain on the east bank was generally broken and heavily forested. Towns and the sparse roads that bound them together would be of decisive importance. The steep, heavily forested hills of the Low Vosges waited north of the Saverne Gap.

General der Infanterie Wiese hoped *Nineteenth Army* could hold the Americans west of the mountains, because he could still move troops laterally across his front to deal with threats as they arose. His pleas for reinforcements went unanswered by the High Command, which faced more pressing threats farther north, and Wiese dreaded the thought of having to hold a static line in the mountains with his weak forces. Indeed, his division commanders were telling him that they could not stop a powerful Allied thrust.[3]

The Germans nevertheless were working furiously to construct fortifications to exploit the defensive potential of the terrain. Hitler on 20 August had authorized a *levée en masse* to provide labor, but without the direction of professional military men, many of the field works were virtually useless. A *Nineteenth Army* directive issued on 16 September put the fortification effort in the hands of its own rear headquarters, and military construction battalions and combat units took charge.[4] The Vosges position defenses were deemed ready for use effective 25 September.[5]

* * *

The 36th Infantry Division crossed the Moselle on 21 September with little difficulty. During the preceding night, Monsieur R. M. Gribelin, mayor of Raon-aux-Boid and a retired naval officer, guided 141st Infantry Regiment GIs through intermittent rain along a forest trail to a good crossing site. The 1st Battalion forded the river with no problem, but the Germans from the *189th Reserve Division* were alerted by the time the 3d Battalion waded into the stream. The Germans waited until the first platoon had reached the east bank, then opened up with machine-gun and mortar fire. The entire platoon was either killed or captured, and the following platoon suffered heavily; the battalion commander went missing and his operations officer was killed. The outfit shifted north and crossed at the site already secured by the 1st Battalion. By noon, meanwhile, the 2d Battalion had secured the half of Eloyes west of the Moselle. Only at Remiremont, where the Germans still held positions on the west bank, did the 36th Division's 142d Infantry Regiment encounter determined resistance.

The 143d Infantry Regiment crossed in the tracks of the 141st Infantry and by dark had a battalion on Hill 783 overlooking the eastern half of Eloyes. A battalion of German infantry on Hill 605, however, fought the Americans from prepared strongpoints all night long. The battalion was well supported by artillery, which the Americans could not locate for counterbattery fire because of fog.[6]

The 45th Infantry Division, still held west of Épinal by the *716th Infantry Division*, managed to get only a single battalion from the 157th Infantry—which formed the division's left wing—across the Moselle by trucking it over a bridge in the sector of the French 2d DB in the neighboring XV Corps zone. Major General Eagles decided to push his 179th Infantry Regiment, which formed his right wing, across at Archettes the next day. The 157th Infantry Regiment's other two battalions also crossed the Third Army's bridge on 22 September, and the 179th Infantry crossed the Moselle as planned. The 157th Infantry attacked generally southward while the 179th Infantry consolidated its bridgehead. The Germans resisted fiercely in spots but usually withdrew after a short fight.

The 180th Infantry Regiment and tankers from the 191st Tank Battalion, meanwhile, were still trying to take Épinal, which was stoutly defended by infantry in prepared positions supported by ample artillery and rocket fire. The 2d and 3d battalions worked into the western outskirts, and fighting raged from house to house as the Germans beat back repeated attempts to reach the river. Finally, late on 22 September, the Germans withdrew across the Moselle and blew the remaining bridges.[7]

* * *

The 3d Infantry Division on 21 September encountered fierce resistance from the *198th* and *338th Infantry divisions* across its entire front and made few gains toward the Moselle. Continuous rain rendered the roads through the rough terrain almost impassable to supporting tanks, and the Germans skillfully exploited the heights and log-bunkered roadblocks to slow the Americans. Artillery shells bursting in the treetops caused heavy American casualties, and in the 30th Infantry Regiment's zone German counterattacks through the dense woods were hitting as often as every half-hour. Major General O'Daniel speculated to Truscott that he was mired in determined German efforts to protect the Belfort Gap, and Truscott told him to be ready to slip two regiments to the north to follow the 36th Infantry Division across the river. He also told the 117th Cavalry Reconnaissance Squadron to take responsibility for tying into the French on his right, where the even slower advance was exposing O'Daniel's troops to troublesome flanking fire from German positions on high ground near Mélisey. The 3d Division continued to encounter almost unyielding resistance during most of the day on 22 September.[8]

A Fighting Withdrawal

Exactly what transpired next is not entirely clear. The official U.S. Army history concludes that *Nineteenth Army*'s commanding general Wiese fought to hold his ground until 25 September, when he proposed to *Generalleutnant* Hermann Balck, a veteran panzer commander who had taken over *Army Group G* from Blaskowitz on 21 September, that he pull back his *LXVI and LXIV corps* about ten miles to between Rambervillers

and Le Tholy. Balck agreed, but Commander in Chief West
Generalfeldmarschall Gerd von Rundstedt authorized a more limited
withdrawal to the line Rambervillers-Grandvillers-St. Ame.[9]

Developments on the ground, however, suggest that German commanders were already disengaging along the Moselle as early as the
evening of 22 September and were not reflecting this fact honestly up the
chain of command. As a defensive line, the Moselle River had already
been rendered useless by XV Corps crossing just to the north; Wiese's
account after the war indicates that he viewed his right flank as exposed
by *First Army*'s setbacks.[10] Moreover, a string of defensive works beckoned to the rear. Organized as strongpoints controlling the east-west
routes into the Vosges Mountains, the defenses consisted of antitank and
machine-gun positions and firing and communication trenches. The
heaviest belt stretched from Rambervillers north through Baccarat, then
toward Rechicourt. Fewer positions had been completed from
Rambervillers south through Gérardmer and Le Thillot. Work continued
apace on a second line along the Meurthe River, farther east.[11] Third
Army's XV Corps had already crossed the Meurthe on 20 September at
Lunéville, however, and German commanders may already have privately
viewed that line as compromised.

By 23 September, Seventh Army judged that only rear guards were
still fighting in Épinal and Remiremont. At other points, entire battalions
from the 45th and 36th Infantry divisions were able to advance against little or no resistance. Reconnaissance troops from the 636th Tank
Destroyer Battalion (attached to the 36th Infantry Division) rolled all the
way to St. Ame before contacting the enemy. Von Rundstedt supposedly
authorized St. Ame as part of a new post-withdrawal line two days later.
Resistance in front of the 3d Infantry Division eased considerably late on
22 September. American patrols that night found no enemy troops, and
the Germans unquestionably had evacuated their positions in much of
the sector the next day, when O'Daniel's troops swept aside a few infantry
and easily made their way to the Moselle River's west bank. The division
crossed the next day and encountered only scattered machine-gun fire.[12]

As of 0635 hours on 24 September, the 36th Infantry Division reported
no enemy activity in its sector and by late that day had two battalions at

St. Ame. The division largely sat in place the following day because Truscott told Dahlquist to do so, not because of enemy action. The only energetic reaction occurred south of Docelles, where the 143d Infantry Regiment menaced one of the key withdrawal routes running northeastward through Bruyères, then to St. Dié, on the Meurthe River. Here the Germans struck back in such force that the regimental reserve had to be committed to stop the thrust.[13]

At this point, only the 45th Infantry Division was reporting that it faced widespread resistance. In some places, such as Girmont, reports that the Germans were evacuating preceded their capture. Across the front, most reported actions were small, probably delaying affairs around road junctions, on high ground, and in villages.

The 3d Infantry Division reported again early on 25 September that patrols were making no contact with the enemy, and advancing troops during the day encountered little but small-arms fire. The exception was on the division's right adjacent to the French, where the Germans were fighting hard around Rupt. The 36th Infantry Division had secured St. Ame overnight, and the 45th Infantry Division that morning reported that only one regiment faced much resistance.[14]

Dahlquist recorded in his diary, "Troops are very wet and disconsolate and morale seems to have gotten very low."[15] But all was not gloom and doom; back at the main bridge in Épinal, GIs erected a road sign. One arrow pointed southwest and read, "St. Tropez, 430 miles." The other pointed northeast and declared, "Berlin, 430 miles."[16]

* * *

The good news of light resistance did not last long. The Germans were now settling into a string of strong positions along the line Rambervillers–Le Tholy. The 36th Infantry Division was still making little headway around Docelles, and a fierce fight was breaking out around Tendon—especially on the forested slopes of Hill 827—where secondary roads offering access to the east intersected the Docelles–Le Tholy road.[17]

Indeed, reports to Truscott from his divisions during 25 September suggested that VI Corps was so extended through the forbidding terrain that the enemy might stop the corps in its tracks. Major General Dahlquist told Truscott, "I am pretty well shot. Got practically everything out. . . . The country is terribly hard [and] wooded. The road up to [the 142d Infantry Regiment] is a jeep trail. I am spread out about as much as I can be. . . . The Germans have been infiltrating. You just can't keep them out. . . . I can only use tanks and [tank destroyers] in two places. They are pretty well immobilized because of the [muddy] roads." Dahlquist noted that the Germans were probing his right flank, and there were reports of troop movements toward Le Tholy.[18]

Those troops belonged to two understrength grenadier regiments of the *198th Infantry Division*, which von Rundstedt had instructed must counterattack the American bridgehead.[19] Wiese, in response, ordered the division to drive the 36th Infantry Division back across the Moselle. (It is difficult to believe that Wiese thought his outnumbered force could accomplish that mission. The order again suggests that he was managing his commanders' expectations while awaiting approval for the withdrawal he had already undertaken.) The Germans attacked about noon through the hills southwest of Le Tholy after moving close to the American outposts, unobserved thanks to misty rain and fog. The Germans punched through the seam between the 141st and 142d Infantry regiments, cut communications lines, and forced both American regiments to pull back their forwardmost units. Confused fighting petered out at dusk. *Army Group G* halted the operation on 26 September. Planned or otherwise, the *198th Division*'s counterattack had taken on the characteristics of an effective stop-thrust.[20]

The new German line did not quite stop VI Corps, but it came close. The 45th Infantry Division on Truscott's left advanced over relatively open ground against an enemy still falling back on the new line near Rambervillers, and the 157th Infantry Regiment—assisted by the neighboring French 2d DB—captured that town on 30 September. Here the Germans held their ground. The 45th Division's history recorded, "Well-mined roadblocks covered by antitank guns and infantry, riflemen deeply entrenched in positions commanding the terrain, extensive minefields, and well-coordinated enemy rocket, mortar, and artillery fire were encountered. . . ."[21]

The 36th Infantry Division would spend the next nearly three weeks crawling a handful of miles to take Bruyères.[22] On 23 October, a full month after the first attacks on the objective, the division still had fighting positions on Hill 827. The 3d Infantry Division, just to the south, would remain stymied at Le Tholy until 19 October.[23]

* * *

Seventh Army Expands

Eisenhower on 26 September transferred Maj. Gen. Wade Haislip's XV Corps, consisting of the 79th Infantry Division, French 2d DB, and the 106th Cavalry Group, to 6th Army Group effective 29 September and established a new interarmy group boundary running roughly Chaumont-Lunéville-Sarrebourg-Landau-Heidelberg. SHAEF promised another infantry division from the 12th Army Group at some future time, plus three divisions arriving from the States to be diverted through Marseille. Ike gave Devers two missions: to protect the southern flank of 12th Army Group, and to destroy the enemy west of the Rhine, secure river crossings, and breach the Siegfried Line.[24]

Devers and Patch visited Truscott on 27 September and told him that they thought he faced only a shell of resistance without reserves behind it. They outlined a plan for VI Corps to advance to Strasbourg on the west bank of the Rhine via the pass at St. Dié, while XV Corps pushed eastward toward the same objective through Baccarat.[25]

Devers on 29 September issued his commanders instructions that assigned to Seventh Army the objective of Strasbourg. French First Army received orders to capture the Belfort Gap, Mulhouse, and Colmar. Devers separated the First Airborne Task Force, which was still fighting along the Franco-Italian border, from Seventh Army and made it a command reporting directly to his headquarters.[26]

Generalleutnant Siegfried Westphal, von Rundstedt's chief of staff, shared Devers' suspicions about the weak German defenses behind the Vosges in Alsace from Strasbourg south to Mulhouse, and he feared that an Allied airborne landing in the German rear could be catastrophic. (Operation Market Garden—the Anglo-American airborne landings in Holland—was only twelve days in the past when Westphal wrote his appreciation on 29 September, and the withdrawal of the First Airborne Task Force can only have made him more nervous when he found out about it.) Westphal's assessment was intercepted and decrypted by Allied intelligence, and thus the senior American commanders knew the huge payoff from breaking through the Vosges or the Belfort Gap.[27]

PLAYING THE GAME LACKING THE RULES

Devers, Patch, and de Lattre entered the autumn battles ignorant of the point of the struggle in the view of the German High Command, a perspective that was to shape the enemy's actions for nearly four months. During the last two weeks of September, Hitler had outlined to his senior generals his plan for a massive counterstroke against the western Allies through the Ardennes Forest, to be launched as early as November if conditions permitted. The goal was to crack the western alliance just enough for Berlin to extract a separate peace, then turn to stave off the Soviet avalanche in the east. Hitler ordered von Rundstedt to defend as long as possible in front of the West Wall fortifications, or Siegfried Line, that guarded the German frontier, which in the 6th Army Group zone ran mainly along the east bank of the Rhine River.[28] Hitler reiterated that order to *Generalleutnant* Hermann Balck when the latter was on his way to take command of *Army Group G*: Balck was to hold Alsace-Lorraine, and under no circumstances could he allow developments to require the diversion of forces from the Ardennes offensive.[29]

On the one hand, this meant that German commanders—well used to sidestepping impractical orders from the Führer to hold every inch of ground—would have the luxury of trading space for time as long as they held the West Wall. *Army Group G* issued orders for its corps to construct fortifications to support a defense that would "delay and wear down" the enemy. Nonetheless, in any event, many senior officers felt themselves constrained from ordering withdrawals and hoping that the junior officers would do the right thing on their own.[30]

Construction of strong fortifications in the Saverne and Belfort gaps was planned but, for technical reasons, could not begin until late November. To prevent high casualties from artillery fire, infantry divisions were instructed to establish a reserve of regimental strength and withdraw most of their forward troops to prepared positions roughly a mile or two behind the front at the first sign of a large enemy attack.[31]

On the other hand, every spare man, shell, and liter of fuel would be needed to build the strategic reserve, so German forces in the south would have to wring the most out of their tight resources. The situation would be tightest for *Nineteenth Army*, in Alsace, because Balck and his staff expected Patton's Third Army to be the main threat along *Army Group G's* front and therefore gave *First Army*, in Lorraine, priority for replacements and supplies.[32] Replacements were often Luftwaffe or navy personnel reassigned to the infantry who required basic training on arrival. Reinforcements were few: During October, *Army Group G* received some twenty additional but poorly equipped infantry battalions, mostly made up of older men grouped into "stomach" and "ear" battalions (units in which the troops shared the same chronic ailment).[33]

Devers, Patch, and de Lattre by early October almost certainly were generally aware of the debate over strategy that had flared in the Allied command tent at the same time that Hitler was plotting his great gamble in the Ardennes. British field marshal Bernard Montgomery, commanding the 21st Army Group, argued that his Commonwealth forces should drive to Berlin on a narrow front, supported by the Americans immediately to his south, while the remainder of the Allied front sat down to watch. American lieutenant general Omar Bradley, commanding the 12th Army Group, pressed for a broad-front offensive that would put his troops east of the Rhine roughly parallel to Montgomery's. Eisenhower opted to pursue the broad-front approach, but he instructed that the main weight of the Allied effort would be in the north along the British axis of advance.

Ike's decision was all well and good, but as he recognized, logistic constraints imposed by continuing dependence on beaches in Normandy for supplies and stiffening German resistance threatened to render the matter moot for some time. Nonetheless, the message for the Allied forces in the south was clear: They would play a supporting role in the war effort. The senior Allied and German commanders were agreed that the issue would be decided far from the Vosges Mountains.

A BLACK OCTOBER

Within Seventh Army headquarters, officers viewed this time as the beginning of what they came to call the "crisis on the western front."

Devers was ordered to adopt a defensive posture, which may have been just as well. His troops—American and French—were spread over a wide front, and shortages of artillery and ammunition prevented necessary support for sustained offensive operations.[34] As of 1 October, or D+45, Seventh Army was three times farther from Marseille and Toulon than logistic planners had calculated would be the case on D+60. Patch imposed an allocation system for the period 1–15 October for 155mm, 105mm, 81mm, and 60mm artillery and mortar ammunition, which supplied on average only roughly one-fifth of a unit of fire per day. The requirement to supply the newly attached XV Corps forced sporadic freezes in deliveries to VI Corps. Even wool underwear and overcoats were in short supply. By 1 October VI Corps had received only 8,300 of the latter, which had to be divided among three divisions.[35]

Indeed, 10 October marked the first day when the supply of artillery shells being hauled by rail from Marseille matched consumption, and the 6th Army Group slowly began to accumulate reserve stocks. Another month would pass before those stocks were high enough to support a full-scale attack. Devers used that time scrounging more heavy artillery from 12th Army Group and speeding agreed transfers from Fifth Army in Italy.[36]

Franco-American tensions blossomed in the midst of the material hardship. French First Army made repeated requests for assistance to Seventh Army, which the latter judged that it met as well as it could. Relations reached a low point when a French colonel provided Seventh Army with a copy of a memorandum to Devers that read in part, "[I]t is truly a thankless situation for an army committed to full-scale battle to thus find itself abandoned without gasoline and without ammunition. On the other hand, it has been proven that, contrary to established forecasts, this army has been discriminated against during the last twenty days in a way seriously prejudicial to its life and to its capabilities for action."

Although Devers acknowledged in a letter to de Lattre dated 2 October that the French were indeed insufficiently supplied and pledged to deal with the problem straightaway, his staff, at least, believed that shortcomings in the French supply service had much to do with the difficulties.[37] Devers' letter did not stop de Lattre from addressing the supply issue with the

U.S. Army Chief of Staff, General George Marshall, when he visited II Corps on 8 October. Marshall's staff had not prepared him to hear this particular complaint, but he promised that the problem would be set right. Not long afterward, the Americans and French were able to reach an agreement on the equitable distribution of supplies.[38]

Back in southern France, the First Airborne Task Force on 13 October was relieved of its duties along the Franco-Italian border and allocated to army group reserve. Devers ordered French First Army to assume responsibility for border defense, with all reliefs to be accomplished by 20 November. All these plans would change in late November, when the 44th Antiaircraft Brigade was given responsibility for a hodgepodge of units along the frontier, and the zone effectively dropped from the combat history of the 6th Army Group.[39]

The Americans Claw Forward

Truscott's VI Corps measured its progress in blood-soaked yards during early October. Its victories were to take a series of small towns and high points that will forever remain obscure except to the few men on both sides who fought there, places with names such as Fimenil and Herpelmon.

The battle was a ground fight, with American air superiority virtually factored out by the rainy and increasingly snowy weather. From 1 October through 19 November, there were only fourteen days clear enough to allow effective air support to the troops.[40] Indeed, now that the line had moved so close to Germany, enemy fighter-bombers started appearing with some regularity, though in much smaller numbers than the Americans, when they could fly.[41]

The Seventh Army recorded a description of what it called "Vosges warfare":

> For the infantry, combat in the woods was in many ways comparable to jungle fighting. Maintenance of direction was particularly difficult, leading to erroneous reports as to location of units and enemy positions. Orders based on inaccurate information at times result-

ed in bitter and unexpected fighting. The compass was in almost continuous use. Fighting at night became impossible unless enemy positions were known beforehand. Otherwise, such disorganization resulted that it took hours after daylight to get the men together again.

Advancing in the woods, foot soldiers found that the enemy allowed them to come up so close that friendly artillery could not be employed. Experiment proved it better to have a force in front of the main body to draw enemy fire. Attacking through forested terrain, the individual rifleman hardly ever saw his target. The enemy was so well hidden that when he fired only the general direction of his position could be located. In addition, the infantry squad leader could see only two or three men of the squad at once, so that it was difficult to bring the fire of his squad to bear on any one point. Tommy guns, grenade launchers, and bazookas were found useful under these circumstances. Forest sectors had to be mopped up thoroughly. Small, dug-in enemy detachments, if not cleared out, would harass supply columns. Skirmish lines were sent to "drag" an area bypassed by an infantry attack.

In the Vosges, it was necessary to give extra care to the organization of positions for defense. Troops dug deep foxholes, covering them over for protection against artillery fire. Dugouts where groups of men could get warm and dry were also built. Possible lanes of enemy approach were covered by .50-caliber machine guns in positions frequently protected by barbed wire.

Regimental patrolling was so extensive that it became the main combat action during much of the period of static warfare. It was kept sufficiently aggressive to hold the enemy along the front in expectation of a full-scale attack. Patrolling also felt out the enemy's weak points, his strong points, and his intentions.

Raiding parties and regular patrols often inflicted on the enemy severe casualties that sapped his strength. . . .

The strain of hard fighting and the exposure to continuous rain and cold had their effects on the troops. Tree bursts from enemy artillery took a heavy toll and gave the men a certain feeling of helplessness. When caught in attack formation or without overhead cover during a barrage, the troops suffered fewer casualties when they stood upright against trees rather than hit the ground. Respiratory diseases, intestinal disorders, trench foot, and exhaustion cases increased, in some organizations more than doubled, during October. Trench foot became a major problem. It increased in the 3d Division from 54 in September to 160 in October to 448 in November. . . .

Supporting arms and services found it necessary to improvise to give maximum assistance to the advance. Artillerymen found tactics in the Vosges different from those in open country. Adjustments by sound, at times as close as 100 yards from the target, became the rule rather than the exception. Shortage of ammunition limited artillery support and slowed the advance. . . .

Armor could give the infantry only limited support. Tanks lost their maneuverability in the steep and wooded terrain of the Vosges and bogged down even on the shoulders of roads, softened by continuous rain; cross-country operations were precluded for the most part. Tanks were vulnerable to enemy rocket fire from concealed positions at close range and easily ambushed at night. Noise of tanks drew down enemy artillery fire, and their own fire frequently had a more disturbing effect on friendly troops than on enemy troops.

Tactical armor was used as an addition to artillery for the support of infantry attacks. After a road had been taken and swept by the engineers, tanks would follow up in support. Tanks and tank destroyers occupied firing positions on high ridges and fired jointly on enemy vehicles or personnel that exposed themselves below. . . . Tank destroyers were extremely vulnerable and of little value to the infantry as a close support weapon in the Vosges fighting. They were difficult to maneuver, and their field of fire was negligible. Tank dozers were used in the Herculean job of removing antitank obstacles and blocks placed by the enemy on nearly every road and trail.

Engineers during October and November worked to keep open communication and supply roads to frontline regiments. Under heavy rains, roads were immediately broken down even by light vehicles. Rubble from smashed stone buildings was found useful in road repair.[42]

The Germans, of course, were closely watching Allied tactics, both American and French. Early on in the Vosges, they saw the Allies applying relatively simple tactics, typically pushing infantry up the mountain roads with strong support from armor and artillery. The Germans found these attacks relatively simple to fend off. Over time, the Allies developed new tactics of moving laterally over the mountains, which created openings to attack the Germans from many directions. This drastically increased the need for German forces, and rising casualties soon resulted.[43]

Still, as Truscott observed to Eagles one day in early October, "The Germans haven't got a lot to bring up, and no matter what our situation, they have it twice as bad. At least our boys eat every day, and that isn't true of the Germans."[44] Moreover, Truscott used the first two weeks in October to pull infantry battalions out of the line one by one to rest a bit and absorb replacements.[45]

* * *

Indeed, despite having reestablished a relatively stable front, the days were dark for the Germans. *Army Group G* commanding general Balck wrote a letter to von Rundstedt on 9 October in which he said, "I have never been in command of such irregularly assembled and ill-equipped troops. The fact that we have been able to straighten out the situation again . . . can only be attributed to the inefficient and hesitating command of the Americans and the French [and that] the troops, inclusive of the irregular hordes, have fought beyond praise." Balck asked that he be given a mountain division and an additional infantry division, plus an assortment of tank destroyer and engineer battalions.[46]

The badly understrength *21st Panzer Division* had joined *Nineteenth Army* and was now responsible for a sprawling thirty-one-mile front north from near St. Dié and was holding on through little more than desperate determination. *Generalmajor* Edgar Feuchtinger had, on average during October, only fifteen or so Mark IV tanks, a few assault guns, and a handful of antitank guns available to back up his panzergrenadiers, who suffered heavy losses.[47]

Resources were so thinly stretched that even troops dedicated to building fortifications were thrown into battle, dramatically slowing the work. On 10 October, the *360th Cossack Regiment* received orders for the front near Gérardmer. By the time several penal and construction battalions would become available in November to accelerate construction, it would simply be too late.[48] Hitler on 14 October finally offered some relief when he ordered that all newly raised fortress (static) and mountain battalions were to be assigned to *Nineteenth Army* for use in the Vosges.[49]

The Parroy Forest

Lieutenant General Patch had issued orders on 29 September that XV Corps was to assist VI Corps, but as the latter became bogged down during October, Maj. Gen. Wade Haislip's corps became the key player in cracking the new German line.[50] Born in 1889, Haislip was an infantry officer who had served on the Mexican border and in the St. Mihiel and Meuse-Argonnes offensives during World War I. He had commanded the 85th Infantry Division prior to taking charge of his corps.[51] Whereas Truscott was on the phone frequently with his division commanders managing the battle, the XV Corps G-3 journal suggests that Haislip communicated with his commanders primarily through written memos and orders.

The Parroy Forest, a vicious tangle of trees and underbrush named after a town just to its north, was the first objective for XV Corps after joining Seventh Army. The woods cloaked low ridges northeast of

Lunéville between the Rhine-Marne Canal on the north and the Vezouse River to the south—a rectangular patch roughly six miles deep and five miles wide.[52]

The corps' divisions—Maj. Gen. Ira Wyche's 79th Infantry Division and General Jacques Leclerc's 2d DB—were both worn out from the push across France from Normandy. Wyche, an infantry officer born in 1887, had served in France during the Great War and had taught at both the field artillery and cavalry schools.[53] The 79th Infantry Division was a battle-hardened outfit that had been engaged almost continuously for four months, first as part of First Army, then under Patton's command in Third Army, and its infantry regiments were well understrength.

Jacques Leclerc, the nom de guerre of Vicomte Philippe Francois Marie de Hautecloque, had been a captain during the fall of France in 1940. After making his way to London to join de Gaulle, Leclerc had fought in Chad and Libya, and beside General Bernard Montgomery's Eighth Army. Leclerc was given responsibility for raising the 2d DB in 1943. His manpower was drawn from Free French in the United Kingdom, Syria, French North Africa, and Equatorial Africa; they were Catholics, Protestants, Jews, Muslims, animists, Communists, reactionaries, socialists, radicals, free thinkers, militant Christians, and Quakers. The engineers were Lebanese Christians, and one infantry battalion came from the navy. By September, the division's vehicles issued in North Africa were worn out, and its armored-infantry battalions were down to about one-third of their authorized manpower. After the division landed in Normandy, Leclerc displayed a pattern of disobedience to his American commanders that drove them to distraction, but he also led with verve. Haislip had studied in France, and he perhaps had gained some insight into managing his troublesome subordinate, who, in turn, had gained greater respect for his American Allies, whom he came to prefer over de Lattre.[54]

The 2d DB took no active part in this phase of the XV Corps fight and, after helping the 45th Infantry Division take Rambervillers on 30 September, settled in to guard Wyche's right flank.[55] Used to dealing with the Americans, Leclerc's division maintained close daily liaison with Eagles' 45th Infantry Division, to the south.[56] Even so, minor wrangling over whether VI Corps cavalry would relieve the French in the village of

Anglemont—taken, lost, and taken again on 1–2 October—revealed issues of unique French sensitivities. An officer from the XV Corps G-3 staff contacted a counterpart at VI Corps on 3 October and advised, "The French are afraid that if the Germans come back into the town again they will burn the town and raise hell all over the area. This is a pretty sore spot with the French. They lost about thirty or forty people taking the place. . . . The French feel they have done you a great favor and feel they will be called on to do the same thing at Baccarat, and their attitude might have an effect on that. I would strongly recommend that even though you wanted to let the town go, go up and take it and put on a little show and some formality." VI Corps predictably rejected the idea as tactically useless.[57]

The *15th Panzergrenadier Division*'s understrength *104th Panzergrenadier Regiment* and the attached *113th Panzer Brigade* barred the way through the Parroy Forest. The division was part of the *Fifth Panzer Army*'s *XLVII Panzer Corps*, although it was resubordinated to the neighboring *LVIII Panzer Corps* on 30 September. The *104th Panzergrenadier Regiment* was a veteran outfit that had fought in Tunisia, Sicily, and Italy, though most of the rankers were young recruits with only six weeks of training.[58]

The 79th Infantry Division attacked into the woods with its 313th and 315th Infantry regiments on 28 September despite bad weather that all but prevented a preliminary air bombardment. The GIs encountered stiff resistance soon after working their way among the trees. High-velocity 75mm cannon fire from Mark IV panzers crashed into the American lines while German infantry fired from hastily dug positions. German machine guns were able to keep American bazooka men away from the panzers, and the GIs had no antitank guns or supporting armor to help out. One battalion of the 315th Infantry cracked and fled out of range before digging in, a turn of events that led to the relief of the commanding officer. The attacking infantry would become grimly familiar with the enemy's successful use of tanks despite the forbidding terrain.

Technically, the 79th Infantry Division was the advancing party on 29 and 30 September, but repeated German counterattacks ignited a seesaw battle that yielded a net American gain of only a thousand yards. Half-track-mounted 20mm flak guns added to the GIs' problems, and efforts to knock them out with mortars came to naught because it was impossible to observe the fire in the thick woods. The Germans, by contrast, had prepared fire lanes and brought down pinpoint artillery and mortar barrages.

Major Gooding, commanding the 2d Battalion of the 313th Infantry, described one German attack the night of 29 September:

> About eighty infantry clustered around a single Mark IV tank, some riding it, others moving close alongside, attacked west down the road at 2330. Although there was a moon, a light haze made vision uncertain. It was light enough to see shapes but impossible to distinguish friend from foe. This made it impossible to send for reinforcements when the attack threatened to break through.
>
> From 2330 to 0300, the Germans made at least six separate assaults. The infantry all seemed to be armed with either burp guns or light machine guns. Company I, which took the brunt of the initial assault, was down to an effective strength of forty men. It could not hold its position and fell back. This made it necessary for 2d Battalion to refuse its right flank. Company E, which had been reduced to between 90 and 100 men by the fighting in the Forêt de Mondon, was pulled back to a ditch running at right angles to the road. . . . The enemy tank came up to the north end of the ditch and began firing down it. Company E withdrew another 30 yards to the west. . . .
>
> The withdrawal of the company in good order was accomplished largely through the personal leadership of the commander, 1st Lt. George Dale, who had assumed command only three days previously. Lieutenant Dale under heavy enemy machine-gun fire maneuvered his men by means of individual orders and kept them from breaking under the attack.

Fighting was at such close quarters that the German tank was afterwards found to have its bogey plates and turret riddled with .30-caliber machine gun bullets. At 0300, the tank was at last destroyed by a bazooka at a range of 15 yards. The man who got the kill was a replacement who had joined the company two days before.[59]

Wyche committed his third regiment, the 314th Infantry, on 1 October and netted another thousand yards in the center. The 315th Infantry Regiment, on the division's left, suffered another day of inch-by-inch fighting and counterattacks, while on the right the Germans held onto positions that they would successfully defend until abandoning them the night of 9–10 October.

Deep in the woods, the defenders were often invisible. They kept their main force hidden to the rear of an outpost line that called down heavy artillery and mortar fire on the Americans as soon as they were heard; small-arms fire was actually surprisingly light. Tree bursts made the incoming fire all the more lethal.

The 79th Infantry Division turned to its own tanks on 3 October and managed to flank and destroy a roadblock just west of the main road junction in the forest. But on the far side of the junction waited only more grueling fighting punctuated by often-successful German counterattacks.

By 9 October, the Americans held only half the forest, but high ground critical to the German defense beckoned within reach of the 315th Infantry Regiment. At 0630 hours, tanks supporting the 313th Infantry Regiment created a diversion by pounding the Germans at the south end of the line, a ruse that drew German artillery fire for much of the morning. The 315th Infantry, meanwhile, pushed off and gained the high ground by 1800 hours. That night, the Germans abandoned their remaining positions and evacuated eastward.

Attacking out of the forest, the 79th Infantry Division made only slightly better progress and took Embermenil—an advance of just over a mile—on 13 October. The Germans now fought from pillboxes and trenches protected by mines and barbed wire on the western slopes of high ground that offered excellent observation to artillery observers.

Wyche's division was worn out. While hard-fought, minor advances and vicious counterattacks continued, Maj. Gen. Robert Spragin's newly arrived 44th Infantry Division gradually relieved the battered regiments beginning on 19 October, with the turnover complete five days later. Sadly, Lt. Gen. Sandy Patch's son, Capt. Alexander Patch, who was a company commander in the 315th Infantry, was killed by mortar fire just before the relief was accomplished—naturally a terrible blow to the Seventh Army commanding general. The 79th Infantry Division retired to Lunéville for its first rest in four months.

On the German side, the *553d* and *361st Volksgrenadier division*s likewise relieved the exhausted *15th Panzergrenadier Division* and the *11th Panzer Division*, still in reserve, when it moved north during late October.[60]

Truscott's Last Surprise

With VI Corps gaining ground at a snail's pace, Truscott came up with a new plan—Operation Dogface—to use maneuver to take St. Dié. The Germans and the terrain would not permit decisive movement on the battlefield, so he would maneuver *behind* it. Truscott ordered up an elaborate plan to shift the 3d Infantry Division from his right wing to a spot behind the 45th Infantry Division while convincing the Germans that he was actually preparing a major attack toward Gérardmer—this despite the fact that Devers had told de Lattre on 29 September that the Americans would take the town within two days and hand it over to the French as a launching point for their own operations. Truscott believed that the French would fill in the frontage left vacant by the 3d Infantry Division.

O'Daniel's division, less the 30th Infantry Regiment, shifted northward in utter secrecy beginning the night of 14–15 October. The deployment coincided with a shift of the Seventh Army–French First Army boundary northward to run roughly Le Tholy-Gérardmer, and troops from the 36th Infantry Division (now reinforced by the Japanese-American 442d Regimental Combat Team) and a battalion each of FFI and French army reconnaissance troops filled in behind the departing men. The 3d Division maintained its radio net at Le Tholy, dummy guns were slipped into abandoned positions, and the 36th Division increased patrolling along the southern end of its line and arranged to "lose" pieces of 3d Division equipment where the Germans would find them. Corps artillery increased the number of observation flights over the sector to suggest preparation for an offensive.

The 3d Infantry Division, meanwhile, settled into carefully camouflaged encampments south of Rambervillers. Reconnaissance parties wearing 45th Infantry Division insignia scouted the battlefield, and guns were registered by moving individual pieces into position well in advance.[61]

On 17 October, Truscott, just promoted to lieutenant general, was summoned to Patch's headquarters, where Eisenhower was waiting to see him. Ike broke the news that Truscott was to take command of Fifteenth Army and be replaced at VI Corps by Maj. Gen. Edward "Ted" Brooks.[62] Born in 1893, Brooks had seen extensive fighting in World War I and was a natural replacement for Truscott. He was a cavalry officer who had commanded the 11th Armored Division in the States, then the 2d Armored Division in northern France.[63]

The 7th Infantry Regiment sprang Truscott's surprise at 1130 hours on 20 October and attacked northeast of Bruyères toward Vervezelles. The kickoff was something of a surprise even to Truscott, because it started early. O'Daniel had ordered the troops to move out because they were taking casualties from German artillery fire hitting their bivouacs, and Iron Mike decided he would lose just as many men if they were fighting. Resistance from the surprised defenders was modest, and the Americans cracked the weak line of the *16th Volksgrenadier Division* (the reorganized *16th Infantry Division*) within the first twenty-four hours.

The 15th Infantry Regiment struck north of Bruyères on 21 October to exploit the hole opened by its sister regiment, while one battalion supported a thrust by the 179th Infantry Regiment to capture Brouvelieures. By late in the day, Truscott was increasingly optimistic that he had punched a hole through the German defenses, and he instructed the 45th Infantry Division to throw a regiment forward on the 3d Division's left flank.

By the next day, the 3d Infantry Division was meeting scattered resistance, and a decrease in artillery fire suggested that the enemy was pulling back his towed artillery. O'Daniel told Truscott, "There is no doubt this thing is broken [open]."[64]

The 45th Infantry Division on 22 October was hung up along the small Mortagne River, which ran roughly parallel to the Meurthe. The 180th Infantry crossed the river but was thrown back to the west bank. Major General Eagles' men confronted not only difficult terrain but also the seasoned *21st Panzer Division*. With that in mind, the division had attached to it an unusual amount of self-propelled tank destroyers, including its usual partner, the 645th Tank Destroyer Battalion, plus the 636th Tank Destroyer Battalion and a company from the 601st Tank Destroyer Battalion.[65]

Truscott ordered Eagles to move his 179th Infantry Regiment across the 3d Division's bridge, while Eagles planned a dawn crossing with the 180th Infantry Regiment. The second attempt by the 180th Infantry to cross the Mortagne succeeded, and a battalion pushed out against moderate resistance, joined by two battalions from the 179th Infantry.[66]

* * *

The 3d Infantry Division's 30th Infantry Regiment, meanwhile, left Le Tholy on 22 October and motored north to join the rest of the division. On 24 October, one battalion attacked northeastward through a gap in the German line between Les Rouges Eaux and the La Salle valley. Late on 24 October, the 7th and 15th Infantry regiments detected the first signs that resistance might be firming up when they encountered panzers and "a lot of Boche" near Les Rouges Eaux.[67] Indeed, *Nineteenth Army* commanding general Wiese by 23 October held a captured map that showed VI Corps' plans, and he acted accordingly. The lead elements of a grenadier regiment from the *338th Infantry Division* were just arriving from the *IV Luftwaffe Field Corps*, to the south.[68] Both the 7th and 15th Infantry regiments came under increasingly intense artillery fire on 25 October—the day that Maj. Gen. Edward Brooks took command of VI Corps—although the battalion of the 30th Infantry Regiment continued to make headway.[69]

Just to the north, the 45th Infantry Division's 179th and 180th Infantry regiments had found the Germans disorganized east of the Mortagne River, but firefights raged across the forested Vosges slopes on

24 October. The 157th Infantry matched the pace of the 3d Division's push at dawn on 25 October and gained a thousand yards to the northeast before stopping in the face of a hail of machine-gun fire at the edge of some woods.

Company C, 601st Tank Destroyer Battalion, was working with the 3d Battalion, 179th Infantry, which was battling to take some high ground not far from Housseras. The GIs took the objective after a hard fight, and, as usual, the Germans counterattacked, at about 1300 hours.

Tank destroyer crews received commando training stateside, and one rarely used part of that training was dismounted tank hunting once a soldier's vehicle had been knocked out. Staff Sergeant Clyde Choate put his training to good use that day, as recorded in his Medal of Honor citation:

> Our infantry occupied a position on a wooded hill when, at dusk, an enemy Mark IV tank and a company of infantry attacked, threatening to overrun the American position and capture a command post 400 yards to the rear. Staff Sergeant Choate's tank destroyer, the only weapon available to oppose the German armor, was set afire by two hits. Ordering his men to abandon the destroyer, Staff Sergeant Choate reached comparative safety. He returned to the burning destroyer to search for comrades possibly trapped in the vehicle risking instant death in an explosion that was imminent and braving enemy fire which ripped his jacket and tore the helmet from his head.
>
> Completing the search and seeing the tank and its supporting infantry overrunning our infantry in their shallow foxholes, he secured a bazooka and ran after the tank, dodging from tree to tree and passing through the enemy's loose skirmish line. He fired a rocket from a distance of 20 yards, immobilizing the tank but leaving it able to spray the area with cannon and machine-gun fire. Running back to our infantry through vicious fire, he secured another rocket, and, advancing against a hail

of machine-gun and small-arms fire reached a position 10 yards from the tank. His second shot shattered the turret. With his pistol he killed two of the crew as they emerged from the tank, and then running to the crippled Mark IV while enemy infantry sniped at him, he dropped a grenade inside the tank and completed its destruction. With their armor gone, the enemy infantry became disorganized and was driven back.

* * *

Early on 23 October, the 36th Infantry Division's 1st Battalion, 141st Infantry, set out along a trail through the forest east of Bruyères to secure the heights above the village of La Houssiere. The Germans soon spotted the intrusion, struck back, and by dark had overrun the battalion command post and driven back the battalion staff. The regiment lost contact with the rest of the outfit, which the press soon dubbed "the lost battalion."

Thanks to a forward artillery observer with a working radio, Major General Dahlquist soon knew that 240 of his GIs under the command of Lt. Martin Higgins Jr.—the senior surviving officer—were cut off a mile north of La Houssiere. When repeated attempts by the 141st Infantry failed to reach the trapped men, the 442d Infantry Regiment-manned by Japanese-Americans, or Nisei—was alerted for action.

About 9 October, the regiment had motored to the front, where it was attached to VI Corps and placed in the line with the 36th Infantry Division. The regiment's 100th Infantry Battalion had already served with great distinction in Italy, and the regiment had proved itself in fighting around Bruyères.

The Nisei attacked on 29 October and closed with the Germans in fierce hand-to-hand fighting with bayonets and grenades. After the GIs cleared a roadblock, tanks moved forward in support. The regiment attacked again the next day after a crushing barrage placed on the ridge separating it from Higgins' command. At 1600 hours, welcome news came over the radio net: "Patrol from the 442d here. Tell them we love them."[70]

* * *

Brooks' VI Corps almost reached the Meurthe River by the end of the month. The 45th Infantry Division, on the left wing, was still short of the crossing at Raon l'Etape, and Brooks decided to relieve Eagles' tired division, which had been in action for eighty-six days, with the fresh 100th Infantry Division.[71]

The 3d Infantry Division, in the corps' center, still strained to reach the river at St. Dié. *Nineteenth Army* commanding general Wiese realized that the American division's drive threatened to shred his defenses. On 28 October, he sent forward four separate infantry battalions and shifted the *106th "Feldherrnhalle" Panzer Brigade* from the sector opposite the French in a bid to prop up the beleaguered *16th Volksgrenadier Division*. He also shifted the *716th Volksgrenadier Division* from southwest of Bruyères to take charge of the line between the *16th Volksgrenadier* and *21st Panzer divisions*. Old hands in the 3d Infantry Division described the next few days of fighting as worse than Anzio.[72]

Staff Sergeant Lucian Adams was awarded the Medal of Honor for his actions on 28 October as the 30th Infantry battled toward St. Dié. His citation described the action:

> Although his company had progressed less than 10 yards and had lost three killed and six wounded, Staff Sergeant Adams charged forward dodging from tree to tree firing a borrowed BAR from the hip. Despite intense machine-gun fire which the enemy directed at him and rifle grenades which struck the trees over his head showering him with broken twigs and branches, Staff Sergeant Adams made his way to within 10 yards of the closest machine gun and killed the gunner with a hand grenade. An enemy soldier threw hand grenades at him from a position only 10 yards distant; however, Staff Sergeant Adams dispatched him with a single burst of BAR fire. Charging into the vortex of the enemy fire, he killed another machine gunner at 15 yards range with a hand grenade and forced the surrender of two support-

ing infantrymen. Although the remainder of the German group concentrated the full force of its automatic weapons fire in a desperate effort to knock him out, he proceeded through the woods to find and exterminate five more of the enemy.

Finally, when the third German machine gun opened up on him at a range of 20 yards, Staff Sergeant Adams killed the gunner with BAR fire. In the course of the action, he personally killed nine Germans, eliminated three enemy machine guns, vanquished a specialized force which was armed with automatic weapons and grenade launchers, cleared the woods of hostile elements, and reopened the severed supply lines to the assault companies of his battalion.

The 30th Infantry Regiment seized high ground overlooking St. Dié on 30 October. Excellent artillery observation points gave O'Daniel the power to control this stretch of the Meurthe River valley by fire.[73]

Leclerc Loosens the Stalemate
Devers and Patch wanted to add the weight of the U.S. XV Corps and the French II Corps to aid Truscott's assault, and Patch therefore on 25 October ordered the French 2d DB to capture Merviller and cut the roads leading out of Baccarat, which would threaten the northern flank of the Germans barring VI Corps' way into St. Dié. The 3d DIA, supported by the Shock Battalion, a tank destroyer battalion, and a combat command from the 5th DB, meanwhile, was to launch a three-day demonstration attack on 3 November against the Germans to VI Corps' right.

Intelligence reports indicated that the Germans—well aware of the armored division to their front—had built two lines of formidable antitank defenses in Leclerc's path. These strongpoints, which consisted of 75mm antitank guns, minefields, and antitank ditches, covered the roads over which the Germans expected tanks to advance because the rains had turned the terrain to muck. Moreover, panzers reportedly lurked in reserve, and a battalion of twenty-two 88mm guns was reported moving into the area.

The French had no desire to play ducks in a shooting gallery. They determined by trial and error that their tanks could move off the roads by following the contours of slopes. Leclerc constructed a plan to slip between the antitank strongpoints by maneuvering across the high ground.

The French struck out of the Mondon Forest early on 31 October as two combat commands attacked down the east side of the Meurthe. (The 2d DB normally employed four combat commands, one more than the standard organization used by other French and American armored divisions.) The *21st Panzer Division*'s patrols had failed to detect the French preparations.[74]

One column from Combat Command V bypassed the antitank strongpoint at Hablainville, captured a bridge across the small Verdurette River, and by noon controlled the northern road out of Baccarat. Other columns reached Motigny by dark and sealed the eastern road. Combat Command D, meanwhile, struck directly toward Baccarat and, after destroying the antitank defenses barring the way, entered the northern half of the town. Thanks to the heroic action of one French soldier, who rushed forward under fire to cut demolition wires, the French captured the bridge across the Meurthe intact. Combat Commands L and R advanced south of the Meurthe to positions just across the river from the town. Leclerc had virtually accomplished his mission in only twelve hours.[75]

France's "Calvary in the Vosges"

The French experience from mid-September to the end of October was extraordinarily frustrating, punctuated by alternating exasperation with the Americans, whose actions all too often hobbled French plans, and with the Germans, who refused to be defeated when they could be engaged.

During the second half of September, Monsabert's II Corps still held positions to the left of Béthouart and his I Corps, which was anchored on the Swiss border. De Lattre longed for the opportunity to mount an offensive. He intended to use I Corps, creating an opportunity for it to rupture the German lines by dropping the 1st RCP into the German rear, much as *Generalleutnant* Westphal feared. A severe shortage of transport meant that the French army could never muster adequate supplies to put this plan into effect. The Americans, de Lattre believed, were monopolizing the transport to support their own offensive. Moreover, de Lattre's army had to cover a front of some 220 miles.

Another factor made it even more difficult for de Lattre to concentrate his forces: the Americans. They had been driving almost south to north and had reached the Moselle, in the process opening up a gap between the southernmost elements of the 3d Infantry Division and the northernmost elements of II Corps. On 23 September, II Corps found itself stopped after some days of pushing back the Germans, but also that day Truscott sent a letter to Monsabert asking him to cover this gap between the two armies.

De Lattre directed Monsabert to agree to Truscott's request. He still held out hopes for a French offensive, so he told his corps commander to devote only one regimental combat team of the 1st DFL and, for the main effort, one combat command of the 1st DB, operating on the Mélisey–Le Thillot axis, to closing the gap.[76]

II Corps' effort kicked off on 25 September and soon expanded far beyond what de Lattre had intended. Monsabert had entrusted General du Vigier, commander of the 1st DB, to personally work out the relevant details with Major General O'Daniel. The well-liked O'Daniel—de Gaulle described him as "lively and sympathetic"—convinced du Vigier to wildly exceed his instructions and commit his entire division, plus the promised regiment from Brosset's 1st DFL, to fill in behind the American division as it progressed north, turning aside toward Chateau Lambert and Le Thillot when they were reached. De Lattre must have been furious when he found out, but by that time there was nothing he could do. Du Vigier's excessive enthusiasm was only partly made up for by the arrival of a regiment of the 2d DIM, newly available after leaving the Alpine front. Monsabert slotted this in on his right, shortening the 1st DFL's frontage.[77]

Combat Command 3, with the 2d Zouave Battalion out front, had to fight its way out of Mélisey to start the 1st DB's move behind the Americans. Though they had help from the maquis, this took until late on 26 September. The next day, the French drove forward from there, having broken through the thick outer crust of the local German defenses. Combat Command 2 also had great success farther south. The result of the two efforts was that by 28 September, the French advances threatened to encircle German positions in the area of Plancher-les-Mines, at the far right of the German forces defending the Belfort Gap. The Germans fought back ferociously at the southern end of the pocket, clearly seeing the danger they faced.

It nonetheless would be difficult for the French to close the noose. To do so would require reinforcements, but Monsabert had no corps reserve. Accordingly, he started to move units from passive parts of his front, feeding them into combat and backfilling for them with FFI units. Finding sufficient infantrymen was only part of his problem, however. II Corps was using munitions faster than they could be replaced. Soon it seemed that II Corps was taking every resource from First Army that was not nailed down.

Put another way, II Corps was making itself the main effort, despite the fact that de Lattre wanted his other corps to launch the offensive. As de Lattre pondered this situation, the notion of an offensive through the upper Vosges grew on him. He could go around the Belfort defenses to the north. The gateway through the Vosges to upper Alsace was the Schlucht Pass. The Americans were reporting that, as part of their relentless drive north, they would soon take Gérardmer, the perfect location from which to drive on the Schlucht. De Lattre envisioned an offensive starting from Gérardmer, going through the Schlucht Pass, pushing across the Route des Crêtes—a mountain road running roughly north-south—then turning southeast to Guebwiller before entering the Alsatian Plain between Rouffach and Cernay. The French could take Belfort from the rear and perhaps even seize Mulhouse, threatening the German lines of retreat to the Rhine.

De Lattre transferred the 3d DIA, now under General Guillaume, from I Corps to II Corps, along with the 3d GTM. These would be the striking forces augmented by the 2d GTM, the 1st RCP, and the Shock Battalion, all of which already belonged to II Corps. Altogether, these amounted to two divisions' worth of troops. De Lattre feared that the ever-enthusiastic Monsabert would throw even more resources into the offensive. To prevent this, de Lattre transferred the 2d DIM, still forming up, to Béthouart as some form of compensation for the units transferred out of his command.

On 29 September, de Lattre went to visit Lieutenant General Devers to discuss this plan. Devers approved it and, according to the French account, assured de Lattre that the Americans would take Gérardmer within two days and would immediately turn it over to the French to use as the starting point for their attack. At the same time, Devers gave de Lattre additional orders, implementing instructions just arrived from SHAEF. These orders called for the Seventh Army to outflank the lower Vosges through the Saverne Gap while the French First Army penetrated it at the Belfort Gap, captured Mulhouse and Colmar, and covered a now lengthened portion of the Alpine front, all while protecting Patch's flank as it receded ever northward. De Lattre opined that this instruction increased the divergence between his army, which was trying to move west to east, and Patch's, which was rapidly moving south to north.

Despite these grave misgivings, de Lattre walked away from the meeting with what he wanted: approval for his offensive and the promise that the Americans would give him Gérardmer. Almost immediately there were hints of trouble. On the morning of 30 September, Patch visited de Lattre and told him that the 3d Infantry Division was meeting stiff resistance in its advance toward Gérardmer. The division was being forced to close up its front, and Patch asked de Lattre to take over a portion of the American division's frontage at the Forest de Longegoutte and the Rupt region. The timing was horrible; the Germans were counterattacking II Corps in one area and stoutly defending their positions elsewhere. Once again, de Lattre did as he was asked.

Later that day, Devers informed de Lattre that he needed the French to take over all of the 3d Infantry Division's sector, because O'Daniel's division was to be withdrawn so that Truscott could reintroduce it by surprise elsewhere. Not only did this mean that the First Army's front increased by twenty miles, the Americans were not going to liberate Gérardmer after all. The French did not have the strength to fight their way to Gérardmer, then launch their offensive from it.[78]

De Lattre was angry and sent a note to Devers in which he said that he could not immediately extend his front: First Army's strength was decreasing at the very time that it was being asked to take on more responsibilities. The French, he noted, had lost 860 men killed and wounded in the last two days—including a battalion commander killed and General Brosset of the 1st DFL wounded—yet were being asked to take on greater responsibilities. Devers responded promptly by postponing, though not canceling, the extension of the French sector.[79]

De Lattre was still steaming the next day when he wrote to a minister in de Gaulle's government: "I have had difficult questions to handle with the Seventh Army concerning our tactical coordination in the Vosges, where the Americans are reluctant to truly fight and would like to leave us to act on intolerable fronts." As was his way, however, de Lattre soon calmed down and got back to the business of war.[80]

In any event, de Lattre realized that the offensive he had envisioned had to be rethought. Monsabert suggested that his corps could jump off from the Longegoutte crest, on the right bank of the Moselle—terrain that the 3d DIA would be picking up from the 3d Infantry Division's 7th Infantry Regiment. This would be a more modest operation, but if the French succeeded in driving through the Hohneck, between Cornimont and La Bresse, then crossed the Moselotte valley, they would eventually come to the Alsatian Plain. Guillaume's 3d DIA was to mount the main effort, reinforced with the 2d and 3d GTMs. The 1st DB with attached FFI elements was to cover Guillaume's southern flank, first by taking Le Thillot, then entering the valley of the Thur River by way of the Bussang and Oderen passes. The 1st DFL was to protect the 1st DB's southern flank and maintain contact with I Corps. De Lattre issued the corresponding orders on 1 October. He obtained agreement from Patch that the 3d Infantry Division would support the launching of the 3d DIA's offensive by conducting local operations adjacent to the 3d DIA's zone.[81]

Despite the best of intentions, "it is a long way from the cup to the lips," as Guillaume wrote in his memoirs, and even this more modest plan soon ran into difficulties.[82] The 3rd DIA was to relieve elements of the 7th Infantry Regiment on 4 and 5 October. Somewhere, communications broke down, and inexplicably the Americans left these positions on 2–4 October.[83] When on 4 October the 3d DIA's 3d and 7th RTA moved into the Forest de Longegoutte to secure the jumping-off point, they were met with German machine-gun and mortar fire. The 3d DIA had in front of it the *338th Volksgrenadier Division*, which, battle weary though it was, showed no intention of withdrawing. Four days of bloody fighting by the tirailleurs and the goumiers, old partners from the Italian campaign, were necessary to take the Germans' well-placed hilltop positions.[84]

On 5 October, the Algerians approached the crest of the hill and resorted frequently to hand-to-hand combat, but the next day the *338th Volksgrenadier Division* counterattacked across its entire front and drove them back. By 8 October, Guillaume's group stood atop the Longegoutte Crest, having clawed and scratched its way there with the liberal use of pistols and hand grenades. They had finally conquered their starting point.[85]

To Guillaume's right, the 1st DB, under du Vigier, and the RCP had an even worse time clearing out the Forêt du Gehan. The enemy clung like grim death to Le Thillot, counterattacking often despite heavy losses.[86]

In short, the first several days of October saw desperate, brutal combat on rough terrain in soggy, bone-chilling weather. Guillaume in later years remembered this as the beginning of the "Calvary of the Vosges."

* * *

Though French attention was clearly focused farther north in II Corps' section, the Germans were nervous about their weakness opposite I Corps. During the night of 7–8 October, the German command ordered the *Spitzmuller Battalion*—then occupying positions between Onans and Bretigney, near Switzerland, opposite I Corps—to take up positions elsewhere. With no unit available to replace the battalion, its neighbors to the north and south lengthened their lines. These units were made up of aviators and sailors, hardly crack infantry, so the Germans organized a deception to conceal their weakness and dissuade the French from attacking.

Since the departure of the *11th Panzer Division*, the defenders of the Belfort area had had no tanks. But on 10 October, tanks were unloaded at the Belfort railroad station and drove ostentatiously around the town before clattering off in the direction of Héricourt. Before long they were sighted in several other towns in the region. By means of deserters and double agents, the Germans allowed the word to go out to French intelligence that the *106th "Feldherrnhalle" Panzer Brigade* had arrived. Having made their demonstration, the German tanks soon left. The deception was short-lived, and by 16 October the French had definitely identified

218 // First to the Rhine

the *Feldherrnhalle Brigade* in the Vosges. Still, the Germans concluded that they had bought themselves some time to reorganize.[87]

The French Struggle Onward

Back in the II Corps sector, the ruthless combination of weather and combat continued to weigh on both sides. By 9 October, the 3d DIA was making progress but had engaged in some brutal combat against tenacious resistance. The First Army G-3 described the action as "at least as violent as during the severest battles of Tunis, Italy, Toulon, and Marseille." The 3d and 7th RTAs had crossed the crest of the Longegoutte forest, reached the edge of the woods on the far side, and even attained the banks of the Moselotte at Les Graviers. Farther to the north, a battalion each of Tunisians from the 4th RTT and *goumiers* from the 3d GTM had actually crossed the Moselotte. Similarly, the *Bonjour Groupement* (3 RSAR and 2d Dragoons) was moving forward. To the northwest of Le Thillot, resistance on both sides of the Morbieux Brook was cleared by the 2d GTM after it surrounded the enemy with help from the 1st RCP coming from the south, and a battalion of the 4th RTT coming from the north. The French losses over a four-day period were high, some hundred killed and five hundred wounded. The only consolation was that losses were higher for the Germans—an estimated five hundred to six hundred dead and more than a thousand taken prisoner.[88]

Worsening the situation, the cold, rain, and fog made combat difficult for the tirailleurs and goumiers, who were not used to such conditions and were still awaiting their winter gear. The tirailleurs' winter uniforms were still on the Riviera beaches, and those of the goumiers were back in North Africa. Meanwhile, the FFI, although full of fight, were poorly armed and equipped and inexperienced, leading to comparatively high losses. Guillaume felt that their morale might suddenly crumble if they were hit hard.

Guillaume was about to have more troubles. On 10 October, "voilà a new limit between the two armies was suddenly decided, practically doubling the extent of my sector, at a moment when all my means were engaged facing Cornimont and La Bresse!" This was the extension of the French frontage that Devers had asked of de Lattre but then briefly deferred. Truly, as one American general put it, "General Devers' two armies are like two dogs tied at the tail who are each pulling in a different direction."[89]

Despite these travails, Monsabert thought that the Germans in front of his corps were weakening, so he gained de Lattre's concurrence to detach the 6th RTM from the 4th DMM and gave it to Guillaume. On 15 October, the 3d DIA and the 1st DB launched a new offensive, this time oriented on the 3d DIA's right rather than its left. The 3d DIA was aimed at the heights to the east of the Moselotte and again toward the Rainkopf Crest, Grand Vetron, and Grand Drumont. On 16 October, it managed to establish a wide bridgehead. The 6th RTM, under Colonel Baillif, grabbed the critical Haut du Faing (Faing Heights), southwest of Gérardmer. Baillif thought he had thereby blown a hole in the German defenses and the way into upper Alsace was now open, but he could not convince the senior commanders of this.

The 1st DB contributed to the French effort as well; Bouvet's African Commando Group occupied the crossroads south of Cornimont at noon against heavy opposition, then moved rapidly forward to the Haut du Tonteux without meeting resistance. They continued their advance the next day. Farther south, the parachutists (who were under the 1st DB at this time) reached the Col du Menil, while CC1 took the Travexin crossroad.[90]

* * *

Following its considerable success of 16 October, the left wing of First Army—primarily the 3d DIA—had to defend itself the next day against an increasingly violent enemy reaction. A local action toward Rochesson by the *Guillebaut Groupement* (which consisted of the 4th RTT and the 3d GTM) ran into a lively counterattack and was hit by artillery fire. Meanwhile on the Haut du Faing the 6th RTM repulsed three counterattacks, inflicting heavy losses on the enemy and capturing fifty prisoners. The Germans even threw two penal battalions into the meatgrinder, one of which took 70 percent losses in trying to drive the Moroccans off the heights.[91]

After the attacks on the Haut du Faing failed, the Germans used the dark of night to creep toward the French positions. They attacked at 0730 the next morning through a driving rain, but the French were ready once again. The thick underbrush forced the defenders to stand up to see their enemies. It was a gruesome slugfest, but the French by far came out on top. Their twenty machine guns mowed down wave after wave of doomed German soldiers as officers ran from one machine-gun position to the next pointing out targets. For a brief period it looked as though the French would be overrun when yet another wave of Germans appeared just as ammunition was running short, but the French pillaged spare ammunition off the bodies of their fallen comrades, and there was enough to turn back this last assault of the day. Even after the combat was over, the cries of dying German soldiers floated through the woods. The position remained disputed for days afterward, and the defenders had to deal not only with numerous additional attacks but with the frightful smell of an ever-increasing number of decaying bodies. All told, in twelve horrific days of combat, the Moroccans suffered 147 killed, 733 wounded, and 103 evacuated with frostbite.[92]

Meanwhile, the 1st DB consolidated its position around Travexin despite heavy artillery fire and cleared out the nearby woods. The African Commando Group faced its own hell that day, leaving ninety-two of its members dead in the woods around the Haut du Tonteux.[93]

* * *

The violence of the counterattacks on 17 October probably confirmed to de Lattre the wisdom of the decision he had already made to suspend the offensive. He informed General Monsabert of this halt at midday. Monsabert and his men thought this was a mistake. They were capturing German prisoners and deserters in ever-increasing numbers, and these men told stories to their French interrogators that made it sound as though the German formations were ready to break. A few more units, a little more artillery, and II Corps would at least be able to reach the Route des Crêtes. These arguments only reminded de Lattre of the folly of World War I, and he was having none of it. The offensive was over.[94]

Accordingly, on 22 October, Monsabert issued General Operations Order No. 43 to his II Corps. He noted that the 3d DIA had succeeded in drawing into its sector numerous enemy reserves coming from both its flanks and even from Germany itself. (The estimate was that II Corps' offensive had drawn into the Vosges six battalions from the Belfort Gap, four from in front of the U.S. VI Corps, seven from Germany, and a division from Norway.) The enemy had been hard hit but, nonetheless, showed every sign of standing fast as long as II Corps did not grow in strength and was not capable of serious offensive action itself. The general ordered his corps to maintain contact with the enemy by deep patrolling; to organize a set of strongpoints, each of which was to be held at all costs; to deny to the enemy any ability to seize and use several key roads leading through the French rear; and to be ready to seize the road network in the Le Thillot area.[95]

For Guillaume, commanding the 3d DIA, the end came none too soon. He thought the whole offensive had been just this side of disastrous. In front of the 3rd DIA was the German *269th Infantry Division*, which had just arrived, rested, from deployment in Norway. "The snow arrived with it, covering all our positions, freezing the feet of the combatants," recalled Guillaume. Moreover, his division, not alone in the French army, felt abandoned; the French people seemed more interested in politics than in the sacrifices being made by the army that was fighting for their liberty. Some Frenchmen were grateful. These were the many displaced persons who continued to make their way to the 3d DIA's lines after the Germans burned them out of their villages. The French forces, poorly supplied themselves, were scarcely able to support these freezing, wretched civilians, some of whom had not eaten for three weeks, but they did what they could.[96]

* * *

When de Lattre ordered an end to the II Corps offensive, he also told Monsabert that the corps would have to give up substantial forces. The reason for this was that SHAEF had decided it needed to use the port of Bordeaux and that, more generally, the various pockets of German troops along the Atlantic coast should be cleared out. The French government had then decided that such operations could be conducted only by French troops—that is to say, by de Lattre's men. De Lattre, accordingly, was ordered to send General de Larminat roughly two divisions, including the 1st DB in its entirety, hundreds of miles to the west, far from Germany. As if that were not enough, Lieutenant General Devers informed de Lattre at about this time that he was soon going to move the First Airborne Task Force from its present position holding down the Alps, and he expected the French First Army to pick up this responsibility. This had the effect of stretching de Lattre's front by another thirty miles just as he was losing more than a division of troops.

It had been a frustrating and lethal month, but de Lattre immediately began planning a new offensive. On 19 October he wrote to General de Gaulle outlining the offensive that in November would make his forces first to the Rhine.[97]

SETTING THE STAGE FOR THE BIG OFFENSIVE

In late October, Devers considered his offensive options. The Germans appeared to be in some straits and passing from "offensive defense" to static or delaying defense as mobile units such as the *15th Panzergrenadier* and *11th Panzer divisions* disappeared from the front. The principal question was where to make his main effort. His orders were to protect the southern flank of 12th Army Group, which argued for using Seventh Army rather than French First Army. Patch also confronted less difficult avenues of advance than did the French, and the objectives were of higher value. French First Army, moreover, had had to surrender two divisions to besiege Bordeaux and nearby towns, still held by an estimated twenty-five thousand German troops.

On 28 October, Devers issued his orders. Patch was to capture high ground along the interarmy boundary near Gérardmer preparatory to launching an "all out offensive" by 5 November, supported by French First Army. Seventh Army's objective was to reach Strasbourg and destroy the enemy west of the Rhine. Patch was to arrange with de Lattre suitable French participation in the liberation of Strasbourg.[98]

Devers at this time demonstrated rather extraordinary sensitivity to the grim conditions his troops faced in the increasingly wintry mountainous terrain. Perhaps he was wise to the danger of high nonbattle casualties after the hard learning experience in the Italian mountains the preceding winter. As noted in the 6th Army Group history, "because of the several active theaters and extended fronts, divisions were kept in the line without relief for much longer periods than was desirable or was the practice in World War I." Devers' staff, looking for a solution, on 25 October conferred with Maj. Gen. Harold "Pink" Bull, Eisenhower's G-3, about arranging the early shipment of the infantry regiments from the three divisions due to arrive from the States through Marseille, those being the 42d, 70th, and 73d Infantry divisions. Because the regiments had relatively little heavy equipment, they could move separately and early, and Devers thought he could assign one to each American division in the army group to spell worn-out regiments in the line. Approved by SHAEF, the idea went to the War Department, which arranged transportation to permit arrival of the fresh regiments between 6 and 8 December. The 100th and 103d Infantry divisions and advanced detachment of the 14th Armored Division, meanwhile, had arrived at Marseille by 25 October and were destined to bulk up Seventh Army.[99]

* * *

Army Group G considered October to have been a relatively good month in the south. *Nineteenth Army* had managed to hold its ground or fall back step-by-step. Only near St. Dié had the Americans threatened to penetrate the Vosges position, and commitment of the *106th Panzer Brigade* had stabilized the line.[100] Von Rundstedt submitted a report on 3 November detailing an inspection trip to the *First* and *Nineteenth armies*, in which he concluded that *Nineteenth Army* had become stronger and was fighting well. The assignment of fortress (static) artillery battalions had boosted firepower, although the infantry situation was still wholly inadequate. Von Rundstedt judged that construction of fighting positions along the crest of the Vosges had made such good progress that *Nineteenth Army* would be able to fall back to that line if necessary as early as 15 November.[101]

The Seventh Army's assessment about the same time acknowledged the enemy's success in averting disaster: "The Germans had gained time, time to revamp a shattered army, time to erect defensive positions that supplemented favorable features. The new offensive would prove which of the opposing forces had employed that time more effectively."[102]

CHAPTER 8

FIRST TO THE RHINE

"Everything is possible with the youth of France when one knows how to show them the right path and give them an ideal. Theirs was clear now: 'Drive the German out of France.'"

—Colonel Raoul Salan

November brought frequent rains, snow, and sleet storms to the Vosges Mountains. Movement by even tracked vehicles was road-bound. Allied tactical air support remained largely absent because of lousy weather and long distances from airfields. When the weather was bad in the Vosges, aircraft could not attack, and often when the weather cleared in the battle zone, it was so bad over airfields two hundred miles distant around Lyon that fighter-bombers could not take off. Sixth Army Group blamed Field Marshal Wilson for delays in supplying aviation engineers and steel planking for construction of advance landing fields in the mud close to the front.

The shortage of air support made the availability of artillery all the more important to the troops at the front. However, artillery ammunition was still in perilously short supply, and there was little prospect of any immediate improvement. After carefully hoarding supplies once the transportation system had improved in October, the army group received word of a War Department report that stocks in the States were practically exhausted, and as little as a third of daily usage could be covered from current production until output could be increased in spring 1945. Devers' staff estimated that at current rates of consumption, reserves would last only until the first of the year.[1]

* * *

Army Group G's chief of staff, *Generalmajor* Friedrich von Mellenthin, had his own problems: "At the beginning of November, our line was far stronger than a month before, and mud and slush could be relied upon to clog the movements of American armor. Yet there was nothing really solid, and nothing dependable about our front. Under the impact of day and night bombing, the [national] supply system worked spasmodically, and ammunition was woefully short. We had hardly any assault guns, and some divisions had none at all. We had a considerable quantity of field artillery, but much of it consisted of captured guns with only a few rounds of ammunition. We had 140 tanks of all types; 100 of these were allocated to *First Army*."[2]

Nineteenth Army was indeed a patchwork army as of early November. The *21st Panzer Division* was under orders to withdraw into Lorraine as the army group reserve, to be replaced by the green *708th Volksgrenadier Division*. It possessed some twenty tanks and relied on miscellaneous French and Russian guns in its artillery battalions, but its panzergrenadier regiments were still in good order. The *16th Volksgrenadier Division* had received some replacements but was still lacking most of its heavy weapons. The *716th Volksgrenadier Division* was little more than a regiment-sized battle group. The *198th Infantry Division* was the best formation in *Nineteenth Army* but had suffered many casualties in the fighting around Le Tholy. The *338th Infantry Division* had been reduced to a regiment-sized battle group and was shifted to the Belfort area to absorb miscellaneous units available there. The *269th Infantry Division*, pulled together from infantry regiments and artillery units withdrawn from Norway, lacked combat experience, but the division was deemed capable of defensive operations. The *159th* and *189th Infantry divisions* at Belfort Pass had filled their ranks with replacements and were also rated suitable for defensive operations. In terms of armor, once the *21st Panzer Division* and *106th Panzer Brigade* were withdrawn in November, all of *Nineteenth Army* disposed of only between ten and fifteen assault guns.[3]

The Seventh Army noted, "The defenses of the Vosges were more impressive than their defenders." The Americans and French confronted two lines of defense west of the Rhine. The pre-Vosges line by mid-November was an almost continuous string of fortifications and fighting positions along the lower heights west of the Vosges Mountains. The main line consisted of strongpoints commanding the passes to the Alsatian Plain beyond.[4]

All through the area around Belfort, the Germans made substantial use of forced labor by French civilians, setting them to work digging antitank ditches and performing other such labors. This apparently free labor came at a grave cost in security, however. Many thousands of French civilians knew the German defenses in detail, and as they were working alongside German units they were also able to identify other key Wehrmacht locations. Starting in late October, the German command began to believe that French artillery fire was sometimes suspiciously accurate. Mortar positions obscured in the woods, battalion and regimental command posts, even two armored cars that stopped at the same place far from the front at the same time every day came under attack.

The Germans put the collaborationist French militia in Montbéliard on the problem. After a short investigation, they fingered the Resistance forces of three particular towns as the sources of the leaks. SS troops swept into those towns, arrested all the adult men, and shot them.[5]

THE BREAKTHROUGH BEGINS

According to Patch's plan, Major General Brooks' VI Corps was to make the main Seventh Army effort and advance to Strasbourg. After rolling four hundred miles from St. Raphael to Rambervillers in late August and early September, VI Corps had eked out a scant fifteen miles during October and the first half of November. Major General Haislip's XV Corps was to punch through the Saverne Gap and support the VI Corps effort. Fortune instead gave the laurels to XV Corps.

* * *

Haislip was to attack toward Sarrebourg, the first major bastion before the gap, with the 44th Infantry Division on the left and the 79th Infantry Division on the right. The French 2d DB was to exploit a breakthrough wherever it occurred.[6] The armored division's mission was to breach the gap and roll onto the Alsatian Plain.

Two or more inches of snow covered the entire 6th Army Group zone when XV Corps kicked off its attack on 13 November as part of a general Allied offensive that, staggered over several days, engulfed nearly the length of the western front. Streams were at flood stage because of heavy rains that had preceded the snow, and the mud seemed bottomless to the GIs. The 44th Infantry Division struck up the road to Sarrebourg with two regiments abreast and carved out rapid gains until encountering heavy artillery, mortar, and machine-gun fire across its entire front at about 0800 hours, courtesy of the *553d Volksgrenadier Division*. The German division was the southernmost formation in *First Army* and was just absorbing five green infantry battalions given it to replace a regiment that it had sent to another division.

Just to the south, the 79th Infantry Division's attack struck the seam between the *First* and *Nineteenth armies*. Here, the untried *708th Volksgrenadier Division*, just formed in Slovakia, had begun to take over the *21st Panzer Division* zone during the night of 9–10 November and had not fully consolidated its positions.[7]

Army Group G transferred the *553d Volksgrenadier Division* from *First Army* to *Nineteenth Army*'s *LXIV Corps* during the afternoon of 13 November to allow the former to concentrate on fighting around Metz. Balck also instructed Wiese to straighten his line by withdrawing to the field fortifications of the pre-Vosges position—a maneuver that Balck had prepared well in advance—which would allow the weary *198th Infantry Division* to pull back and act as a reserve.[8]

* * *

On 15 November, the German line in front of the 79th Infantry Division all but collapsed after GIs from the 315th Infantry Regiment hit the German reserves just as they were assembling for a counterattack. M10s from the 813th Tank Destroyer Battalion and Shermans from the 749th Tank Battalion destroyed most of the *708th Volksgrenadier Division*'s assault guns during the engagement.[9]

By 16 November, *Army Group G* doubted that the *708th Volksgrenadier Division* could hold much longer, especially against 79th Infantry Division attacks around Blamont. German troops—per a scorched-earth order from Balck dated 2 November—burned St. Dié and other towns and villages in the areas opposite XV and VI corps, which suggested that commanders expected to be forced out of these positions in the near future.

THE FRENCH ATTACK

Through most of October, de Lattre had considered an offensive by Béthouart's I Corps. There were particular advantages to this option: The corps' right flank was well protected and fixed, unlike the French far left flank, which kept expanding as the Americans moved north. The right flank, of course, was Switzerland, whose neutrality the Germans were unlikely to violate at this stage of the war, and which had, in any event, moved substantial forces to its borders.[10]

If, launching from the Doubs, I Corps could break through the German defenses, its right wing could round the corner of Switzerland, then turn to the east, secure the eastern exits of the Belfort Gap around Dannemarie, and with some good broken-field running make it to the Rhine. Simultaneously, I Corps' center and left would secure the industrial area around Montbéliard, which was suffering horrible predations at the hands of the Germans.[11]

Making such an approach doubly attractive was the fact that because Monsabert was battering against the German line farther north, reliable intelligence indicated that the enemy was moving forces from the Montbéliard area to the Vosges. From de Lattre's point of view, the Germans were moving left, so he would move right. It was in this context that de Lattre had ordered Guillaume's 3d DIA to maintain an aggressive posture. It was important to keep those German forces up north.[12]

When on 17 October de Lattre brought Monsabert's bloody but ineffective offensive to an end, Béthouart had ready a draft plan for an offensive in the south. A week later, de Lattre issued his Personal and Secret Instruction No. 4 to Béthouart, in essence approving the latter's plan.[13] The 2d DIM, under General Carpentier, would be responsible for the main effort of breaking through the German defenses north of the Doubs River. To its right was the 9th DIC, which was deep in the *blanchiment* process and had many white soldiers with less than a month in service. To partially make up for the division's weakness, Béthouart gave its commander, General Magnan, control of many experienced, if slightly unruly, FFI units. Magnan's force was to operate between the Doubs and the Swiss border, eventually driving its armor toward the valley of the Allaine River and beyond, opening up the way toward the Rhine-Rhône Canal.[14] The

1st DB less one combat command was to stay back to exploit any hole that the two infantry divisions managed to create.

De Lattre gave Béthouart the 5th DB, a combat command of the 1st DB, and two armored regiments (the 7th RCA and the 1st RSAR). Béthouart would also receive a regimental combat team from the 4th DMM; it included the 6th RTM, under Colonel Baillif, which had held out so valiantly on the Haut du Faing; the 1st GTM; the Shock Group; and the 9th Zouaves. There would also be substantial artillery reinforcements. Devers even chipped in some American 240mm and 8-inch howitzer battalions arriving from Italy. Critically, however, all these units were to move into their positions at the last possible hour so as to ensure surprise.[15]

The French were comforted that when the local weather permitted it, they could finally rely on French I Air Corps, which, supported by some American units, had 120 fighters, 80 bombers, and 20 reconnaissance aircraft.[16] Three days into the offensive, the French daily situation report would proudly note: "For the first time since the invasion, aviation, entirely French, of the French I Air Corps supported the action of our troops. Thirty-one direct support and close support missions totaling 175 sorties were made during the course of the day. The assistance given our units was extremely efficient."[17]

All during the planning period, however, de Lattre worried that the withdrawal of more than two divisions to liberate the Atlantic ports could preclude the offensive. Particularly problematic was the withdrawal of the 1st DB, which was slated to begin the exploitation phase of the French offensive. Keeping the matter almost entirely to himself so as not to throw off the good work being done by Béthouart, the French commander begged, pleaded, and cajoled Devers to postpone the move. It was only two days before the French launched their offensive that Devers put off the withdrawals until the very end of November.[18]

Even as de Lattre battled to keep his forces, he turned to the French intelligence services to draw a curtain of uncertainty and deception around his emerging plan. On 20 October, he signed phony orders laying out a plan for a major new offensive in the Vosges, again aiming at the Schlucht and Bussang, substantially to the north of Belfort. This misleading document was handed to a brave French double agent to carry to the

Germans. Unfortunately, vigilant tirailleurs from the 2d DIM arrested him as he crossed the French lines. The agent was lucky to escape with his life, but eventually he was released and successfully made it to German lines. Soon he found himself standing before *General der Infanterie* Wiese, explaining that he had obtained this vital document from a staff secretary at the headquarters of the French I Corps. Because Wiese had already received reports that air reconnaissance had spotted French convoys moving northward, he was inclined to believe the story. Meanwhile, in support of the deception, the 5th DB was making ostentatious preparations for an attack toward Plombières. On 7 November, another French agent, this one in Switzerland, gave the Abwehr (Germany's defense intelligence service) a copy of another fake document from de Lattre explaining the importance of pushing through the Vosges and deviously indicating that reinforcement in the Doubs area was necessary to keep the Germans from perceiving the truth of the plan for a renewed attack in the mountains. Wiese was so convinced that between 8 and 10 November he reinforced his defenses in the Vosges at the expense of those around Belfort. Finally, to seal the deal, on 12 November de Lattre issued an order of the day to his army promising a long-deferred period of leave to many of his soldiers in the second half of November.[19] Some of the troops probably believed de Lattre, but the savvy ones had already noticed that their officers were being called more and more frequently to headquarters for meetings.[20]

The offensive was due to begin on 13 November, but when the time came to start moving the additional forces forward four days earlier, disaster struck. The horrible rains, punctuated occasionally now by snow, had caused flooding and washed out or weakened key bridges in the French rear and made much of the countryside an impassable morass. At midday on 11 November, General Béthouart proposed to de Lattre that the offensive be postponed; his forces simply would not be in place and ready.[21]

De Lattre was disappointed and annoyed, but he was not going to waver with Devers' eyes upon him. He demanded that Béthouart at least start his offensive in the 9th DIC sector on schedule. Béthouart's armor must be ready on 14 November, a day late.[22] On the night of 12 November, many thousands of French soldiers quietly and carefully took up their positions in the woods and settled in for a cold and nerve-wracking night, thinking that bloody combat awaited them in the morning.[23] When day broke, however, the ground was covered with snow. In fact, the snow was still falling, and visibility in some areas was just a few yards. The offensive would have to wait another day after all, and the infantry would have to spend another freezing night in the woods praying that they would not be discovered.[24]

On the morning of 14 November, there was a pause in the storm. Béthouart and his division commanders conferred. The weather was still lousy, but they agreed that the 2d DIM could go at 1145 hours and the 9th DIC would start at 1330. Béthouart called de Lattre. "I'm going," he told his commander. Later de Lattre confessed to his corps commander that he thought the weather was so bad that he would never have dared to order his forces into it.[25]

The French had a stroke of luck in the opening artillery barrage. Opposite the 2d DIM was the *338th Volksgrenadier Division*, commanded by *Generalmajor* Oschmann. On the morning of 14 November, the general left his command post to inspect the division's forward positions in the forests near Bretigney. At about 1120, artillery fire erupted all around, sending the general running for a nearby foxhole. The bombardment lasted for an hour, then silence fell. The general got out of his foxhole, still not fully realizing that this was the beginning of a major French attack. The 8th RTM, however, had already infiltrated into the woods. A Moroccan caught the general with no cover and shot him dead. The Moroccans captured a map showing the *338th Division*'s defensive positions and a copy of the latest orders from the general. They included this notation: "The French are on the defensive. There is no indication of an attack soon."[26]

Between the 2d DIM and the 9th DIC proper was Colonel Salan's group, attached to Magnan's 9th Division. Because the fog was still thick in the rest of the 9th DIC's sector in the Jura Mountains, only the left wing of Magnan's forces was to launch at 1400 on 14 November. The rest of the division would go on the following morning. Mines were a serious problem in front of the 9th DIC, and the demining effort—which hadn't begun until 0100 on the morning of 14 November—had to be finished by late that morning. The engineers sprang into action and by 1030 had opened three breaches in the snow-covered minefield belts, some of them in minefields that were under enemy fire.[27]

Salan's group, consisting largely of the 6th RIC and a demi-brigade of "Fabien's" FFI, was to attack into the "*boucle du Doubs*," a great looping protrusion of the river pointing to the northeast. The ground on the inside of the loop was held by the Germans. Under the command of Lieutenant Colonel Dessert, the 6th RIC moved through the breaches in the minefields and quickly took Écot, an essential bastion for the German resistance in the region. The French already knew from documents found on a prisoner a few days earlier that the German code word for Écot was *edelweiss*. French signal intelligence units heard the German defenders radio "*Edelweiss ist genommen*" just before the senior German officer there surrendered with the last of his men. The Germans now knew that only French soldiers—and civilians, of course—were in the town, and they brought it under withering artillery fire. Soon the German infantry arrived to counterattack, still well supported by artillery. The combat was ferocious and developed into nighttime street fighting in the biting cold.[28]

At 0400 hours on 15 November, the field phone on Salan's desk rang. It was Colonel Dessert, in Écot, who wanted to call in artillery fire on his own position. The French responded with a thunderous barrage, expertly directed by an artillery liaison officer in the town, who called in artillery all around Dessert's position. Though shells fell perilously close, the liaison officer's expertise, and the French artillery's minute preparations for the attack, had made it unnecessary to honor Dessert's self-sacrificing request.

When day broke, the French were still in the town and the German counterattack was broken. The 6th RIC and the 9th DIC, to its right, surged forward. The engineers cleared mines from Écot and nearby towns.[29]

Securing roads was a serious issue. Colonel Salan, commanding the 6th RIC, was nearly killed on 14 November as he drove through the snow to visit his men at Écot. His convoy of two jeeps came to a small stone bridge, which showed signs of the recent passage of trucks. They stopped and examined the surroundings, but everything seemed in order, so they got back in their jeeps. Salan led the way, his jeep carefully staying inside the tracks of the trucks that had preceded them. The vehicle made it across and climbed up the road on the far side of the stream. Suddenly an explosion made him look back; he saw the bodies of the three soldiers in the jeep behind him flying through the air, surrounded by parts of their vehicle. The men were dead, of course, their bodies in grotesque, broken poses inside their greatcoats. The Germans had rigged an improvised explosive device out of 155mm shells.[30]

In fact, when night fell on 14 November, the French were well pleased with their progress. In some places they had pushed back the Germans as much as ten miles. De Lattre was positively glowing and urged the I Corps forward, releasing to Béthouart the 1st DB's command staff and its CC3.[31]

On the morning of 15 November, the center and right of the 9th DIC moved out of their positions and into battle. They made good progress as well, though with more difficulty. Only on the far right was there no significant advance. The 9th Zouaves took 25 percent casualties in their first day of combat. The 6th RTM, on the 9th DIC's extreme right, ran into Germans in strong defensive positions. They were all the more difficult to attack because they were so close to the Swiss border that the French could make little use of artillery for fear of sending shells into Swiss territory.[32]

The 2d DIM continued its advance on 15 November. Its efforts came at the cost of the commander of the 5th DB's CC5, one of the two combat commands attached to the 2d DIM for the exploitation phase. He was felled by an artillery shell. That day the 2d DIM defeated the last of the meager reserves of the unfortunate *338th Volksgrenadier Division*: a reinforced battalion of infantry, including a company of bicycle troops. The 9th DIC's left wing, as well, had definitively broken the first line of German defenses, and in one spot even the second line of defense.

The *338th Division* had no tanks to counter the French, and the volksgrenadiers were about to suffer for it. On 16 November, French tanks went into action and shattered the German defenses in front of the 2d DIM. On the left, CC4 attacked along National Route 83 toward Belfort and reached the town of Aibre. The infantry followed behind them for three miles. Combat Command 4 then turned to the right and fell upon the rear of St. Marie, a town that the Germans were ferociously defending against a frontal attack by CC5 and supporting infantry. It took house-to-house fighting, but by late afternoon the battle was over. Combat

Command 5 also pressed on toward Montbéliard while, just to its right, CC3 and the 6th RIC working together made progress as well.[33]

The most important gains came on the 9th DIC's far right. The 9th Zouaves broke through the German defenders, and the 23d RIC infiltrated through the woods and took out key fortresses right on the Swiss border, opening the way for the 6th RTM to surge forward.

De Lattre and Béthouart saw that now was the time to exploit their successes. If the French could get across the Lisaine and Gland rivers, the Germans would be playing catch-up. De Lattre ordered the right wing of Monsabert's II Corps to go over to the attack. De Lattre and Béthouart, drawing on their reserves, formed a "special exploitation group" under General Molle, to the left of the 2d DIM—between II and I corps—but under General Carpentier's command and sent it toward the Lisaine River with the goal of seizing the bridge at Chagny. The 2d DIM was also to drive for the Lisaine to seize further crossings between Héricourt and Montbéliard and make a maximum effort to drive over the river to Belfort. The 9th DIC was to go for Hérimoncourt, cross the Gland River, reach Abbévillers, then commit its tanks.[34]

The Germans immediately realized the threat to the Héricourt area, the key to the entire Lisaine-Gland line. From all directions they rushed infantry battalions and engineer battalions used as infantry.[35]

These battalions were not used to fighting together, however. Some had just been force-marched to their new positions, none was familiar with the terrain, and they had insufficient time to coordinate with the artillery intended to support them. Moreover, these units had few anti-tank weapons and no tanks whatsoever with which to counter the rampaging Shermans and the determined Moroccans.

With the 1st *Cuirassiers* leading the way, the French erupted out of the woods and hit the German positions with full force. They sliced through the German lines so quickly that the Germans were unable to call in fire support. The French grabbed the bridge over the Lisaine before the enemy could react. Soon, however, the Germans came out of their stupor and fought back with panzerfausts and whatever else they had at hand. The cuirassiers hung on like grim death waiting for the main body of CC4. When it arrived, some German units panicked and ran or surrendered themselves by the hundreds. Stiff fighting was still necessary. With darkness falling, de Lattre himself came to watch the battle. By the light of a burning tank next to the bridge—the tank commander, a major, lay writhing in pain next to it—the general watched as legionnaires of the *Régiment de Marche de la Légion Etrangère* (RMLE), determined to exploit across the bridge, used hand grenades to clean out the buildings on either side of the main road.

Soon enough the remaining Germans fled into the night, abandoning their wounded, and the French were able to push more than a mile beyond the bridge. They had also secured crossings of the Lisaine on either side of Héricourt. Farther north, General Molle's "Special Exploitation Group" had also reached the Lisaine.

Having crossed the Lisaine, the 2d DIM struck toward Belfort. The Moroccans of the 8th RTM soon encountered the Fort du Vaudois and machine-gun and mortar fire. Having failed in their first frontal assault, the Moroccans soon surrounded the fort, but *Leutnant* Ulrich, who had seized command from an officer willing to surrender, refused to surrender. Soon, high-caliber artillery was pounding the fort, but still the stubborn Ulrich held out. The artillery bombardment's only major effect was to knock out the fortress' one radio, which had kept it in communication with the German headquarters at Belfort. As soon as darkness fell, Ulrich dispatched a runner to Belfort. At 0200 hours, the runner returned with an order to evacuate.

As Héricourt was falling, the 5th RTM, the 1st RCA, and local maquis seized Montbéliard, the tanks going in a broad flanking movement around the north of the town at 1515. The enemy attempted to fend off the French tanks with panzerfausts, but at 1630 the tanks forced their way into the town. They were closely followed by the maquis, who promptly took the bridges and prevented the Germans from executing their preparations to destroy them. They soon cleared the village of German stragglers.[36]

On Béthouart's right, the 9th DIC had done good work as well. The Zouaves filtered into the woods above Hérimoncourt, fell upon the town from an unexpected direction, and took it in fifteen minutes. This action, plus other vigorous efforts by the 23d RIC, two squadrons of tanks from

CC3, the Colonial Artillery Regiment of Morocco, and the 9th Zouaves shattered German resistance and opened the way for exploitation.[37]

DRIVING TO THE RHINE

As late as 17 November, the Germans were still assessing the French attack as a feint, albeit a dangerous one, but the French were ready now to drive through the shattered German defenses and exploit fast and deep.

That day, de Lattre and Béthouart conferred. The corps commander proposed to regroup the three combat commands of General du Vigiers' 1st DB; add to them the RICM, the RCCC, the 9th Zouaves, and Colonel Baillif's 6th RTM; and drive them through the gaping holes opened by the 9th DIC. Their objective would be the Rhine between Brisach and Switzerland. The 9th DIC would obliterate the German forces remaining to the rear and protect the left flank of the armored division.[38]

The 1st DB moved out on the evening of 17 November. The next morning, Béthouart met with his G-2, who told him "the route from Mulhouse is open" and the Germans would not be able to close the hole in their defenses. Du Vigier believed that what German forces were in reserve would be drawn toward Belfort, which was increasingly menaced by the 2d DIM and attached forces. Thus, the far right wing of his armored division, being farthest from Belfort, would be most able to make rapid progress.[39]

Du Vigier was absolutely correct. His troops there under Lieutenant Colonel Le Puloch, the commander of the RICM, were held up briefly on the morning of 18 November. The combined actions of the RICM and 9th Zouaves cleared all impediments and led to the capture of 250 German prisoners. Le Puloch could not have been less interested in this haul of prisoners. He immediately pushed forward his reconnaissance forces as fast as they could go. Elsewhere on the I Corps' front, the disorganization of the enemy appeared total, and Le Puloch's men faced virtually no enemy at all. They lunged ahead twenty miles. Combat Command 3 under Colonel Caldairou followed.[40]

At 1400 hours on 19 November, the RICM, still driving relentlessly ahead, reached Seppois, the first town to be liberated in Alsace. The Germans put up a fight, but the colonial troops left fifty dead Germans and another hundred wounded littering the battlefield before driving on. The tanks of the RICM and the attached Zouaves kept on going. They were still only halfway to the Rhine from their starting point, but it seemed they could almost smell the water. As they drove forward, occasionally there would be a small flurry of gunfire as they surprised some small group of Germans or blew into some lightly defended town.

Before long the column crossed the Ill River, the last water obstacle. By 1700, the advance became a charge. A detachment under Lieutenant de Loisy, consisting of a company of Sherman tanks and a platoon of Zouaves, took the lead, driving at top speed. The town of Rosenau loomed ahead. The finish line was in sight. They charged into Rosenau and paused to accept the surrender of fifteen flabbergasted Germans who had no idea the enemy was anywhere near. It was about to get dark, and they were tantalizingly close to their destination, so de Loisy urged his men forward. His little force erupted out the other side of the town. Five hundred yards ahead they saw a line of trees. It was the Rhine![41]

At 1830 on 19 November, the RICM and the Zouaves reached the river. They were euphoric. Moments later more units arrived, headlights on. A battery of the 68th Artillery Regiment arrived, set up, and fired a few artillery shells into Germany, the first French shells to land in that country in four and a half years. The next morning, someone had the idea to bring out an RICM flag and dip it in the Rhine, a less violent gesture but equally defiant.[42]

Colonel Caldairou, informed of the RICM's coup, ordered all his forces to follow, headlights on, driving through the night, and take up positions along the Rhine.[43]

The Fall of Strasbourg

In the XV Corps zone, Major General Haislip on 16 November fed the first elements of the 2d DB into his drive to protect the flanks of the 44th and 79th Infantry divisions. On 18 November, the 44th Infantry Division cracked the heretofore energetic resistance offered by the *553d Volksgrenadier Division*, while the *708th Volksgrenadier Division* continued to dissolve before the 79th Infantry Division's remorseless pressure.[44] The time was ripe for Leclerc and his armored division to roll.

The 2d DB shattered the German line on 19 November when it captured Cirey, its bridge across the Vezouse River intact, and spread out in all directions. Leclerc's pre-offensive orders gave his commanders the freedom to choose their own routes once they were on the loose, with the general proviso that they were to seek out less obvious secondary roads rather than plunge straight through the center of the gap, where the Germans would most expect them. XV Corps immediately ordered the 79th Infantry Division to leave the capture of Sarrebourg to the 44th Infantry Division and move by all available transport to exploit the French breakthrough and protect the corps' right flank.[45]

Combat Command L rolled out of Cirey toward the minor Wolfsberg Pass, south of the gap, early on the afternoon of 19 November. Its task forces operated in parallel, driving up every minor road that pointed in the right direction and maneuvering to assist one another when resistance was encountered. All roads joined into one at the mountain village of Dabo, however, and German resistance mounted as the French troops approached the defiladed pass.

About 1600 on 20 November, Leclerc committed his reserve Combat Command V, and the French armor rolled through pouring rain toward Dabo with headlights on full. They wanted to make certain they arrived in time. The extra weight enabled Combat Command L to smash through Wolfsberg Pass about 1400 on 21 November.

Leclerc had meanwhile dispatched Combat Command D to exploit the 44th Infantry Division's progress toward Sarrebourg. Advancing in two task forces, the French armor swung west of Sarrebourg, then sharply east, while the 44th Infantry Division moved into the town. The Germans—most of them from *First Army*'s retreating *361st Volksgrenadier Division*—held Task Force Quilichini before Phalsbourg, the gateway to Saverne Pass, but Task Force Rouvillois plowed through disorganized German resistance along a minor road north of the gap and reached the Alsatian Plain the evening of 21 November.[46]

Forming part of Rouvillois' forces were the 12th *Cuirassiers*, a tank regiment originally raised in 1688 as the Dauphin Cavalry. It had taken part in such famous battles as Jena and Austerlitz. Now it had another chance to add to the proud regimental history. A few days earlier the regimental commander had gathered his men and told them they were going to shock the enemy with their audacity in the Alsatian Plain. "Our lives do not matter," he said.[47]

On 21 November, the 12th Cuirassiers, having crossed the Marne-Rhine Canal and now moving north-northwest, encountered the first scattered opposition around Héming, but they soon dealt with it and the tanks pushed on, leaving their prisoners behind in the hands of local civilians. It was important to keep the momentum going if they were to achieve tactical surprise of the bigger German forces ahead of them. The Americans following behind could clean up any pockets of Germans who had not yet raised the white flag.

The next town was Keprich, where there was much more resistance; 81mm mortar rounds fell around the tanks, and German infantrymen were in the upper floors of the buildings firing down with rifles and machine guns. The French Shermans took out some of the machine-gun positions with their 75s, but the column scarcely slowed down before exiting the other side of the town, leaving the defenses largely intact. A few of the tankers exchanged comments among themselves that they would like to stop and kill Germans, but the cuirassiers' job was to pierce the defenses, not to take vengeance on every defender.

The French column had a good head of steam up now. In Langatte, it destroyed two German horse-drawn artillery pieces. The artillery crew members took off running across the fields, but a tank drove a shell right into their midst, and none of them moved again. Passing a wounded horse, a French officer stopped long enough to put the poor beast out of its misery with his revolver. Then he got back into his vehicle, and the charge continued.

The cuirassiers entered Haut-Clocher from the south and the west. Exiting out the north side of the town, they surprised a column of German heavy artillery. The French attacked it with machine guns and 75s. They had to do very little killing before the rest of the Germans, tired and clearly shocked by the unexpected arrival of the French army, surrendered. Again, the French left the prisoners for the Americans and got back on the move. This was not quite as satisfying as the charge of a horse-cavalry regiment, but it felt good to crank up the machines and go barreling across the country dispatching unsuspecting Germans. "We are taking way too many prisoners," one cuirassier commented to his pal.

Machine-gunning their way through more lightly defended towns, the regiment arrived at Sarre, where the Germans had rigged the bridge with explosives but fortunately had lacked the presence of mind to actually blow it. While the engineers rendered the bridge safe, an infantry patrol pushed forward to Oberstinzel, where it met a rapturous welcome and an impressive number of pretty girls, all smiles and flowers. There was no time to take advantage of these opportunities for rest and relaxation, however. The main force soon caught up with this infantry patrol, and the advance continued, heading for Rauwiller.

The Germans in Rauwiller were totally surprised and put up no resistance. The French spent the night there—an eventful night, as it happened, because German vehicles kept approaching the town in the dark, unaware that it had fallen into the enemy's hands. The French took great joy in killing the few who did not immediately give themselves up and in capturing the rest. The Germans, in fact, were in such disarray that during the night the phone rang in what had been the town's German headquarters. On the other end was a Gestapo officer asking if the town's defenders had any information about the location of French forces. The French soldier who had answered the phone politely reported in perfect German that the French forces had been stopped far from Rauwiller by German tanks that had arrived as reinforcements.

In fact, later in the morning, German tanks did arrive at Rauwiller. Perhaps the Gestapo officer had not been entirely convinced by what he had heard. The Germans burned much of the town, but they arrived too late to find the 12th Cuirassiers. They had already moved on.

Seventh Army was now through the Vosges Mountains. Patch's G-2 reported, "In the Army's northern zone, resistance offered by remnants [of the] *553d* and *708th division*s appears to have collapsed."[48] Patch decided to commit the 45th Infantry Division, which had been resting under Seventh Army control, to reinforce Haislip's effort.[49]

The two French armored columns swung toward the Saverne Gap from the north and south and linked up in the town of Saverne shortly after 1400 hours on 22 November. There, French troops captured

Generalmajor Hans Bruhn, commander of the *553d Volksgrenadier Division*. A task force pushed westward through the gap and hit the German defenses at Phalsbourg from the rear, safe from most of the 88s ensconced in positions facing westward. German resistance ended when the 79th Infantry Division's 314th Infantry Regiment linked with the French troops on 23 November.[50]

Leclerc, however, was focused by this time on Strasbourg, not the gap. Capital of Alsace, the city was a political objective of the first order for French pride, albeit of no great military significance for control of the Alsatian Plain. Leclerc received authorization from XV Corps at 1130 on 22 November to advance on Strasbourg to assist VI Corps in its capture, or to take it himself if VI Corps could not do so.

Leclerc ordered Combat Commands L and V to strike toward the prize while Combat Command D finished up clearing the gap and Combat Command R pushed down the Vosges chain toward Mutzig. Combat Command L was to approach the city from the north while its running mate, now accompanied by an attached battalion of the 79th Infantry Division's 313th Infantry Regiment, executed a hook to arrive from the south. Sixteen forts controlled the avenues of advance; they were connected by an antitank ditch that stretched in an arc from the Rhine-Rhône Canal, south of the city, to the Rhine River, on the north. Speed was of the essence if Leclerc's troops were to bash through before the Germans could establish a coherent defense—to say nothing of one objective defined by Leclerc's orders: to force a surprise crossing of the Rhine River by capturing and traversing the Kehl bridge.

Though some of the soldiers were the worse for wear after having spent the previous evening drinking Alsatian wine, the French armor rolled out at 0715 on 23 November and charged across the flat ground toward the Rhine. The main columns of both combat commands encountered delaying resistance as they approached the antitank ditch and forts, which stopped them in their tracks.[51]

Leclerc, however, had sent Task Force Rouvillois of Combat Command L racing eastward from the gap to Brumath, on the Zorn River, where it turned southward toward the northern outskirts of Strasbourg.[52] In the morning, a detachment of Rouvillois' forces under Lieutenant

Briot, centered on tanks of the 12th Cuirassiers set off for Strasbourg with the tank *Evreux*, commanded by Sergeant Gélis, in the lead.

As the detachment approached Strasbourg, the number of German soft-skinned vehicles became more numerous. South of Mommenheim, a German car drove right up to the *Evreux*, its driver clearly unaware that French forces were in the area. When the horrible realization came, there was a squeal of brakes and the car came to a shuddering halt. Three Germans got out of the car and ran into a nearby building. The *Evreux*'s gunner put a round right into the car, leaving it a twisted hulk, but spared the soldiers. The gallop continued.

Somehow in the confusion, as the *Evreux* kept charging ahead, dealing death and destruction on every side, its crew progressively lost track of where the other friendly forces were. Suddenly Sergeant Gélis awoke to the fact that the only other French vehicle with him was a half-track carrying infantry. Between his tank and that half-track, they were only seventeen French souls. As Gélis was pondering this fact, his loader, a soldier named Mounier, reported that the tank was getting low on ammunition, and there were only eighteen rounds left for the main gun.

Did they have enough ammunition to fight whatever enemy lay ahead? Gélis wondered. They would deal with that problem when it came up, he decided. The driver accelerated hard and was soon in fifth gear heading for Strasbourg and the Pont de Kehl.

As this little column of two vehicles flew by, some German soldiers hidden behind the parapet of a bridge let loose two panzerfausts. The rounds flew harmlessly by, but the *Evreux* turned its turret toward them, the gunner punched the trigger and . . . nothing! A useless main gun *was* something to worry about. Suddenly, the cavalry rode over the hill in the form of the *Djemila*, one of the tanks that the *Evreux* had so cavalierly left behind. By this time the gunner and the loader on the *Evreux* had determined that the shell they had loaded would have to be removed out the muzzle of the gun. The *Djemila* sheltered the *Evreux* while its annoyed crew members got out and cleared the gun. As this was going on, the rest of the column drove up.

Now reunited, the French column pressed on, soon passing a sign: "Strasbourg 3km." At 0930 Lieutenant Briot's tanks entered the northern suburbs of Strasbourg. Nobody there was expecting the French army. One German officer walking quietly with his wife was cut down by a French machine gun. The detachment barreled toward the center of the city. In the heat of the moment, the crew of the *Evreux* lost track of what they were doing and ran out of main gun ammunition shooting Wehrmacht automobiles in front of Strasbourg's famous cathedral. No matter; where shells had served, now bluff and the last few hundred machine-gun rounds would have to do.

Meanwhile, a few hundred yards to the *Evreux*'s left, more French tanks, led by Lieutenant Briot, in the *Lisieux*, were pushing toward the Pont de Kehl. They came across seven antitank guns being prepared for action by their frantic crews. The French tanks paused, calmly took aim, and one by one destroyed these guns before they ever got off a round.

Briot had ordered the tank *Paris* to drive as fast as possible for the Pont de Kehl without stopping no matter what kind of fire it came under. This was a tough order, especially because just at this point *Paris*' main gun jammed and was useless for several minutes. Finally, the crewmen got the gun working again. They drove down a large avenue, then paused for a moment to dispatch some Germans. One crew member, Jean-Claude Henriot, suddenly saw a German antitank gun. "Forward! Antitank to the right!" Before the driver could react, a thunderous blow rocked the tank, then a second, then a third. By rights they should have been dead, but somehow the tank was intact, not even burning, and the crew was alive. *But for how long?* Henriot wondered as the tank scooted away. As they escaped, they happened to see a French jeep behind them get hit by a shell. The driver went flying out of the vehicle, his body in two pieces.

The *Paris* followed the *Lorient* and the *Fyé* through a tunnel. As the *Paris* emerged back into the light, German soldiers dropped grenades onto it, destroying all the gear that the soldiers had strapped to the outside of the tank. Henriot stuck his head out of the tank and looked back. He saw "corned beef everywhere" on the tank's back deck. This was infuriating but would not stop their progress.

The two lead tanks turned left onto a street that led straight to the Pont de Kehl. As the *Paris* turned the corner to follow them, Henriot was forced to duck back under cover. Germans were everywhere, letting loose with everything they had. A soldier in the back of the half-track that followed the *Paris* collapsed, shot dead. Moments later another soldier went down. The Shermans opened up, blowing big holes in the buildings on either side of the street. The Germans, wherever they were hidden, must have had to keep their heads down, but the fire did not abate. Panzerfaust rounds bounced off the tanks. Henriot opened fire on every window he could aim at.

The situation was untenable. The tanks and the half-track went into reverse and backed up. Scarcely had they started to move when the *Lorient* and the *Fyé* both came to a halt. Perhaps the German fire had disabled some critical parts, or perhaps it was just everyday mechanical breakdowns. Whatever it was, the *Paris* had to tow them both out, one by one. Miraculously, all the tanks made it out and managed to retreat back through the tunnel and take up defensive positions at an intersection on the other side.

Strasbourg was taken, but the French would not take the Pont de Kehl. The next day the *Paris* left Strasbourg heading south. "I never saw the cathedral," Henriot recalled. "Because, whatever they may tell you, you don't see much from inside a tank."

* * *

About 1300 hours, Combat Command V worked its way across the antitank ditch and into the southern quarter of Strasbourg, where the attached American infantry battalion took over the job of clearing the route of advance.

Leclerc's division had most of the city in hand by dark. Since 17 November his men had taken 12,500 prisoners and claimed to have killed 2,000 enemy troops, as well as to have destroyed 39 tanks and assault guns and 120 antitank guns (75mm and 88mm).[53]

VI CORPS ATTACKS

Major General Brooks commanded a very large corps, and his plan of attack took full advantage of that fact. From north to south, he disposed of the 100th, 3d, 103d, and 36th Infantry divisions, and on 19 November he received Combat Command A of the 14th Armored Division to use for exploitation. The 100th Division, going into battle for the first time, was to protect the left flank and maintain contact with XV Corps while the 3d Infantry Division struck northeastward through the Saales Pass to Strasbourg. The 103d Infantry Division was to take St. Dié and the nearby high ground, then advance southeastward. The 36th Infantry Division was to simulate preparations for an attack to the southeast to draw off the enemy, then hold a blocking line at Gérardmer and maintain contact with the French First Army.[54]

The corps had continued to press along its front before the official kickoff of the offensive in order to improve its positions. The 100th Infantry Division was able to advance unhindered east of Baccarat and around Raon L'Etape as the Germans fell back before XV Corps' assault. The 103d Infantry Division finally established firm control over all of the high ground west of St. Dié, and the Germans withdrew from the part of that town south of the Meurthe River. Otherwise, gains were tactical and hard-bought.[55]

During the wet pre-dawn darkness on 20 November, the 3d Infantry Division's 7th and 30th Infantry regiments quietly crossed the Meurthe River between Clairefontaine and St. Michel. At 0615, the division fired its most intense artillery preparation since Anzio, initially concentrated on the German main line of resistance only two hundred yards ahead of the hidden GIs.

By the time the infantrymen stormed the extensive German earthworks, the defenders from the *716th Infantry Division* were no longer in much of a fighting mood. Haislip's XV Corps to the north and de Lattre's army to the south were already achieving breakthroughs, and the outflanked German center opposite VI Corps was ready to cave in. The long-sought town of St. Dié, over much of which the maquis had effectively established control on 18 November, finally fell to the 103d Infantry Division on 22 November.[56]

As German forces clearly withdrew before his corps, Brooks late on 21 November ordered his divisions to organize fast-moving strike forces consisting of motorized infantry, tanks, tank destroyers, artillery, engineers, and reconnaissance to pound toward their objectives. The columns rolled out, delayed here and there for a day to extirpate resistance at one town or another, but the fall of Strasbourg had rendered the Vosges positions untenable. Captured Germans reported that morale had broken down, many units were short of food, and disorganization was rampant.

At Rothau, 3d Infantry Division troops captured the first SS-run concentration camp, complete with gas chambers disguised as showers and a crematorium. Sadly, the Nazis had already evacuated most of the prisoners.

On 26 November, 3d Infantry Division troops reached the Alsatian Plain at several points along the line, and the 103d Infantry Division made it the next day. The 36th Infantry Division by 28 November held the crest line in its sector and had begun to shell Germans moving about on the Alsatian Plain.[57]

Panzer Lehr Counterattacks

Hitler reacted to his misfortunes by ordering a counterattack to cut off the XV Corps with a stroke toward Sarrebourg from the north. The *Panzer Lehr* division was detached from strategic reserve on 21 November, and *Army Group H* was instructed two days later to transfer the *256th Infantry Division* to *Army Group G* and send it to Haguenau. Von Rundstedt told Berlin that these divisions would not be enough to salvage the situation and that he could prevent the loss of Alsace only if given another infantry and two panzer divisions from the strategic reserve. The next day he was informed that Hitler had no intention of diverting more divisions from his Ardennes offensive even at the cost of more territorial losses in the south. Von Rundstedt was to box in the penetration by holding the area south of Strasbourg around Colmar, preventing any American advance northward between the Vosges and the Rhine, and pressing the *Panzer Lehr* counterattack in the hope of cutting XV Corps' supply lines.[58]

Army Group G commanding general Balck at least professed to believe the attack would work. "The American XV Corps finds itself momentarily spread out over a wide area and in a moment of weakness," he wrote von Rundstedt. "*Panzer Lehr*'s counterattack . . . promises complete success."[59]

Indeed, the Third Army had only just taken Metz, sixty miles northwest of Saverne, on 22 November, and XV Corps commanding general Haislip's left was but thinly screened by the attached 45th Cavalry

Reconnaissance Troop. XV Corps knew trouble was coming: Prisoners warned that three divisions with twenty thousand men would attack south through Haguenau, and reconnaissance detected heavy road movement in the *First Army* area.

In light of this threat, Haislip had to keep the bulk of the 44th Infantry Division (reinforced by the 45th Division's 157th Infantry Regiment) west of the mountains and added the remainder of the 45th Infantry Division, which was released to him at midnight on 23–24 November. The 45th Infantry Division's 179th and 180th Infantry regiments took up positions on high ground, supported by tanks from the 191st Tank Battalion, and waited for what was to come. As elements of the 79th Infantry Division moved through the Saverne Gap, Haislip directed them toward Haguenau to secure his eastern flank.[60]

Panzer Lehr had required two days to move into position, because air attacks forced it to travel only in the dark, and even the lead elements were not into position to attack until late on 23 November. The division had been in reserve and rebuilding, and it was short one panzer regiment. The available panzer regiment—nominally thirty-four each of Mark IVs and Panthers—was missing a dozen Mark Vs because the new tanks had mechanical problems; only three of the panzergrenadier battalions had transportation; and the antitank battalion was short twenty-four Jagdpanzer IVs.

The panzers caught troopers from the 106th Cavalry Group eating a turkey dinner for Thanksgiving in Weyer, and *Panzer Lehr* easily recaptured Baerendorf and several other towns by dark. Almost out of fuel, the Germans settled in to await the arrival of their trains, but Balck demanded immediate forward movement. Running on fumes, *Panzer Lehr* pushed on and took Hirschland before halting in the face of heavy artillery and tank fire early the next morning.

Unknown to division commander *Generalmajor* Fritz Bayerlein, the *361st Volksgrenadier Division*, just to his west, was collapsing, and on 24 November, elements of the 4th Armored Division (part of Third Army's XII Corps) overran *Panzer Lehr*'s artillery positions and entered Baerendorf. *Panzer Lehr* had to redirect its attention to fighting this new threat, although part of the division continued to push south in accordance with the original mission. Von Rundstedt and Hitler acknowledged that the counterattack had no hope and ordered the division to break it off late on 25 November.[61]

GERMAN ATTACK AND DISASTER

De Lattre was delighted that his forces had reached the Rhine. There were many Allied armies in the west, but it was not the Canadian army that had first reached the Rhine, nor the combined airborne army, nor the British armies. Not even the several American armies had been first to the Rhine. That honor fell to de Lattre's beloved French First Army. One of de Lattre's main goals was to use his army to redeem the honor of France and thereby lay a solid foundation on which a fully reconstituted French army could take its rightful place in post-war Europe. Being first to the Rhine was a big step in that direction, something in which Frenchmen of all political persuasions could take pride. What de Lattre did not know was that his First Army would be the last of the Allied armies to *cross* the Rhine.

But that was still in the future. On the afternoon of 20 November, Colonel Caldairou's combat command turned north and attacked Mulhouse where the headquarters of *General der Infanterie* Wiese's *Nineteenth Army* was located. He scarcely had a large enough force to do this, but the French Shermans plunged into the city nonetheless. The French were unable to wipe out the defenders before dark fell, and the Germans damaged the bridges over the Rhine-Rhône Canal. The battle went on into the night, Caldairou's tankers finding help from the FFI. Caldairou personally contributed to the battle. During the night, he and his adjutant, armed only with pistols, approached the building that housed the German *Feldpost*. Inside they found twenty soldiers sorting the mail while upstairs another sixty soldiers slept. These dedicated postal workers thought the gunfire they had been listening to for several hours was merely a German exercise. All eighty of them obligingly surrendered to the two pistol-toting French officers. The battle for Mulhouse raged into the next day, drawing in virtually all of CC3, plus Moroccan infantrymen.

Meanwhile, on 20 November, the 1st DB's CC1, under Colonel Gruss, was engaged to the left of Caldairou's forces heading for Altkirch, south and west of Mulhouse. One of his columns had a nasty encounter with

Panther tanks from the *30th SS Division*, the same division that had lost two battalions of Ukrainians to mutiny back in August but was now part of Wiese's army reserve. Nonetheless, another French column entered Altkirch from a different direction, and the Germans fell back.

But other problems loomed as word came that German commandos and heavy tanks had driven south at the narrowest part of the French penetration and cut the major road running near the Swiss border. This road was the very lifeline of the 1st DB and its forces at Mulhouse and on the Rhine. This interruption forced CC2 to reverse course to deal with the setback, in which task they were aided by colonial troops and a combat command of the 5th DB, which was just coming up to enter the fight for the first time.[62]

By the end of 22 November, there had been progress elsewhere as well. The 2d DIM and supporting forces had attacked Belfort—which would still hold out for a few days.[63]

* * *

Back on 19 November, Monsabert's now denuded II Corps had also started to push forward to keep the Germans fixed in place. The 1st DFL and attached FFI units kept up stiff pressure on the Germans and supported the efforts of the 2d DIM. By 22 November, the 1st DFL had taken Giromagny.

Sadly, this effort came at the cost of an important leader. On 20 November, General Diego Brosset, the personable and effective commander of the 1st DFL, was visiting his frontline units. Driving faster than was safe, he suddenly spotted a mine in the road and swerved to avoid it. The vehicle went out of control on the slippery road and skidded into a river. The fast-flowing waters carried away his body and drowned him.

The result of these various actions was that by the evening of 22 November the French positions resembled a giant letter "U," with its base sitting on the Swiss border. To the west, the Germans faced the 1st DFL and below it the 2d DIM. The 5th DB held the western end of the base of the "U," and the 1st DB held the eastern end of the base and the west bank of the Rhine, roughly along a line connecting Seppois and Mulhouse. The Germans were in the middle, still in communication with their comrades to the north, but cut off from the Rhine and the Reich to the east by the 1st DB.

FIRST TO THE RHINE // 251

Rather than immediately pulling his troops rapidly northward and attempting to extricate them from this pocket, Wiese decided that he would go for broke. If he could drive to the Swiss border, he could cut the French forces in two, then destroy the isolated 1st DB, snatching at least a draw from the jaws of defeat. He began by dissolving the *LXXXIV Corps* and firing its commander. He also fired the commanders of the *189th* and *338th divisions* (the latter was the replacement for the even more unlucky commander who had been killed little more than a week before).[64]

Wiese formed a strike force with the *198th* and *269th Infantry divisions*, what passed for the best of his army, which he ruthlessly stripped off the Vosges front. To these he added the understrength *30th SS Division*, a marginal unit at best, and an armored unit. After the war, senior German officers recalled this latter as the *106th Panzer Brigade*, but lower-level German soldiers on the ground and French intelligence perceived it as somewhere between eight tanks and a brigade's worth of Jagdpanther tank destroyers, or Panther tanks, depending on which reports one chooses to believe. In any event, the armored unit arrived by train directly from Germany. (In the forthcoming battle, the French destroyed armored vehicles that had rolled out of the factory on 11 November 1944.) With these forces, Wiese struck hard toward Switzerland.[65]

The leftmost prong of Wiese's attack was the *30th SS Division*. It got as far as Friesen and the Seppois electrical station, near the Swiss border, and was stopped by the RCCC and a battalion of the 6th RTM.[66]

To the right of the *30th SS Division*, the *198th Infantry Division* struck, led by the *490th Grenadier Regiment* and some Jagdpanthers. The fighting was fierce. The Germans suffered considerable losses, particularly at the town of Suarce, where the French fiercely defended at the town cemetery. The *490th Grenadier Regiment* reached the Swiss border but was cut off there. Over the next few days, the regiment's position got more and more confined. Eventually, most of the men crossed into Switzerland.[67]

By 24 November, it was clear to Wiese that his efforts to cut the French in two had come to naught, and things would now get rapidly worse.[68] The French had punched through the German defenses at their far southern end and had progressed significantly into the Belfort Gap itself, but there had been no progress in the Vosges. De Lattre urged Patch to move southward, particularly with the 2d DB, and catch the Germans in the rear, but unyielding German resistance north of Colmar stopped VI Corps' efforts to comply. The French First Army would have to finish off Wiese by itself.

Instead, de Lattre and his corps commanders devised a maneuver under which I Corps forces at Mulhouse were to strike to the west and II Corps forces were to strike to the east. The two forces were to meet up at Burnhaupt and complete the encirclement. Meanwhile, French forces to the south were to continue to protect the 1st DB's precarious supply lines along the Swiss border and push north. This was all very well in the abstract. However, the division of II Corps positioned to move eastward was the 1st DFL, which was scheduled to assemble in the rear on 28 November for shipment to the Atlantic coast.

Monsabert could use the 1st DFL for only the first few days of the attack, but to mount the main effort he was forced to use the 2d DIM, by now moved to his control, and its attached armor. The operation was to kick off on 25 November. When the day dawned, II Corps discovered that the Germans had disengaged along most of the II Corps' front, though they still grappled with Guillaume's 3d DIA to the north. With his attacks to the south thwarted, Wiese had realized the danger of encirclement and was moving vigorously to forestall it, pulling back his forces to a more defensible position along the St. Nicolas and Suarcine rivers.

The Germans were not, however, pulling back in front of I Corps, though Béthouart thought for a time that they must be. The 1st DB in particular had to fight hard, losing several tanks and armored cars. Combat Command 4 of the 5th DB and a supporting FFI brigade, driving northwestward from the bottom of the French "U," also ran into stiff resistance from the *76th Infantry Regiment* of the *30th SS Division*, supported by self-propelled guns and other assorted units, all defending the village of Ballersdorf. The combat progressed slowly, seemingly yard by yard. In the end, the French took the town, and the Germans left behind twenty burned out armored cars of the twenty-four that they had brought to the town. This violent engagement did not prevent the French commander from detaching a subgroup during the battle and sending it onward to Dannemarie, the combat command's intended destination.

The French were intent on collapsing the German pocket. Combat Command 4, victorious in Ballersdorf, pressed on, harassing and mauling the *30th SS Division* as it went. At the eastern edge of the base of the "U," CC5 and foreign legionnaires were also destroying elements of this unfortunate division, whose members were suffering from "*Panzerpanik*." Their performance led one battalion commander to conclude an order with, "Cowards. I will not tolerate them in my battalion." This officer's complaints did no good. By the end of November, the division had taken some 80 percent losses among its infantrymen as a result of its collision with the French armor.[69]

In general, though elements of the *198th Infantry Division* once again briefly cut the French lifeline along the Swiss border, the French were making good progress against the German pocket from the south. The pincers meant to converge on Burnhaupt from the east and west were having a much harder time.[70]

Wiese now started to pull his forces north out of the pocket. Determined not to let him do it, on the evening of 27 November de Lattre urged his men forward. The next morning, the Germans slipped away from the St. Nicolas line pursued by Moroccans. The German lines elsewhere were weakening, probably in part as the result of withdrawals. At 1430 hours on 28 November, the junction was made at Burnhaupt. Ten thousand Germans were surrounded. "The battlefield is strewn with German corpses," de Lattre wrote to his superiors.[71]

STRASBOURG SECURED

Back in Strasbourg, sporadic artillery fire from east of the Rhine crashed into the city to support the remaining German troops. *Panzer Lehr*'s counterattack had provoked serious discussion back at Seventh Army headquarters of completely evacuating the city, but no action was taken.[72]

Much of the city's population was, in fact, German. Leclerc issued a memorandum on 24 November that read, in part: "The General is determined to use his authority to put an end to the activity of snipers in Strasbourg. . . . 1) For every French soldier killed in the city, five German hostages, chosen among those taken by the General, will be shot. 2) All snipers will be immediately shot. 3) Any person who gives shelter to a sniper or who helps him in any way will be shot."[73]

The remnants of the German garrison retreated into several forts the morning of 25 November, and the French set about reducing them with artillery fire followed by infantry assaults. By day's end, six hundred Germans, including the garrison commander, *Generalmajor* Vaterrodt, surrendered.[74]

That same day, an Allied special technical collection "T Force" subordinated to the 6th Army Group arrived in the city, where it found that much of the populace was hostile to the reestablished French rulers. On 27 November, the first American GIs from the 3d Infantry Division arrived to relieve Leclerc's division and take over the fighting to clear remaining German resistance from the west end of the Kehl bridge and the hippodrome area of the city. Franco-American relations quickly became tense when the Americans disavowed Leclerc's decree as being at variance with international law, and Seventh Army put up posters around the city stating that the "liberators" would respect the Geneva Convention—after the French military governor refused to publish that statement in the local newspaper.[75]

Hitler, meanwhile, on 26 November put *Reichsführer SS* Heinrich Himmler in command of all forces south of Bienwald along the upper Rhine with orders to prevent a river crossing.[76] He was to report directly to the Führer, access that might guarantee him the resources he needed to hang on at Colmar.

The Germans blew the last Rhine bridge at Strasbourg on 1 December and extracted their rear guard. The Allies held the Alsatian capital, but a substantial German bridgehead held out south of Strasbourg and north of the French First Army positions. Centered around Colmar, this pocket was supplied by two railroad and three pontoon bridges across the Rhine.

Combat Command A, 14th Armored Division, which had swung through the XV Corps zone, attacked southward from the vicinity of Erstein on 28 November in conjunction with a sweep by the French 2d DB, which the preceding day had been attached to VI Corps. The inexperienced American combat command ran into stiff resistance and counterattacks, and it was thrown back at all points with heavy losses. Leclerc's veterans advancing just to the east encountered similar trouble but held their ground.

Operations the next day by the 14th Armored Division made some-what better progress until stopped by blown bridges. The French armor pushed slowly southward for several more days, battling panzers and anti-tank guns and undergoing constant shelling from east of the Rhine River. After clearing villages as far south as Herbsheim and Benfeld at the cost of rising casualties, the division hunkered down to stay the night of 2–3 December, its offensive dash finally spent. Plans were already in the works for the 2d DB to be transferred to French First Army.[77]

The 103d Infantry Division and elements of the 36th Infantry Division, meanwhile, had reached the city of Selestat on 1 December, where the Germans held out for three days. All ideas of a quick entry into Colmar, farther south, evaporated; it looked as though the Germans intended to hang onto a bridgehead west of the Rhine after all. The capture of Selestat nevertheless completed the VI drive southward.[78]

THE SPOILING ATTACK THAT DID NOT COME

Sixth Army Group records suggest that Devers wanted Eisenhower to modify his strategic plan and exploit 6th Army Group's unexpectedly rapid advance to the Rhine by letting him cross the river. Seventh Army in October had formulated a plan to cross the Rhine at Rastatt, north of Strasbourg, preparatory to advancing on Stuttgart. Patch was confident that his men could manage the assault crossing—because he had available amphibious equipment sufficient for six infantry battalions—as well as breach the Siegfried Line defenses on the far bank. Any exploitation, how-ever, might require support from 12th Army Group.

Eisenhower, Devers, and Bradley met in Vittel on 24 November to discuss the matter. Devers argued that Seventh Army patrols across the Rhine had found the West Wall defenses empty, and he could best help Bradley by crossing the river and pushing northward. Bradley preferred that Devers closely support his operations west of the Rhine, and Ike con-curred after an evidently heated exchange with Devers. The 6th Army Group commander was bitter over what he saw as a lost opportunity, but Eisenhower was simply remaining true to his determination to destroy the German armed forces west of the Rhine first so that nothing substan-tial would be left to defend the Reich on the far side.

The interarmy-group boundary was therefore bent northeastward through the Siegfried Line on the west side of the Rhine, thereby reducing Bradley's frontage.[79] That same day, 6th Army Group instructed French First Army to reduce the Colmar Pocket and Seventh Army to hold its line along the Rhine and attack northward to assist Third Army, with XV Corps west of the Vosges and VI Corps between the mountains and the river.[80]

Recalling the German strategic imperative to hold roughly the West Wall line in order to launch the Ardennes offensive, this decision may have blocked a Rhine crossing by Devers' forces that would have forced the German High Command to at least weaken the reserve available for the attack in order to contain a politically damaging American breakthrough into the German heartland. Eisenhower, of course, had no idea that such an offensive was coming and made a rational decision given the information available to him.

*　*　*

Responding to the new orders, Haislip instructed the 45th Infantry Division, now rejoined by the 157th Infantry, to push northward on 27 November. While the 180th Infantry improved its defenses, the sister regiments advanced against mere screening forces. The division continued to gain ground, and the Germans had to divert precious mobile formations to stop the advance. The *25th Panzergenadier Division* moved in front of XV Corps, and resistance began to firm up from west to east on 28 November. The Germans pushed back with local counterattacks across the front on 29 November, when half-tracks and light armor signaled the presence of an armored reconnaissance battalion. By 30 November, the 45th Infantry Division found panzers supporting the defenses all across its front.[81]

Sixth Army Group during November had suffered 19,932 battle casualties (3,103 of whom were killed in action), about equally divided between the Seventh and First French armies.[82]

CHAPTER 9

STOPPED AGAIN

The long spearhead that had cleared the Saverne
Gap and reached the Rhine was a narrow lane,
tenuous and vulnerable on both its flanks.

—After-Action Report, Seventh Army

Eisenhower's directive of 24 November and the continued German occupation of the Colmar Pocket meant that Seventh Army would have to spend December attacking in opposite directions along the west bank of the Rhine, all the while coordinating with French First Army around the pocket. Devers realized that this situation was far from ideal, and effective 5 December he attached the French 2d DB and the 36th Infantry Division to French II Corps for operations aimed at Colmar, marking the first time that an American division would fight under French command.

If anyone thought the hard fighting was over with the cracking of the Vosges line—one intelligence report referred to the Germans' "hopeless tactical situation"—that illusion was soon shattered. The 6th Army Group's advance to the north put Seventh Army on a course toward the German-held fortifications on both sides of the frontier: the Maginot Line on the French side and the Siegfried Line on the German side. To the south, a German document captured in early December stated that troops west of the Rhine were considered expendable and were to hold out to the end.[1]

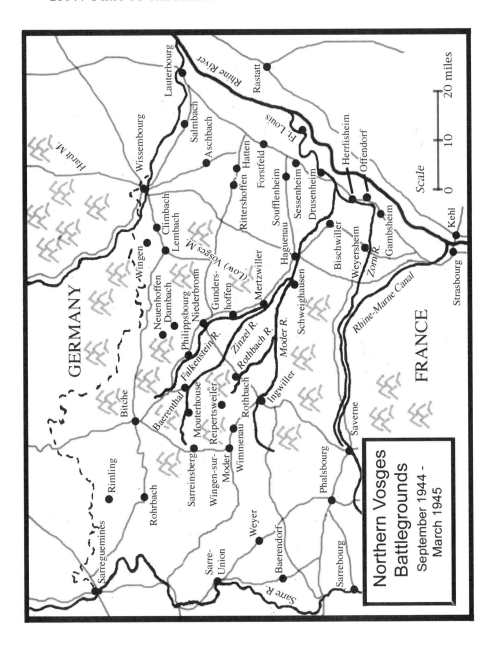

Northern Vosges
Battlegrounds
September 1944 -
March 1945

SEVENTH ARMY PUSHES NORTH

By 5 December, Seventh Army had reorganized its two corps for the drive northward toward the German border. XV Corps, west of the Vosges, now consisted of the 44th and 100th Infantry divisions plus the newly arrived 12th Armored Division. VI Corps controlled the 45th Infantry Division, on its left, and the 79th Infantry Division, abutting the Rhine River on its right, plus the 14th Armored and 103d Infantry divisions, in assembly areas, and the 3d Infantry Division, in Strasbourg. Major General Robert Frederick, formerly commanding the airborne task force and now at age thirty-seven the youngest division commander in the U.S. Army, had taken charge of the 45th Infantry Division after a mine explosion wounded Eagles on 30 November. The front ran roughly along the line of the Moder River except in the 45th Infantry Division's area, where a bridgehead around Mertzwiller reached almost to the Zinzel River.

After fighting *Nineteenth Army* since Operation Dragoon, Patch now faced the battered *First Army* instead. Patch's G-2 estimated that a mere fourteen thousand German troops held the line against seven American divisions. The *245th Infantry* and *256th Volksgrenadier divisions* defended the Alsatian Plain, and the *361st Volksgrenadier Division* held the eastern slopes of the mountains. These divisions were subordinated to *LXXXIX Corps*, which was also to receive the weak *21st Panzer Division* on 8 December to use east of the Vosges. *XC Corps*—Petersen's renamed *IV Luftwaffe Field Corps*—was shifted to the zone just to the west of *LXXXIX Corps*, at Bitche, where it took charge of the *25th Panzergrenadier Division* and elements of *Panzer Lehr* operating along the western slopes. The infantry formations were all well under their authorized strength.

The Germans had the weather and terrain on their side. Clouds, drizzling rain, and fog blocked American tactical air support except for five days during December, and the wet ground was cold enough to create misery for American troops in foxholes but not cold enough to freeze and support heavy vehicles. East of the Vosges in the VI Corps' area, the Haguenau Forest—eighteen miles long and six miles deep—transformed the rolling farmland of the Alsatian Plain into prime defensive ground. A three-mile corridor ran between the woods and the Rhine on the east; a six-mile gap between the forest and the mountains on the west was broken up by four small rivers and many villages. West of the mountain crest in the XV Corps area, the advance would be along the gradually sloped mountains themselves, which were cut by rivers running roughly east to west, including the Moder and the Zinzel.

The German frontier, also running roughly east to west, lay about ten miles distant along the entire front. Aerial photography showed little sign that the Germans were constructing fighting positions except at Bitche—the strongest point in the Maginot Line—which suggested that *First Army* intended to use the Maginot Line merely as a delaying position while strengthening the West Wall fortifications on the German side of the border, where intensive work was visible.[2]

VI Corps Reaches Germany

The VI Corps drive began as a two-division push up the Alsatian Plain, with the 45th Infantry Division on the left, adjacent to the mountains, and the 79th Infantry Division on the right, abutting the Rhine River. The drive did not begin auspiciously. A battalion of the *245th Volksgrenadier Division* counterattacked the 45th Infantry Division's 180th Infantry Regiment in Mertzwiller on 6 December with infantry and panzers and drove the GIs back across the Zinzel River. Unfazed, Brooks continued to position his pieces.

The 103d Infantry Division relieved the westernmost elements of the 79th Infantry Division on 7 December. That same day, the 94th Cavalry Reconnaissance Squadron—attached to the 79th Division—attacked the stubbornly held town of Gambsheim, a settlement just west of the Rhine, which had to be secured before the division could advance farther north. The 103d Infantry Division then relieved the 180th Infantry Regiment at Mertzwiller the night of 7–8 December.

The 79th Infantry Division pushed off on 9 December, when the 313th Infantry Regiment surprised the Germans at Bischwiller by attacking at dawn with no artillery preparation. As the GIs neared the town's bridge across the Moder, they spotted German soldiers readying to destroy the span. The Americans gunned down the Germans and raced across the bridge. The 314th Infantry Regiment had more trouble at

Haguenau, the tough nut in the forest that had to be cracked before the division could go any farther. The regiment needed two days to eject troops of the *256th Volksgrenadier Division* from the village.[3]

The 103d Infantry Division, meanwhile, attacked across the rain-swollen Zinzel into Mertzwiller and took the northern half of town for good. H. K. Brown, a machine gunner with the 410th Infantry, recorded in his diary, "[T]he corps artillery opened up—all forty-eight artillery pieces, plus heavy mortars and 4.2-inch chemical mortars. It was terrific—for the next twenty minutes or so the exploding artillery rounds traversing up and down the opposite bank, the town, the rail yard, the hills and woods, seemed to light up the whole area. As the barrage began to slacken, the rifle troops began to start across the railroad bridge." By dusk, the 103d Division was ready to drive toward Wissembourg, just shy of the border.[4]

The 45th Infantry Division's 157th Infantry struck at 0630 hours that same day and drove the Germans from Niederbronn by dark. It appeared that the Germans were pulling back in the area and leaving only outposts and delaying forces to impede the American advance. The next day, the 180th Infantry Regiment breached the German defenses along the Zinzel when it attacked through the 179th Infantry at Reichshoffen and Gundershoffen. The 157th Infantry, meanwhile, pushed ahead from Niederbronn.[5]

* * *

The Moder and Zinzel positions lost to them, the Germans on 11 December withdrew to their next delaying line, and the VI Corps divisions advanced, impeded by little but mines and occasional rear-guard actions. The 117th Cavalry Reconnaissance Squadron joined the corps and secured the west bank of the Rhine River as the 79th Infantry Division moved north. The 14th Armored Division, meanwhile, entered the line on 12 December and advanced toward the German border with little difficulty.[6] The division's informal history recorded, "There was no resistance, no firing; the men and women in the black Alsatian clothes lined the streets, crying and shouting and throwing kisses. . . ."[7]

Also on 12 December, the commander of the 158th Field Artillery Battalion called Col. Walter O'Brien, commanding the 157th Infantry

Regiment. "Colonel, from where we are, we can put a barrage across the border. Say the word, and we can toss a concentration into GERMANY!"

"What are you waiting for?" asked O'Brien. "Fire away!"[8] The 45th Infantry Division had been fighting toward this day since Sicily.

LXXXIX Corps offered its next stiff delaying action at the Maginot Line. The Germans fought back against the 45th Infantry Division on 14 December near Lembach, a heavily fortified city in the heart of the former French defenses. Rather than become trapped in urban fighting, the Germans set up their lines along the north side of the Lembach-Wingen valley and left only a few strongpoints to be rooted out in both those towns. The 45th Infantry Division needed only twenty-four hours to push back the defenders.[9]

Indeed, 14 December revealed a growing German determination to fight back all across the VI Corps front. The 103d Infantry Division ran into renewed resistance at Climbach, where elements of the *21st Panzer Division* appeared for the first time. The 14th Armored Division found determined defenders in Riedseltz, and the 79th Infantry Division dealt with its own scrap at Lauterbourg.

The 79th Division's 315th Infantry Regiment put its first patrols into Germany on 15 December at Scheibenhardt.[10] Patrols from the 45th Infantry Division crossed the border early in the afternoon.[11]

* * *

Before dawn on 16 December, Hitler launched a three-pronged offensive along a seventy-five-mile front in the Ardennes. In the north, the SS-heavy *Sixth Panzer Army* struck toward the Meuse River and Antwerp. In the center, the *Fifth Panzer Army* attacked toward Brussels. The *Seventh Army* pushed forward in the south to reel out a line of infantry divisions to protect the flank of the operation. *Army Group G* had achieved its objective: Nowhere had the Americans or French penetrated the West Wall before the offensive could be launched.

All German troops in the VI Corps zone were now ordered to fall back into the Siegfried Line.[12] *Army Group G* commanding general Balck had new orders to prevent any breakthrough on his front, pin as many American units in place as possible, and watch for the withdrawal of American forces for use in the Ardennes. In the last case, previously designated German units would also shift northward. If the American line pulled back, he was to pursue.[13]

The 45th Infantry Division crossed the border in force near Bobenthal and Nothweiler, just west of the point where the frontier parts ways with the Lauter River and the West Wall defenses consequently lay somewhat deeper inside Germany. The 103d Infantry Division simultaneously entered Germany north of Wissembourg, where the Lauter ran inside France for several miles, while the 14th Armored Division occupied that town and dispatched a small force across the frontier near Schweighoffen.

The 79th Infantry Division put patrols across the Lauter River the night of 15–16 December, and during the day constructed a Bailey bridge and moved tanks to the north bank near Berg. The 315th Infantry Regiment crossed at Scheibenhardt against no opposition.[14]

VI Corps commanding general Brooks was optimistic and told his commanders to "go rugged" and find what he anticipated would be weak spots in the German line. Patch called Brooks that evening to pass along the news that the Germans had launched their counteroffensive in the Ardennes. "Now we want to get just as aggressive as humanly possible," instructed Patch.

"That's what I am doing," replied Brooks. "I have given instructions to everybody to turn loose tomorrow." Brooks called Brig. Gen. Albert Smith at the 14th Armored Division headquarters the morning of 17 December and reiterated, "Be on your toes and ready to drive right in."[15]

But reports arrived in growing numbers that the Germans were resisting firmly from Siegfried Line positions, and fresh troops appeared to be available to the enemy. The VI Corps' advance stopped abruptly in the face of a pillbox- and bunker-studded line that ingeniously exploited terrain to create a solid barrier. The *245th Infantry Division* barred the way of the 45th and 103d Infantry divisions between Bobenthal and Bundenthal; the *21st Panzer Division* manned the line opposite the 14th Armored Division, where the terrain was relatively open; and the *256th Infantry Division* opposed the 79th Infantry Division. As Seventh Army recorded in its after-action report, "Against these forces entrenched in the

Siegfried Line, the VI Corps prodded and attacked for five days, for the most part ineffectively and, as it turned out, in vain."[16]

XV Corps Has a Bitche of a Time

On the morning of 5 December, Haislip's XV Corps, like VI Corps, confronted an enemy who had seemingly recovered from the collapse of his Saverne Gap defenses. During the preceding week, the 44th Infantry Division, on the corps' left, and the 100th Infantry Division, on the right, had eked out but a few miles northward against suddenly ferocious German resistance. Now the 44th Division was embroiled in a stiff fight at Ratzwiller that lasted into the next day and resulted in only the shortest breathing space. On 7 December, the 44th Infantry Division ran into heavy resistance again at Maierhof, Petit Rederching, and Montbronn.

The 100th Infantry Division had been tied up in bitter fighting at Wingen for three days and received a pleasant surprise on 5 December, when the Germans pulled out toward Lemberg. The 399th Infantry Regiment approached Lemberg late on 6 December to find that Jerry had settled in to fight back again.

On 8 December, Maj. Gen. Roderick Allen's 12th Armored Division entered the line on the corps' left—actually in the Third Army zone, to relieve the exhausted 4th Armored Division—and charged north along the boundary between Seventh and Third armies. By 10 December, XV Corps had reached positions only four miles southwest of Bitche.

The Germans had no intention of fighting a mere delaying action at the Maginot Line west of the Vosges. They intended to hold the ground.

The 44th Infantry Division reached Sierthal on 11 December, but its advance the next day stopped under crushing artillery fire from Fort Simserhof, in the Maginot Line's "Ensemble de Bitche." Four large interconnecting forts ran along the border in the stretch before the 44th and 100th Infantry divisions, each supported by a constellation of smaller bunkers. Unlike the defenses along most of the Maginot Line, these had had fields of fire into France as well as Germany, and they had held out in 1940 until the armistice. Troops from the *25th Panzergrenadier Division* manned the western portion of the line, and the *361st Infantry Division* occupied the eastern stretch. Planners assessed that the capture of Fort

Simserhof by the 44th Infantry Division and Fort Schiesseck by the 100th Infantry Division would suffice to unhinge the German line.

On 14 December the 44th Infantry Division's 71st Infantry Regiment captured the first pillboxes, which covered the gap between Forts Simserhof and Schiesseck. Two battalions held the ground for four days against counterattacks while the GIs scouted out the next set of bunkers. Engineers and tank destroyers went to work on the personnel and ammunition entrances, blowing holes through which Bangalore torpedoes, satchel charges, and phosphorus grenades were dropped, and the diesel power plant was destroyed.

XII Tactical Air Command conducted close-support bombings against the fortifications on 17 December, and that evening American troops penetrated the fort and explored twenty-three flights of stairways. The next day, division artillery pounded the Germans with remarkable effectiveness: Three pillboxes were so badly damaged that the enemy abandoned them. Deep in the bowels of the fort, where the Germans were fighting back in the tunnels, the engineers blew up the stairway and the ventilation system.

By the time the division launched its general assault on the northern pillboxes of Fort Simserhof on 19 December, it encountered no resistance. Prisoners reported that morale had crumbled after the electricity and ventilation were knocked out, and the Germans had retreated north of Hottviller.[17]

* * *

The 100th Infantry Division plan issued on 12 December called for the 398th Infantry Regiment to breach the Maginot Line at once if it were only partially defended. The regiment's 1st Battalion moved out of the woods west of Bitche on 15 December and was pinned down by overwhelming fire from the fortifications. Clearly, this was going to take some work.

The 100th Infantry Division used the same general approach to reduce Fort Schiesseck that the 44th Infantry Division was employing just to the west. The division pounded the Germans with air attacks, tank and tank-destroyer direct fire, and indirect fire from its organic artillery—backed by five additional artillery battalions, including 240mm howitzers and 8-inch guns—for thirty-six hours before moving in on 17 December. After advancing under observed shellfire and dispatching a lone remaining machine-gun turret, the GIs from the regiment's 3d Battalion quickly blasted their way into the first fortifications with satchel charges. The defenses fell on 20 December, and subsequently the Americans concluded that no more than 350 German troops had ever occupied the bunkers, albeit with orders (ignored, as usual) to fight to the last man.[18]

THE FIRST CRACK AT COLMAR

On 2 December, Devers gave the 2d DB and the U.S. 36th Infantry Division to de Lattre and his First Army. At the same time, however, the 1st DFL was detached, imminently to be sent to the Atlantic coast to help collapse the pockets of Germans there—an operation that, though far away, was to be under Devers' overall command. Moreover, the French also now received responsibility for the northern sector facing the Colmar Pocket manned by the two divisions transferred from Seventh Army. The net result of these changes was that the French position became, if anything, slightly weaker.[19]

Nonetheless, de Lattre intended to have a crack at collapsing the Colmar Pocket. In the south, Béthouart's I Corps was to use the 9th DIC, 4th DMM, and 2d DIM, all supported by General Sudre's 1st DB and one combat command of the 5th DB, to clear the banks of the Rhine and attempt to break out to Brisach. Meanwhile, Monsabert's II Corps, comprising the 2d DB (with an attached parachute regiment), the U.S. 36th Infantry Division, Guillaume's 3d DIA, the goumiers, and a combat command from the 5th DB, was to push generally toward Kaysersberg, then toward Colmar, then toward Brisach to link up with I Corps.

Unfortunately, the weather was frightful, so the French offensive had to be delayed two days. It finally kicked off on 7 December. I Corps started, moving out from its left flank to approach the city of Thann. The engineers performed miracles of bridging unusually broad rivers, but the flooding and strong German defenses prevented any serious advances. Moreover, when the French finally did get to Thann, they faced a particularly serious fight. Thann contains a spectacular Gothic church, which the French were eager to preserve, and the artillery had been forbidden to fire on the city. Thus, the infantry and armor had to overcome German defenses that had not been at all softened up before their arrival.

I Corps was making little progress. On 12 December, de Lattre acceded to a request from Béthouart for a few days' rest for his corps.

Things had gone no better in the II Corps' sector. In fact, the Germans had launched a spoiling attack against the 36th Infantry Division on 6 December, the day before the French offensive was started. Five German divisions plus an armored brigade faced Monsabert's corps, enough strength to bring the French effort to a halt. By 11 December, even Monsabert, who was usually aggressive to a fault, was forced to scale back his plan.

For the next few days, the French and their attached American division had to fend off several substantial counterattacks. They were successful every time, but each German blow took its toll, keeping the French off balance and further tiring their forces. Intelligence showed that the Germans were sending reinforcements from all over the Reich to the Colmar Pocket. One such attack even led to a company of the 4th RTT being cut off in the mountains for four days surrounded by Germans, having inadequate medical supplies, and ultimately running out of ammunition. It was protected in the end only by three feet of snow, which kept not only the Germans but their French rescuers at bay.

On 12 December, in the midst of the German counterattacks, de Lattre realized that the offensive was going nowhere. Perhaps, he thought, if he scaled back the plan and gained more forces, he would be able to make some progress, even if the Colmar Pocket would not be crushed as soon as the Allies had hoped. He wrote to Devers asking him to return the 1st DFL. Devers acceded immediately to the request, probably because SHAEF itself was no longer pushing the Atlantic operations as such a high priority. Accepting that concession, de Lattre then wrote another letter to Devers asking for two more infantry divisions. This letter was dated 16 December, coincidentally just as the Germans were launching their Ardennes offensive. Devers' response two days later was hardly sympathetic. In fact, Devers ordered de Lattre in no uncertain terms to push the Germans back across the Rhine by 1 January.[20]

After launching the Ardennes offensive, the Germans kept up the pressure on the 6th Army Group with numerous small attacks in Alsace against the French. The French also received intelligence reports, including numerous alarmist articles in the Swiss press, indicating a German buildup opposite their positions in Alsace. The French First Army's G-2, Lieutenant Colonel Carolet, correctly assessed that these were merely efforts using double agents and other means to hold the 6th Army Group in place to prevent it from sending forces to the Ardennes. An order had, in fact, been given at least within the German *LXIV Corps* and probably much more broadly: "By an incessant activity of shock detachments we must deceive the enemy and make him believe that we intend to attack. By a marked activity, it is necessary to prevent the enemy from withdrawing formations from in front of the *Nineteenth Army* to engage them elsewhere."[21]

Given the state of the French forces and the German efforts to hold down the allies in Alsace, Devers probably knew that the destruction of the Colmar Pocket was not in the cards for what was left of 1944. In any event, it did not happen. De Lattre's two corps did go back into action, and though Monsabert's corps got within five miles of Colmar at one point, the overall effects were negligible. The Germans fought ferociously, repeatedly going on the tactical offensive. By 22 December, Devers realized the futility of the operations and agreed with de Lattre that the next real effort against the Colmar Pocket would take place in January.[22]

Back on a Shoestring

Eisenhower, at a meeting of his senior officers at the 12th Army Group Headquarters in Verdun on 19 December, ordered Devers to halt offensive operations and take responsibility for much of Third Army's sector to fill in behind Patton's counterattack against the growing German salient in the Ardennes. Devers had to cover an additional thirty miles of front without receiving any additional divisions with which to do so. Eisenhower followed up his verbal orders with a cable to his commanders in which he announced his intention to launch counterattacks against the enemy's flanks in the Ardennes. "I am prepared," he added, "to yield ground in areas unessential to this main purpose. . . . The Southern Group of Armies will be prepared to yield ground rather than endanger the integrity of their forces."[23]

Seventh Army had to surrender to Patton's Third Army two hundred men from each regiment of the newly arrived 42d, 63d, and 70th Infantry divisions. More ominously, SHAEF informed 6th Army Group that it could expect few men, if any fresh manpower, for the next several weeks, or perhaps a month or more. Seventh Army responded and established a crash program to convert to riflemen 10 percent of infantry support, cavalry, combat engineer, chemical mortar, and divisional artillery personnel. The original three Dragoon assault divisions were given priority for allocation of junior officers, because they were judged to have exhausted their supply of officer material in the enlisted ranks during two years of sustained combat. But there was no easy fix for the shortage of tank crews. The losses suffered by the 14th Armored Division alone consumed all available replacements.

The supply situation also tightened again. Seventh Army held less than a day's supply of gasoline in its depots as of 17 December, and a strict rationing program was introduced that allowed the army to build up a slim reserve equivalent to 2.7 day's usage by the end of the month. At year's end, Seventh Army was short nearly a hundred tanks, assault guns, and tank destroyers, or roughly two battalions' worth of armor. Shelter halves and raincoats—critical needs for GIs living in the open—were in short supply, although the stock of winter uniforms and shoepacs (arctic overshoes) had almost caught up with demand. Ammunition shortages, at least, eased somewhat when Third Army transferred control over a dump at Insming containing nine thousand tons of munitions.[24]

CHAPTER 10
OPERATION *NORDWIND*

The German Army struck in the closing hours
of the old year with fanatical force.

—*Report of Operations, Seventh Army*

Six days into the Ardennes offensive, the German High Command
ordered *Army Group G* to exploit the thinning out of American lines
along the southern end of the western front by retaking the Saverne Gap
and cutting off much of Seventh Army. Code-named Operation
Nordwind (Northwind), the attack was to take the form of two pincers,
the first formed by *General der Infanterie* Obstfelder's *First Army* driving
southward from the area of Bitche, and the second by a northward thrust
out of the Colmar Pocket by elements of *Nineteenth Army*. *Nineteenth
Army* since 10 December had been subordinated to the newly created
Army Group Upper Rhine, commanded by *Reichsführer SS* Heinrich
Himmler, which controlled forces in the Colmar Pocket and in defenses
along the east bank of the Rhine. The anticipated meeting point was
Sarrebourg, just west of the gap.[1]

Shortly after the beginning of the Battle of the Bulge, the Ultra signals
intercept system revealed that the Germans were preparing a secondary
offensive against the 6th Army Group. Tidbits, such as aerial reconnaissance orders to the Luftwaffe, identified possible river-crossing sites, and
by the last week of December, the *First Army*'s dispositions were fully
known. The information was strong enough for Devers' intelligence officers to conclude that the main German attack would hit XV Corps west of

the Vosges, while VI Corps would confront a smaller effort on the Alsatian Plain. The intercepts did not reveal German plans to attack out of the Colmar Pocket or across the Rhine near Gambsheim, but locally gathered information pointed in that direction.[2] French intelligence, though not entrusted with Ultra materials, was coming to a similar conclusion.[3]

Responding to the intelligence developments, SHAEF ordered Devers on 26 December to earmark an armored and an infantry division, plus a corps headquarters, for SHAEF reserve, and he so flagged the 12th Armored and 36th Infantry divisions. These formations, plus the French 2d DB, which was being transferred back to the Seventh Army sector, were to be ready to counterattack any German penetrations and were available for use only on Devers' orders.[4] Eisenhower's operations officer, Lt. Gen. "Pink" Bull (promoted in late October), orally passed to Devers' staff Eisenhower's instructions to shorten the 6th Army Group front by establishing its main position along the line of the Vosges Mountains, instructions Devers passed to Patch that evening.[5]

Devers told de Lattre of Eisenhower's orders at a meeting the morning of 27 December, and the French commander was reported to be in accord with Devers' instructions except for a few minor details. On 28 December, Devers issued a letter of instructions that outlined a series of planned defensive positions, the last of which ran along the eastern slopes of the Vosges Mountains.[6] At this time, by Devers' own private admission, he and Patch disagreed with Eisenhower's plan to retreat before any German blow had been struck and were slow-rolling the execution of SHAEF's instructions.[7]

Foreshadowing problems to come, the SHAEF deputy operations officer contacted 6th Army Group headquarters on 30 December to say that General Alphonse Juin, the French chief of staff, was most anxious that Strasbourg be held and had offered three FFI "divisions" for use in the city's defense. Devers sent an inspection team to Paris to ascertain the combat value of these purported divisions. (The team's conclusion on 6 January would be that the FFI units were not capable of combat operations.) Devers was clearly concerned with French staying power. He cabled SHAEF the next day: "The French First Army is short approximately 8,000 infantry replacements, is composed largely of colonial troops who present a serious morale problem due to the shortage of officers with experience in handling colonial troops, and is badly in need of complete refitting and retraining. To bolster this army, I am leaving the U.S. 3d Infantry Division with it for the time being. . . ."[8]

* * *

The 6th Army Group headquarters on 30 December transmitted a message to Patch's headquarters warning that "a hostile attack against your flank west of Bitche may force you to give ground from your main position. . . . [R]econnaissance and organization of a reserve battle position will be instituted without delay along high ground on the general line: Hill east of Landroff-Benestroff-Sarre-Union-Ingwiller."[9] This line ran parallel to the French-German border at a distance of roughly ten miles to the south, nearly entirely in the XV Corps zone.

Seventh Army held an eighty-four-mile-long front from its junction with Third Army a few miles west of Saarbrücken to the Rhine, as well as the west bank of the river down to Strasbourg. Haislip's XV Corps had arrayed from west to east the 103d, 44th, and 100th Infantry divisions, and the 106th Cavalry Group screened the far left flank. Brooks' VI Corps manned the ten-mile line in the lower Vosges abutting XV Corps with the brigade-sized Task Force Hudelson. The 45th and 79th Infantry divisions held the stretch to the Rhine, backed by the 14th Armored Division less one combat command. Task Forces Harris, Herren, and Linden, composed of infantry regiments of the 63d, 70th, and 42d Infantry divisions, respectively, were strung along the length of the Rhine in Seventh Army's sector and were deemed "insufficiently trained for full-scale combat operations."[10]

* * *

On 31 December, the 1st DFL was in the process of relieving the 2d DB, the northernmost French division, deployed adjacent to the American positions. As the DFL's staff typed up the operations order for New Year's Day, the words they read were ominous. The enemy had been significantly reinforced in the Colmar Pocket and probably had fifteen thousand infantry alone, though aside from a few SS units these were generally troops of mediocre quality. Moreover, the order noted, on the other side of the Rhine about a dozen German divisions, "certainly reinforced with modern tanks," had gathered. The 1st DFL "may therefore expect the possibility of an enemy offensive."[11]

* * *

On New Year's Eve, Patch visited the XV Corps command post and told Haislip and Brooks, who had traveled from the VI Corps headquarters, that they could expect an enemy attack in the early hours of the new year. He related that plans were already in train to move the Seventh Army's command post from Saverne to Lunéville, which his operations report characterized as "a more central position for the direction of both XV and VI corps defense"—though, in fact, it was far less central and just happened to be beyond the reach of the planned German pincers. Both corps were to hold their line until ordered to withdraw, at which time they were to fight delaying actions as they slowly pulled back to the second line of defense.[12]

At 1400 hours, Brooks ordered all his divisions and task forces to instruct troops that there would be no New Year's celebrations of any kind. Ten minutes later, word was passed to put troops on alert for enemy action and to send out stronger and more numerous patrols than usual.[13]

Stopping the Northern Pincer Arm

The German plan required that two *First Army* infantry attack groups capture the key road centers that the mobile divisions needed to launch their high-speed drive toward Sarrebourg. *Attack Group I* (essentially SS *Gruppenführer* Max Simon's *XIII SS Corps*), consisting of the *19th* and *36th Volksgrenadier divisions* and the *17th SS Panzergrenadier Division*, was to strike west of Bitche toward Rohrbach, where it would link up with the main attack. According to *Army Group G* operations officer *Oberst (I.G.)* Horst Wilutzky, Hitler viewed this as the main thrust, but the army group staff believed that this attack was doomed to fail at the Maginot Line and saw it mainly as a feint to increase the chances of success farther east. Nevertheless, Hitler saw to it that three massive Jagdtiger tank destroyers and some seventy assault guns—nearly all those available to *First Army*—were assigned to the *17th SS Panzergrenadier Division*, although many of the assault guns were in such poor condition that they could not be used. The division also received an additional battalion of panzergrenadiers.

Attack Group II was to execute what *Army Group G* privately viewed as the main drive east of Bitche aimed toward Wingen-sur-Moder, for which the High Command allocated *General der Infanterie* Hoehne's *LXXXIX Corps*, controlling the *361st* and *256th Volksgrenadier divisions*, plus the *6th SS Mountain Division* (in transit from Denmark) and Petersen's *XC Corps*, incorporating the *559th* and *257th Volksgrenadier divisions* and battle groups from two more. The *25th Panzergrenadier* and *21st Panzer divisions*, which formed the *XXXIX Panzer Corps*, were held in *First Army* reserve, ready to exploit any breakthrough.

One hour before midnight on 31 December, a cable arrived at *Army Group G* revealing that Hitler had ordered an immediate expansion of the operation. Hitler assigned to the *XXXIX Panzer Corps* additional formations that were to concentrate just west of the Rhine behind *First Army* lines. These included the *10th SS Panzer Division, 11th Panzer Division, 7th Airborne Division*, and elements of two infantry divisions, plus additional artillery. Hitler also ordered *LXXXII Corps*, tentatively assigned two or three infantry divisions, to gather east of the Rhine for employment only if the drive around Bitche failed; in the event of success, the corps would be used farther west along with *XXXIX Panzer Corps* to recapture Metz.[14]

* * *

In the XV Corps zone, the assault by the German *Attack Group I* concentrated its icy fury on the lines of the 44th Infantry Division, which ran from Sarreguemines to just west of Rimling.[15] The division's main line of resistance, manned by all three regiments, occupied the commanding terrain along the Blies River. Within a few hours of the first German probes, the entire division front was deeply embroiled in fighting.

The *XIII SS Corps* attacked without artillery preparation, confident that it would surprise the Americans. Thanks to a bright moon, outposts in the 71st Infantry Regiment's zone, on the division right wing, spotted the attackers about midnight, and the *36th Volksgrenadier Division*, in the *XIII Corps* center, stumbled into a killing zone resembling the Union attack at Fredericksburg. Machine guns, rifles, mortars, and artillery lashed the screaming attackers, and German dead piled up in what the GIs came to call "Morgue Valley."

At some points along the line, the sheer weight of attacking bodies drove several companies out of their positions. In almost every case, a counterattack supported by the 749th Tank Battalion restored the main line, in part because the Germans had no armor support of their own. Divisional and corps artillery, meanwhile, pounded German reinforcements moving forward. The appearance of a handful of assault guns and half-tracks from the *17th SS Panzergrenadier Division*, attacking on the German left wing, during the afternoon did nothing to restore German momentum. That night, the 71st Infantry pulled back in good order to a second prepared line of defense. (The regiment over the next two days faced further German attacks, but a combat command from Leclerc's 2d DB and two infantry battalions from the 255th Infantry Regiment arrived on 3 January to guarantee that the Germans achieved no breakthrough.)

On the 44th Division's left wing, the 114th Infantry Regiment, using concentrated artillery fire, crushed an attempt by the *19th Volksgrenadier Division* to break out of a small bridgehead south of the Blies River. The 324th Infantry, in the center, turned back three assault crossings of the Blies.[16]

The 100th Infantry Division, which held the sector east of the 44th Division, initially was straddled by the German operation. The 397th Infantry Regiment, on the left flank, defended Rimling against *Attack Group I*, while the 399th Infantry Regiment, on the right, abutted the *Attack Group II* drive against Task Force Hudelson.[17]

Colonel D. H. Hudelson's command was doomed to a mismatch from the start. The task force was built around Combat Command Reserve (CCR) of the 14th Armored Division, less the tank battalion that would normally give CCR its main punch. Instead, the light armored vehicles of the 94th and 117th Cavalry Reconnaissance squadrons, backed by Company B, 645th Tank Destroyer Battalion, were supposed to do. Hudelson had but the 62d Armored Infantry Battalion to hold ground, and a single company of chemical mortars for extra indirect-fire support.[18] Late on 31 December, the 1st Battalion, 540th Engineer Regiment, was attached to the task force to fight as infantry.[19] For the veterans of Task Force Butler in the 117th Cavalry Squadron, the mix looked somewhat familiar, but instead of a mission to exploit against a disorganized foe, Task Force Hudelson was supposed to stop a thoroughly prepared enemy.

The *LXXXIX Corps' 361st* (on the German right) and *256th Volksgrenadier divisions* struck southeastward from Bitche without a preparatory barrage. Because of the broken and forested terrain, the

Germans needed to quickly reach the north-south roads behind the Americans in order to approach their objectives. They intended to bypass any strongpoints and were fortunate to have received a few assault guns to support the infantry.[20]

At 0015 hours, the 2d Platoon of Troop B, 117th Cavalry Squadron, reported large numbers of enemy soldiers outside its wire, and the German attack developed rapidly from there. By 0100 hours, most of the squadron was heavily engaged, and the German grenadiers, screaming and shouting, pressed forward with no apparent concern for the minefields and wire entanglements in their path. Despite supporting artillery fire called down within twenty-five yards of the American line, the cavalrymen gave way under the crushing pressure, and the squadron ordered a general withdrawal to a new line at about 0330.

The squadron commander contacted Hudelson to report the critical situation and was told that the 19th Armored Infantry Battalion had been assigned and would come to his aid. By the time the armored infantrymen arrived at about 1000, German infiltration of the cavalry's positions was so advanced that they could do little but plug some of the holes in the line.

The 62d Armored Infantry Battalion similarly was hit around midnight. The 14th Armored Division's history records, "A trip flare went off in front of [Company A's] outposts and there, 50 yards away, was a German patrol, crawling across the snow in white camouflage suits. The infantrymen had been holding their guns inside their clothing to keep them warm enough so they would not freeze and cease functioning; now they were ripped out. The chatter of a single machine gun, first, then instantly all the guns slashed through the night. . . . The Germans attacked, yelling and screaming, firing automatic weapons. It was an attack by madmen." The battalion found its positions at the risk of encirclement by German infantry supported by tanks, as did the 94th Cavalry Reconnaissance Squadron.

Once he realized the gravity of the situation, Hudelson ordered the entire task force to fall back on a prepared delaying line around Sarreinsberg and Reipertsweiler—where his troops subsequently held firm until relieved. His withdrawal nonetheless opened the door for the Germans to press toward Baerenthal and Phillipsbourg. The 117th

Cavalry Reconnaissance Squadron lost so many of its vehicles during the retreat that VI Corps conducted an investigation of the unit's conduct.[21]

The 540th Engineer Regiment's Company A had been sent north from Baerenthal to find elements reportedly cut off by the Germans but found the advancing *361st Volksgrenadier Division* instead. Lieutenant Albert Philips reported:

> About 1200, one of my outposts observed German troops moving south down the draw. I notified [company commanding officer Capt. Robert] Irvin, and a few minutes later he gave me the order to withdraw and take up a defensive position at [a] road junction. . . . We were fired on as we were withdrawing, and we killed or wounded several of the enemy by rifle fire. We reached our new position about 1230 and joined with the 2d and 3d platoons in forming a line.
>
> About 5 minutes later, the enemy was advancing on us from the hills, at the same time throwing lots of [machine-gun] and mortar fire at us. My .50-caliber [machine gun], which was on the half-track, knocked down quite a number of the enemy, and a couple of minutes later the 'track was blown up by enemy fire. Two American [tank destroyers] were setting up . . . and when they observed enemy tanks coming down the road, they immediately withdrew. . . . About 1240, due to a superior enemy force, we were forced to withdraw toward our bivouac area. The enemy machine-gunned and dropped mortars on us for nearly a mile before we were out of range.[22]

Task Force Hudelson's retreat forced the 100th Infantry Division to bend its right flank back to the south and commit a battalion of its 255th Infantry Regiment to hold the extending line. That night, the 36th Infantry Division's 141st Infantry Regiment relieved the Century Division troops in the sector abutting VI Corps.[23]

The 45th Infantry Division, which held positions east of Task Force Hudelson, experienced only minor trouble on 1 January in the form of an attack on Dambach by poorly briefed and hence disoriented troops from the *256th Volksgrenadier Division*. The situation was cleared up by dusk. Brooks attached to the division the 70th Infantry Division's 275th Infantry (part of Task Force Herren), which assembled near Niederbronn and occupied defensive positions around Baerenthal and Phillipsbourg on the left flank of the 45th Division. The 79th Infantry Division's 313th Infantry (less the 3d Battalion) likewise assembled near Reichshoffen and moved into positions on high ground north of Reipertsweiler at the far left wing of the 45th Division's rapidly expanding sector. The 1st Battalion from each of the 79th Division's 314th and 315th Infantry regiments were also attached to the 45th Division as its reserve, and after dark the 36th Engineer Combat Regiment took over the sector of the 179th Infantry on the division's right wing.[24] Major General Frederick now commanded what amounted to a disjointed corps.

In response to the German gains, Frederick moved the 179th Infantry Regiment from his far right to the Wingen-sur-Moder area, on his extreme left flank, to buttress the line established by Task Force Hudelson. The 2d Battalion encountered troops from the *257th Volksgrenadier Division*, in Sarreinsberg, where it formed the left wing of *XC Corps*. House-to-house fighting raged throughout the day, and the other two battalions tangled with German troops as each side set up roadblocks and probed the enemy's positions.[25]

Brooks on 2 January extended the 45th Infantry Division's sector even farther westward to take responsibility for the 276th Infantry, southeast of Bitche, and he attached the regiment to the division as a task force. To the east, the 45th Infantry Division took charge of the 313th Infantry Regiment, southeast of Lembach. Frederick's unofficial corps now held a twelve-mile-long curving line, the left half of which was under strong German pressure. He ordered his 157th and 180th Infantry regiments back from positions against the Siegfried Line to a new main line of resistance in the Maginot fortifications.[26]

Fracas with the French

Eisenhower called Devers on 1 January and ordered that VI Corps withdraw promptly to positions in the Vosges, and he authorized

Devers to use the divisions he had placed in SHAEF reserve. Patch ordered Brooks in the wee hours of 2 January to complete the withdrawal in three days. Brooks was to delay at three lines: the Maginot Line by dawn, the Bitche-Niederbronn-Bischwiller line on order, the Bitche-Ingwiller-Strasbourg line on order, with the final withdrawal also to be executed on order. Devers called Patch later in the morning to relate that Ike had called him to underscore his concern that much of VI Corps could be cut off on the Alsatian Plain, and Eisenhower had emphasized that the bulk of the corps should be withdrawn to the Vosges line while light mobile forces held the front, falling back only under pressure. The Seventh Army operations report records that the withdrawal was to occur "regardless of the political repercussions and the evacuation of the Strasbourg area."[27]

De Gaulle had also acted on 1 January, when he ordered de Lattre to defend Strasbourg even if VI Corps pulled back.[28] The political repercussions began the morning of 3 January, when an impassioned plea from General du Vigier, French military governor of Strasbourg, not to abandon the city arrived at Patch's headquarters (now in Lunéville) by courier. Du Vigier asserted that an Allied evacuation would result in a massacre of the population by the Germans. Almost simultaneously, Devers arrived and instructed that Strasbourg be evacuated regardless of any political pressure to hold the city."[29]

De Gaulle that same day approached Eisenhower and admitted that Ike's plan made military sense, but he said that the loss of Strasbourg would be a political disaster for France. De Gaulle even raised the prospect that a popular revolt might break out in France if Strasbourg were abandoned. He handed over a letter in which he threatened that the French army would act independently to defend the city if necessary.

Eisenhower told de Gaulle that he would receive no more supplies if he so acted. Ike nevertheless agreed to modify his orders to ensure that the withdrawal would not affect Strasbourg. Ike later explained that the possibility of a popular revolt that could sever his supply lines turned de Gaulle's political problem into his military problem.[30]

* * *

If de Gaulle played the good cop with Eisenhower, General Juin played the bad cop. In a separate meeting with Ike's chief of staff, he threatened to cut off all Allied railroads and communication lines through France if the Americans embargoed equipment deliveries to the French. This may well have played a larger role in Ike's decision than he later admitted.[31]

While de Gaulle and Juin talked, de Lattre acted. His army was not going to abandon Strasbourg. His thoughts turned to the 3d DIA. It was horribly tired and battered, but it was a good division, perhaps the best de Lattre had, and it was commanded by General Guillaume. FFI troops would have to fill in for the hole left by the withdrawal from the line of the 3d DIA, but de Lattre was willing to accept more risk there to save Strasbourg. De Lattre gave Guillaume his marching orders.[32]

While Devers was still at Patch's headquarters, the new orders arrived from SHAEF that Strasbourg was to be defended. To accomplish that, VI Corps' pullback into the mountains had to stop. Devers approved a proposal by Patch's chief of staff that VI Corps stand its ground at the Maginot Line.[33]

The Thunderbirds Stand Fast

Back at the Bitche penetration, the right wing of the German offensive ground to a halt as the completely stymied *XIII SS Corps* ended its offensive operations on 3 January.[34] Farther east, Major General Frederick's command continued to tilt with the enemy. Along most of the western half of the division's zone, company- and battalion-sized units on both sides attacked and made modest gains, most of which amounted to nothing in the big picture. The exception was the southeast extreme of the German salient, where the American line blocked access to the river valleys that ran across the rear of the VI Corps zone. Continuing attempts by *XC Corps* to envelop Phillipsbourg and Reipertsweiler indicated that the enemy was trying to secure key road junctions to permit exploitation.[35]

At Phillipsbourg, a German infantry battalion supported by the *256th Volksgrenadier Division*'s assault guns drove Task Force Herren's 1st Battalion, 275th Infantry, through the streets until it held but a weak toehold in the southern outskirts. German infantry infiltrated through the surrounding woods at the same time, and by dark every company in the 275th Infantry's 3d Battalion was fighting desperately and out of contact.[36]

At Reipertsweiler, German infiltrators flanked the 313th Infantry Regiment's 1st Battalion and severed contact with its Companies A and C. The 2d Battalion beat off direct assaults on its positions north of town during the morning, after which the enemy disengaged.[37] Appeals by *Army Group G* to shift assault guns from the stymied *17th SS Panzergrenadier Division* to reinforce the attack at Reipertsweiler went unanswered by higher command.[38]

That night, the 1st and 2d battalions, *12th SS Mountain Regiment, 6th SS Mountain Division*, infiltrated between the 313th and 179th Infantry regiments to enter a third key node in the road net at Wingen-sur-Moder. The Germans arrived just as the 276th Infantry Regiment's 1st Battalion, attached from Task Force Herren to the 45th Infantry Division, was trucking from Wingen-sur-Moder to nearby Wimmenau, and the SS ambushed Company B as it was moving into position. An estimated eight hundred German troops were spotted in Wingen-sur-Moder itself.[39]

* * *

By 4 January, Frederick had shifted another regiment from his right to his left wing. Overnight, the 180th Infantry Regiment trucked to the area east of Wingen-sur-Moder and at about 1030 hours attacked northward into the gap between the 179th and 313th Infantry regiments. The shift occurred too late to prevent the SS mountain troops from reaching Wingen-sur-Moder, but it wreaked havoc on the German effort to follow up. The *361st Volksgrenadier Division*'s *951st Volksgrenadier Regiment* attacked toward Wimmenau at about the same time and ran head-on into the American advance. After a sharp meeting engagement, the Germans tried to fan out in three columns but were repulsed at every point. The SS troops in Wingen-sur-Moder were cut off.[40]

Frederick ordered the 276th Infantry Regiment to recapture the village, and the 1st Battalion jumped off at 1330 from west of Wingen-sur-Moder, supported by ten tanks and heavy mortar fire. The 1st Battalion, to the east, was to lay down supporting fire and prevent the Germans from escaping. The SS mountain troops had no such idea and fought back fiercely inside Wingen-sur-Moder.[41]

* * *

Back in Phillipsbourg, two isolated companies from the 275th Infantry's 3d Battalion reestablished contact on 4 January, but Company I's fate remained unknown. At 0935, the 1st Battalion, which had moved forward from reserve positions near Niederbronn, attacked Phillipsbourg under heavy artillery and small-arms fire. By dark, the effort had managed to reclaim only half the town.[42] *Stars and Stripes* described the action:

> While headquarters tried desperately to re-establish contact with the lost companies, the battalions struck at the enemy. . . .
>
> Machine guns set up in houses and on the outskirts of the town swept every angle of approach. German 88s were zeroed in on the crossroads. When Lt. Col. John T. Malloy, Paso Robles, Calif., 275th executive officer, reached Philippsbourg, he found five tanks and seventy-five men clinging to the edge of town but disorganized and ready to withdraw.
>
> Ordering the tanks to follow him, he marched up the middle of the street through a hail of lead, guiding the tanks to the most important enemy position, a machine-gun nest at the upper end of the block. Just beyond the crossroads, he was wounded by fragments of an 88 [shell]. At 150 yards, however, the lead tank fired point-blank at the machine gun, blowing off a corner of the house and wiping out the emplacement. With this threat gone, elements of the [274th and] 275th . . . stormed through the rest of the town in savage house-to-house fighting. [The attack actually burned out after recapturing half of the town, because two of the supporting tanks from a platoon of the 47th Tank Battalion, 14th Armored Division, were destroyed.]
>
> Late that night, Companies A and L made their way to safety; next day Company I was located and relieved.[43]

The fifth day of the offensive saw desultory fighting along most of the salient wall. The 275th Infantry's 1st and 2d battalions, supported by a battalion from the 274th Infantry that had been rushed to the scene, cleared

Phillipsbourg. It was only after the Germans evacuated the town at about 1440 that the 275th Infantry was able to make contact with Company I.[44]

The 276th Infantry, backed by fire from the 45th Infantry Division's artillery, recaptured most of Wingen-sur-Moder, where the action became completely detached from the overall German operation and, for the Americans, amounted to mopping up a stubborn bypassed point of resistance behind their lines.[45]

The *OKW*, perhaps influenced by reports from Himmler that the Americans were thinning out near Strasbourg, concluded that there would be no breakthrough in this sector for their mobile divisions to exploit. The night of 5 January, the *21st Panzer* and *25th Panzergrenadier divisions* received orders to shift eastward almost to the Rhine for an attack south across the Alsatian Plain. *Army Group G* and *OB West Generalfeldmarschall* Gerd von Rundstedt fruitlessly objected and argued that a breakthrough in the Bitche salient was still possible if mobile divisions were committed there. The divisions were subordinated to the newly arrived *XXXIX Panzer Corps* headquarters.[46]

The Maginot Line Lost

The reason for the end of German offensive operations around Bitche on 5 January was already becoming apparent thirty miles to the southeast. That morning at about 0745 hours, the *553d Volksgrenadier Division*, part of *Obergruppenführer* Erich von dem Bach-Zelewski's *XIV SS Corps*, drove a spike into VI Corps' plans when it forced a crossing of the Rhine at Gambsheim, nearly eight miles behind the Maginot Line. The volksgrenadiers entered battle supported by some thirty Hetzer tank destroyers, an assault gun battalion, and five artillery battalions. The Germans had an excellent picture of American dispositions, because they had maintained an aggressive outpost and long-range patrolling program after withdrawing to the east bank of the river in November.

The volksgrenadiers encountered only a few sentries when the first infantry battalion crossed the river from forest-shrouded assembly areas on the east bank. The troops quickly occupied Drusenheim, Gambsheim, and Bettenhofen. An infantry regiment followed, and 88mm guns and an antitank company were quickly ferried into the bridgehead.

Elements of Task Force Linden (attached to the 79th Infantry Division), made up of the infantry elements of the 42d Infantry Division, under the command of Brig. Gen. Henning Linden, were responsible for a thirty-one-mile stretch of the Rhine bank. The task force's battalions were in various stages of relieving 79th Infantry Division regiments when the Germans gained their foothold. The 42d Division had arrived at the front with a poor training evaluation and was not to have been committed to battle without more training; for that reason, it had been assigned a quiet flank sector. Circumstances, however, had suddenly forced the men into on-the-job training.[47]

Linden tried to dislodge the Germans with two weak task forces. Task Force A consisted of four infantry companies drawn from the 222d, 232d, and 242d Infantry regiments and a platoon of medium tanks from Company A, 781st Tank Battalion. The inexperienced troops drove southeastward toward Gambsheim astride the road from Weyersheim. Checked at the small Landsgraben Canal by automatic weapons fire, the GIs flanked the defenders on the right, and two rifle companies pushed into the western outskirts of the objective.

The small command was out of communication with all other elements in the operation, so it could not even call for artillery support when five Sturmgeschutz IV assault guns and some infantry counterattacked from the direction of the Rhine. The infantry had no means to communicate with the supporting Shermans, which were buttoned up, short of waving their arms in front of the periscopes to get the crews' attention. One attempt to get the tanks to help the men in Gambsheim resulted in a Sherman firing on friendly troops, after which the tanks withdrew. The GIs had been issued no bazooka ammunition and had only rifle grenades to defend themselves against the panzers. Darkness fell, and inexperience and the ad hoc nature of the command began to tell: The men lost contact with the left flank element and pulled back behind the canal to reorganize.[48]

Task Force B, meanwhile, consisted of roughly a battalion of riflemen drawn from the 222d and 232d Infantry regiments, two medium tank platoons from Company A, 781st Tank Battalion, some fifty FFI, and the 232d Infantry's Cannon Company. The task force struck northward toward Gambsheim, but heavy artillery fire stopped the men north of

Kilstett, well short of the objective. The Germans had secured a bridge-head two miles deep and five miles long.

Major General Wyche, commanding the 79th Infantry Division, spoke with Brooks, who told him to clean out the pocket "pronto." Wyche moved two battalions from his 314th Infantry Regiment to the Bischwiller area to add weight to the counterattack. Brooks attached a reconnaissance troop and a medium tank company from the 14th Armored Division to Wyche's sprawling command to help out.

Early on 6 January, Task Force A managed to enter Gambsheim, where its GIs fought from house to house for two hours before a German counterattack threw them back across the Landsgraben Canal. Task Force B tried to reach the village again from the south, but the assault was poorly organized and broke down. The 314th Infantry Regiment's two infantry battalions attacked the pocket farther north, and the 2d Battalion clawed its way into the southern fringes of Drusenheim by dark.

Still, Major General Wyche admitted to Brooks that things were not going well. "The real trouble is this mushroom organization, plus the greenness of the troops and lack of communications," Wyche reported. He doubted that Task Force Linden, which had suffered heavy casualties and amply demonstrated its training and organizational shortfalls, could take Gambsheim. "They've been in and out twice," he lamented.[49]

Decisions made on both sides on 7 January guaranteed that the small constellation of towns just west of the Rhine from Gambsheim north would become the setting for some of the most vicious and ultimately meaningless fighting of the war. Hitler instructed that his forces mount steady pressure out of the pocket to assist operations elsewhere. The 314th Infantry Regiment's 2d Battalion, in Drusenheim, noticed the impact almost immediately, when it was pushed back through town by a battalion of infantry supported by eight to ten panzers and lost five of its own supporting tanks.

Army Group G now committed the *21st Panzer Division*, which attacked southward parallel to the Rhine in the Aschbach area, where the 313th Infantry Regiment manned the Maginot Line. The division had been hurriedly rebuilt in late December and had about twenty Mark IV and fourteen Mark V panzers available, to be joined on 8 January by twenty Panzerjäger IV tank killers.[50] The Germans captured Aschbach and several nearby villages, but the American main line withstood five strong attacks.

* * *

Devers ordered Patch on 7 January to organize a reserve battle position along the line Landroff-Benestroff-Sarre-Union-Ingwiller and an alternate position along the Moder River from Ingwiller to Haguenau. Withdrawal to these positions, he instructed, would occur only under strong enemy pressure. At the same time, the boundary between the Seventh Army and the French First Army was shifted north of Strasbourg to give the French responsibility for defending the city.[51]

Patch gave the 12th Armored Division to VI Corps, and Combat Command B, attached to the 79th Infantry Division, moved to Bischwiller to attack into the Gambsheim Pocket toward Herrlisheim. Intelligence estimated that between 800 and 1,200 German troops were in the pocket, and CCB assembled what should have been the larger force. Task Force Power consisted of the 714th Tank Battalion, less one company, and an armored-infantry company; Task Force Rammer controlled the 56th Armored Infantry Battalion, less a company, and Company B of the 714th Tank Battalion.

The combat command advanced through Rohrwiller early on 8 January in a column of task forces, with Task Force Power leading. By 1400 hours, Sherman tanks took up positions from which they could fire directly into Herrlisheim, and the armored infantry clambered off the decks ready for action. Two 14th Armored Division tanks supporting the 314th Infantry, farther north, were just visible, and patrols moved forward to check the bridges. The operation almost immediately ground to a halt at a blown bridge across the Zorn River.

About mid-afternoon, the 56th Armored Infantry Battalion, supported by the fire of the 714th Tank Battalion, west of the Zorn, moved out and reached some fields outside Herrlisheim under heavy and accurate mortar fire, which claimed a heavy toll in casualties. A planned move into town after dark for some reason never took place, and the armored infantry pulled back to a waterworks building on the Zorn. That night, several German tanks accompanied by infantry ground up outside the complex and shelled it until one was damaged by bazooka fire. More than one GI probably considered the implications of the fact that the Germans had tanks near Herrlisheim, whereas their own were stuck on the far side of the river. Engineers were supposed to be building a Bailey bridge for the tanks, but no sounds of construction disturbed the night.[52]

* * *

French II Corps, meanwhile, on 7 December absorbed an attack northward out of the Colmar Pocket by the *198th Infantry Division*. The weak jab gained some ground near Erstein but sputtered out after a day and proved irrelevant to the fighting in the VI Corps zone.

* * *

Patch on 8 January informed his corps that, effective 13 January, XXI Corps—just released by SHAEF—was to take responsibility for the 103d Infantry Division and 106th Cavalry Group, on the army's left wing. Haislip's XV Corps was to control the 36th, 44th, and 100th Infantry divisions, Task Force Harris less one regiment, and the French 2d DB. Brooks' VI Corps was to command the 45th and 79th Infantry divisions, the 12th and 14th Armored divisions, and Task Forces Herren and Linden.[53]

* * *

The German effort to reach the pocket by driving down the Rhine resumed on 9 January, when the *21st Panzer Division*, now supported by elements of the *25th Panzergrenadier Division*, shifted its efforts some three thousand yards to the southeast and struck the 242d Infantry Regiment's 1st Battalion at Hatten. The regiment was part of Task Force Linden, which was attached to the 79th Infantry Division. The division, particularly with the further attachment of three combat commands from the 12th and 14th Armored divisions, was the size of a small corps. Major General Wyche concluded that he had to divide his sprawling force into three pieces, commanded by himself, his assistant division commander, Brig. Gen. George Wahl, and Brigadier General Linden, from the 42d Infantry Division.[54] Hatten fell under Linden's purview.

The American defenses exploited the Maginot Line fortifications, which at this point ran north to south, with Hatten sitting just west of the defenses at about the center of the battalion's zone. The village of

Rittershoffen lay some 1,500 yards due west. The 1st Battalion was seeing action for the first time.

An early-morning two-battalion assault by infantry and tanks from the *25th Panzergrenadier Division* struck the lines held by Company A. Panzergrenadiers infiltrated around two pillboxes northeast of Hatten and fired into the foxhole line from the rear. The company called down mortar fire on its own positions, which briefly restored the situation, but by mid-morning the 1st Battalion had committed its entire reserve, and German pressure continued to mount. Flamethrower tanks forced the Americans in one bunker to surrender, and all of Company B save one platoon was over-run. The battalion CO radioed his company commanders, "Hold your positions, let the tanks pass, and fire at the enemy foot troops."[55]

One GI recalled, "The snow had been falling all night and had obscured the advance until they were almost upon us. Shells screamed overhead and burst to the rear of us. The roar was deafening. Fire was coming from the tanks at very close range. Soon the snow churned, like sand in a box, by the shells landing all around us."[56] Only a chain of daisy mines hastily strung across the main street in town stopped a Panther from reaching the battalion's command post, but it did not stop two panzers from firing directly into the building.[57]

A second German attack spearheaded by twenty-five to thirty panzers enveloped the town on three sides and reached the area south of Rittershoffen. South of Hatten, Sherman crews from the 14th Armored Division's 48th Tank Battalion (1st Platoon, Company A) were ready for one assault group. "We took up positions just in front of town and waited for the attack we knew was coming," recalled one lieutenant. "We didn't have to wait long. Six German tanks began moving along the railroad track from Hatten. They were on our left, and they apparently didn't see us, so we let them get within 600 yards, and then we let go! A Mark IV was leading the advance. One of our tanks opened fire and, before the Krauts knew what was coming off, had poured four rounds into the hull." Within five minutes, all of the panzers were smoking hulks.[58]

The Germans had better luck inside Hatten. According to one dough-boy, "The enemy overran our positions, and we were forced to fight in small, dispersed groups in defense of the town." Master Sergeant Vito

290 // FIRST TO THE RHINE

Bertoldo, who was at the battalion CP when the main line of resistance collapsed, was awarded the Medal of Honor for his role in the fight. His citation read in part:

> On the close approach of enemy soldiers, [Bertoldo] left the protection of the building he defended and set up his [machine] gun in the street, there to remain for almost 12 hours driving back attacks while in full view of his adversaries and completely exposed to 88mm, machine-gun, and small-arms fire. He moved back inside the command post, strapped his machine gun to a table and covered the main approach to the building by firing through a window, remaining steadfast even in the face of 88mm fire from tanks only 75 yards away. One shell blasted him across the room, but he returned to his weapon. When two enemy personnel carriers led by a tank moved toward his position, he calmly waited for the troops to dismount and then, with the tank firing directly at him, leaned out of the window and mowed down the entire group of more than twenty Germans.
>
> Some time later, removal of the command post to another building was ordered. Master Sergeant Bertoldo voluntarily remained behind, covering the withdrawal of his comrades and maintaining his stand all night.

A heavy concentration of artillery and tank-destroyer fire broke the German momentum, and the 1st Battalion, supported by two platoons of Shermans from the 48th Tank Battalion, counterattacked. "We left our commanding ground and eased down past the Jerry tanks burning like steel torches to guide our way in the darkness," recalled one tanker. "The night was cold; the wind was sharp. We stamped our feet on the floor of the tank. . . . From out of Hatten came a vehicle. We wet our chilled lips. One tank fired, two and three, and the Jerry vehicle burst into flames." The American pressure forced the panzers back to the east, but the GIs failed to dislodge the Germans from the eastern part of Hatten.[59]

* * *

The staff of the 2d Battalion, 315th Infantry Regiment, was just sitting down for a noontime meal when orders arrived for the outfit to rush to Rittershoffen and send two companies to help restore the line at Hatten. Lieutenant Colonel Earl Holton, commanding, ordered his men to contact friendly tanks that he had been assured were deployed just outside Hatten. The first patrol ran into only Germans and lost half its troops to machine-gun and panzer fire. Other patrols could find no sign of the American armor—the platoon of Shermans from the 48th Tank Battalion that had knocked out six panzers during the afternoon—which was hunkered down on a hill closer to Rittershoffen.

Companies F and G nevertheless made their way into the village and tied into the 242d Infantry's positions. They were under fire from the first moment and discovered that the Jerries were only a few yards away in the darkness. A platoon of M18s from the 827th Tank Destroyer Battalion— one of several such battalions in the segregated army, consisting of black enlisted men and mostly white officers—also arrived, and the Shermans from the 48th Tank Battalion rolled to the rear at 2230 hours.[60]

That was the first day at Hatten.

* * *

Back at Herrlisheim, all three rifle companies of the 56th Armored Infantry Battalion advanced into the village on 9 January under supporting fire from much of the 714th Tank Battalion and two nearby 14th Armored Division tanks. Company B suffered 50 percent casualties to mortar and small-arms fire on the way to the objective, but the other companies arrived in good shape. All contact between the tanks and the infantry broke down at this point. Fortunately the engineers completed a Bailey bridge across the Zorn, and the tanks turned by company toward the crossing.

High-velocity fire from concealed panzers and antitank guns near Herrlisheim crashed into the tempting targets moving broadside along the river. Tanks erupted into flames throughout Company B. "All of our tanks were like ducks in a shooting gallery," lamented company commander Captain Leehman, who obtained permission to withdraw to reorganize. Companies A and C's tanks, meanwhile, backpedaled westward with their fronts facing the enemy to reduce target area.

The armored infantrymen in Herrlisheim moved from house to house, clearing snipers and machine-gun nests. All went well until the men ran into a platoon of Mark IVs spread out in their path. Lacking tank support and a radio link to the artillery, the men pulled back a bit and set up defenses in the houses.

During the night, white-caped Germans infiltrated around the battalion and assaulted the American-held buildings one by one. One sergeant recalled, "The Krauts seemed to have a system of first firing at a building with tracers to mark it, and then blowing it up with a bazooka or [antitank] gun." Panzers fired into some buildings, and German infantry assaulted others with hand grenades. The GIs shot only when they had to—out of fear of exposing their positions.[61]

* * *

To the north in Hatten on 10 January, *XXXIX Panzer Corps* took charge of the battle, and the Germans reinforced their positions in the eastern part of town and stopped cold every effort to eject them. The 2d Battalion, 315th Infantry, meanwhile moved Company H into town. The outfit almost immediately took heavy casualties when one platoon, while assaulting a row of houses, came under a withering crossfire from panzers and friendly tanks located in Rittershoffen. Nearby, Company F reported that it was under attack by a dozen panzers, and men later said that only the deterrence posed by a crippled M10 tank destroyer, which the GIs "manned" like a scarecrow, allowed the company to hold that afternoon. A push by two panzergrenadier companies and five tanks, meanwhile, drove a platoon of tank destroyers from the 827th Tank Destroyer Battalion, which had relieved the tanks on the hill near Rittershoffen during the night, back into that village, with the loss of two vehicles. Seven miles still separated the German forces at Hatten and the Gambsheim Pocket.

Sherman tanks from Company A, 48th Tank Battalion, had provided fire support from outside Hatten during the day's fighting. The remainder of the 48th Tank Battalion arrived during the afternoon, and Company B took up positions south of Rittershoffen, while Company C deployed south and east of the town. Brigadier General Albert Smith, commanding the 14th Armored Division, now took control over the disparate infantry units north of the Haguenau Forest.

A nearly mirror-image reinforcement on the German side occurred at the same place at about the same time: Elements of the *125th* and *192d Panzergrenadier regiments* from the *21st Panzer Division* appeared at Rittershoffen during the day. Attempts to secure the key terrain around Hatten by the 48th Tank Battalion armor and riflemen from the 315th Infantry Regiment ran into deadly fire from panzers and antitank guns. Five Shermans from Company B were hit, as were three from Company C. "As my section crossed [the railroad tracks]," recollected one platoon sergeant, "we were fired on from somewhere to the south of Hatten. . . . Behind me, Captain Elder's tank was hit twice in quick succession. Four more tanks were hit, and still we couldn't pick up the flashes. . . . Your whole body goes tense; you're scared to your fingertips." All further attacks were called off.

That night, artillery fire hit the 2d Battalion's rear CP in Rittershoffen and severed all phone lines to the companies in Hatten. Bad communications characterized the fighting in the two villages from that point onward.[62]

* * *

On the west bank of the Rhine that same day, the eleven surviving Shermans of Company B, 714th Tank Battalion, crossed the Bailey bridge over the Zorn and rolled into Herrlisheim under cover of the pre-dawn darkness. Captain Leehman had no idea where he was, or where the armored infantrymen were either, so he set out to reconnoiter with a second tank. Cruising the empty streets, he came upon a panzer, and his gunner destroyed it at point-blank range. Leehman finally spotted an American soldier, who led him to the surviving captain who commanded the battered battalion elements in town. Leehman radioed that it did not look possible to hold the village, but higher command disagreed and ordered more forces into Herrlisheim. By now, however, German antitank fire interdicted vehicular traffic, and late in the day withdrawal orders were issued, and the command retreated back across the Zorn River after nightfall.[63]

* * *

While German artillery crumped into Hatten early on 11 January, panzergrenadiers quietly infiltrated the northern end of Rittershoffen through concealing snow and mist. Soon, more grenadiers and panzers followed the first wave into the village. When the 1st Battalion, 242d Infantry, CP came under assault, the headquarters displaced rearward and set up defenses using cooks and motor pool personnel. The 3d Battalion, 315th Infantry Regiment, which had arrived during the night, lost its main line of resistance and fought all day at close quarters merely to contain the penetration.

Street fighting continued to rage in nearby Hatten, and shortly before noon a pincer attack from the north and south by fifteen panzers isolated the 2d Battalion, 315th Infantry, in the southwest corner of town. Three panzers jockeying from the west, however, had a fatal encounter with four M18s from the 827th Tank Destroyer Battalion that had arrived in town the night before. Sergeant Spencer Irving ordered his speedy vehicle forward from behind some buildings and caught the panzers in a most embarrassing situation. Standing in his turret, Irving asked the GIs dug in nearby, "How does you want them, one-two-three, or three-two-one? Ah thinks Ah'll take them one-two-three." His gunner picked them off in that order, and the GIs shot down the escaping crews.

Combat Command A, 14th Armored Division, received orders to attack eastward from Kuhlendorf to clear Rittershoffen and roll on to relieve the men in Hatten. The American tanks were stopped four hundred yards from the first objective, though elements of the 68th Armored Infantry Battalion worked their way into town at about 1600 hours. The remnants of the 1st Battalion, 242d Infantry, departed at this time, reduced in fifty-two hours from 781 officers and men to 264 souls.

German panzers had more luck than CCA, and by dusk had cut off the 3d Battalion in Rittershoffen.[64] Still, it was apparent to the German commanders that the *XXXIX Panzer Corps'* attack was bogged down, and Hitler ordered that the *7th Airborne* and *10th SS Panzer division*s drive south from their assembly areas in the Forstfeld-Blenheim region and link up with the *553d Volksgrenadier Division*.[65] The following day, Hitler transferred control over *XXXIX Panzer Corps* to Himmler's *Army Group Upper Rhine*, less the *21st Panzer*, *25th Panzergrenadier*, and *47th Volksgrenadier division*s, which went to *LXXXIX Corps*.[66]

* * *

Combat Command A, 14th Armored Division, attacked again on 12 January and succeeded in reaching northern Rittershoffen, but the

Germans held out in a cemetery in the southeast corner of town. Rather than continuing eastward, pushing the Germans before them, CCA's tankers found themselves boxed into town with the infantry. They remained stuck there for the duration of the fighting in the area.[67] The division's informal history recorded, "Tank-infantry teams were organized, eight infantrymen along with each tank. The tanks inched ponderously a few yards down the street, heavy cannon searching out machine-gun nests [and] enemy strongpoints; the infantrymen moved along with them, running, dodging from building to building, throwing grenades in the cellar windows, going through each small [house] room by room, rifles at the ready, hand grenades ready; the artillery and mortar fire screamed into the street and exploded the roofs, and the German machine-gun fire swept the street in quick, nasty blasts."[68]

Combat Command B was committed at 1115 hours to break through to the men in Hatten. Machine-gun and small-arms fire pinned down the armored infantry five hundred yards from town, and direct fire from panzers knocked out the first two Shermans to expose themselves. This command, too, stayed stuck where it was, and, despite orders to carry on the attack, a de facto defensive line emerged from Hatten to Rittershoffen; it remained in place until a general withdrawal one week later.

Fighting raged in Rittershoffen throughout the day on 13 January. The Germans reinforced their positions with *flakwagens*, flamethrowers, and more panzers. Combat Command A and the 3d Battalion made slight gains, only to be thrown back late in the day by a heavy counterattack from the northeast.[69]

Meanwhile, Combat Command B attempted to outflank Hatten, but it pulled back in the face of heavy artillery and antitank fire from Buhl. While tank duels raged, a German company tried to infiltrate Hatten from the south, but it ran into Lt. Luther Harrell's platoon of Company E positioned in the upstairs windows of a row of houses. Harrell was a "rabid proponent of the automatic-fire school," his company commander later noted, and the lieutenant had somehow scrounged up Tommy guns, Browning automatic rifles (BARs), or light machine guns for almost every man in the platoon. Harrell waited until the Germans were within a hundred yards, then loosed a storm of fire that virtually wiped out the attacking force. (Harrell was killed during a German assault several days later.)[70]

The 14th Armored Division's last resource, Combat Command R, entered the battle. From the perspective of the GIs in town, the first attack about 0900 "turned into a rout" after heavy losses in men and tanks. A second effort after reorganization finally managed to blast a path from the west to the remnants of the 2d Battalion. The Americans gained control over much of the town by dusk, but once again a vigorous counterattack reversed most of the gains that night.[71]

Indecisive but bitter fighting rocked both villages the next day. Nevertheless, German reconnaissance forces slipped southwest of the villages and worked their way to the Haguenau Forest. With the discovery that only light American forces were in the area, *Army Group G* concluded that conditions existed for successful commitment of the full weight of *XXXIX Panzer Corps*.[72]

Quiet descended on Rittershoffen on 15 January, but elements of the *7th Airborne Division*'s *20th Airborne Regiment* supported by panzers appeared in Hatten and by 1715 hours had nearly overrun the troops of 2d Battalion and CCR. Several days after the action, Sergeant Wolf related, "[T]he last assault of the day consisted of five tanks that seemed particularly determined to break the American stranglehold on [one] street. The tanks were methodically destroying all of the remaining houses one-by-one this trip. They would sit back and, with machine guns and 88s going full blast, hammer holes through what walls were still standing. Then the flamethrowers would follow in for the kill, pouring Satan's brimstone through the apertures. Or they would follow [high-explosive] shells by tracers, setting fire to the hay in the numerous barns."[73] Men from the 315th Infantry and CCR were tormented over the coming days by memories of the screams of civilians trapped in burning basements that could be heard over the sounds of battle.

Unlike the white-clad panzergrenadiers, the paratroopers wore dark uniforms that gave them the appearance of demonic shadows moving among the burning ruins, and the effect demoralized the exhausted GIs. About 1600 hours, 2d Battalion commanding officer Lieutenant Colonel Holton made brief radio contact with the rear and said he would have to have help if he were going to hold Hatten.

The situation was not quite that dire, and CCR's 19th Armored Infantry Battalion counterattacked to reclaim lost ground. An army historian who interviewed company grade officers who participated in the action recorded:

> By the time Company C was ready to jump off, two medium tanks of Company A, 47th Tank Battalion, were positioned on the main street to support the attack. Four more tanks stayed in the rear [to provide] covering fire. At 1915, all units began their advance through the rubble of houses lining both sides of the main street. Close contact was necessary due to the poor visibility in the darkness, which was not helped any by the smoke and dust that enemy HE shells were kicking up. . . . A medium tank kept pace with the men of Company C and slowly clanked up the rubble-littered main street. . . .
>
> At "Y" intersection, the advancing units were halted in anticipation of making close contact with the enemy in the next few moments. The tank sought the cover of "Y" street running south off the main street. As the group moved forward once more, the tank jockeyed into a position [that left it] silhouetted against a burning building. From the west end of the main street, two 75mm rounds from an American tank found their marks in the turret and engine compartment. . . . [The other crew] thought the silhouetted tank to be an enemy. The stricken tank caught fire. Small-arms and 75mm shells within the vehicle began to explode. . . .
>
> Company C "mouseholed" through the devastated buildings until enemy bazooka [and] intense small-arms and machine-gun fire halted [it]. The [second] supporting tank relieved the situation by speeding past the burning tank and firing into the enemy. Company C again pressed forward. The tank pulled to the south side

of the main street, out of the field of fire from the slight bend in the road ahead. This bend was the crucial point in the entire village. Jerry tanks were around the eastern side of the bend, [and] American armor commanded the western side. . . .

After gaining the rubble of two more buildings on both sides of the main street, the enemy once more held up the advance with bazooka, machine-gun, and small-arms fire.

The American medium [tank] again came forward and fired its 75mm and machine gun into suspected enemy positions. The Germans quickly retaliated with a barrage of bazooka fire that forced the tank to withdraw. In an effort to flank the enemy . . . , Capt. Harold S. Persky led a platoon of tanks to the south. . . . Three of these tanks were knocked out by German bazooka and artillery fire. The remaining two tanks withdrew.

[The armored-infantry troops gained one more building.] The operation had taken five hours to accomplish, and Company C men were weary. . . . A German counterattack was not long in coming.[74]

The VI Corps troops again held half the village.[75]

* * *

Troops from the *47th Volksgrenadier Division* relieved the panzer-grenadiers in and around Hatten and Rittershoffen beginning 16 January, a signal that the mobile forces would be put to better use elsewhere. The commitment of the 315th Infantry's 1st Battalion to Rittershoffen on 17 January nevertheless had no effect on the stalemate, and the pattern of punch and counterpunch continued in both villages through 19 January, when German efforts shifted to the east.[76]

A battlefield survey conducted in March, after American forces reclaimed the ground, recorded the locations of the hulks of thirty-one M4 medium and nine M5 light tanks from the American side and sixteen panzers and eight self-propelled guns from the German side in and around Hatten and Rittershoffen. The German total did not include vehicles that had been salvaged.[77]

Pointless Sacrifices in the Bitche Salient
The 45th Infantry Division recognized as early as 6 January that the enemy in the salient had gone over to the defensive and intended only to hold his gains, so Frederick set about trying to take away those gains. The result was two weeks of bloodshed that yielded no important advance over ground much of which was destined to be handed back to the Germans because of developments along the Rhine's west bank.

The greatest tragedy unfolded on the eastern shoulder of the salient, where the 157th Infantry Regiment attacked on 14 January to clear the valley between Baerenthal and Mouterhouse. The regiment was supported on its left by a battalion of the 180th Infantry. The 157th Infantry's 3d Battalion drove a salient into the German lines, only to be enveloped by the *6th SS Mountain Division*. Repeated efforts by the 157th Infantry to reach the trapped battalion failed, as did a last-ditch effort by the 3d Battalion to break out. On 20 January, the SS troopers overran the last defenses, and only two men made it back to American lines.

During this period, VI Corps commanding general Brooks concluded that, given his problems with the Bitche salient, his position east of the Vosges would be much more secure with an experienced division in the line. Patch agreed, and on 13 January he initiated relief of Task Force Herren by the 103d Infantry Division.[78]

Battle of the Bridgehead
Back on the west bank of the Rhine, the remainder of the 12th Armored Division had moved into the area of the Gambsheim bridgehead and received orders to attack on 16 January. Combat Command A struck eastward across the Zorn River amid snow and bitter cold. Combat Command B pushed off on a southeastward axis just to the north near Rohrwiller, aiming to link up with CCA in Herrlisheim. Both commands encountered determined resistance from the *553d Volksgrenadier Division* and made little headway, and CCA's 43d Tank Battalion lost a dozen tanks to antitank guns hidden in woods and in the village of Offendorf.[79]

At the same time that the 12th Armored Division attacked the pocket, the *XXXIX Panzer Corps* pushed off down the west bank of the Rhine with the objective of linking up with the pocket. In addition to the fresh *7th Airborne Division*, already pressing the Americans at Hatten, the powerful *10th SS Panzer Division* had arrived, which the corps committed to the drive down the road that ran between the Haguenau Forest and the Rhine. The 232d Infantry Regiment of Task Force Linden, which defended a line from Sessenheim to the river, was the first victim. The initial SS probes on 16 January briefly threw an American listening post out of Dengolsheim and scouted the Sessenheim area.

The storm broke on 17 January, when SS troops captured Roeschwoog, Stattmatten, and Dengolsheim, the last of which was only some two miles from the German lines in the pocket. Brooks attached almost two battalions of the 313th Infantry Regiment and a platoon of light tanks from the 117th Cavalry Reconnaissance Squadron to the 232d Infantry in hopes of restoring the situation, but plans for a counterattack never came off.

Meanwhile, some five miles to the south, CCA's 43d Tank Battalion and 17th Armored Infantry Battalion (with the tank battalion's light tanks providing direct support) attempted to envelop Herrlisheim from the east and south, respectively. Companies A and B of Maj. James Logan's armored infantry battalion established a foothold in the southern part of town. Lieutenant Colonel Nicholas Novosel simultaneously led his medium tanks toward the southeastern fringes. Two Shermans were hit by antitank fire from the rear on the way in, and Novosel ordered his command to rush into the village at full speed. The lead tanks crossed a railroad track near the station and encountered an assault gun, several antitank guns, and an unknown number of infantry.

As usual, the Germans counterattacked almost immediately, spearheaded by at least six panzers. Tankers taken prisoner later agreed that the men were SS troopers. Some of the tankers were able to establish physical contact with a few of their own armored infantry, but that word never filtered up to Logan's infantry CP, only several hundred yards away in southern Herrlisheim.

German soldiers with panzerfausts stalked the American medium tanks that had crossed the railroad tracks in eastern Herrlisheim. Some of their comrades had rolled several railcars down the tracks to block the crossing, and the Shermans west of that point were bottled up. Without infantry to protect them from close assault, the tanks were sitting ducks; about a dozen of them were later found destroyed by rocket penetrations. "Things are very hot," Novosel reported in his last message from eastern Herrlisheim, after his own tank had been knocked out. When asked what assistance he required, he replied, "About 2,000 infantrymen." Novosel was hit shortly afterward and recalled nothing more until he woke up in a German military hospital.

The elements of the 43d Tank Battalion that could escape evidently pulled out of Herrlisheim at some point around mid-afternoon in a desperate bid for survival and deployed for all-around defense in some nearby woods. Aerial reconnaissance the next day revealed that fourteen of the twenty-eight medium tanks with which the battalion had first attacked had been knocked out in that area. A survey of the battlefield in February identified the wrecks of twenty-seven Shermans that had belonged to the 43d Tank Battalion in and around Herrlisheim. Supposition centered on some sort of antitank gun ambush as the explanation for the final destruction of the command.

That same day at 0700, the 23d Tank Battalion, now subordinated to CCA, attacked toward Offendorf, but after some four hours it received new orders to drive northward on a wide front to capture Drusenheim. This maneuver would entail crossing the track of the assault on Herrlisheim or bypassing the town to the east. The battalion reached Herrlisheim, where, after making contact with the 17th Armored Infantry Battalion, Major Edwards, commanding, committed his tanks to helping the infantry withstand the German counterattacks. The tankers nailed one panzer advancing from Offendorf but lost a Sherman to another German tank in town.

Sergeant Carl Lyons, who belonged to Company A, 17th Armored Infantry Battalion, witnessed the beginning of the end and later recalled, "[About 1800 hours,] we saw four enemy tanks approach the railroad embankment, but instead of coming over, [they] turned and moved to the left, behind some buildings. In another half hour we looked around and saw men moving through the houses 50 yards to our rear. Upon looking

302 // First to the Rhine

closer, we saw that they wore camouflage suits: They were Krauts! A few shots were exchanged, but nothing serious. They were now in position to cut us off from the company. . . . A Tiger tank moved up the street with these Krauts and was soon pumping shells into the houses our men were in. Two of our tanks in town were burning. Our bazookas just bounced off the sides of the Kraut tanks. By nightfall, things were completely confused; Kraut patrols walked the streets. They had split the company in half."

At dark, Edwards pulled back his tanks to the south edge of town because the armored infantry were too busy to provide security, and German infantry had crept to within thirty yards of his vehicles. A visitor to the 17th Armored Infantry Battalion's CP at about 2100 hours reported that battalion CO Logan thought that about two hundred of his men were still in action. A street lined with burning buildings more or less demarcated the line of control.

That night, panzers and an estimated thousand troops from the *10th SS Panzer Division* cut off the armored-infantry troops huddled among the buildings, most of whom were then killed or captured. Logan radioed at 0400 that his CP was surrounded, which was the last word heard from his command.[80]

* * *

Combat Command B, meanwhile, encountered heavy artillery, mortar, and small-arms fire and gained no ground on 17 January. Early the next day, a task force consisting of a company each of tanks and armored infantry tried to make its way into Herrlisheim to relieve the CCA men thought to be holding out there, but the Germans prevented any gains. Combat Command B elements attacking elsewhere that day had no better luck.

One reason was the sudden appearance of the *10th SS Panzer Division* on the 12th Armored Division's front. Early on 18 January, the SS surrounded the 232d Infantry Regiment elements defending Sessenheim and shoved other elements west into the woods by about 1430. The German bid to link its penetrations on the Alsatian Plain and the Gambsheim Pocket had finally succeeded.

Two hours later, SS troops supported by ten panzers seized the bridge across the Landsgraben Canal on the Weyersheim-Gambsheim road and crossed the Zorn. A blistering American artillery barrage knocked out eight of the panzers and stopped the thrust, but in the space of the next forty-five minutes two infantry forces, each backed by some seventeen panzers, crossed the Zorn at Herrlisheim and again over the Landsgraben Canal.

The 12th Armored Division fought back with artillery and tank destroyers and claimed to have knocked out twenty-six panzers for the loss of eleven tanks. Despite this success, Combat Command B was instructed to withdraw west of the Zorn under cover of night, and the division withdrew to defensive positions between Weyersheim and Rohrwiller.[81]

Patch had asked Brooks as early as 17 January whether he wanted to use the 36th Infantry Division, and Brooks now took advantage of the offer. He ordered Maj. Gen. Dahlquist to relieve the 12th Armored Division, which had already lost 1,200 men and seventy vehicles. The infantry relieved the armored troops during the afternoon of 19 January despite continued attacks by the *10th SS Panzer Division*, and the battered American armored division went into reserve before being sent south to French First Army on 22 January.[82]

Brooks' VI Corps was looking tattered almost across the board as of 19 January. The 12th Armored Division and Task Forces Linden and Herren were judged to be in "unsatisfactory" condition for further combat. Only the 36th and 103d Infantry divisions were in very good shape. Combat fatigue and shortages of riflemen plagued all formations. Patch informed Devers that he could not hold his existing line, and Devers authorized VI Corps to withdraw across the Moder River to its preplanned defensive positions there.

The American withdrawal took place during the night of 20–21 January over dangerous, icy roads. The 14th Armored Division's CCA screened the 79th Infantry Division's move, while small infantry rear guards covered retrograde operations elsewhere and blew the bridges behind them. The new line, considered east to west, ran north along the Zorn from just west of Gambsheim to its confluence with the Moder at Rohrwiller; west along the Moder to Pfaffenhoffen; then northwest, initially along the small Rothbach River. The French 3d DIA had taken responsibility for the remaining sector between the Rhine and the Zorn south of Gambsheim. By the end of 21 January, the corps was well positioned and had been able to create substantial reserves. Patch told Brooks, "I think [the enemy] is getting tired. I think we will be able to hang on alright."[83]

The Moder Line Holds

The German attempt to crack the Moder line kicked off the night of 24–25 January with a three-pronged attack by the bulk of six divisions. The *553d Volksgrenadier Division* first launched diversionary attacks against the 3d DIA south of Gambsheim, but the main effort aimed for the open ground southwest of the Haguenau Forest.

To the west, in the Vosges foothills, defended by the 103d Infantry Division, German infantry and tank forces had vigorously probed the American lines on 23 and 24 January and established a small bridgehead at Rothbach. On 25 January, the *6th SS Mountain Division* broke through the positions of the 410th Infantry Regiment and captured Schillersdorf, nearly a mile south of the Rothbach River. A counterattack by the reserve 1st Battalion contained the German advance at Schillersdorf, and a company made its way into the village and engaged the SS men in house-to-house fighting.

The 410th Infantry Regiment struck back on 26 January with heavy artillery support and tanks from the 781st Tank Battalion. The attack drove to the Rothbach and cut the German supply line through Muhlhausen and thereby isolated the SS troops in Schillersdorf, who were cleared out by the next day.

The *36th Volksgrenadier Division* in the meantime subjected the rest of the 103d Division's line to heavy pressure. Brigadier General Anthony McAuliffe, who had, as assistant and acting division commander of the 101st Airborne Division, delivered the famous reply of "Nuts!" to the German surrender demand at Bastogne, now commanded the 103d Division.

Between Neuborg and Schweighausen, the *47th Volksgrenadier, 25th Panzergrenadier*, and *7th Airborne division*s hit the 222d Infantry Regiment of Task Force Linden, which was still attached to the 79th Infantry Division. The Germans had driven the American outpost line south of the river on 23 January and plastered the defenses with artillery during the following day.

At 2005 hours on 24 January, German infantry attacked out of the dark in the woods west of Schweighausen, a town on the south bank of the Moder. The Germans quickly surrounded the 2d Battalion's Company E, which fought until its ammunition ran out; only two officers and thirty GIs managed to get back to friendly lines. German infantry, meanwhile, worked their way into the northern portion of Schweighausen but failed to pry the 2d Battalion out of the southern half.

Early on 25 January, the 1st Battalion's Company B counterattacked against the Germans in the woods. They were unable to eject the foe, but they secured positions that effectively contained the German bridgehead. Major General Wyche reestablished the task force he had used during the fighting around Hatten, including the 222d, 232d, and 314th Infantry regiments and CCB, 14th Armored Division. The 232d Infantry's 2d Battalion moved forward and hit the Germans in Schweighausen from the east while the regiment's other two battalions concentrated south of the woods. At 0730 on 26 January, the regiment drove forward and discovered that the Germans had pulled back across the Moder River during the night.

The third prong also hit Task Force Linden along the positions held around Haguenau by the 242d Infantry Regiment. German infantry paddled across the Moder in rubber rafts at three points at 0100 hours on 25 January. The German assault carried forward only some five hundred yards before running into determined resistance and petering out. The 2d and 3d battalions counterattacked early in the afternoon and eliminated the small bridgehead by 1700 hours.[84]

PREPARING FOR THE NEXT ROUND

With the abysmal failure of the attack across the Moder, Hitler on 25 January pulled the plug on Operation Northwind and ordered the mobile formations involved back into reserve. Stopping Hitler's last offensive had cost Seventh Army more than fifteen thousand men killed, wounded, or captured.[85]

The Führer had to turn his eyes and remaining resources toward the East: On 12 January, the Soviets had launched their greatest offensive of the war. Over the next week, 180 divisions shattered the German line in East Prussia and Poland. By 27 January, Soviet troops were within a hundred miles of Berlin and had overrun the strategic Silesian industrial basin. After pondering the loss of the coal mines there, Hitler's armaments wizard Albert Speer wrote the Führer a memo that began, "The war is lost." Hitler shifted his panzer strength from the western front, and by February nearly every new or repaired panzer to leave a German factory was shipped eastward.[86]

West of the Vosges, fighting had burned out by the end of January, and German divisions began disappearing from the XV Corps front. By 10 February, all known German reserves in the Saar-Palatinate area, north of the border, had departed. Task Force Harris dissolved, and its elements were resubordinated to the 63d Infantry Division, while the Third Army's 10th Armored Division arrived to replace the French 2d DB, which was sent south to the Colmar Pocket. The 12th Armored Division in turn relieved the 10th Armored Division once it completed its mission in the Colmar area in mid-February.

Major General Haislip launched a limited-objective offensive on 17 February along his front west of Bitche to straighten his line. His divisions handily pushed back the weak German forces some two miles to the Siegfried Line along most of the front by early March, and the 70th Infantry Division penetrated the first belt of defenses and seized high ground overlooking the city of Saarbrücken from the south.

On 18 February, XXI Corps returned to Seventh Army from the Colmar Pocket (its operations there are covered in the next chapter) and took charge of the left wing, encompassing the 70th Infantry, 63d Infantry, and 12th Armored divisions, plus the 101st Cavalry Group. Haislip's XV Corps retained the 44th and 100th Infantry divisions and the 106th Cavalry Group.

East of the Vosges, the Germans by 31 January had evacuated hard-fought Gambsheim, and the 36th Infantry Division, supported by CCB, 14th Armored Division, reclaimed most of the former pocket during the first week of February.

The VI Corps zone was otherwise generally quiet during February, and the 101st Airborne Division joined VI Corps to relieve the regiments of Task Force Linden and the 79th Infantry Division. SHAEF decided to reclaim the airborne division almost as soon as it had deployed in the line, and the 36th Infantry Division had to extend its line to the west to fill the gap. Task Force Linden dissolved, and its regiments rejoined the 42d Infantry Division.

An influx of infantry replacements finally reached Seventh Army at this time, and divisions set about training and absorbing the new men.[87]

CHAPTER 11

CRUSHING THE COLMAR POCKET

Elsass bleibt Deutsch. [Alsace will remain German.]

—German graffiti painted
throughout Alsace[1]

In early January 1945, the Allies were growing weary of dealing with the Colmar Pocket. The Germans were using the pocket to tie down as many Allied forces as possible so they could transfer forces to the eastern front and free up time to organize a strong defense of the Reich with those German units that remained in the west. Thus, crushing the Colmar Pocket would pay big dividends to the Allies. Unfortunately the French who contained it scarcely had the resources to deal with the problem.[2]

I Corps was weak. Its 3d DIA had been sent north to defend Strasbourg under II Corps command and was on its last legs in any event. The 9th DIC was made up largely of new recruits who had scarcely two months of service in the regular army, having joined it as part of the *blanchiment* process. General Béthouart felt that he could give that division only the simplest of tasks. He was also about to receive the 10th Infantry Division (DI), under General Billotte, but this division was newly formed of FFI from the Paris area and was probably not up to playing an important role in any major offensive. Béthouart placed the 10th DI in a quiet sector in the Vosges. That left only the 2d DIM and 1st DB to do the hard work of any I Corps offensive. It was not enough.[3]

II Corps had its own problems. The 1st DFL was very low on manpower. Ever since the big November offensive, it had been racking up casualties and receiving no replacements. It had lost 1,600 men in the Vosges and another 1,700 men in the first half of January. The impact of these losses was felt all the more because so many officers, especially junior officers, had fallen. There was also a shortage of equipment for the soldiers. This deficit had started with the *blanchiment* process, during which all too often one set of personal equipment had to be divided between the tirailleur and the Frenchman who was replacing him. The lack of proper winter clothing and boots was particularly telling in the seemingly arctic weather of Alsace that winter.[4]

Despite the fact that the Germans viewed the Colmar Pocket as an economy of force measure, they still had significant strength within it. The forces inside the pocket belonged to the *Nineteenth Army*, now commanded by *Generaleutnant* Siegfried Rasp, whom Heinrich Himmler had appointed in mid-December after removing Wiese. *Nineteenth Army* had two corps, comprising eight infantry divisions and one panzer brigade. The *106th "Feldherrnhalle" Panzer Brigade* and one infantry division were the army's reserve. That infantry division, however, was in the process of being transferred east, and its scheduled replacement, the *2d Mountain Division*, had yet to appear.[5]

All of Rasp's divisions were understrength and short on equipment. They had only some 30 to 40 percent of their antitank weapons and about sixty-five tanks and assault guns, although they made good use of those they did have. Artillery pieces were numerous, but there was little ammunition to shoot from them. Much of the infantry that was available consisted of new recruits or hastily trained fillers. Many were not even Germans. Even among the Germans, there was no telling where they might have come from. There were SS and NCO training units that were full of fight, but many other units were far from it. The Germans had certain advantages, however. They had short interior lines of communication (though they would be somewhat impeded by the weather); plenty of small-arms ammunition; and terrain that heavily favored the defense, crisscrossed as it was with numerous rivers and streams and dotted with built-up areas. Finally, they had atrocious winter weather on their side. Temperatures hovered at around 0 degrees Fahrenheit, and there was three feet of snow on the ground. "Anyone with a roof over his head—and that was not the attacker—had a master card in the struggle," de Lattre wrote in his memoirs.[6]

Despite the strength of the Germans holding the pocket and the challenges posed by the terrain and the weather, "there was no question of passivity," General Béthouart, I Corps commander, remembered later. "The weaker one is, the more one must be active. The best solution would be to attack. The Allies demanded it, and for us it was a duty. But with what?" Béthouart went looking for reinforcements.

De Lattre provided the 4th Moroccan Mountain Division (DMM) from the First Army reserve, and more ammunition, but he made clear that, with respect to artillery, the cupboard was bare. "You'll have to manage with what you have," he said. Béthouart walked away confident that he could launch a strong offensive from the south against the Colmar Pocket.[7]

But de Lattre kept thinking about the discussion with Béthouart. He realized that Béthouart would not be able to liquidate the Colmar Pocket by himself. Béthouart could attach his corps "like a leech to the south of the pocket," but that, de Lattre feared, was about it. Soon he envisioned a two-pronged offensive against the pocket, from the north as well as the south. However, just as Béthouart had needed reinforcements, so, too, would de Lattre if this bigger plan were to succeed.[8]

On 11 January, de Lattre went to see Devers to ask for those reinforcements. The American was immediately amenable; it looked as though the operation would come off. De Lattre wrote an optimistic letter to Béthouart passing on the good news. He warned Béthouart, however, that there was word of an increase in "5th column" and German intelligence activities, such as clandestine radio stations in Alsace, including in Strasbourg, Mulhouse, and Altkirch. "For the love of God, no telephone carelessness, papers, confidences." He even fretted about the discretion of two of Béthouart's division commanders.[9]

Four days later, and after raising the issue with Eisenhower, Devers ordered de Lattre "to launch without delay and by surprise, with all the means now at your disposal, powerful offensive operations converging in the direction of Brisach and aimed at total reduction of the Alsace bridgehead." In order to make this all possible, he gave de Lattre Leclerc's 2d DB and the U.S. 28th Infantry Division—though the latter came with the proviso that it be used initially, at least, on a defensive sector because it had just been savaged in the Ardennes. There was even a possibility, Devers told de Lattre, that he would soon be able to provide the U.S. 12th Armored Division.[10]

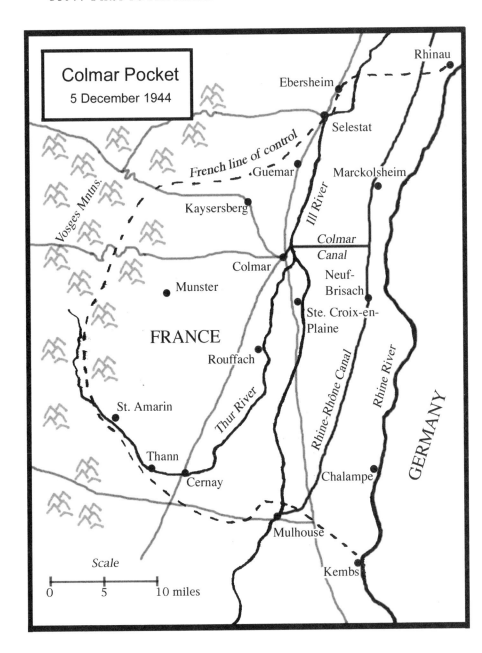

Colmar Pocket
5 December 1944

For de Lattre, this was enough. He intended to trap all the Germans in the Colmar Pocket, not allowing them to escape to fight another day. It would be a double envelopment. His forces would drive toward Brisach, two miles east of Neuf-Brisach—another fortress town designed by Vauban—and take the single-track reinforced railway bridge there. The Germans had given the bridge an honorary Iron Cross for surviving so many Allied bombing raids. It was the key to the *Nineteenth Army*'s ability to maintain a defense and to escape, should that become necessary. The move on Brisach would also quickly cut off Chalampe, near the southern base of the Colmar Pocket, with its bridge that de Lattre had considered seizing back in November.[11]

I Corps was to kick off on 20 January, seeking the enemy's reserves. It would direct its main effort at cutting the road network in the Cernay-Guebwiller area, then exploit in the direction of the Rhine bridges at Brisach. Béthouart conceived the breakthrough operation of I Corps as a "crushing attack in depth," a surprise attack launched on a rather narrow front with the 4th DMM on the west and the 2d Moroccan Infantry Division (2d DIM) on the east. The 9th DIC would protect this main effort by establishing itself along the Ill River (which ran north-south between the French positions and the Rhine). All the divisions would be reinforced by elements of the 1st DB.

II Corps was to follow on 22 January, driving south between Colmar and Selestat, bypassing Colmar itself to the northeast, and driving in the direction of Brisach. If all worked according to plan, those German forces that were not destroyed outright would be cut off and have no way of getting back to the Reich. The 10th DI, holding down the Central Vosges front, was to remain quiet until the Germans' exit was blocked.[12]

It was a good plan, but de Lattre was still concerned about the weather and the terrain—and the lengthy time that the Germans had had to improve the latter. In the face of all this, de Lattre decided he needed an extra edge. Perhaps he could at least lull the Germans into complacency. He issued phony orders dispatching the 1st DB north to Strasbourg and made sure that the Germans received a copy. He supported this deception with phony radio traffic. He and Béthouart even used a social function with civilian luminaries from Mulhouse to play out a little charade, in the course of which de Lattre wished his I Corps commander a pleasant and well-earned period of rest and relaxation in sunny North Africa.[13]

There was one other problem, however. As of 13 January, the French First Army had six days' worth of fuel. Then came flooding of the Doubs River, followed by a freeze that stopped the barges that carried fuel northward. At the same time, the pumping stations on a key American pipeline also froze. Fuel trucks were immobilized by bad weather, unable to drive to Marseille to pick up their loads. By 19 January, the fuel reserve was down to a scant twenty-four hours, and the offensive was due to start on 20 January. American service units sprang into action to help Lieutenant Colonel Allard, de Lattre's logistics officer, with his problem. Though the American and French forces had often clashed over logistics during the pursuit from Provence up to the Vosges, in the intervening time relations had improved. Allard had complete confidence that the Americans would be able to sort things out. He had so much confidence that he risked his career and the offensive by not even telling de Lattre about the problem until after it had been resolved. By 25 January, the crisis was over, and the French First Army had fuel stocks sufficient for eight days of combat.[14]

ATTACK FROM THE SOUTH

At 0800 hours on 20 January, after a thirty-minute artillery preparation, I Corps soldiers moved forward into a snowstorm and battle. They had achieved surprise and were able to exploit a seam between the German *159th Infantry* and *716th Volksgrenadier divisions*. On the French left, in front of the 4th DMM, resistance was particularly weak, but progress was still slow because of the weather and its effects on the roads. The weather, indeed, was a problem at least as big as the German defenses. The snow was now more than three feet deep. Vehicles could scarcely move, and wounded soldiers had to be evacuated on toboggans. All these effects disorganized the French attack as units became disoriented in the snowstorm and had trouble moving. Persistent German artillery fire did not help either. The 4th DMM made insignificant progress. "It seemed that Himmler's SS had made a pact with the devil and that all the forces of nature were mobilized in their service," de Lattre commented.

In front of the 2d DIM, resistance was stronger, and the Germans even managed a local counterattack. Nonetheless, the 4th RTM, on the left, and the 5th RTM, on the right, made relatively rapid progress, advancing some three miles. To the east, on I Corps' right, the 9th DIC did unexpectedly well despite an added obstacle beyond the relatively built-up nature of the terrain: a small river that had to be crossed almost immediately. The 5th Company of the 23d Colonial Infantry Regiment solved that problem; jumping off half an hour before the rest of the division, the men forded the river—literally a death-defying act in its own right, given the weather—and seized a factory on the other side.

This bridgehead allowed some degree of protection behind which the engineers quickly created footbridges. The German infantry resisted the 9th DIC attack, but they had scarcely any artillery support and paid a heavy price for it. Overall, I Corps moved forward several miles on the first day, but the *159th Infantry Division* managed to hold onto Cernay, just opposite the French jumping-off positions. It was clear that getting to Ensisheim, the first major objective for the French, would be very hard.[15]

The weather on 21 January was, if anything, worse. Furthermore, the Germans launched a series of small counterattacks supported by armor, which were all the more difficult to repulse given that the French had spent a frigid night sleeping in the hills, whereas the German attackers had had (relatively) warm nights. The effect of all this was that the French were unable to exploit any of their reasonable successes of the previous day.[16]

At first, neither Himmler nor Rasp thought much of the I Corps' attacks. At most, they figured, they were diversionary actions meant to reduce the pressure on Strasbourg, far to the north. With no inkling that anything bigger was afoot, for which reinforcements might be more urgently needed, Rasp felt comfortable requesting armored reinforcements to snuff out the effort, and Himmler was immediately willing to send one of its two mobile antitank units and the *106th Panzer Brigade*.[17]

By the next morning, 22 January, the weather had improved somewhat and the French were able to move forward again.[18] That day Béthouart visited the forward positions of the 9th DIC. The division commander, General Morlière, and his chief of infantry, General Salan, were there in animated discussion. The division had reached a position surrounded by woods out of which converging German attacks might emerge at any moment. Morlière wanted to pull back from this exposed position, but Salan was dead-set against it. Béthouart pondered the matter and decided that with a few precautions it would be safe to stay. He issued the corresponding order and returned to his command post, where he spoke with his corps artillery commander and told him to prepare to pound the wood lines around the forward position. Béthouart was going to cold-cock anything that came out of those woods.[19]

A victim soon presented itself. During the night, an Alsatian deserter came over to the French lines and announced that the *106th Panzer Brigade*, to which he belonged, would attack at the break of day. Béthouart's corps artillery was ready.[20]

The attack that came the next morning involved a battalion of tanks, led by the brigade commander himself, and infantry from the *716th Volksgrenadier Division*. The assault was savage, and the defenders were hard-pressed, even with the copious artillery support. By midday, however, the battle was over, and the French held the field. The Germans had lost sixty men dead, seven tanks, two armored cars, and a hundred prisoners.[21]

With the 9th DIC making slow but nonetheless steady progress on the corps' right, Béthouart shifted his main effort from the center-left to the right. It made little difference. The Germans continued to resist firmly, helped by the fact that the slow pace of the French advance allowed them to retreat in good order. The weather also played a part, slowing vehicular movement to a crawl and inflicting on the French a mounting list of frostbite casualties. On 26 January, de Lattre telegraphed Béthouart and urged him to move his I Corps faster toward a juncture with II Corps, but Béthouart could not do it. I Corps even lost a division commander on 30 January when General de Hesdin was seriously wounded in the hills above Cernay, which his 4th DMM had still not been able to wrest from the Germans.[22]

Eleven days after the kickoff of the offensive, after hard fighting in atrocious weather, I Corps had reached none of its objectives. The French infantry was at the point of exhaustion, and repair crews had been run ragged trying to put the outclassed Shermans back into action after they had clashed with Jagdpanthers. Given these disappointing results, Béthouart ordered a day of rest for 31 January.

On 1 February, I Corp again made modest gains against Germans supported by powerful artillery and protected by minefields. The next day, word came that the American XXI Corps had entered Colmar and that Allied infantry was near the Rhine bridges at Brisach (covered below). This made it imperative that I Corps renew its efforts to hasten the crumbling of German resistance west of the Rhine. By the end of 3 February, I Corps was near Ensisheim, its initial objective. Perhaps most importantly, the French also had secured bridges near Ensisheim, across the Ill and Thur rivers. These now provided a base from which I Corps could drive northward to join up with the Americans at Rouffach, which would doom the remnants of four German divisions still in the mountains to the west.[23]

DRIVE FROM THE NORTH

On 18 January, before the beginning of I Corps' offensive, de Lattre wrote to his superior, General Juin, the chief of staff, to explain the plan. Juin had responded, "[T]he matter is well organized and we share your confidence. Does it not seem to you, however, that the means allocated to the northern operation are rather meager, especially in infantry? They ought to have given you two U.S. divisions. . . ." De Lattre conveyed these sentiments to Devers just hours before II Corps came out of the starting blocks. On 23 January, Devers turned him down, but he was seized with the problem. His staff estimated that the 6th Army Group overall would be short 13,300 infantrymen by February, a mere week away. He asked Eisenhowever to reconsider his allocation of replacements. Behind the scenes, actions were under way that would eventually save the Colmar offensive.

In the meantime, the burden for the offensive would remain on the weary 1st DFL (minus one of its own brigades, but supplemented with a combat command from the 2d DB) and the American 3d Infantry Division, augmented by the 63d Infantry Division's 254th Infantry Regiment and a combat command of the 5th DB. De Lattre had great admiration for this American division and its commander, Major General O'Daniel.[24]

Under Monsabert's plan, the 1st DFL was to drive east while protecting the 3d Infantry Division's left flank. The 3d Infantry Division's attack, the II Corps' main effort, was called Operation Grandslam. O'Daniel's plan called for his four infantry regiments to launch successively in an innovative and unpredictable zigzag maneuver. The first was to break through the German lines on the Ill River between Guemar and Ostheim, push east for a few miles, then drive south for five to ten miles. The next regiment was then to pass through the lines and attack east for a few miles before turning south in turn. By repeating this process, O'Daniel hoped that he could sideslip the entire division southeast to the Colmar Canal and beyond, in the process opening a path for a final drive by the French 5th DB on Neuf-Brisach, the ultimate target. The 3d Infantry Division itself would then be in a position to push on south toward Rouffach, Ensisheim, and even Chalampe to join up with I Corps.[25]

At 2100 hours on 22 January, O'Daniel's 7th Infantry Regiment kicked off the offensive with no artillery preparation, an attempt to enhance surprise. The 30th Infantry, under Col. Lionel McGarr, followed at about midnight.[26] The 7th Infantry's 1st Battalion, led by Lt. Col. Mackenzie Porter, set out from Guemar in the dark and the cold. Wearing their white snow camouflage and carrying inflatable boats, the men immediately crossed a bridge over the Fecht River. While crossing, they took several casualties. Later, the battalion almost lost Porter and his command group to a bounding mine that miraculously did not go off, and all the companies successfully met up on the other side of the Colmar Forest.

Here the men came to the Ill River, sixty feet wide with steep banks. The troops were so cold that they could not stand still, so the battalion decided not to wait for engineers to come build a footbridge. Instead, they built an improvised bridge using their boats. Inevitably, three or four men fell into the river, and others got wet. Their uniforms promptly started to freeze, forcing some evacuations due to hypothermia. The remaining men got across the river successfully, then crossed the Orchbach, scarcely more than a stream, some 1,500 yards north of La Maison Rouge, and proceeded south toward that village. Along the way, a sniper shot a squad leader from Company A in the chest, then nailed a "new man." A private took the point and with a miraculous shot picked off the troublesome sniper when he poked his head out of his hole. Lieutenant Lombardi, a platoon leader, remembered, "a Tommy gun, a beautiful shot, right between the eyes, about 50 yards."[27]

The rest of II Corps started on the morning of 23 January. The 1st DFL crossed the Ill River at dawn north of the 3d Infantry Division's crossing point. The division had to go through heavily mined terrain, but it soon reached Illhaeusern, at the confluence of the Fecht and Ill rivers. In a stroke of luck, the foreign legion's 1st Brigade de la Légion Etrangère (BLE) burst into the city and seized three bridges across the Ill, including an eighteen-ton bridge, which allowed combat vehicles to cross the water obstacle. The 2d BLE then pushed through the city and carried the offensive forward. Less than a mile past the town, however, the men were stopped dead by heavy German fire and were forced to take up defensive positions around Moulin.

At 1900 the Germans counterattacked, supported by two tanks and a storm of artillery. The legionnaires were thrown back into Illhaeusern. The Germans penetrated back into the town, but close combat with bayonets soon ejected them, with heavy losses. In the end, it took three days of fighting before the town was fully secure. Another cause of serious delay in the area was the fact that the Germans had liberally laid nonmetallic mines, which had been covered over by snow and a thick layer of ice. There was no means of demining other than the use of bayonets to probe the earth.[28]

Debacle at Riedwihr

Back in the 30th Infantry Regiment, Company A, in the lead, pushed on and soon occupied the bridge across the Orchbach at La Maison Rouge. It kept going south along the Orchbach and entered the Riedwihr Woods—the Orchbach ran right along the west edge of the trees—with Company B following. By midday on 23 January, both companies were in Riedwihr Woods, but Company A found itself in a neck of the woods dangerously exposed to German tanks and infantry beyond the wood line. The Americans laid low, and, as one GI related, "the Germans made a lot of racket; they talked loud as hell. . . . We stayed there several hours and fortunately were not spotted. The ground was too hard for digging. If they had known we were there, they would really have blasted us."[29]

After kicking off at 2100 on 22 January, the 3d Battalion had gone straight through Colmar Forest, then seized the bridge across the Ill River at La Maison Rouge. The 3d Battalion then turned south and pushed along the length of the Riedwihr Woods to attack Holtzwihr, at the far end. Meanwhile, the 2d Battalion followed and entered the forest to act as a reserve.

The Americans were preparing to face tanks. By 1300 on 23 January, two platoons of 57mm antitank guns were across the Ill at La Maison Rouge and in position, alongside Company C of the 1st Battalion and Company G of the 2d Battalion. Getting tanks into the fray was proving difficult, because the bridge across the Ill was too weak to support them. Engineers were already working to strengthen the bridge. At 1510, the regimental commander told Lieutenant Colonel Porter, the 1st Battalion commander, that in an hour and a half the engineers would have completed a bridge and Shermans would be able to cross the Ill River.

The lack of tanks was becoming an increasing concern. The 1st Battalion's Companies A and B were eyeing "too much enemy armor," as one GI put it, in the open area between the Riedwihr Woods and the town of Riedwihr beyond. The regimental executive officer assured the 1st Battalion that armor would be coming as soon as possible and instructed that it was imperative that the regiment seize the bridges across the Colmar Canal, which ran east-west south of the Riedwihr Woods, by that night. He ordered the 1st Battalion to get into Riedwihr, then turn south to Wickerschwihr, on the canal. Similarly, he ordered the 3d Battalion to clear the Riedwihr Woods and drive south to take Holtzwihr, slightly north and west of Wickerschwihr. "I hope to hell our tanks get here before we have to go to Riedwihr," said the Company A commander.

Something was still holding up the tanks back at the bridge when Company A heard that it must launch its attack straightaway with Company B to follow. The company dutifully set out across the mostly open countryside. The Germans let the Americans get within a few hundred yards of Riedwihr before they opened up with machine guns and a tank, and the GIs were immediately pinned down. "We must have been under fire for an hour. Not a damn person could move," one soldier remembered.

Meanwhile, the companies of 3d Battalion were moving south toward Holtzwihr and the Colmar Canal. As Company I approached Holtzwihr, it came under fire from a German machine gunner in the steeple of the town church. Much of the company was pinned down in the field. Suddenly, the men heard even more small-arms fire in the town. Trying to seize control of the situation, Company I returned fire. The men felt some concern because they had briefly spotted a couple of tanks, but they had no sense that they were in serious peril.

Before long, Company I's fire into the town evoked angry shouts in English. Company K, which had approached Holtzwihr by a different route, was actually in town, clearing houses and now receiving friendly fire from Company I. By now, Company K had another problem. The GIs heard a tank coming, so they sent forward a "new man" with a bazooka. The first bazooka round went high, the other low. The tank ground to a halt, then backed around a corner out of sight. "We were elated and thought we had a chance and continued to organize a defensive position," 2d Lt. Frank Harrell remembered.

About ten minutes passed, then the German counterattack struck. From the beginning until the next morning, such confusion reigned that it is difficult to determine the timing and sequence of events. What is clear is that by 1800 the Germans were ruthlessly striking with tanks, tank destroyers, and infantry from the front and both flanks of the 30th Infantry's penetration. The German attack was perfectly timed, just as if "they'd had a liaison officer with us," as one American put it later; none of the three American battalions was in a good defensive position.

In Holtzwihr, German infantry worked its way up the street, capturing American soldiers who thought *they* were clearing the houses. Germany infantrymen broke into one house where the Company I and K commanders were conferring and grabbed both of them. When Holtzwihr was finally freed two days later, the locals said that the Germans had taken about a hundred prisoners. Some American soldiers heatedly replied that many of those hundred had been taken because the locals had pointed out their hiding places.

Meanwhile, Mark VI tanks appeared and drove all before them. Most of the remaining men of Companies I and K fled across the open fields around the town. To their surprise, they reached the woods on the other side, still alive. There "we kept milling around, keeping out of the way of the [enemy] infantry, and praying for it to get dark," one lieutenant remembered. Second

Lieutenant Harrell recounted, "[W]e could hear the tanks circling the woods, and we could hear the infantry getting off a tank when it would stop. They were laughing and joking and talking loud. They didn't have a care in the world. They must have known they had us by the balls."

After what seemed like an eternity, night fell. "The men were so panicky in the woods that it was impossible to keep them together," Harrell told a combat historian later. "Every once in a while, two or three would slip off and not be seen again." In small groups, the men made their way back across the open spaces toward the Ill River. Eventually, most got safely across the river at La Maison Rouge.

While the 3d Battalion's Companies I and K were being defeated, the 2d Battalion's Companies E and F were digging in inside Riedwihr Woods behind the 1st Battalion, which was attacking Riedwihr itself. Company G was back at the bridge over the Ill. The 2d Battalion sent out a patrol to make contact with the 1st Battalion, but that patrol was driven back to its starting positions by the fierce fighting that was now engulfing Companies A and B.

Company L was down at the southern end of Riedwihr Woods at about 1600 hours when it heard that American armor would be coming in about twenty minutes and that it should be ready to go. The company formed up on the road, and the men soon heard the noises of a tank coming along the road through the woods. Though they could not tell where the noise was coming from, they assumed that it was one of theirs coming down from the north. They got off the road to let it pass, and suddenly a *German* tank appeared from the *south*. As soon as the panzer arrived, it opened fire on the building that housed the CP. Standing outside the building, an American soldier with a bazooka fired two or three rounds, which hit but bounced off. The 3d Battalion and Companies E and F never recovered their cohesion.

As the chaos erupted all around, the regimental commander ordered the battalions to consolidate their positions and set up a defense. The 2d Battalion reported, "There is one Kraut tank on [the] road and three in [the] field that we can see."

"Shoot them with artillery, call fires now," the regimental commander ordered. He could sense enough of the developing panic to tell the 2d Battalion to get its men under control.

321 CRUSHING THE COLMAR POCKET // 321

The commander was correct in sensing panic in his regiment. Across the battlefield, dramatic vignettes played out as men struggled between their duty to obey and their instincts to survive. In one instance, a platoon sergeant stood over his men brandishing his Tommy gun and forcing them to use up all their ammunition, then destroy their guns before he would allow them to flee.

At the Ill bridge, antitank gunners swiftly made ready for battle as soon as their guns and ammunition trucks arrived. They could hear "a hell of a lot of firing going on" and knew something big was happening. As soon as the armor crossed the river, Company C was to move forward with the tanks and sort things out. Behind them, the antitank gunners could hear a long line of Shermans revving their engines. One drove out onto the bridge, and there was a tremendous crash, then a splash and shouts of dismay. The tank had fallen through. Things had just gone from bad to worse.

When the German attack struck 1st Battalion, the outfit was off balance and stretched out between the bridge over the Ill and the outskirts of Riedwihr. The battalion called in artillery wherever it saw the enemy, but it did little good. The German attack continued unabated. As the gunners back at the bridge completed their preparations, the Company A commander and thirty "scared, wet, dirty" soldiers appeared. German tanks were clearly audible behind them. The Company A commander said his men had "nothing to fight with and were being chewed to ribbons." He could not account for his other hundred-odd men. An officer stopped one of the men streaming toward La Maison Rouge and asked him what was going on. "Beaucoup Mark VIs up there!"

"How many is "beaucoup"? the officer asked.

"About half a dozen," the desperate soldier answered. How many did you actually see, the officer wanted to know. "Well, I only seen one . . . , but he was coming right for me!"

Much of the rest of Company A was with Lieutenant Lombardi, one of the platoon commanders. After being pinned down for about an hour toward the rear of the column that had been approaching Riedwihr, Lombardi saw three men get out of the ditch along the road where they were taking cover and start running to the rear. A German tank blew them apart. Lombardi crawled along the ditch, hoping to find someone with a phone line so he could call in artillery fire, but he found no one and began to feel that the situation was hopeless. At this point, the men of Company A started moving past him toward the rear along the ditch; "somebody," they said, had ordered a withdrawal. Lombardi decided to follow them.

Getting back into Riedwihr Woods, Lombardi cobbled together some sort of defense using the men of the 1st Platoon and a few from each of the other platoons and the company headquarters. They could hear armored vehicles crashing through the woods behind them. Soon they decided to pull back to a line along the Orchbach in the woods, where they met up with remnants of Company F from the 2d Battalion. They stayed there only about fifteen minutes until they realized that there were no Americans nearby. There were, however, German tanks and 88s moving all around them in the dark. Lombardi and his ragtag group waded across the creek and followed its west bank north. The men were "panicky as hell," according to Lombardi. As they got near La Maison Rouge, most of them broke entirely, all discipline gone, and ran across the field, scrambled over the broken bridge across the Ill, and sought shelter in a water-filled ditch.

In the hours leading up to midnight, as one army combat historian writing just a few weeks later put it, "Maison Rouge became a great vortex for hundreds of scared, cold, often wounded, and in many cases defenseless men." Officers were unable to find their men. To the extent that there was an organized defense, men were in line behind the high shoulder on the north side of the road between the Ill and the Orchbach. One captain observed, "It was like a God-damned scene from Civil War days. Men were lying right next to each other along the road. Officers were running around." Occasionally, when they thought no officers were looking, small groups of men would break off and make their way through the dark to the rear, across the broken bridge over the Ill.

Companies G and C were protecting the river crossing and the broken bridge over the Ill River at La Maison Rouge. Farther north along the Ill, the 1st Battalion command post and a ragtag group of soldiers were also defending the river line. Even before the first panzers appeared, the men of Company G started to withdraw. Companies G and C were now hopelessly intermixed. When, sometime after 2130, the German tanks arrived at La Maison Rouge with their supporting infantry and shattered the American antitank defenses, the line gave way.

Lieutenant Wright, a Company G platoon commander, sent his and the other platoon sergeants to round up as many men as they could and directed them to rally at a bend in the Ill River. After a short time, the sergeants returned with twenty-one soldiers. Wright told them to follow him forward toward the enemy, and he started out. After a brief time, he marched around a bend. Moments later his runner caught up with him and told him that the men were "taking off." Wright ran back and saw "blurred shapes moving a good distance down the bank and going fast." After a brief pursuit, he caught up with them. Gathering up another eleven stray men for a total of thirty-two, he laid down the law. "I told them I was putting a sergeant in front of them and was bringing up the rear and that I would shoot anyone who turned back because I was pretty pissed off that they'd run off on me that way." Wright's men soon found themselves back at the northern end of where Companies C and G had defended the bridge, where they dug in.

The Americans called in more artillery between La Maison Rouge and the area immediately north of Riedwihr. The 3d Infantry Division Artillery recalled it as the most intense fire that its guns had laid down on a counterattack since Anzio, but the barrage did little good. The defensive line along the Ill, consisting of pieces of Companies A, B, C, D, and G, slowly weakened over the course of the night. Company H's mortar platoon had exhausted all of its ammunition, dropped its mortars in a well, and retreated across the river.

At about 2030, Iron Mike O'Daniel ordered the 15th Infantry Regiment, previously held in reserve, to ride to the rescue: "Make plans to take over [the] 30th Infantry attack with same objectives...; [the] plan now is to hold [the] bridgehead and line along [the] Ill River. We will get [the] bridge that tank fell thru back in, send armor across, and attack again."[30]

At 0400 hours on 24 January, two companies from the 15th Infantry's 1st Battalion crossed the Ill and moved southward to expand and secure the tenuous bridgehead. There was scant resistance from the Germans, who, it turned out, had virtually abandoned the crossing sites at Maison Rouge. Seeing the thousand yards of wide-open fields stretching ahead of them in a "ghostly whiteness," Lt. Eugene Koschkin, a platoon leader in the 15th Infantry Regiment, cried out to his commander, "It's suicide! A man hasn't got a chance out there!" Some soldiers of the 15th Infantry found foxholes previously dug by the 30th Infantry that they could occupy. One found a foxhole occupied by a dead German and just pushed the body into the bottom of the hole and stood on him. The rest had to dig into the frozen ground. As daylight dawned, one company first sergeant went on a last-minute inspection. "Get those God-damned holes in the ground!" he yelled. "We're going to catch hell!"[31]

The first sergeant was right. A German armor attack came at about 0800. Having inexplicably left the Maison Rouge area and its crossing points the previous day, the Germans were now intent on getting them back. Many of the 15th Infantry troopers were "new men" in their first battle, and there were also difficulties calling in artillery fire support. Most decisive of all was the fact that there was still no American armor to duke it out with the panzers.

The German attack rolled right through the American positions. Some GIs were crushed in their foxholes. Lieutenant Koschkin's prediction of suicide came true: He tried to surrender his platoon but was shot and killed for his troubles. Most of the other Americans fled, "hollering and screaming like they was scared to death." One platoon commander ordered his men to retreat, and one of his soldiers remembered later, "I don't know if anybody left before the order was given, but everybody was sure ready to go. We all practically had one foot out of the foxhole. He didn't have to give the order very loud!"

By 1030 the only organized resistance east of the Ill was the 1st Battalion CP, which consisted of Lieutenant Colonel Porter, nineteen officers and men, and a platoon's worth of men from the 15th Infantry in and around La Maison Rouge. Most of the officers east of the Ill had long since decided that they could not keep their men in line on that side of the river. They had devoted their efforts to withdrawing them and reconstituting a defense on the other side of the river, where there were tanks and tank destroyers. Initially, there were some 150 to 200 men in these positions, but when dawn came there were only 60 men left. Many fled all the way back to the positions they had held at the kickoff of the offensive.

These two small groups held out in the face of German attacks with the help of devastating artillery support, but it was a near-run thing. At one point, a German tank came within 150 yards of the 1st Battalion CP, but it seemed to develop motor trouble and had to pull back. A short time later, a German tank destroyer put three rounds directly through the battalion switchboard, but the Americans stuck it out.

Finally, at 1400, the 15th Infantry came through the area in force with attached tanks and tank destroyers. "If that ain't a beautiful sight, I never seen one!" a soldier crowed. This time the regiment successfully threw back the Germans. Meanwhile, efforts were under way to police up the widely dispersed members of the 30th Infantry, many of whom were still hiding in the Riedwihr Woods. Not only were many men wounded, but many others were suffering from hypothermia. The regimental commander urged the maximum effort in these regards, "for it is apparent that we will be committed again tomorrow. . . ."

The offensive was a disaster for the 30th Infantry Regiment, but not an irretrievable one. The average company went from 111 men on line to 73. Companies I and K were almost totally destroyed. The regiment had left some 80 percent of its equipment strewn across the battlefield. Fortunately, however, the Germans had devoted little effort to capturing or destroying this equipment, and most of it was recovered and put back into service. The regiment might otherwise have been forced to completely retire from the Colmar offensive, given the slow rate of replacement and repair for automatic weapons then prevailing in the Seventh Army. By the night of 25 January, most of the regiment had been found, treated, reorganized, and re-equipped. That night, the troops were put back in the fight and finally took Holtzwihr and Wickerschwihr.

On 25 January, the 15th Infantry Regiment, now supported by American and French armor, pushed forward east and south from Maison Rouge. During the day's fighting, every officer in Company B other than 2d Lt. Audie Murphy became a casualty. Murphy later described the attack from one dogface's perspective: "Our armor pulls ahead of us with gun barrels traversing. From the woodland comes a crash of shells. Two of the tanks burst into flames. Their escape hatches open, and the still living members of the crew bail out. Blazing like torches and screaming horribly, they roll in the snow. . . . As we advance, the fighting develops into individual duels. Once I am pinned behind a tree by a stubborn Kraut using a huge pine tree for cover. Only a few yards separate us. We snipe at one another, but neither of us scores a hit. [One of Murphy's comrades eventually wounds the German soldier.] I nail him in the side. As he drops to his knees, I finish emptying the ammo clip into his body."[32]

Only the next day, Murphy earned the Medal of Honor when a German counterattack overran his company's positions. The citation records: "2d Lt. Murphy commanded Company B, which was attacked by six tanks and waves of infantry. 2d Lt. Murphy ordered his men to withdraw to prepared positions in a woods, while he remained forward at his command post and continued to give fire directions to the artillery by telephone. Behind him, to his right, one of our tank destroyers received a direct hit and began to burn. Its crew withdrew to the woods. 2d Lt. Murphy continued to direct artillery fire, which killed large numbers of the advancing enemy infantry. With the enemy tanks abreast of his position, 2d Lt. Murphy climbed on the burning tank destroyer, which was in danger of blowing up at any moment, and employed its .50-caliber machine gun against the enemy. He was alone and exposed to German fire from three sides, but his deadly fire killed dozens of Germans and caused their infantry attack to waver. The enemy tanks, losing infantry support, began to fall back. For an hour the Germans tried every available weapon to eliminate 2d Lt. Murphy, but he continued to hold his position and wiped out a squad, which was trying to creep up unnoticed on his right flank. Germans reached as close as 10 yards, only to be mowed down by his fire. He received a leg wound, but ignored it and continued the single-handed fight until his ammunition was exhausted. He then made his way to his company, refused medical attention, and organized the company in a counterattack, which forced the Germans to withdraw. His directing of artillery fire wiped out many of the enemy; he killed or wounded about fifty. 2d Lt. Murphy's indomitable courage and his refusal to give an inch of ground saved his company from possible encirclement and destruction, and enabled it to hold the woods that had been the enemy's objective."

Himmler's Hideout

The 7th Infantry Regiment, meanwhile, had been progressing in the direction of Colmar. This brought it to the Chateau de Schoppenwihr, a strong position from which the Germans could seriously impede progress along the north-south road to Colmar.

The men of the 7th Infantry had their own reasons for wanting into that chateau. Heinrich Himmler was reputed to have slept there recently, and they wanted to see what a Nazi chieftain's hideout looked like. They also suspected that there were good "souvenirs" to be taken.[33]

The task fell to the 1st Battalion. Early on the morning of 24 January, Companies B and C got into position in the Rothleible Woods east of the chateau to have a look at their target. It lay in a wooded area, but between them and it was a wide-open field, flat and covered with white snow, gently gleaming in the moonlight. The chateau itself consisted of a number of large stone buildings surrounded by a seven-foot-high stone wall. Immediately to the east of the chateau, a roadway, raised several feet about the adjacent fields, ran north-south.

This was not going to be a walk in the park. The battalion commander decided that Company A, with attached tanks, would assault the chateau from the north while Companies B and C would go in from their positions in the woods to the east.

Kicking off the assault, Company A moved south down the main road to the chateau with the understanding that everything north of the chateau was in friendly hands. Looking ahead, they saw soldiers dressed in white snow camouflage. Suddenly one of the Americans yelled, "Those guys don't look like GIs to me!" Staff Sergeant De Bona ordered a soldier to go forward to identify the mysterious soldiers in white. The soldier walked forward a short distance and he shouted "Are you GIs?" The answer became clear as the unidentified soldiers leapt into foxholes and slit trenches. Within moments the Germans were firing on Company A with small arms and machine guns. The men scrambled wildly to find holes or hollows in the flat terrain. Sergeant De Bona knew that his platoon was in a "bad spot," and he dispatched another sergeant to the rear for instructions.

Before too long, an American tank clanked its way forward. It opened up with its 75mm and its machine guns and killed several Germans in their holes. One of the tank's tracer rounds set a haystack on fire in the middle of the field, which sent several nearby Germans scurrying away. Riflemen quickly picked them off as they became silhouetted against the blaze.

Germans in the chateau opened fire, spewing out an enormous volume of machine-gun and rifle bullets. Slowly, Company A fell back into the Rothleible Woods, where the men set up defensive positions, still supported by the tank that had saved their bacon. Now it was time for Companies B and C to have a go.

After a strong artillery barrage, Company B moved out in three waves across the open field followed by Company C. Company B's 1st Platoon led the way as skirmishers trudged through the deep snow with the 2d and 3d platoons in support. The 1st Platoon advanced some four hundred yards, almost two-thirds of the way to the raised roadway near the chateau's eastern wall. Suddenly all hell broke loose as Germans behind the far bank of the road unleashed machine-gun, rifle-grenade, and small-arms fire. Moments later, a panzer appeared on the road 150 yards to the south and opened fire on the American troops.

The men had no cover whatsoever and were rapidly taking casualties. The Company B commander kept his head and rapidly realized that there was no place to go but forward. Following his lead, the GIs advanced, firing from the hip, and soon reached the comparative safety of the eastern bank of the highway, where they bunched together seeking to make themselves small. Just across the road not more than twenty yards away, German voices could be heard above the noise of the weapons. Behind them, the GIs could hear moans and cries for help from wounded comrades who had walked by their sides just minutes before.

Company C was also having a hard time of it. The company commander was shot dead along with two other men. As German fire played across the field, twenty more men went down wounded. A lieutenant assumed command and pulled back the company into the Rothleible Woods.

This left Company B all by itself hugging the eastern bank of the road as the Germans on the other side fired rifle grenades at the men. The panzer was now in position to fire directly at them as well. A private decided he was going to take on the tank. He fired two rifle grenades at it, but as he prepared to launch a third, the tank fired again with its main

gun, killing the private and unleashing screams from several more soldiers wounded by the blast.

With that, something just snapped in the mind of a Lieutenant Kerr.
He rose and climbed up onto the roadway yelling at the GIs, "Let's go!"
Electrified by Kerr's action, the rest of the company poured over the road
after him, screaming at the top of their lungs and firing from the hip at
everything that moved. The Germans on the other side were stunned by
this sudden turn of events. Many dropped their weapons and gave themselves up on the spot. Others had to be routed out of their foxholes with
grenades or killed at point-blank range.

Company B's momentum swept it forward through the wooded area.
In less than half an hour, the men reduced the outer perimeter defenses
and, despite the fire of retreating Germans, reached the seven-foot wall
surrounding the chateau grounds. The American artillery barrage had
blasted holes in the wall, which enabled the Americans to work their way
through. Once inside the wall, they encountered no organized resistance.

Company B's desperate actions turned the tide. As it had surged forward, two bazooka teams had moved through the woods and gotten into
position less than fifty yards from the troublesome panzer. The bazooka
men soon drove it off, preventing it from making any attempt at another
reversal of fortunes.

The next day, 25 January, the 7th Infantry, which had started this
offensive alongside the now decimated 30th Infantry, was able to drive
directly south from Ostheim almost halfway to Colmar. Upon reaching
Houssen, the regiment had to repel a few small counterattacks.

The Assault on Jebsheim

With the 3d Infantry Division still in a stiff fight around La Maison Rouge,
the Allied effort to gain a firm foothold east of the Ill River continued elsewhere on 24 January. Combat Command 5, French 2d DB, which was
attached to the 1st DFL, launched an attack in the direction of Elsenheim.
The combat command's reconnaissance forces ran into an enemy counterattack from heavy tanks concealed in the Elsenheim Woods, which forced
a hasty retreat by the French forces. The next day, CC5 was again to make
scant progress in the face of the panzers' resistance. Meanwhile, the 5th DB

received orders to advance as quickly as possible from Illhaeusern to Neuf-Brisach, which is on the French side of the Rhine.

Also on 25 January, the American 254th Infantry Regiment had assembled in the Colmar Forest, ready to attack Jebsheim, a strongpoint in the German defense of the Rhine crossing, which lay east of Riedwihr. The Americans knew that the Germans would desperately defend Jebsheim. At 0245 on 26 January, four artillery battalions laid down preparatory fire on the unfortunate French town, and immediately afterward the 1st and 2d battalions of the 254th Infantry attacked. The German will to hold the town and fire from the adjacent Jebsheim Woods were so strong that by 0430 both American battalions had to withdraw to defensive positions.[34]

Now the 254th Infantry sent its 3d Battalion from Riedwihr—which had been liberated the day before—into the Jebsheim Woods to clear it out. This horrible task took the 3d Battalion a day and a half, during which time the 1st and 2d battalions renewed their attack on Jebsheim. At midnight on the night of 26 January, eight artillery battalions pounded Jebsheim for fifteen minutes. An hour later, four infantry companies entered the town and worked for the next three days to clear out the place, ultimately with the help of the 5th DB and the 1st DFL, at the cost of six hundred Allied troops dead.[35]

THE PUSH GAINS STEAM

On 27 January, the by now somewhat recovered 1st and 2d battalions of the 30th Infantry Regiment and a combat command of French tanks had passed through the positions of the 15th Infantry to gain control of the crossings of the east-west Colmar Canal between the north-south Ill River and Muntzenheim, which they were able to do by 2000 hours.[36] German commanders were growing increasingly concerned. The German High Command that day empowered *OB West* von Rundstedt to withdraw as necessary to straighten up his line between the Ill and Rhine rivers. These orders even foresaw a withdrawal beyond the Rhine as soon as defenses had been erected. German engineers immediately set to work enhancing the ability to move soldiers and equipment east across the Rhine.[37]

The Führer had approved the withdrawal of the right wing of the *Nineteenth Army*, but he also directed von Rundstedt to examine how far the army's front could be bettered by pressing forward the main line of resistance along the axis Selestat-Col du Bhonhomme-Le Valtin, and he authorized the use of the *6th SS Mountain Division* for that purpose. On 29 January, von Rundstedt indicated that it was impracticable to mount an attack for the purpose of advancing the main line of resistance of the *Nineteenth Army* and that it was more important to strengthen the army's bridgehead on its pre-existing front. The *6th SS Mountain Division* could not be released from the *First Army* in view of the large-scale attack expected by Patton against the Moselle Gap. The *2d Mountain Division*, moreover, was not fit for offensive action after all the abuse it had taken. Accordingly, an order was issued the following day that it was essential to keep the bridgehead active and to pin down enemy forces.

The Germans were not the only ones with problems. The tough fighting in the Colmar Pocket had been running down the already low infantry strength of de Lattre's First Army. De Lattre continued to lobby Devers for reinforcements, letting Devers' chief of staff sit in on a conference of division commanders to hear their various tales of woe. Devers recognized the difficulties posed by the weather and kept representing de Lattre's concerns to Eisenhower, even though privately he felt that the French lacked "the punch or the willingness to go all out." Soon, Eisenhower decided to transfer five additional American divisions to the Seventh Army and later handed over twelve thousand service troops to support them. Accordingly, Devers decided that the American XXI Corps would slot itself into the French First Army sector between de Lattre's two existing corps, thus shortening the French lines. XXI Corps was to command the U.S. 3d and 28th Infantry divisions, already on the scene, and the 75th Infantry Division, which by 25 January had started moving from the Ardennes region. De Lattre promptly added the 5th DB—which had previously been divided into combat commands, each supporting one of the infantry divisions of II Corps—to the American XXI Corps order of battle.

XXI Corps was given the mission of attacking in the direction of Neuf-Brisach and seizing the bridges across the Rhine, while also maintaining contact in the Vosges and containing the enemy there. In making this decision, de Lattre was depriving his own II Corps of the mission of exploiting toward Brisach. Instead, II Corps was to cover the left flank of the American XXI Corps as it went for the gold. II Corps would now also be free to continue its attack to Marckholsheim and the Rhine. It was then to clear the area between the Ill and Rhine rivers and between Erstein and Marckholsheim.

XXI Corps took over its sector at 0900 on 28 January and launched its attack toward Neuf-Brisach exactly one day later. The 28th Infantry Division, still sitting west of the Ill River, was to mount a strong demonstration, conduct aggressive patrolling and raiding, and vigorously follow up any German withdrawals. The 5th DB was to attack in multiple columns when ordered by the corps commander. The 75th Division was to assemble one regimental combat team by noon on 30 January and have the other two assembled by the next day. Meanwhile, the XII Tactical Air Command was to concentrate on Brisach and the bridges behind it, optimistically wanting to cut off what the Allies hoped would soon be a German retreat.

The 3d Infantry Division again mounted the main effort. The 7th and 15th Infantry regiments attacked abreast behind a rolling artillery barrage across the Colmar Canal between Colmar and Artzenheim. There was little resistance, though traffic jams delayed some bridging equipment, which caused further backups. There were particular delays in getting tanks across the canal, which did not happen until the morning of 30 January. Both infantry regiments made solid progress south of the canal, snuffing out an enemy counterattack the morning of 30 January and clearing Muntzenheim and other little villages between Muntzenheim and Colmar.[38]

That night, the 75th Division's 289th Infantry Regiment took over most of the positions held by the 7th Infantry Regiment. One battalion of the 7th Infantry drove forward to take Horbourg, a suburb immediately west of Colmar.

The 2d Battalion of the 7th Infantry Regiment, under Major Duncan, was given the task of taking Horbourg. This would cut the main highway through Andolsheim to Neuf-Brisach, the last escape route of Germans west of Colmar.[39] Major Duncan's battalion had suffered tremendous losses, and all of its companies were down to about thirty men each. The

Germans defended the approaches to Horbourg from foxholes and trenches in the fields around the town. Duncan realized that help would be advisable. Fortunately, a mere two hundred yards away was Wihr-en-Plaine, occupied by a French armored unit. Duncan attempted to persuade the French commander to aid the attack with his armor. To Duncan's intense annoyance, the French commander said he would not move his vehicles until the road junction east of Horbourg had been secured. He absolutely refused to budge. Disgusted, Duncan ordered his battalion to begin the attack at 2100 on 30 January without support from the French.

The battalion formed a column of companies to advance along the road toward the town. Company E led the assault through the open fields, followed by two American tanks. The GIs got to within twenty yards of the first house on the eastern edge of Horbourg when two German machine guns opened up from a house. A third machine gun fired from the field, approximately sixty yards south of the road along which the company was traveling. Five men were wounded, and the others grimly hugged the slushy, muddy ground, but soon were crawling forward again as one of the American tanks swung into action and blasted away at the machine guns in the house. The Germans inside fled, but before long they set up again in another house. The tank now swung its cannon toward the machine gun in the field and destroyed it.

Soon, Company E's 2d Platoon was in position to rush the first house. The men occupied it with no opposition and from there laid down covering fire for the 1st Platoon as it assaulted the second house. The German machine gunners fled, abandoning their weapon. But now another threat appeared as a German antitank gun opened fire directly down the street, which forced the American tank to seek shelter behind a house.

It seemed a good idea to find a different way into Horbourg, particularly if Company E wanted support from that tank. The platoon and its tank looked for another point of entry, but in the darkness the Sherman fell into a German tank trap and was out of the action.

A runner went to the rear to summon a second tank, which soon rumbled up out of the dark. With this new tank available and seeing that the German antitank had withdrawn, Company E resumed its advance. The tank fired into buildings ahead of the infantry as the troops moved forward from house to house using hand grenades liberally along the way. Companies F and G moved up and occupied houses on both sides of the street.

But now things got tough. A storm of German antitank, panzerfaust, and machine-gun fire broke out. The fire became so intense that the men had to run for the cellars. The Americans had a toehold in Horbourg, but progress was halted. The Germans were resolved to hold the road junction.

The Americans spent an uneasy night hunkered down in the houses of Horbourg. At daylight, the Germans brought their positions under heavy mortar fire. The GIs had a grim breakfast of K rations as the buildings they occupied slowly got pounded into dust. After what seemed like an eternity, the Americans had to raise their heads to beat off an attack by German infantry, which tried to infiltrate into the houses.

The Americans drove back that attack. Finally at 1300 on 31 January, the French armor and some infantry arrived and pushed through the 2d Battalion's positions. The combined Franco-American force now broke the German resistance, taking seventy prisoners, many of them wounded, and killing about forty, all of which left the Americans to wonder whether this could not have been accomplished earlier, if the French had only come when asked.

There was still sporadic resistance from the western and southern edges of town, including some artillery fire. Suddenly the German prisoners broke and ran to the east, spooked by the artillery fire of their comrades. But they were not the only ones suffering. Two French infantrymen soon followed the Germans, screaming in pain and horror. Both men had arms blown off. Quickly pushing the attack, the tanks and infantrymen cleared house after house.

As evening approached, Horbourg was still taking German artillery and mortar fire. This was the third consecutive night of fighting for the 2d Battalion. The GIs were out of food and were forced to eat whatever they could find in the houses around them. Relief, however, was finally coming. At 2300 on 31 January, elements of the 289th Infantry Regiment, 75th Infantry Division, relieved Duncan's exhausted battalion.

The Germans, knowing that their escape route from Colmar was in grave peril, still fought fiercely with antitank guns, infantry weapons, and artillery, but the Americans held on until more tanks of the 5th DB arrived and broke the German positions. By 2300 on 31 January, the town was clear—though the Germans persisted in dropping artillery shells on it.

At that very time, one German commander, describing the tense situation in the bridgehead, reported that the enemy was only five miles from the bridge at Brisach and the maximum width of the bridgehead was only twenty-five miles. He inquired whether it was necessary to maintain the bridgehead for a protracted time and whether the *Nineteenth Army* was not in danger of being cut off. The dilemma facing the Germans was that both *First* and *Nineteenth armies* were understrength for the tasks facing them. Because the *Nineteenth Army*'s bridgehead was nearly wiped out, von Rundstedt suggested that forces be withdrawn altogether to help the *First Army* ward off the anticipated attack by Patton's Third Army. The Führer refused to sanction such commonsense measures and forbade the evacuation of the bridgehead. He ordered the formations still in the pocket to deploy against attacks in the Colmar and Cernay-Mulhouse sectors, though he did indicate that the Vosges sector was to be only lightly held.

On 1 February, the 254th Infantry Regiment (attached to the 3d Infantry Division) supported by French armor reached the Rhine-Rhône Canal north of its junction with the Colmar Canal. The evening of 1 February saw the 15th and 30th Infantry regiments fighting alongside French tanks pushing south along the Rhine-Rhône Canal to just north of Neuf-Brisach, only about a mile from Neuf-Brisach and about two miles from the Rhine bridge. The 3d Infantry Division was now in Biesheim, northeast of Neuf-Brisach; the 75th Infantry Division was approaching from the northwest; and the city of Colmar was ripe for capture.

Now that Colmar was cut off from Brisach and the Rhine, the Germans had, in essence, two pockets of troops in Alsace, the one in the Vosges now almost cut off. On 1 February, the 28th Infantry Division, which had been holding the Vosges line and probing the German positions, attacked toward Colmar, seeking to crush that pocket. By the morning of 2 February, the division's 109th Infantry Regiment had fought its way through increasingly strong German resistance and arrived at the northern gates of Colmar. Here the Americans paused and allowed the

French tankers of the 5th DB to have the honor of being the first to enter the city, where they were met by deliriously happy Alsatians. The French tankers—doubtless after receiving their fair share of kisses and bottles of wine—split into three groups. One left the city to the west to block the valley of the Fecht River in the Vosges, a route along which German forces to the west now facing isolation might attack. Another group drove straight through the city and pushed on south, blocking egress from the Vosges west and south of Colmar. A third group stayed to help clear the city of Germans alongside the American infantry of the 28th Infantry Division, who soon entered.[40]

On 2 February, French First Army intelligence saw a general German retreat from the territory between the Ill and the Rhine, from Colmar in the north to Krafft-Erstein in the south. To the relief of the French, this lifted any remaining threat to Strasbourg. Also on 2 February, French intelligence picked up signs of the German evacuation of the Alsace pocket via railroad bridges, pontoon bridges, and ferries, and reports indicated that traffic east across these crossings was very heavy. Hitler, it seemed, had changed his mind, or perhaps his forces were doing the right thing despite their Führer's wishes.[41]

The escape route for the Germans in the Vosges was down to the thinnest thread: the road through Rouffach. Now that Colmar had fallen to the XXI Corps, the Americans decided to push as fast as possible along the Colmar-Rouffach road to join up with I Corps, which was still slogging its way northward. The U.S. 12th Armored Division, which earlier had been attached to Monsaberts' II Corps for operations much farther north near Strasbourg, was now given to the XXI Corp to attack south through the 28th Infantry Division, which was still tidying up Colmar itself.

The 12th Armored Division attacked on 3 February. Two CCB task forces got to the Ill and seized bridgeheads across it at Sundhoffen and Ste. Croix-en-Plaine. The third task force got a scant eight hundred yards before being stopped cold. The combat command held its positions during the night of 4–5 February, then was relieved by the 28th Infantry Division's 109th Infantry Regiment.[42]

* * *

General Jean-Marie de Lattre de Tassigny (left) led the French First Army under the command of Lt. Gen. Jacob Devers (right), commanding general of the 6th Army Group. *NARA, 6th Army Group records*

Lieutenant General Alexander "Sandy" Patch commanded the Seventh Army. *NARA, Signal Corps photo*

GIs from the 141st Infantry Regiment, 36th Infantry Division, exit their landing craft on the beach east of St. Raphael on 15 August 1944. *NARA, Signal Corps film*

Americans from the 509th Parachute Infantry Battalion and British comrades from the 2d Independent Parachute Brigade, both part of the First Airborne Task Force, rest beside a farmhouse in southern France on 15 August 1944. *NARA, Signal Corps photo*

A maquis machine-gun crew covers a road on 22 August 1944. The Resistance fighters were good at gathering intelligence, harassing German troops, and guarding supply lines, but they often did not take well to infantry life in the regular army and performed poorly as infantry when supporting American forces. *NARA, Signal Corps photo*

The Sherman tank *Vesoul* of the 4th Squadron, 2d *Cuirassiers*, fires during the fighting around Notre Dame de la Garde cathedral, in central Marseille, on 25 August 1944. *NARA, Signal Corps photo*

Butler Task Force's 117th Cavalry Reconnaissance Squadron advances near Riez on 18 August 1944. *NARA, Signal Corps photo*

Wreckage of German vehicles clogs Highway 7 near Montélimar on 28 August 1944. *NARA, Signal Corps photo*

GIs from the 399th Infantry Regiment, 100th Infantry Division, man positions in a Vosges forest in early November 1944. *NARA, Signal Corps photo*

French First Army and U.S. Third Army troops link up at Autun, France, on 13 September 1944. *NARA, Signal Corps photo*

Seventh Army tanks on 8 November 1944 are almost inundated after forty-three hours of rain. *NARA, Signal Corps photo*

The 1st Battalion, 30th Infantry Regiment, conducts training just before Truscott's surprise in mid-November 1944. *NARA, Signal Corps photo*

Commandos d'Afrique on 24 November 1944 fire a 57mm antitank gun to blast the Germans out of the Chateau du Belfort. *NARA, 6th Army Group records*

The French 2d DB enters Strasbourg on 25 November 1944. *NARA,*
Signal Corps photo

French troops battle Germans still holed up on the French bank
of the Rhine at Huningue on 30 November 1944. *NARA, Signal*
Corps photo

GIs from the 44th Infantry Division examine a captured casemate at Fort Simserhof, in the Maginot Line, in mid-December 1944. *NARA, Signal Corps photo*

The 3d Battalion, 175th Infantry Regiment, works with an M10 during street fighting in Niederbronn on 10 December 1944. NARA, *Signal Corps photo*

Combat Command A, 14th Armored Division, operates in Wissembourg, which lies on the Franco-German border, on 16 December 1944. *NARA, Signal Corps photo*

The 275th Infantry Regiment sets up to defend Phillipsbourg on 1 January 1945, only hours after the beginning of Operation *Nordwind*. *NARA, Signal Corps photo*

The 714th Tank Battalion, 12th Armored Division, readies for its fruitless counterattack on Herrlisheim on 8 January 1945. *NARA, Signal Corps photo*

The 75th Infantry Division advances near Colmar on 31 January 1945.
NARA, Signal Corps photo

French tanks and infantry work their way into Colmar under sniper fire on 2 February 1945. *NARA, Signal Corps photo*

Riflemen from the 3d Infantry Division enter Zweibrücken as Seventh Army begins its final sweep west of the Rhine River in March 1944. *NARA, Signal Corps photo*

Seventh Army troops cross the Rhine River at Worms. *NARA, Signal Corps photo*

A 3d Infantry Division GI takes cover from sniper and machine-gun fire during fighting in Nürnberg on 19 April 1945. *NARA, Signal Corps photo*

Lieutenant General Jacob Devers accepts the surrender of Army Group G from *Generalfeldmarshall* Albert Kesselring on 5 May 1945. *NARA, Signal Corps photo*

Combat Command A did better. It was held up for a day outside Hattstatt by strong German antitank defenses, but the next day it took the town. At 0200 hours on 5 February, it pushed in the direction of Rouffach, over-running German positions along the way, destroying numerous German horse-drawn transports, and generally sweeping all before it.[43]

Shortly after 0500 on 5 February, 1st Lt. Charles Ippolito, leader of the 2d Platoon, Company D of the 43d Tank Battalion, the leading edge of Task Force Scott, reached a roadblock at the northern edge of Rouffach. He wanted some knowledge of where the enemy was before he entered the town, so he dismounted his tank and walked up to the first house he came to. A civilian inside told him that the Germans had left. Leaving that house, he encountered the owner of a nearby chateau, who told Ippolito that he had just come from the far side of Rouffach. The civilian had seen French forces there, but they were not strong enough to move northward, so the Americans would have to go south to effect a juncture. Most of the Germans had left the town, the civilian added, leaving only a few who intended to blow the bridges just east of Rouffach. There were, however, two tanks sitting astride the north-south rail line just east of the bridges.

Shortly after this, Ippolito's superior, Major Hall, showed up. With additional elements of Task Force Scott now available, Hall directed another tank platoon to move east of Rouffach to knock out the reported German tanks and cut off the escape of any Germans still leaving the town. Hall was concerned that the reported presence of Germans imme-diately east of the town might mean there were Germans in the town as well. He did not relish leading his tank-heavy force into the confined streets, where they potentially would be in great danger. He radioed back that, given this possibility, he would need more than the company of infantry that he had. With dawn breaking, the order went out for infantry all down the column stretching north from Rouffach to bypass the tanks and hightail it to help Hall.

As all these urgent preparations were going on for a full-scale assault on Rouffach, the friendly civilian volunteered to go tell the French on the other side of town about the American presence. A French-speaking American sergeant volunteered to go with the civilian, and the two set off, not entirely sure that they might not meet German soldiers along the way. They soon returned, however, reporting that the French force consisted only of a few scout cars, a light tank, and some infantry. The French apparently were delighted to know that the Americans were coming. The French were from the 4th Regiment of Moroccan Spahis of the 4th DMM.

It was time now to link up the two forces. The Americans sealed the exits to the town. Ippolito ordered one of his tanks to ram the roadblock in an effort to knock it down. It seemed like a good plan, but instead the tank rocketed up and over the roadblock, crashing down on the other side. The tank was in perfect working order, but it failed in its task. It took a tank's towing cable to pull apart the roadblock.

The American forces carefully entered the town. After all this preparation, not a shot had to be fired. The Americans took fifteen German prisoners. The French civilians, awakened early from their slumber, poured into the streets and began to celebrate. The Americans quickly reached the other side of town. The spahis removed the mines from their roadblock, and the Americans and Moroccans met. By 0800 the senior French and American officers had agreed on their combined plans for defending the town.

The two corps had linked up, and the Colmar Pocket was cut in two. Elements of four German divisions were surrounded, and now the remaining German forces could be diced even smaller.[44]

* * *

All that remained now was for XXI Corps to sweep forward, scattering the by-now shattered German resistance. By the morning of 6 February, the 7th Infantry Regiment had sealed off Neuf-Brisach. Victory was at hand.

On the night and early morning of 5–6 February, patrols from the 30th Infantry Regiment probed Neuf-Brisach, finding few Germans. At about 0930, a platoon moving south along the Rhine-Rhône Canal met a civilian who led them into a dry moat and showed them a sixty-foot tunnel that led into the city. An hour and forty-five minutes later, Neuf-Brisach was cleared. A grand total of seventy-six enemy troops were there. The record is not clear, but they may not even have been Germans, because they told the Americans who took their surrender that the night before, their officers had urged them to resist to the last man, then had left them to their fate.[45]

By the morning of 9 January, all the German units west of the Rhine had surrendered or been destroyed. Devers' forces were everywhere at the Rhine. The offensive had had something of the quality of the folktale of the man who made stone soup. Repeatedly, commanders from Béthouart to de Lattre to Devers himself had argued that it was a good offensive, but it could be even better if they had more resources. This repeated wheedling had worked.

Despite the fact that I Corps, which had kicked off the offensive, had essentially been stopped in its tracks, and despite the shocking setback of the 30th Infantry Regiment, which might have thrown a lesser outfit than the 3d Infantry Division off-kilter and seriously demoralized it, and despite the occasional minor squabbles between French and American officers, it had been a masterful offensive. De Lattre and all his attached subordinates, both French and American, could feel justifiably proud. Three corps, two of them multinational, had pounded the last major German toehold in France out of existence. It was fitting that de Lattre had commanded the liberation of the last bit of occupied French soil, the long-disputed land of Alsace. Ahead lay the Reich.

But if de Lattre's army was to play any role worthy of the name in Germany, it would have to do it on the cheap. The army had been wobbly, but willing, going into the Colmar offensive. Now it was flush with victory, but very weak.

CHAPTER 12

ACROSS THE RHINE

If he wishes to live and fight another day, the
enemy must choose to fight and run away.

—6th Army Group G-2 Intelligence
Summary, 10 March 1945

After the Franco-American offensive that finally crushed the Colmar
Pocket, the French army rested. In fact, it was ground down and had little
choice. It was a tribute to French determination—sheer cussedness, the
Americans might have said—and the willingness of Africans and others
to suffer and risk their lives for their colonial masters that de Lattre's army
had gotten this far at all.

During this rest period, however, the French continued laying the
foundations for their post-war army. They completed amalgamation of
the FFI into the regular army and replaced all but a few of the colonial
troops. With the increasing number of maquis available, the army raised
another division as well, the 14th DI, the "Colmar and Mulhouse Division."

Despite the fact that the 14th DI was added to the French First Army's
order of battle, the number of divisions at de Lattre's disposal did not
grow. De Lattre lost the 2d DB back to the Americans, and he also lost the
10th DI. Furthermore, he had to cough up the 1st DFL to go to the Alps.[1]

The other Allies did not envision a significant role for the French in
Germany and had allocated no occupation zone to France. Under a plan
called Eclipse, in case of a sudden German collapse a French corps was to
cross the Rhine in the wake of the right flank of the Seventh Army, holding territory for it as it moved on to occupy new regions. Moreover, the

1st and 5th DBs had to lend most of their bridge-building units to Patch's army. At the same time, the eighty British and American divisions manned a frontage of about 355 miles, whereas the seven French divisions covered 135 miles.[2]

Despite the fact that the French army was resting and recuperating, underequipped and overstretched, de Lattre still had every intention of entering Germany. He viewed this as both a duty and a right. In March, an opportunity would arise for the French to take their war to Germany.[3]

* * *

Eisenhower had long insisted that his armies clear the west bank of the Rhine before crossing it. Field Marshal Bernard Montgomery, commanding the 21st Army Group, launched Operation Veritable on 8 February and after three weeks of hard fighting closed to the Rhine. The U.S. Ninth Army, which had been under Montgomery's command since the Battle of the Bulge, crossed the Roer River on 23 February, paced on its right by elements of First Army. The 9th Armored Division on 7 March accomplished what Leclerc had hoped to in Strasbourg when it seized an intact railroad bridge across the Rhine at Remagen. Patton's Third Army attacked into the Palatinate on 1 March, and his marauding divisions quickly reached the Rhine at Koblenz. From there they could cut off the Germans manning the Siegfried Line north of Seventh Army if they turned southeastward across the Moselle River and advanced down the west bank of the Rhine. On 13 March, Third Army kicked off to do just that.

Anticipating that the Germans would soon have to withdraw from the Siegfried Line in front of Seventh Army, the 101st Cavalry Group and 70th Infantry Division patrols energetically felt out the enemy at the left end of the XXI Corps line, which once again faced northward toward the Palatinate adjacent to Third Army's sector. Already on the morning of 13 March, the patrols detected the first signs that German activity had decreased sharply.

In response to verbal orders, two regiments of the 70th Infantry Division surged nearly two miles into the vacuum, to the banks of the Sarre River, where they encountered nothing but a few delaying forces at roadblocks. The Germans were now penned into a roughly triangular space formed by the Saare and Lauter rivers on the south, the Rhine on the northeast, and the Moselle on the northwest. Devers' planners assessed that either the Seventh Army penetrating the Siegfried Line or Patton crossing the Moselle would render the entire area indefensible. They had spent early March putting together a plan to crack the West Wall, which on 8 March was dubbed Operation Undertone.

Reinforced by the 4th Infantry and the 6th and 13th Armored divisions, Seventh Army hit the Germans with three corps controlling eight infantry and three armored divisions. Haislip's XV Corps, in the center, was to make the main effort and attack from the Rimling area through Zweibrücken toward Kaiserslautern. On the right, Brooks' VI Corps was to reclaim the territory it had lost during Northwind, penetrate the Siegfried Line, and continue on to Landau and Neustadt. The French 3d DIA, attached to VI Corps along with elements of the 5th DB, was to cover its advance by clearing the west bank of the Rhine. On the left, Maj. Gen. Frank Milburn's XXI Corps was to cross the relatively short distance—some ten miles—to Neukirchen and isolate the defenses in Saarbrücken from the east. The XII TAC was to block all rail lines prior to D-day and hit transportation and supply dumps. On D-day, the Eighth Air Force was to pummel Zweibrücken, Kaiserslautern, Homburg, and Neukirchen; the 9th Bomb Division was to hit Pirmasens, Neustadt, and Landau; and the 42d Bombardment Wing was to carpet bomb defenses in front of Seventh Army.

Looking ahead to a quick defeat of German forces west of the Rhine, 6th Army Group dusted off its plans for a river crossing. The amphibious equipment it had gathered the preceding fall had been carefully maintained, and the old plans were easily adapted to new crossing sites. The 3d and 45th Infantry divisions were flagged to conduct the operation and received orders on 2 March to undertake ten days of special training. Their attached tank battalions—the 756th and 191st—sent tank crews to train on duplex drive Shermans such as had been used during the Operation Dragoon landings. On 9 March, XV Corps was ordered to ready itself to cross the Rhine near Worms, and the 3d and 45th Infantry divisions joined the corps from SHAEF and Seventh Army reserve, respectively, two days later.[4]

When Devers briefed him on the plan for Undertone, de Lattre immediately realized that it would put the 3d DIA very near the

Pforzheim Gap, between the Black Forest and the Oden Wald in Germany. Better yet, the West Wall did not fully cover the gap. This was an entry point into the Reich that his weakened forces could deal with, if only they could get to it. De Lattre vowed that somehow they would. Without informing Major General Brooks, the VI Corps commander to whom Guillaume officially reported, de Lattre wrote a note to Guillaume directing him "to go as far as possible, no matter what the orders," to get as close as possible to the Pforzheim Gap with sufficient frontage on the Rhine to effect a crossing in force. Though the French had to put up with some halfhearted protestations from Brooks and had to beg from Devers some further boundary adjustments, de Lattre soon had what he wanted.[5]

* * *

D-day for Operation Undertone was 15 March. The Germans really did not stand much of a chance. Haislip's XV Corps struck first. At 0100 hours, the 45th and 3d Infantry divisions moved out silently through the lines of the 44th Infantry Division and easily overran the forward German defenses. The two assault divisions pushed on deeper into Germany, bypassing strongpoints as they went, and reached the main West Wall defenses around Zweibrücken by 17 March—an advance of between five and ten miles. Only at Utweiler, in the 3d Infantry Division's area, did the Germans counterattack vigorously, and briefly managed to surround a battalion of the 7th Infantry Regiment.[6]

On the corps' right, the 100th Infantry Division attacked with the objective of capturing Bitche. The GIs from the 398th Infantry Regiment, in the center, had to retake Fort Schiesseck, which turned out to be little trouble because the division had so thoroughly demolished the defenses there the preceding December. The 398th Infantry Regiment seized Fort Otterbiel, north of Bitche, the next day, and the now isolated town fell to the regiment's 2d Battalion. The 100th Infantry Division then pushed northward to the Siegfried Line, turning over Bitche to the newly arrived 71st Infantry Division.[7]

* * *

In the VI Corps zone, the 42d Infantry Division, on the left wing, attacked at 0645 hours against German defenses that enjoyed the benefits of the Vosges terrain. The attacking regiments avoided the mined and blocked roads and clambered over the hills, moving supplies forward by mule trains. The 242d Infantry Regiment reached high ground overlooking Baerenthal, and its capture of that town the next day sent the Germans all along the line retreating northward to avoid being cut off. The 42d Division pushed forward against almost no resistance until it entered Germany on 18 March and encountered the Siegfried Line.

The 103d Infantry Division, just to the east, attacked simultaneously on 15 March against little resistance and pushed to the Zinser River. Here the Germans tried to delay the advance from dug-in positions, but the 103d Division captured Zinswiller and Oberbronn and sent the Germans retreating through Reichshoffen. As in other areas, the German withdrawal continued to the Siegfried Line, and the 103d Division advanced easily into Germany on 18 March, even capturing intact two bridges built by American engineers back in December.

The 36th Infantry Division, on the corps' right wing, pushed off at the same 0100 H-hour as XV Corps and by 1045 had overrun the German line. Dahlquist's division, too, was in a headlong rush toward Germany by the next day. It was delayed occasionally by holding actions as the Germans pulled back toward the West Wall defenses, which the Americans reached late on 19 March. The 14th Armored Division's CCA took up positions facing the Siegfried Line on the 36th Division's right on 20 March.

The attached French 3d DIA joined the action at 0745 hours on 15 March and experienced a similar advance to the German frontier. The original plan had been for the division to revert to French control upon reaching the Lauter River, which marked the border, but that would have meant that the division would halt offensive operations. Instead, a task force under the command of General Monsabert was created on 19 March to continue pushing north under Seventh Army control. The task force crossed the river the next day and pushed northward against spirited resistance until it reached the Siegfried Line on 20 March.[8]

* * *

Whereas Seventh Army's other two corps had to advance to the West Wall from their lines of departure, XXI Corps' divisions already confronted those fortifications. The corps attacked with only its 63d Infantry Division at 0100 on 15 March. The 70th Infantry Division and 101st

Cavalry Group, on the left wing, had only to hold the enemy in place around Saarbrücken, while the 12th Armored Division waited to exploit any hole the assault division might create.

The 63d Infantry Division had the hardest fight in Seventh Army during the initial assault. For three days the division struggled to overcome thick minefields, determined resistance from pillboxes, and frequent tank-infantry counterattacks.

The 70th Infantry Division finally went into motion on 19 March. Despite a tremendous pre-assault pounding by everything from antiaircraft guns to heavy artillery, the Germans at first fought back stubbornly from their pillboxes. Reconnaissance flights nonetheless reported that German troops and civilians were heading northward. By evening, advancing GIs found empty pillboxes. The division captured Saarbrücken the next day without the loss of a single soldier.[9]

* * *

While Seventh Army's troops were gaining momentum along the front, Eisenhower and Patton flew to Lunéville on 17 March to meet with Devers and Patch. Ike asked whether Patch would mind if Third Army were assigned objectives in Seventh Army's zone, to which Patch replied, "We are all in the same army."[10]

Patton intended to take Kaiserslautern, then turn two divisions south to link up with VI Corps, on the Rhine. He sent XX and XII corps pounding eastward, and within two days the 11th Armored Division had almost drawn a noose around *XIII SS* and *LXXX corps.* On 20 March, the 4th Armored Division fought its way into Worms, and German resistance before Third Army degenerated into panicked chaos.[11]

* * *

A vacuum to their rear sucked at the staying power of the Germans in front of Patch's troops, and on 20 March the 63d, 45th, and 3d Infantry divisions all breached the Siegfried Line. The 6th Armored Division raced through the gap created by the 63d Division and raced across the German rear to Rhine-Durkheim, on the banks of the Rhine, which it reached at noon on 21 March. Patrols entered Worms and made contact with Third Army elements.

After two days of tough fighting, GIs from the 42d Infantry Division in VI Corps discovered the pillboxes in front of them to be empty when they attacked on 21 March. The next day, German implosion spread east to the 103d Infantry Division's area, where prisoners indicated that some units had been ordered to fight until dusk, then pull back to the Rhine. Elements of the 14th Armored Division rolled through the hole created by the 103d Division and struck toward the Rhine against scattered resistance. Resistance in front of the 36th Infantry Division, another step to the east, crumbled on 23 March and began to give way before General Montsabert's French task force.[12]

SS *Oberstgruppenführer* Paul Hausser had taken command of *Army Group G* on 25 January. His operations officer, *Oberst (I.G.)* Horst Wilutzky, later described the collapse from the German perspective: "It was only on 18 March 1945, when *First Army* had already started its retreat, that *Army Group G* was authorized to partially give up the Saar district—but it was already too late. . . . Orderly withdrawal of the main formations became impossible, as the mobile formations of the enemy had driven deep wedges into our front and, cooperating with their air forces, cut off and destroyed a number of German divisions, comprising almost all formations of *Seventh Army* (excluding the *6th SS Mountain Division*), the divisions of *LXXXII Corps*, and elements of *LXXXV Corps*. . . . It was at least possible to move to the Rhine formations of *XIII SS* and *XC corps*, employed on the left wing of *First Army*, in more or less intact condition. Very little had been done for the defense of the eastern bank of the Rhine."[13]

Advancing American troops found the Palatinate in a state of chaos. Zweibrücken and Homburg were in flames, the corpses of humans and horses lay everywhere, and looting and small riots were breaking out. In Bad Durkheim, a wine and liquor center, drunken civilians pillaged their own city. Now that Seventh Army had entered Germany, these were its problems to deal with, because the Americans could not turn over such matters to the French as they could have previously. Patch's staff moved military government units forward as quickly as the combat situation allowed.

By 25 March, Seventh Army was settled in along the length of the Rhine in its entire zone, and it readied to cross the river at the first opportunity.[14] Haislip's XV Corps occupied the stretch between Gernsheim and Mannheim, and its engineers quickly readied rafts and ferries to support the crossing.[15]

Seventh Army Crosses the Rhine

The 6th Army Group, having held much of the Rhine's west bank for four months, was relegated to last place in the Allies' crossing of that river. Worse yet, from the French perspective, de Lattre's army received no support for a crossing at all.

Wade Haislip's XV Corps was to jump the Rhine in the Worms area on 26 March. The 3d Division was to cross south of the city while the 45th Division made its assault to the north. Patch instructed XXI and VI corps to prepare contingency plans to establish a bridgehead in the Speyer-Germersheim area in case something went poorly.[16] In a slight twist of fate, the remnants of the German *Seventh Army* held the far bank against its American opposite number.[17]

The 6th Army G-2 as of 24 March assessed, "*Army Group G* has been reduced to merely an expression. . . . The enemy is restricted to a single capability: to withdraw into the interior of Germany before our advancing forces."[18] Indeed, other than the elements that had escaped the debacle on the west bank of the Rhine, *Army Group G* had in reserve only two training divisions that it judged unfit for combat.[19]

Nevertheless, the assault divisions had little idea what awaited them on the far bank, and Seventh Army doubted that even the Germans had any real notion of what units they had there after the rout west of the river. Commanders were able to fly over the terrain that they would be crossing, albeit under vigorous antiaircraft fire. Aerial reconnaissance and information from prisoners indicated that the 45th Infantry Division faced some home guard and two regiments of the *553d Volksgrenadier Division*, but a four-man nighttime patrol led by the commander of the 1st Battalion, 180th Infantry, which paddled across the Rhine the night of 24–25 March, found no mines, no barbed wire, and no emplacements. Later reconstruction based on prisoner interrogations indicated that elements of the *36th* and *159th Infantry divisions* were also in the area.[20]

The plan called for an assault at 0230 hours without an artillery preparation that would alert the Germans, who in fact knew that the assault was coming thanks to intercepted radio messages. The 45th Infantry Division history recorded the scene early on 26 March: "At 0230 hours, in a heavy spiraling fog through which the moonlight picked out the dim figures of the 3d and 45th division infantrymen, the crossing of the Rhine was forced. Even before the engines of the assault boats began to roar, the wary Germans probed into the mists with streams of fire. Then as the small craft reached the eastern shore, heavy resistance met the assault troops as the Germans strove to hold them back, supported by fire from 88mm guns, 20mm flak guns, and machine guns."[21]

In the 45th Infantry Division zone around Worms, the 180th Infantry Regiment confronted the strongest resistance, and half the initial wave of assault boats was lost to German fire. Once the remaining GIs scrambled up the east bank and suppressed the guns, no further serious resistance stood in the way. By dusk, the 45th Division had carved out a forty-square-mile bridgehead.[22]

The 3d Infantry Division's engineers came under heavy artillery fire even before the assault boats were in the water. Surprise obviously lost, the division's artillery replied in kind, and one battalion of the 7th Infantry jumped off four minutes early to take advantage of the friendly barrage and thereby became the 6th Army Group's first outfit to cross the river. In contrast to the 45th Division's experience, the men encountered little fire, but resistance built as the GIs worked eastward. German troops (probably officer reserve candidates from the Frankfurt area and elements of the *159th Infantry Division*) even counterattacked the 30th Infantry Regiment at Burstadt and Lampertheim in the course of the morning, but they were driven off. At Sandhofen, the 7th Infantry's 1st Battalion became enmeshed in house-to-house fighting that lasted all day and required commitment of the 2d Battalion to resolve.[23]

INTO THE REICH

The 3d and 45th Infantry divisions surged toward the Main River on 27 March, the 44th Infantry Division filled in behind the 3d Division to secure the right flank, and the 12th Armored Division crossed the same day—the first of a huge surge to follow. The first two divisions of XXI Corps were across by 29 March, and VI Corps worked eastward the next day. Haislip's corps had cracked the last coherent German "line" that Seventh Army would face in the war.

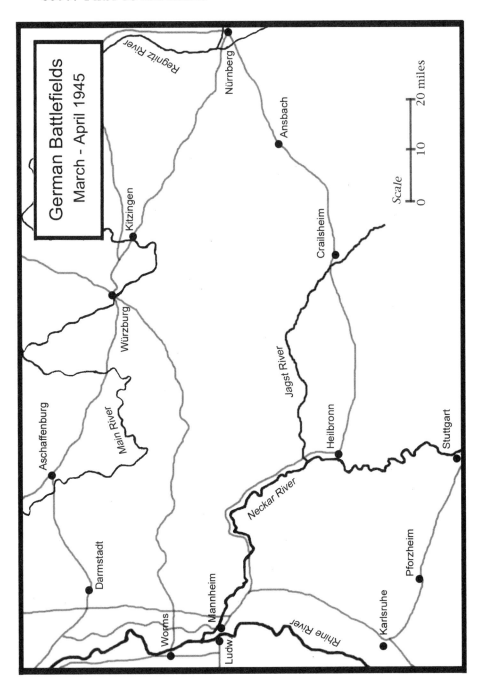

German Battlefields
March - April 1945

Scale

0 10 20 miles

Regnitz River
Nürnberg
Ansbach
Kitzingen
Crailsheim
Würzburg
Jagst River
Aschaffenburg
Main River
Heilbronn
Stuttgart
Neckar River
Pforzheim
Darmstadt
Mannheim
Worms
Karlsruhe
Ludw
Rhine River

Seventh Army charged eastward, XV Corps on its left, XXI Corps in the center, and VI Corps on its right, with a general mission of protecting the right flank of Bradley's 12th Army Group. Over the next four weeks, Seventh Army would race 120 miles northeastward to the Hohe Rhön hills, 100 miles east to Nürnberg, and 120 miles southeast to the Danube. Many columns moved so fast that they had to be supplied by air.

As of 28 March, Seventh Army judged that only six thousand poorly organized combat troops were present on its front.[24] Henceforth, isolated but often tough resistance generally would be found in towns or military facilities such as flak batteries and barracks, or along short stretches of a river.

Or in cities. On 28 March, the 45th Infantry Division arrived at Aschaffenburg, which proved to be the first of several tough urban battles. *Army Group G* was attempting to construct a line along the Main River and had transferred *LXXXV Corps* from *First* to *Seventh Army* to execute the mission. *OKW* had ordered the *413th Division*, slapped together from training units, to reinforce positions north and south of Aschaffenburg. The army group was hurriedly refitting the *36th Infantry* and *17th SS Panzergrenadier divisions* from its dwindling stocks and planned to bring them forward as soon as possible.[25]

The 45th Division crossed to the east bank of the Main River and found an organized defense anchored in pillboxes and trenches and backed by artillery and mortars. The GIs encountered elements they initially identified as the *553d Volksgrenadier Division*, although *Oberst* Wilutzky's account indicates that the troops belonged to the *413th Division*. The 2d Battalion, 157th Infantry Regiment, which had crossed the Main over a railroad bridge, attacked Aschaffenburg, where it encountered heavy small-arms, machine-gun, and antitank fire that slowed the advance to a painstaking crawl.[26]

After getting a first taste of the resistance, the division reported that an estimated 3,500 "Krauts" were in Aschaffenburg.[27] The division's AAR records the following for 29 March: "Enemy resistance . . . soared to a peak of fanaticism. . . . Civilians without [*Volkssturm*, or militia] armbands fighting in Schweinheim and Aschaffenburg necessitated searching every house and building. Enemy reinforcements arrived steadily, and elements of the *36th Infantry Division* were identified. Many of the enemy soldiers were 16- and 17-year-old boys who refused to surrender and had to be killed in their foxholes and trenches." The division's history added, "[Garrison commander] *Major* von Lambert organized old men, women, and young girls to resist the division's advance. They hurled grenades from roofs and second-story buildings." (Von Lambert had permitted all civilians who wished to leave to do so by 29 March.)

The 2d Battalion pounded Aschaffenburg while tank destroyers fired at a church steeple serving as an observation post (OP) and at strongpoints, and numerous fires flared around the city. The 3d Battalion struggled to clear nearby Schweinheim to open a route that would allow the regiment to envelop Aschaffenburg from the east. Three battalion-sized counterattacks hit the Americans in the course of the day before the Germans withdrew to the northern part of town.

Commanders the next day ordered up air strikes against targets in Aschaffenburg, including von Lambert's headquarters in the Gestapo building. A chemical mortar battalion rained white phosphorus on the city, igniting yet more blazes. The 3d Battalion managed to reach the last row of houses in Schweinheim by dusk, but German troops reinfiltrated behind the Americans. As a result, when the 2d Battalion moved forward for a day of house-to-house fighting in Aschaffenburg, the 3d Battalion had to refight the battle in Schweinheim.

Finally, on 2 April, the regiment was able to commit all three of its battalions to Aschaffenburg, which continued to shudder under air and artillery bombardment. Self-propelled 155mm guns were brought into the city to fire point-blank into buildings. At 0900 hours on 3 April, von Lambert approached the lines of the 2d Battalion and capitulated. One German officer estimated that the defenders had suffered 1,500 personnel killed and wounded, and another 3,000 were taken prisoner. The GIs, recalling their toughest fight in Italy, henceforth called the ruined city "Cassino-on-the-Main."[28]

The Germans had expended almost everything they had in front of XV Corps at Aschaffenburg. From here, the Americans would encounter almost no organized resistance until they reached Nürnberg.[29] Irreparable holes had emerged between *Army Groups G* and *B*, and between the armies within *Army Group G*.[30]

* * *

On 28 March, Devers ordered the French to cross the Rhine with a corps of at least two infantry divisions and an armored division. Their tasks, important in light of later developments, were to capture Karlsruhe, Pforzheim, and Stuttgart. Jubilant, de Lattre called a commanders' conference and announced that on 31 March the French forces should be prepared to cross the Rhine. Monsabert's II Corps would take the lead.[31]

The next day, de Lattre was at General Béthouart's headquarters when he received a message from de Gaulle saying that it was vitally important that the French army get to Karlsruhe and Stuttgart immediately. The crossing would have to be moved up a day. Béthouart and his senior staff watched in silent astonishment as de Lattre dealt with the matter. He had a call placed to Monsabert. "Allô, Monsabert, you will cross the Rhine tomorrow." There was silence in the room. Nobody could hear Monsabert's response. Suddenly de Lattre spoke again. "What do you mean 'we will try'?! It is not a question of trying. It is an order." And with that, de Lattre hung up the phone.[32]

The crossing would now happen on the night of 30–31 March, no matter how ready Monsabert was. The key thing, in de Lattre's mind, and de Gaulle's as well, was to prevent the Americans from occupying the German territory into which the French intended to go. The fact that only a tiny and motley collection of boats was available did not matter. The French army was going to cross the Rhine, an event that had not taken place since the Napoleonic era.

At 0230 hours on 31 March, the French "invasion" started near the town of Speyer. The 3d RTA of the 3d DIA received the honor of crossing first. The crossing started with only a single inflatable rubber boat. In the first three hours of the operation, scarcely more than a platoon crossed the river. Then four more rubber boats appeared. By dawn, an entire company was across. Then seven motorboats arrived. By 1000 an entire battalion was across.

This battalion started taking losses as the Germans brought the tiny bridgehead under fire, but the Frenchmen held on and created a deep enough position to provide at least a little bit of protection for the engineers. By 2200 on 31 March, the engineers were building a ten-ton bridge.

Shortly after first light on 31 March, two other crossings started farther south in the 2d DIM's sector, one by the 151st Infantry Regiment (RI), the other by the 3d Battalion of the 4th RTM. The latter set out with a magnificent ten boats, but the enemy was alerted and ready. Between enemy action and mechanical breakdowns, only three boats of the first wave got across. They were carrying a platoon of men, who were forced to take cover beneath the riverbank under fire from a German blockhouse. More boats attempted the crossing and more soldiers drowned in the river, but slowly, painfully, the French forces built up. By 0800, a company of troops held a bridgehead of 50 meters by 150 meters. Soon that force was more than doubled, despite the artillery shells raining down. Every once in a while the artillery would pause for a German infantry attack. The Moroccans were stuck between Wehrmacht fire and Rhine water and forced to repel four successive attacks, but they held. Eventually the 151st RI and 4th RTM bridgeheads merged, but they could have been wiped out at any time had the Germans been able to mount a sufficiently sizable attack or find a few tanks. The spirit of the day can be summed up by the message from one small unit radioed back from the east bank as the battle raged: "Ten killed, thirty wounded, eight able-bodied men. We will hold on."[33]

The 4th RTM and the 151st RI crossing was preceded at 0400 by a violent artillery barrage softening up the German positions on the east bank of the Rhine. The German forces opposing the French crossing were from the *2d Mountain Division*. They had virtually no reserves ready to throw at the French and had to rely primarily on artillery and mortar fire to make life miserable for this insignificant crossing. They also raked the surface of the river with machine-gun fire. However, as the morning wore on, the French forces grew. At some point, the German division decided that it should attack, but it was in such a weak and disorganized state that it managed to find only a company to do the job. The French forces fended off attack after attack, and soon they were strong enough that the Germans had to pull back.[34]

All the sacrifice and suffering paid off. On 1 April, the 3d DIA and the 2d DIM moved across the Rhine in force and pushed as far as fourteen miles into the German heartland.[35] De Lattre was relieved and euphoric.

His haste had prevented Seventh Army's fourteen divisions from filling up the Pforzheim Gap themselves and blocking out the French. De Lattre now urged his men on toward Karlsruhe, Pforzheim, and Stuttgart.[36]

Over the coming days, the French forces continued to expand and surged forward, annihilating pathetic *Volksturm* and Hitler Youth units, finally wiping from the map the remnants of divisions, such at the *198th Infantry Division*, that had fought them to a standstill a few months earlier in the Vosges.[37]

The Germans were running out of troops and running out of space, as well. On 4 April, the day that the 9th DIC, which had crossed the Rhine south of the 2d DIM, took Karlsruhe, an order came down from the German High Command that Allied penetrations would no longer lead to a withdrawal of German forces to establish a new line farther back. Henceforth, German forces were to stay in place and attack the flanks of the penetrating Allied units. In the *16th Volksgrenadier Division*, one officer, upon hearing of this order, commented sarcastically, "So much the better, if we have to remain in place. We'll be taken prisoner more quickly." The next day, French tanks encircled the division's headquarters and gave this man his wish.[38]

With French forces on the verge of victory, there is some evidence that their discipline was starting to fray. A soldier of the 3d DIA traveling with three buddies in early April recalls visiting a small town in which an antitank unit was staying. They found the town in an uproar because Moroccan goumiers, encamped in the nearby woods, had come to town and taken some of the local women into the woods with them. The French soldier and his buddies decided not to get involved.[39]

* * *

Army Group G on 3 April wrote off its *Seventh Army*, which was then reeling back toward Eisenach, as beyond its ability to control and decided to fight on in southern Germany using only its *First Army*. At roughly the same time, it unilaterally subordinated to itself *Nineteenth Army*, opposite the French, which had lost all contact with *OB West Generalfeldmarschall* Albert Kesselring, who had succeeded von Rundstedt in March and had been controlling *Nineteenth Army* directly. Berlin on 4 April appointed *General der Infanterie* Friedrich Schulz commanding general of *Army Group G*, perhaps in lieu of troops it could not provide. The unfortunate general arrived fresh from a meeting with Hitler bearing orders to stage a massive counterattack that he could not even pretend to carry out. Schulz evidently shrugged his shoulders and set about planning an organized retreat through the Franconian and Schwabian uplands to the Danube river.

First Army's XIII SS Corps was just then trying to slow the American surge at Würzburg.[40] The 42d Infantry Division, part of XXI Corps, fought from 3 to 5 April to clear the city. Civilians, police, and firemen joined the German troops in battle, and the defenders never did surrender en masse. The city was simply secured after a last-gasp counterattack by two hundred men was wiped out. After that, XXI Corps had almost a clear run to Schweinfurt.[41]

Hellacious Heilbronn

VI Corps' 100th Infantry Division had perhaps an even tougher fight at Heilbronn, which it attacked across the Neckar River on 4 April. Hills to the east and north dominated the town and gave German artillery observers a perfect view of the bowl below, and German guns had excellent lines of fire. The First Army's XIII Corps (an army staff commanded by Generalleutnant Max Bork, not to be confused with XIII SS Corps) had collected elements of some old Seventh Army foes here: the 246th and 553d Volksgrenadier divisions, the 198th Infantry Division, the 17th SS Panzergrenadier Division, and the 2d Mountain Division. They held a string of strongpoints anchored in Heilbronn and running forty miles north along the Neckar River, then northeast along the Jagst River. Inside Heilbronn, large numbers of Hitler Youth formed battle groups to support the regular troops. The defenders had panzerfausts in abundance, and even a few panzers.

The 398th Infantry Regiment's 3d Battalion crossed the Neckar before dawn in assault boats, intent on establishing a bridgehead amid the factories on the far bank so the engineers could build a bridge. The GIs seemed to have surprised any defenders in the neighborhood, and all went well at first. At 0900 hours, however, Germans counterattacked from three directions, and the 3d Battalion reeled back toward the river with heavy losses. Two platoons were cut off and captured. The 3d Battalion attacked again but succeeded only in establishing a line some thousand yards from the Neckar.

The 10th Armored Division, which was trying to put in a bridge nearby at Neckargartach, was also hit by a counterattack supported by artillery. The Germans nearly drove the armored infantry, which had established a bridgehead, back into the river. At first, VI Corps commanding general Brooks was disbelieving. "They don't have enough stuff to counterattack with," he told the 10th Armored Division operations officer. "They don't have a sizable force there."

For a time, direct fire sweeping the river prevented reinforcements from joining the fight in Heilbronn. The 2d Battalion, 397th Infantry Regiment, managed to cross the Neckar during the afternoon to attack beside the battered 3d Battalion. It was turned back with heavy casualties. Heavy artillery fire in the meantime sank the rafts that the engineers had brought forward to ferry tanks across the river and stopped every effort to build a bridge.

The 63d Infantry Division, meanwhile, had encountered resistance along the Jagst River. Brooks decided to send the 10th Armored Division on a wide circling maneuver to get behind the enemy at both points. This would have been a brilliant plan if the Germans had still been worrying about lines of communication instead of waging a last-ditch defense.

On 5 April, the 397th Infantry's 3d Battalion joined the fighting in Heilbronn. The GIs fought their way from building to building without any tank support; accurate German artillery fire still prevented any work on a bridge. Burning buildings lit the riverbanks so well at night that engineers continued to draw heavy artillery fire, which prevented work on a desperately needed span. VI Corps frantically arranged for the delivery of ten DD Shermans to the 781st Tank Battalion, which was attached to the 100th Infantry Division.

German counterattacks on 6 April included panzers for the first time. The GIs had only their bazookas to handle the armor, and they knocked out two tanks. Friendly artillery fire destroyed another two, but more than two hundred riflemen were killed, wounded, or captured before the German pressure abated.

After crews received a day of minimal training, the 781st Tank Battalion's DD Shermans entered the water on 7 April, but they were unable to climb the other side, and three sank. Finally, on 8 April, two tank platoons made the trip across a temporary bridge, which was immediately knocked out by enemy artillery. On 12 April, American riflemen and tanks pushed the German artillery out of range of the bridging sites, and the next day Heilbronn fell.

The 10th Armored Division's envelopment operation, meanwhile, turned into a bit of a fiasco. Combat Command A easily rolled thirty miles into Crailsheim on 6 April; a task force occupied the town while two others pressed on. Small groups of German troops, probably from the *1st Alpine Regiment*, which by chance had just arrived in the area, slipped behind the command and closed the single narrow road that was the armored outfit's supply line. Perhaps because the Luftwaffe saw no point in hoarding fuel or aircraft, air strikes by German fighter-bombers increased as Allied forces progressed deeper into the Reich. Me-110 bombing runs against the troops in Crailsheim that day suggested that there was still some coordination going on with ground forces, and more air attacks in support of ground assaults took place over the next several days.

"For four days," noted *Stars and Stripes*, "the fighting at the tip of the Crailsheim finger was the most bitter along the western front." Brooks had to commit CCB from corps reserve along with a cavalry squadron and an infantry regiment from the 44th Infantry Division to flush the German combat groups from the length of the road and the villages alongside it, which took until 10 April.

Inside Crailsheim, as many as seven hundred SS troopers from a school at Ellwangen attacked Combat Command A on 8 April from three directions and inflicted numerous casualties. When sixty C-47 transports were ordered to land at the captured Crailsheim airfield to deliver supplies and evacuate casualties on 9 April, German fighter-bombers appeared and strafed and bombed the aerodrome. A battalion-sized SS force attacked the Americans again on 10 April. Once the 10th Armored Division linked up with the 63d Infantry Division, which had also had a rough time with the SS, it abandoned Crailsheim rather than fight to hold the unimportant town. Within a day after Heilbronn's capture, the SS had largely been wiped out or slipped away.[42]

According to a fairly substantial body of German post-war accounts, after this and other stiff actions involving the SS—at a time when the war was clearly lost, and GIs increasingly resented the idea of being killed for no good reason—some American troops summarily executed groups of captured SS men.[43] It is possible that the liberation of a growing number of concentration camps also contributed to these ugly violations of the rules of war.

Nazi Nürnberg

The 45th Infantry Division on 7 April pivoted from its northeastward axis of advance toward the southeast for the first time in its long experience in battle. Munich lay 450 miles distant.[44] Not far ahead, the headquarters of *OB West* moved to Nürnberg on or about 10 April, and *Generalfeldmarschall* Kesselring reestablished direct control over *Nineteenth Army* as well as *Army Group G.*[45]

Nürnberg, the scene of massive Nazi Party rallies in happier times for Hitler, was the last big fight for Seventh Army. This last job, as had the first, fell to the 3d and 45th Infantry divisions. The two veteran outfits approached Nürnberg on 16 April in an envelopment maneuver. The 3d Division advanced southeastward to capture the part of the city north of the Pegnitz River, while the 45th Division, on its left, wheeled past the city to the east and advanced into its southern outskirts with three regiments abreast.[46]

A ring of 88mm flak batteries around the city offered the first resistance but was reduced during the day, while a few battalions of Luftwaffe ground troops and *Volksturm* militia defended the streets. The 45th Infantry Division's drive into the city proper began on 17 April and made good progress against infantry and more flak batteries. An attempt that day by the *17th SS Panzergrenadier Division* to break into the city to reinforce the garrison failed. Progress slowed the following day as resistance built from house to house, but by 19 April the GIs had pushed to the ancient stone walls of the old city, where an estimated two thousand German troops clearly planned a last stand.[47]

On 20 April, the 3d Infantry Division's 2d Battalion, 7th Infantry, entered the part of the old city north of the river. At about noon, it made contact with elements of the 30th Infantry, marking the end of organized resistance in that zone. The 45th Infantry Division's 180th Infantry Regiment in the meantime faced such stiff resistance from sniper, small-arms, machine-gun, bazooka, and mortar fire that it committed all three of its battalions to house-to-house fighting. Resistance collapsed about 1600 hours, except for a last stand by some two hundred die-hards who had holed up in an underground passage. The GIs finally eliminated this last strongpoint at 2250.[48]

XV Corps had taken the last major Nazi stronghold that would defy American arms and sent Hitler its own special birthday present.

The French Enter the Black Forest

As de Lattre's army passed through the Pforzheim Gap, it was able to move briskly on its left. To its right, however, it was increasingly bogged down in the Black Forest, defended by the *Nineteenth Army*, a shadow of its former self but still needing to be reckoned with.[49]

Nineteenth Army, commanded since mid-March by *General der Panzertruppen* Erich Brandenberger, had three nominal corps but only a single division—the *198th Infantry*—still worthy of the name. Otherwise, Brandenberger had regiment-sized remnants of several volksgrenadier divisions and a mix of police, militia, and border guard units supported by some fortress artillery battalions. By and large, these formations were immobile.[50]

De Lattre decided that he would seize the bull by the horns and send his forces through the forest. This was, of course, attacking on terrain that strongly favored the defense. It was traversed by small, winding roads and hemmed in on all sides by trees. Ambushers could get near the French troops without being seen. A few felled trees and mines could hold up a column for hours. This effort, undertaken by forces of II Corps, was to meet up with I Corps elements, still recovering back in France, which were to cross the Rhine at Strasbourg and drive to Freudenstadt, roughly in the center of the Black Forest. This would cut the *Nineteenth Army* into two pieces and, hopefully, sound its death knell.[51]

French forces plunged into the Black Forest on the night of 11–12 April. Elements of the 9th DIC drove south in the area between the Rhine and the Black Forest to secure the banks of the Rhine opposite

Strasbourg, where the Germans were still shelling the city from time to time. On 16 April, Béthouart's troops staged a glorious parade in Strasbourg in front of a grateful crowd that practically screamed itself hoarse. The parade was merely an excuse to assemble forces to cross the river. That day infantry and spahis rafted across. More followed, and a junction was made with the 9th DIC. *Nineteenth Army* commanding general Brandenberger threw his only reserve, the remnants of the *16th Volksgrenadier Division*, into a counterattack, but as the general later noted, "The French attack was hardly slowed down."[52] The German defenders fell into disorder. Sensing this, General Linarès, recently given command of the 2d DIM, told his troops, "Push to the limit—by night and without concern for alignment." Freudenstadt fell on 17 April.

I Corps spent 19–27 April enveloping the southern part of the Black Forest and in the process destroyed the *XVIII SS Corps*. This corps, commanded by SS *Obergruppenführer* Georg Keppler, struck hard but unsuccessfully on 25 April to break free, then denied the French a proper surrender. Béthouart's forces had the corps surrounded and taking tremendous punishment, so he wrote a letter to Keppler in which he pointed out that he and his men were doomed. Before a way could be found to get the letter to Keppler, he held a meeting of his officers; they agreed to cease resistance and allow each man to escape on his own as best he could.[53]

THE END, AND THE BEGINNING

The last weeks of the war brought to the surface the French pattern of recalcitrance toward the Allied military command that was to roil relations between Paris and its presumptive partners for the next half-century.

Despite—or perhaps because of—the fact that the French were routing the Germans in and around the Black Forest, the Americans were not pleased. On 16 April, Devers sent de Lattre a letter of instruction saying that the French First Army should clear out only the eastern bank of the Rhine and, as a secondary matter, attack Stuttgart from the west. It was not to move east from the Black Forest. Instead, the Americans would move southeast down the east side of the Black Forest, a maneuver that would hem in the Germans—but also the French. In any event, there should not be "a premature advance by the French First Army."[54]

The French were having none of this. At a conference in the still-burning Freudenstadt on 18 April, the French turned their attention to capturing Stuttgart and clearing out the southern half of the Black Forest. The former task fell to Monsabert's II Corps, the latter to Béthouart's I Corps, most of which was still crossing the Rhine in the Strasbourg area.[55] Béthouart had further orders. De Lattre told him, "Eisenhower has given me the order to stop, but I refuse. . . . You will cross the Danube on the 22d. I want Constance and Ulm on the 25th."[56]

Having earlier been the first Allied unit to reach the Rhine, the 1st DB on 21 April became the first to cross the Danube. Having crossed the river, the 1st DB turned eastward, going parallel to the Danube, driving toward Ulm, just as de Lattre wanted it to and just as Devers did not.[57]

As two combat commands of the 1st DB rolled along the south bank of the Danube, the Americans, moving along the north bank of the river, stayed with them. As it approached Ulm, about forty miles outside the French First Army's zone, VI Corps found that French troops had moved into its path of advance to the southeast. Major General Brooks ordered the 44th Infantry Division to stop the French advance if possible, but it was too late. Brooks next contacted Maj. Gen. William Morris at his 10th Armored Division headquarters. "If necessary, you put a tank at right angle across the road and physically block their traffic. . . . You tell them that they are out of their territory, and the commander of the 6th Army Group tells them to get back in their own zone."[58]

The French met no resistance worthy of the name, and on 24 April they reached Ulm. They arrived ten hours before the American 44th Infantry Division, which thought that it was going to attack the city. The French and American commanders on the spot reached a modus vivendi, and they mounted a coordinated attack into the town.[59]

The French presence in Ulm soon had repercussions. Devers protested to the French that they were not supposed to have moved in this direction, let alone taken the city.[60]

To de Lattre, it was important to get to Ulm for symbolic reasons, namely that Napoleon had once been wounded there. There were two more important reasons in his mind. First, he wanted to get behind the German forces still defending in the general Stuttgart area (a task that the

Americans, per orders, were executing). He envisioned Monsabert's II Corps, which was fighting in that area, driving these German forces onto the rocks of the I Corps positions at Ulm.

The second reason was more strategic and political. All the Allies were concerned that the remnants of the German military would retreat into Bavaria and man an "Alpine redoubt," postponing the destruction of Nazism and forcing the Allies to pay tremendous human costs attacking into the mountains. By taking Ulm, de Lattre believed he was ensuring that France would own part of the front if the Allies were forced to attack an Alpine redoubt.[61]

In American eyes, these were insufficient reasons for outright disobedience of orders. Devers again issued instructions telling de Lattre to get his forces out of the way, but the French troops took two days to comply. The 6th Army Group blamed this delay for prolonging the fighting before *Army Group G* offered to surrender.[62]

Ike, moreover, had already reached a quite different prescription for the redoubt problem than did the French. The reason that VI Corps was in the Ulm area was that on 16 April, he had turned the 6th Army Group south in part to eliminate any danger that the Germans would man such a redoubt and fight on. Seventh Army was to drive down the Neckar valley to the area of Tübingen, then exploit eastward toward Munich, southward to the Swiss border, then westward to assist the French in mopping up elements of *Nineteenth Army*. This last part represented the order that would, in de Lattre's view, have confined much of the First Army to the borders of the Rhine.[63]

There was also a serious inter-Allied confrontation over Stuttgart. The 3d DIA assaulted the city from the north while the 2d DIM and the 5th DB, which had moved through the Black Forest, attacked from the south. The day before the 3d DIA attacked, its indomitable commander, General Guillaume, took several pieces of shrapnel in the head as he sat in his jeep, but he stayed in command and on duty. On the afternoon of 21 April, French tanks of the 5th DB entered Stuttgart. They had outstripped the French infantry. The city was far from under control, with shooting all around, but this did not stop joyous celebrations from breaking out. The German inhabitants of Stuttgart were not happy to see the

French army, of course, but also inhabiting the city were many thousands of forced laborers from all over Europe: Poles, Russians, Dutch, Yugoslavs, Italians, even twenty thousand Frenchmen who somehow found or made innumerable Tricolors. French infantry arrived from the south at about 2000 hours in the form of the 4th RTT. Not long thereafter, the 49th RI (formerly the Pommiès Free Corps of the FFI) effected a juncture from the north with the tanks of CC6.[64]

As Devers' headquarters saw this action, "General de Lattre apparently did not accept [the] Army Group conception of the maneuver and launched a premature main effort through his center [that] frightened the German so he started running to the rear [and] carried his troops across the Neckar into the zone of action of VI Corps." Devers fired off several cables ordering de Lattre to hold back his center, to no effect. When Devers and de Lattre conferred directly, the American stood firm but offered a face-saving ceremony to honor the French capture of the city. De Lattre, however, felt obliged to tell Devers that, sadly, he could not obey his orders in this, because he had received quite unambiguous orders from de Gaulle, his ultimate superior, to keep a French garrison in the city and furthermore to set up a military government there. In the confusion, a goodly portion of *Nineteenth Army*'s remaining strength escaped the net.[65]

For several days, the 100th Infantry Division and the 3d DIA jostled each other for control of Stuttgart. This confrontation contained the seeds of disaster. One French veteran of Guillaume's division recalls the use of tanks from the 5th DB to deter American encroachment. Furthermore, as the 6th Army Group saw it, the "French procedure for occupying a German city is traditionally different from that of U.S. forces." Devers himself visited Stuttgart to investigate reports of French-inspired "disorders" coming from the 100th Division and to smooth things out.[66]

Certainly, all was not well in Stuttgart. A soldier from the 49th RI recalled having engaged in looting of the cellars of a wine merchant there. "In the exploration of the city, we were on the lookout for anything. One day, some men discovered the cellar of a wine merchant. At once . . . guys flocked to help themselves. With my buddies, we went there in a jeep and collected all that we could, just in time because security elements were arriving to stop the pillaging. . . . These acts of plundering got to the ears of the Americans, and in the affair in which we opposed them for the possession of Stuttgart, they took these incidents as pretext for saying that the French command did not have its men under control." [67]

Appalled by the plundering and rape that he had observed, Devers angrily ordered the French out again and told de Lattre in blunt terms to get his men in hand.[68]

General Guillaume, the senior French officer on the spot, had already issued orders to "prevent all looting," and he worked himself into high dudgeon in response to Devers' accusations. Guillaume wrote a memo to General Monsabert on 27 April about what he saw as mendacious reports of bad French behavior in the city. Guillaume attributed these accounts to a variety of misunderstandings as well as the fact that American reporters were freely circulating in the town eager to collect horror stories from recently defeated Nazis. Guillaume said the looting was primarily the work of the foreigners who had been forced laborers in Stuttgart. In particular, he said, this was the work of Russians. It was true, he wrote, that one of his regiments, which had arrived without organic transport, had seized a large number of automobiles from the Germans, but these consisted of vehicles previously stolen from France. As far as the rapes were concerned, there had been some initially, but he had summarily executed the criminals and made sure that all his men knew it. In the past six days, only six more rapes had been reported.[69]

Like Guillaume, de Lattre was stung by this cable from Devers, but his concern was more that its orders put him in an untenable position. He could obey the orders of his political master, de Gaulle, or he could obey the orders of his military master, Devers. He could not do both. He immediately cabled the new developments to de Gaulle, then dispatched a representative to Devers to show him—informally—the orders he had from de Gaulle forbidding him from leaving the city, and the cable he had just sent to de Gaulle.[70]

With the military commanders stymied, the matter was taken up at the level of governments. According to de Lattre, on 28 April word came that Eisenhower had backed down and agreed to let the French keep Stuttgart.[71] According to American accounts, Eisenhower told Devers to stick to his guns. De Gaulle in Paris remained defiant, even after President Harry Truman, who had been sworn in after Franklin Roosevelt's death on 12 April, intervened with a sharply worded message to de Gaulle. Eisenhower informed the French that he would advise the Combined Chiefs of Staff that he could no longer rely on the use of French forces in future operations and threatened to curtail the delivery of equipment to the French army. Only then did de Gaulle relent and order his troops to evacuate Stuttgart. In any event, Devers, ever graceful, made a point of personally attending a celebration of the festival of Saint Joan of Arc, put on by the 3d DIA at Stuttgart a week after V-E Day.[72]

* * *

Speed and low casualties were the priority as the 6th Army Group proceeded onward from Ulm and Stuttgart. The Seventh Army's operations report recorded, "The assault spread through little countryside villages that, according to orders, were taken under fire if there were no white flags flying. When evidence was found of civilian sniping and of German soldiers who had changed into civilian clothes, the town was destroyed. The orders had been, 'If you run into any resistance in the towns, particularly the big ones, I don't want you to take casualties. Use phosphorus, [tank destroyers], and everything else, and chew them to pieces.' "[73]

Despite the scattered nature of the fighting during April, Seventh Army lost more than 10,000 men killed, wounded, or missing during the month—nearly equal to its losses during Operation *Nordwind*. French losses during the same period amounted to more than 9,700 men.[74]

* * *

The free-for-all continued in the last few days of war. The French continued grabbing whatever key objectives were in their reach, irrespective of what the Americans intended. Even the 2d DB, under more direct American control than the divisions in de Lattre's army, got into the act. One officer of that division recalled:

> May 2d in the evening, after bounding forward [270 miles], our Spahis . . . rejoined us. . . . A gap had opened between the 12th Armored Division and the U.S. 4th Infantry Division. We hoped to take advantage of it, but

for the 3d, the order was not to go past Inn. That day there was a sudden burst of winter weather, and we advanced in a snowstorm. Nevertheless, ahead of our schedule, we took a coffee break about 8AM. The water was boiling when the chief of the "message center" . . . arrived in a feverish state. The yellow paper he handed me indicated: New objective Berchtesgaden . . .

The coffee was forgotten. I tore off in my jeep to catch up with and direct our Spahis to the new objective. Happily, they had had the same idea as us, and I found them right at the crossroads from which our new itinerary would start. It was a stroke of luck. And like us a short time ago, they forgot their "juice" and set off like a whirlwind to Berchtesgaden via Inzell.[75]

Evading Americans along the way, the French arrived at their destination on the afternoon of 4 May. The Nazi leadership compound was largely deserted, but they did find a terrified Belgian who admitted that he had been Göring's personal cook. The soldiers were suspicious of this man's story, so he proved his bona fides and ingratiated himself by showing them the way to Göring's collection of fine port. Mollified, the French soldiers drank themselves into a stupor.[76]

The Americans were angered by this latest French insubordination and also by a recent incident of French pillaging, so they ordered Leclerc's division out of Berchtesgaden on 6 May. But, as one colonel in the division put it, "The occupation of Berchtesgaden by the French army is something that will always stick in Uncle Sam's craw."[77]

* * *

Devers on 1 May worked out a change in boundary with SHAEF that transferred Salzburg from Third Army to Seventh Army. Devers sent XV and XXI corps charging eastward, and by the time 3d Infantry Division troops entered Austria on 3 May, the first surrender proposals were reaching Allied commanders up and down the western front.[78]

Sandy Patch's chief of staff called Major General Brooks at VI Corps headquarters at 1830 hours on 5 May and told him, "A representative of

German *Army Group G* has surrendered effective 1200 6 May. General Patch would like you to freeze your troops in place."

Brooks was not to be topped. "I have just completed surrender terms with [*Nineteenth Army* commanding general] Brandenberger effective 1800 tonight on the fronts of the First French [Army], VI Corps, and a portion of XXI Corps. I have told my troops to move into certain towns. Does he want me to freeze them in place where they are now?"

"You had better go ahead."[79]

* * *

Nineteenth Army, after battling the 6th Army Group all the way from the French beaches, had been reduced to some seven infantry battalions and seventeen thousand men, most of them supply troops.[80]

The line between the European and Mediterranean theaters was fast disappearing. On 3 May, elements of the 103d Infantry Division had linked up with Fifth Army's 88th Infantry Division south of Brenner Pass. The 44th Infantry Division met Fifth Army's 10th Mountain Division in Resia Pass late on 6 May.[81]

* * *

Late on 7 May, a highly irritated *General der Panzertruppen* Erich Brandenberger contacted the 44th Infantry Division to complain that the French were still attacking his men. The Germans were firing only in self-defense, and Brandenberger wanted higher authority to force French compliance with the terms of surrender. He further complained that the French were committing atrocities against the civilian population. Brandenberger's demand flew up the American chain of command.

Patch called Brooks at VI Corps headquarters shortly after 0900 on 7 May. "General Devers directed me to direct you to send a representative to the French and tell them to cease fire immediately." Brooks said that Maj. Gen. William Dean, commanding the 44th Infantry Division, believed that Brandenberger seemed to be doing the best he could on his side.

That evening, another call came in to VI Corps from the 44th Infantry Division: "We have a problem. We have a [company] in Tannheim, and yesterday a French general came in with troops and proceeded to take over the town. The company CO told him it was his town and he would occupy it. The French have looted the town and have already had two or three rape cases—a very unpleasant situation—and American troops have threatened to put French troops out forcibly."[82]

* * *

With the final German surrender, the declarations of victory displayed the unique American and French perspectives on the object of their military actions. On 8 May, Devers issued an order of the day to the men and women of his army group that began simply, "The enemy has been vanquished." De Lattre issued his own order of the day to French First Army on 9 May from the ruins of the German capital, declaring, "The day of victory has come. I have the honor to sign in Berlin in the name of France, in your name, the solemn document of Germany's surrender. . . . Your victories mark the milestones of the French revival."[83] The Germans may have shared a somewhat political perspective on the French role; upon spotting the French flag at the surrender ceremony, *Generalfeldmarschall* Wilhelm Keitel muttered, "Ach! The French are here. It lacked only that!"[84]

A Mighty Contribution

The Franco-American armies had indeed played "damned fools damned well," if fools they had ever been. The Operation Dragoon undertaking had contributed substantially to the Allied victory, whether viewed primarily in military or political terms.

It is doubtful that Eisenhower could have prosecuted his broad-front strategy as well as he did without Operation Dragoon. The Allies by early September had killed, wounded, captured, or bottled up in coastal ports some 450,000 German troops. The Dragoon forces had accounted for roughly one-fifth of that total despite their small size relative to the massive bulk of the Overlord armies. As a near crisis in logistics that month had brought the Overlord forces to a virtual halt, 6th Army Group contributed three corps to the effort, supplied entirely through ports it had captured. By the end of September, it had taken on the burden of one of the Overlord corps.

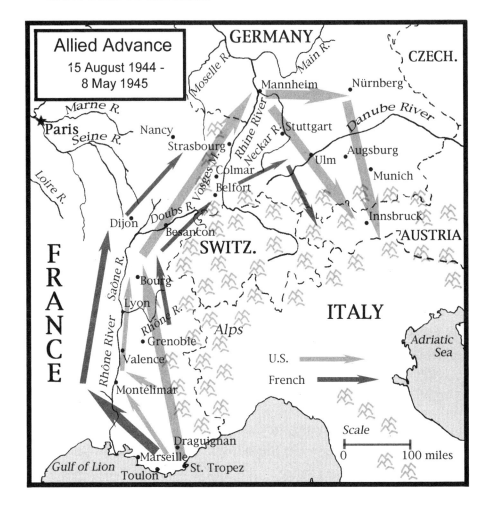

The operation had brought the French into the war on a large scale. In rolling from the French Riviera to Austria, 6th Army Group suffered the loss of 23,303 men killed, another 107,583 wounded, and 15,266 still accounted missing in action as of 30 May 1945.[85] Roughly half of those men wore the Tricolor, to which one must add the unknown number of FFI who died supporting Devers' command. Absent the French, the Americans and British would have had to pay some of that blood toll, and both of their armies were hard enough pressed during the awful autumn fighting to replenish the ranks of riflemen. The French, moreover, contributed most of the armor to the drive that brought the Allies to the Rhine at the only place they reached it in 1944.

Should Eisenhower have ordered Devers to cross the Rhine in November 1944? Perhaps. But the question differs little from that regarding the wisdom of Field Marshal Montgomery's repeated proposals to Ike that his 21st Army Group make a single "full-blooded" thrust along the coast toward Berlin. Neither fit into Eisenhower's broad-front strategy, which aimed to destroy the German armed forces west of the Rhine before driving into the Reich. Monty's idea at least established a route of advance that led through and to strategic objectives—the Ruhr industrial basin and Hitler's capital. Southern Germany contained no such strategic objectives.

The two armies of the 6th Army Group fought very different wars. The U.S. Seventh Army was simply one of several American armies fighting in a foreign land. The Americans viewed the war as a dirty business to be gotten over with as efficiently and quickly as possible so that they could go home. They did not share Churchill's strategic post-war vision or the apparent obsession of the French with symbolism and faded glory. The point of Operation Dragoon was to pin down Germans, put more troops into France to kill Germans, establish the logistic capability to kill yet more Germans, and end the whole unwelcome conflict.

The French First Army was, in essence, *the* French army fighting on its own territory. General Patch and General Devers had the freedom to fight the war on the purest of military merits. General de Lattre did not have that option. Indeed, it would have been impossible for him to have done so, because de Gaulle would not have stood for it. Perhaps the French insistence on defending Strasbourg best exemplifies the political circumstances that so profoundly influenced the French First Army's behavior. To the Americans, this was French cussedness at its height. For their part, the French were no more willing to surrender Strasbourg to the Nazis, no matter what the military exigencies, than the Americans would have been to surrender Boston or Detroit.

The decisions de Lattre made that subverted the spirit or violated the letter of the American-authored plans, as vexing as they sometimes were to American generals, were uniformly decisions that gave the French more opportunities to fight rather than fewer. French officers from lieutenants to corps commanders were often overly enthusiastic and eager to get straight into combat even when it was unwise or contrary to orders. Not surprisingly, the French resented the fact that many Americans manifestly held them in contempt.

De Lattre also had to think about the future and the unity of his nation in ways that Patch and Devers did not. The First Army was the best foundation available for a post-war French army that would be able to defend the security of both France and the western democracies. The alternative was an army founded on the left-leaning and much less competent French Resistance. Would an army built on that basis have been able to defend France against Communist aggression? Would an army built on that basis and with heavy participation by the Communist FTP have wanted to defend France against Communist aggression?

The 6th Army Group's achievements, and the precedent of Franco-American cooperation, should not be forgotten. It is worth recalling the day when the Americans and French fought a great crusade together, especially in times such as these, when the French prefer to ignore the preponderant American contribution to recovering their country (the Defense Ministry's website in 2005 offered a pictorial homage on the sixtieth anniversary of the *Liberation*—and ignored the Americans except for the few units that fought under French command), and the Americans all but ignore de Lattre's army in education and literature about the conflict. The Americans stormed the beaches, and the French were first to the Rhine.

APPENDIX A

BASIC DIVISIONAL ORDER OF BATTLE, KEY UNITS

AMERICAN

3d Infantry Division

  7th Infantry Regiment

  15th Infantry Regiment

  30th Infantry Regiment

  3d Reconnaissance Troop (mechanized)

  Usual armored attachments: 746th Tank Battalion, 636th Tank
    Destroyer Battalion

12th Armored Division

  Combat Command A

  Combat Command B

  Combat Command R

  23d Tank Battalion

  43d Tank Battalion

  714th Tank Battalion

  17th Armored Infantry Battalion

  56th Armored Infantry Battalion

  66th Armored Infantry Battalion

  92d Cavalry Reconnaissance Squadron

14th Armored Division

  Combat Command A

  Combat Command B

  Combat Command R

  25th Tank Battalion

47th Tank Battalion

48th Tank Battalion

19th Armored Infantry Battalion

62d Armored Infantry Battalion

68th Armored Infantry Battalion

94th Cavalry Reconnaissance Squadron

36th Infantry Division

141st Infantry Regiment

142d Infantry Regiment

143d Infantry Regiment

36th Reconnaissance Troop (mechanized)

Usual armored attachments: 753d Tank Battalion, 636th Tank
    Destroyer Battalion

42d Infantry Division

222d Infantry Regiment

232d Infantry Regiment

242d Infantry Regiment

42d Reconnaissance Troop (mechanized)

Usual armored attachments: None

44th Infantry Division

71st Infantry Regiment

114th Infantry Regiment

324th Infantry Regiment

44th Reconnaissance Troop (mechanized)

Usual armored attachments: 749th, 772d Tank battalions, 776th
    Tank Destroyer Battalion

45th Infantry Division

157th Infantry Regiment

179th Infantry Regiment

180th Infantry Regiment

45th Reconnaissance Troop (mechanized)

Usual armored attachments: 191st Tank Battalion, 645th Tank Destroyer Battalion

70th Infantry Division
274th Infantry Regiment
275th Infantry Regiment
276th Infantry Regiment
70th Reconnaissance Troop (mechanized)
Usual armored attachments: None

79th Infantry Division
313th Infantry Regiment
314th Infantry Regiment
315th Infantry Regiment
79th Reconnaissance Troop (mechanized)
Usual armored attachments: 813th Tank Destroyer Battalion

100th Infantry Division
397th Infantry Regiment
398th Infantry Regiment
399th Infantry Regiment
100th Reconnaissance Troop (mechanized)
Usual armored attachments: 781st Tank Battalion, 824th Tank Destroyer Battalion

103d Infantry Division
409th Infantry Regiment
410th Infantry Regiment
411th Infantry Regiment
103d Reconnaissance Troop (mechanized)
Usual armored attachments: 756th Tank Battalion

FRENCH

1st *Division Francaise Libre* (DFL; Free French Division, also known as Motorized Infantry Division)

1st Brigade
13th *Demi-Brigade de la Légion Etrangère* (DBLE; half brigade of the foreign legion)
2d Brigade
4th Brigade
1st *Régiment de Fusiliers Marins* (RFM; Marine Fusilier Regiment; light tanks)

1st *Division Blindée* (DB; armored division)
Combat Command 1
Combat Command 2
Combat Command 3
2d *Régiment de Cuirassiers* (tank regiment)
5th *Régiment de Chasseurs d'Afrique* (RCA; tank regiment)
2d *Chasseurs d'Afrique* (tank regiment)
9th RCA (tank destroyers)
Three bataillons de Zouaves
3d RCA (reconnaissance)

2d *Division d'Infanterie Marocaine* (DIM; Moroccan Infantry Division)
4th *Régiment de Tirailleurs Marocains* (RTM; Moroccan Infantry Regiment)
5th RTM
8th RTM
3d *Régiment de Spahis Marocains* (RSM; Moroccan Spahis Regiment; light tanks)

2d *Division Blindée* (DB; armored division)
4 combat commands (also known as *groupements tactiques*; designated CC1–CC4 or by the first initial of the commander's last name)
501st *Régiment de Char de Combat* (RCC; tank regiment)
12th RCA (tank regiment)
12th *Régiment de Cuirassiers* (RC; tank regiment)
Régiment Blindé de Fusiliers Marins (RBFM; naval/marine

Armored Fusilier Regiment, or Tank Destroyer Regiment)

Régiment de Marche de Spahis Marocain (RMSM; Moroccan Spahis "March" Regiment, Armored Reconnaissance Regiment)

Régiment de Marche du Tchad (RMT; Chadian "March" Regiment, or Armored Infantry Regiment)

3d *Division d'Infanterie Algerienne* (DIA; Algerian Infantry Division)

3d *Régiment de Tirailleurs Algériens* (RTA; Algerian Infantry Regiment)

4th *Régiment de Tirailleurs Tunisiens* (RTT; Tunisian Infantry Regiment)

7th RTA

3d *Régiment de Spahis Algériens de Reconnaissance* (RSAR; Algerian Spahis Reconnaissance Regiment; light tanks)

4th *Division Marocaine de Montagne* (DMM; Moroccan Mountain Division)

1st *Régiment de Tirailleurs Marocains* (RTM; Moroccan Infantry Regiment)

2d *Régiment de Tirailleurs Marocains* (RTM)

6th *Régiment de Tirailleurs Marocains* (RTM)

4th *Régiment de Spahis Marocains* (RSM; light tanks)

5th Division Blindée (DB; Armored Division)

Combat Command 4

Combat Command 5

Combat Command 6

1st *Régiment de Chasseurs d'Afrique* (RCA; tank regiment)

6th RCA (tank regiment)

11th RCA (tank regiment)

1st *Régiment Etranger de Cavalerie* (REC; foreign legion)

1st *Régiment de Cuirassiers* (tank destroyers)

126th *Régiment d'Infanterie*

152d *Régiment d'Infanterie*

9th *Division d'Infanterie Coloniale* (Colonial Infantry Division)
    4th *Régiment de Tirailleurs Sénegalais* (RTS; Senegalese Infantry
        Regiment)
    6th RTS
    13th RTS
    Régiment d'Infantrie Coloniale du Maroc (RICM; Moroccan
        Colonial Infantry Regiment)
    Régiment de Chasseurs de Chars (RCCC; tank destroyers)

Goums Maroccains (Moroccan goum)
    1st *Groupement de Tabors Marocains* (GTM; Moroccan Tabor
        Group)
    3d GTM

Note: French "regiments" in some cases, such as tank regiments in armored divisions organized along American lines, were actually the size of battalions.

Sources (sites current as of May 2007):
U.S. Army Center of Military History online,
    www.army.mil/cmh-pg/documents/eto-ob/etoob-toc.htm.
"French Organizations in Italy,"
    http://members.aol.com/Custermen85/Units/FrenchOrg.htm.
"La Deuxieme Division Blindee Francaise,"
    http://perso.orange.fr/did.panzer/2-FR-DB.htm.
"L'Armée Francaise de la Libération de la Provence,"
    http://perso.orange.fr/forum-julii/DEB-F%20FRANCAISES.htm.
"Les Insignes des Unités de la 5e Division Blindée,"
    http://mapage.noos.fr/4edmm/insignes_5e_db.htm.
"Section Rhône-Alpes de l'Amicale des Anciens de la 5e Division
    Blindée," http://membres.lycos.fr/anciens5db69/Accueil.html.

APPENDIX B
TABLE OF EQUILVALENT RANKS

U.S. Army	German Army and Air Force	German Waffen-SS
None	*Reichsmarschall*	None
General of the Army	*Generalfeldmarschall*	*Reichsführer SS*
General	*Generaloberst*	*Oberstgruppenführer*
Lieutenant General	*General der*	*Obergruppenführer*
	Infanterie	
	Artillerie	
	Gebirgstruppen	
	Kavallerie	
	Nachrichtentruppen	
	Panzertruppen	
	Flieger	
	Pioniere	
	Luftwaffe	
	Fallschirmtruppen	
	Flakartillerie	
	Luftnachrichtentruppen	
Major General	*Generalleutnant*	*Gruppenführer*
Brigadier General	*Generalmajor*	*Brigadeführer*
None	None	*Oberführer*
Colonel	*Oberst*	*Standartenführer*
Lieutenant Colonel	*Oberstleutnant*	*Obersturmbannführer*
Major	*Major*	*Sturmbannführer*
Captain	*Hauptmann*	*Hauptsturmführer*
Captain (Cavalry)	*Rittmeister*	None
First Lieutenant	*Oberleutnant*	*Obersturmführer*
Second Lieutenant	*Leutnant*	*Untersturmführer*

Source: Hugh M. Cole, *United States Army in World War II, The European Theater of Operations, The Lorraine Campaign*. Washington, DC: Historical Division, Department of the Army, 1950.

GLOSSARY

AAR	After-action report
AFHQ	Allied Forces Headquarters
AP	Armor-piercing
BLE	(French) Foreign Legion Brigade
Capt.	Captain
Col.	Colonel
CP	Command post
Cpl.	Corporal
DB	(French) armored division, *division blindée*
DFL	(French) Free French (Infantry) Division
DI	(French) Infantry Division
DIA	(French) Algerian Infantry Division
DIC	(French) Colonial Infantry Division
DIM	(French) Moroccan Infantry Division
DMM	(French) Moroccan Mountain Division
Dough/doughboy	American infantryman
ETO	European Theater of Operations
FFI	(French) Resistance, the maquis
FTP	(French) Communist Resistance movement
G-2	Intelligence staff
Gen.	General
GI	American infantryman
Goum	Company-sized unit made up of Moroccan goumiers
Goumier	Ethnic Berber Moroccan mountain infantryman
Grenadier	Honorific for the German infantry
GTM	(French) Regiment-sized "Group of Moroccan Tabors"
HE	High-explosive
Lt.	Lieutenant
Lt. Col.	Lieutenant Colonel
Maj.	Major
MATAF	Mediterranean Allied Tactical Air Force
NCO	Non-commissioned officer
OB West	German Commander in Chief West
OKW	German High Command
OP	Observation post

Panzer	German tank
Panzergrenadier	German armored infantry
Pvt.	Private
RCA	(French) Regiment of African Chasseurs (tank or tank destroyer regiment)
RCCC	(French) Regiment of Chasseurs (tank destroyer regiment)
RCP	(French) Regiment of Parachute Chasseurs (airborne infantry)
RCT	Regimental Combat Team
RI	(French) Infantry Regiment
RIC	(French) Colonial Infantry Regiment
RICM	(French) Moroccan Colonial Infantry Regiment
RMLE	(French) Foreign Legion Infantry Regiment
RSAR	(French) Regiment of Algerian Reconnaissance Spahis
RTA	(French) Regiment of Algerian Tirailleurs (infantry)
RTM	(French) Regiment of Moroccan Tirailleurs (infantry)
RTS	(French) Regiment of Senegalese Tirailleurs (infantry)
RTT	(French) Regiment of Tunisian Tirailleurs (infantry)
SAS	Special Air Service (commandos)
Sgt.	Sergeant
S/Sgt.	Staff Sergeant
S-3	Operations staff
SHAEF	Supreme Headquarters Allied Expeditionary Force
SP	Self-propelled
Spahi	French colonial reconnaissance soldier
Tabor	Battalion-sized unit of made up of goums
TAC	Tactical Air Command
Tirailleur	Literally, sharpshooter, colonial infantryman

BIBLIOGRAPHY

BOOKS AND BOOKLETS

La 2e DB Général Leclerc Combattant et Combats en France. Paris: Arts et Métiers Graphique, 1945.

The 45th. Paris: *Stars and Stripes*, 1945.

Ancell, R. Manning, with Christine M. Miller. *The Biographical Dictionary of World War II Generals and Flag Officers*. Westport, CT: Greenwood Press, 1996.

Bennet, Ralph. *Ultra in the West: The Normandy Campaign of 1944–45*. New York: Scribners, 1980.

Béthouart, Général. *Cinq Années d'Espérance: Mémoires de Guerre 1939–1945*. Paris: Librairie Plon, 1968.

Bimberg, Edward L. *The Moroccan Goums: Tribal Warriors in a Modern War*. Westport, CT: Greenwood Press, 1999.

The Blue and White Devils. Paris: *Stars and Stripes*, 1945.

Bonn, Keith E. *When the Odds Were Even*. Novato, CA: Presidio Press, 1994.

Booth, Waller B. *Mission Marcel-Proust: The Story of an Unusual OSS Undertaking*. Philadelphia: Dorrance, 1972.

Breuer, William B. *Operation Dragoon: The Invasion of Southern France*. Novato, CA: Presido Press, 1987.

Brooke, Field Marshal Lord Alan. *War Diaries: 1939–1945*. London: Phoenix Press, 2002.

Carter, Capt. Joseph. *The History of the 14th Armored Division*. The Division: nd. [1945].

Churchill, Winston S. *The Hinge of Fate*. Boston: Houghton-Mifflin, 1950.

———. *Triumph and Tragedy*. Boston: Houghton-Mifflin, 1953.

Clarke, Jeffrey J., and Robert Ross Smith. *Riviera to the Rhine: United States Army in World War II, The European Theater of Operations*. Washington, DC: Office of the Chief of Military History, Department of the Army, 1993.

Clayton, Anthony. *France, Soldiers and Africa*. London: Brassey's Defence Publishers, 1988.

Conombo, Joseph Issoufou. *Souvenirs de Guerre d'un 'Tirailleur Senegalais.'* Paris: L'Harmattan, 1989.

De Gaulle, Charles. *The War Memoirs of Charles de Gaulle: Salvation 1944–1946*. New York: Simon and Schuster, 1960.

De l'A.O.F. aux Bords du Rhin: Juillet 1943–Janvier 1945, 9e Division d'Infanterie Coloniale. Lyon: np., nd. [1945].

De Lattre de Tassigny, Jean. *The History of the French First Army*. London: Allen and Unwin, 1952.

———. *Reconquérir: 1944–1945*. Paris: Plon, 1985.

De Trez, Michel. *First Airborne Task Force*. Wezembeek-Oppem, Belgium: D-Day Publishing, 1998.

Duroc-Danner, Jean. *Face aux Marocains: Italie-France-Allemagne*. Le Puy, France: Xavier Mappus, nd. [1946].

Eisenhower, Dwight D. *Crusade in Europe*. Garden City, NY: Doubleday and Company, Inc., 1948.

Funk, Arthur Layton. *Hidden Ally: The French Resistance, Special Operations, and the Landings in Southern France, 1944*. New York: Greenwood Press, 1992.

Gilbert, James L., and John P. Finnegan, eds. *U.S. Army Signals Intelligence in World War II: A Documentary History*. Washington, DC: Center of Military History, United States Army, 1993.

Gras, Yves. *La 1ère DFL, Les Francais Libres au Combat*. Paris: Presses de la Cité, 1983.

Grossjohann, Georg. *Five Years, Four Fronts: The War Years of Georg Grossjohann, Major, German Army (Retired)*. Bedford, PA: The Aberjona Press, 1999.

Guillaume, Augustin. *Homme de Guerre*. Paris: Éditions France-Empire, 1977.

Heek, Clifford, Jr., ed. *Five Years—Five Countries, Five Campaigns, An Account of the One-Hundred-Forty-First Infantry in World War II*. Munich: 141st Infantry Regiment Association, 1945.

Heller, Joseph. *Now and Then: From Coney Island to Here*. New York: Alfred A. Knopf, 1998.

The Historical Board, 45th Infantry Division. *The Fighting Forty-Fifth: The Combat Report of an Infantry Division*. Baton Rouge, LA: The 45th Infantry Division, 1946.

Hobbs, Joseph P. *Dear General: Eisenhower's Wartime Letters to Marshall*. Baltimore, MD: The Johns Hopkins Press, 1971.

Horne, Alistair. *A Savage War of Peace: Algeria 1954–1962*. Harmondsworth, England: Penguin Books, 1977.

Howard, Michael. *Strategic Deception in the Second World War*. London: Pimlico, 1992.

Keegan, John. *Six Armies in Normandy: From D-Day to the Liberation of Paris*. New York: Penguin, 1982.

Lawler, Nancy Ellen. *Soldiers of Misfortune: Ivoirien Tirailleurs of World War II*. Athens: Ohio University Press, 1992.

Lockhart, Vincent M. *T-Patch to Victory: The 36th Infantry Division from the Landing in Southern France to the End of World War II*. Canyon, TX: Staked Plains Press, 1981.

MacDonald, Charles B. *The Battle of the Bulge*. London: Guild Publishing, 1984.

———. *The Last Offensive: United States Army in World War II, The European Theater of Operations*. Washington, DC: Center of Military History, United States Army, 1990.

Markey, Michael A. *Jake: The General From West York Avenue*. York, PA: Historical Society of York County, 1998.

Muelle, Raymond. *Le 1er Bataillon de Choc*. Paris: Presses de la Cité, 1977.

Murphy, Audie. *To Hell and Back*. New York: Henry Holt and Company, 2002.

Notin, Jean-Christophe. *Les Vaincus Seront les Vainqueurs: La France en Allemagne 1945*. Paris: Perrin, 2004.

Paillole, Colonel Paul. *Fighting the Nazis: French Military Intelligence and Counterintelligence 1935–1945*. New York: Enigma Books, 2003.

Porch, Douglas. *The French Foreign Legion*. New York: Harper Perennial, 1993.

Ritgen, Helmut. *West-Front 1944*. Stuttgart: Motorbuch Verlag, 2001.

Salan, Raoul. *Mémoires: Fin d'Un Empire*. Paris: Presses de la Cité, 1970.

Shirer, Willam L. *The Rise and Fall of the Third Reich*. New York: Fawcett Crest, 1983.

Shirley, John. *I Remember*. Livermore, CA: Self-published, 2003.

Southern France. CMH Pub72-31. Washington, DC: U.S. Army Center of Military History, nd.

Steidl, Franz. *Lost Battalions*. Novato, CA: Presidio Press, 2000.

The Story of the 36th Infantry Division. Germany: 36th Infantry Division, 1945.

Taggert, Donald G., ed. *History of the Third Infantry Division in World War II*. Washington, DC:

Infantry Journal Press, 1947. This volume is, in effect, the official division history and was written by division staff.

Terrify and Destroy: The Story of the 10th Armored Division. Paris: *Stars and Stripes*, 1945.

Thompson, Major General Julian. *Ready for Anything: The Parachute Regiment at War.* London: Fontana, 1990.

Trailblazers. Paris: *Stars and Stripes*, 1945.

Truscott, Lt. Gen. Lucian K. *Command Missions.* New York: E. P. Dutton and Company, Inc., 1954.

Turner, John Frayn, and Robert Jackson. *Destination Berchtesgaden: The Story of the United States Seventh Army in World War II.* New York: Charles Scribner's Sons, 1975.

Von Mellenthin, F. W. *Panzer Battles.* New York: Ballantine Books, 1971.

Whiting, Charles. *America's Forgotten Army.* New York: St. Martin's Press, 1999.

———. *The Other Battle of the Bulge: Operation Northwind.* Chelsea, MI: Scarborough House, 1990.

Wilmot, Chester. *The Struggle for Europe.* Ware, England: Wordsworth Editions Limited, 1997.

ARTICLES AND INTERNET RESOURCES

2d Armored Division. www.angelfire.com/wa2/FJ6/French2nd.html (as of May 2005).

The 12th Armored Division Memorial Museum.
www.acu.edu/academics/history/12ad/Museum.html.

Amicale des Anciens de la 5e DB. http://membres.lycos.fr/anciens5db69/Historiq.html.

Axis History Forum. www.axishistory.com.

Blumenson, Martin. "Politics and the Military in the Liberation of Paris," *Parameters*, Summer 1998, 4–14. Reproduced online at the U.S. Army War College,
http://carlisle-www.army.mil/usawc/Parameters/98summer/blumenso.htm.

Bolling Haxall Personal Account, August 11, 1987.
www.acu.edu/academics/history/12ad/Museum.html (downloaded 31 May 2004).

Brown, Arthur. "The Jedburghs: A Short History."
www.freespace.virgin.net/Arthur.brown2/index.htm (as of May 2004).

Brown, H. K. "H. K. Brown's WW II 1944–1945 Diary."
www.eastmill.com/103rd/compos/410/hk/index.htm.

Butler, Brig. Gen. Frederic. "Butler Task Force," *Armored Cavalry Journal*, published in two parts, January–February 1948, 12–18, and March–April 1948, 30–38.

Corson, William. "Captured in Hatten, Part 3: Captain William Corson's Speech." www.tank books.com/stories/schmidt3.htm.

De la Guéronnière, Isabelle. "*Le Général Diego Brosset.*"
www.stratisc.org/pub/pub_G%20SALKIN.html (downloaded 20 June 2004).

"De Neucheze Rober Jean-Marie." www.gers.pref.gouv.fr/acvg/documents/regiment3.htm (from the website of the Department of Gers).

Debray, Pierre. "*Souvenirs de Pierre Debray.*" www.marechal-leclerc.fr.st/ (downloaded 9 January 2004).

Devers, Jacob L. "Operation Dragoon: The Invasion of Southern France," *Military Affairs*, Summer 1946, 2–41.

Echenberg, Myron. " '*Morts pour la France*': The African Soldier in France During the Second World War," *Journal of African History*, Volume 26, Number 4, 369–371.

Faure, Henri. "*Etais-je un terroriste ? . . .*", Tome II.

http://war.megabaze.com/page_html/012-Resistance-Parachuting (downloaded 22 May 2005; this memoir is dated 1985).

Fremeaux, Jacques. "*Les Contingents Africain et le Débarquement de Provence (Août 1944).*" www.stratisc.org/partenaires/ihcc/ihcc_44prov_Fremeaux.html (downloaded 24 June 2004).

Frizzell, Art, et al. "Office of Strategic Services Operational Groups." www.ossog.org (as of May 2004).

Guelton, Frédéric. "*Les Chefs Militaires Francais et la Realité de la Menace Militaire Soviétique, 1946–1950*" in Delmas, Jean and Jean Kessler, eds., *Renseignement et Propaganda Pendant la Guerre Froide (1947–1953)*, Éditions Complexe.

"Initial Assault on Herrlisheim by the 56th Armored Infantry Battalion and the 714th Tank Battalion," Seventh Army. www.12tharmoredmuseum.org.

"*Journal de Marche du 1er Regiment de Chasseurs d'Afrique.*" www.chars-francais.net/archives/jmo/jmo 1rca.htm (downloaded 19 August 2005).

"*Journal de Marche du 8e Regiment de Chasseurs d'Afrique, 1ère partie.*" www.chars-francais.net/archives/jmo/jmo 8rca.htm (downloaded 19 August 2005).

Kaminski, Alexandre. *Les Batailles de la Liberation et de la Revanche 1944–1945 Avec le 2eme Cuirassiers.* www.chars-francais.net.

"*Le Corps Franc Pommiès—49 R.I.*" www.gers.pref.gouv.fr/acvg/documents/regiment3.htm (this website of the Department of Gers indicates that the material in this document comes from the book *L'Epopée du Corps-France Pommiès*, written by Dominique Lormier).

"*L'embuscade de Glainans, 7 septembre 1944.*" http://perso.wanadoo.fr/clerval/histoire/embusca.htm (downloaded 10 April 2005; this website is quoting *Les Panaches Rouges: Historique du 3e régiment Algériens de Reconnaissance*," 1947).

Les Cahiers de la Liberation de Toulon. www.ordredelaliberation.fr/fr_compagnon/155.html (downloaded 22 March 2004).

Lescastreyres, Raymond. "*Souvenirs de Guerre d'un Jeune Francais.*" www.duhamel.bz/souvenir/ (downloaded 20 August 2005).

"One-Man Stand at Holzwihr." www.tankdestroyersociety.com/audie_murphys_one.htm (as of June 2005).

Saint-Hillier, General. "*L'armée Francaise dans le débarquement de Provence.*" www.france-libre.net/temoignages-documents/1_6_1_20debarquement_provence.htm (downloaded 13 June 2004).

Sorobey, Ronald B. "Ukrainians Fight for France," *World War II*, September 2004, 42–48.

"Tarzan, un blindé du 2eme RSAR." www.memoire-net.org/article.php3?id_article'170 (downloaded 5 February 2005).

Woodfork, Jacqueline. "The Levée of the Masses and the Elite: Subjects and Citizens in the French Colonial Army in the Second World War," paper presented at the Society for Military History annual conference, Charleston, SC, 2005.

Unpublished Studies

Blaskowitz, *Generaloberst* Johannes. "Fighting By Armeegruppe 'G' in Southern France until the middle of September 1944." MS # B-800, 16 May 1947. National Archives.

Brandenberger, *General der Panzertruppen* Erich. "Seventh Army from 16 December 1944 to 16 January 1945. Nineteenth Army from 28 March to 5 May 1945." MS # A-934, 15 May 1950. National Archives.

Degener, *Generalmajor* Joachim. "189th Infantry Division (Kampfgruppe Degener) (15 Sep–16 Nov 1944)." MS # B-253, nd. National Archives.

Drews, *Oberstleutnant* Werner. "Remarks Regarding the War History of the Seventh U.S. Army (15 Aug–14 Sep 1944)." MS # A-881, 15 January 1950. National Archives.

"Employment of Panzer Forces on the Western Front." Interview with *Generaloberst* Heinz Guderian. ETHINT-39, 16 August 1945. National Archives.

Feuchtinger, *Generalleutnant* Edgar. "21st Panzer Division in Combat Against American Troops in France and Germany." MS # A-871, 17 December 1949. National Archives.

Grundmann, *Obserstleutnant* Hasso, et al., "The Landings of the American Seventh Army in Southern France August 1944." MS # C-086, 1952. National Archives.

Hauser, *Generalmajor* Wolf-Rüdiger. "Report on the Combat Engagements Within the Framework of the First Army During the Period From 24 March to 2 May 1945." MS # B-348, 12 September 1946. National Archives.

Hüther, *Generalmajor* Gerhard. "Commitment of 553d Volksgrenadier Division, December 1944 to March 1945." MS # B-177, 6 October 1950. National Archives.

"The Invasion of Southern France." Interview with *Rittmeister* Wilhelm Scheidt. ETHINT-19, 17 September 1945. National Archives.

Matthews, Herbert L. "Patch Will Avoid French Disputes." *The New York Times*, August 19, 1944, 5.

Philippi, *Generalmajor* Alfred. "361st Volksgrenadier Division (24 Dec 1944–12 Jan 1945)." MS # B-428, 22 February 1947. National Archives.

Schaefer, *Generalmajor*. "244th Infantry Division, Marseille, 19–28 August 1944." MS # A-884. National Archives.

Schramm, *Major* Percy Ernst. "OKW War Diary (1 Apr–18 Dec 1944)." MS # B-034, nd. National Archives. The "war diary" was an unofficial compilation (circa March 1945) of notes and summaries based on meetings and original documents, many of which were destroyed.

Simon, *Generalleutnant* of the Waffen SS Max. "Comment on the Report of 20 Nov 47 on Operation 'Nordwind' ('Sylvester-Offensive') by Oberst Einem." MS # C-039, November 1948. National Archives.

Taeglichsbeck, *Generalmajor* Hans. "LXIV Corps Defensive Construction (16 Sep 1944–25 Feb 1945)." MS # B-504, nd. National Archives.

Von dem Bach-Zelewski. *General der Waffen SS* Erich. "The XIV SS Corps in November-December 1944." MS # B-252, 7 December 1946. National Archives.

Von Einem, *Oberst* Kurt. "Bericht Über die Kämpfe des XIII. S.S. A.K. in Lothringen in der Zeit vom 8. November 1944–12 January 1945." MS # B-780, 20 November 1947. National Archives.

Von Mellenthin, *Generalmajor* Friedrich, and others. "Army Group G in the period of September to the beginning of December 1944." MS # A-999, 11 July 1950. National Archives.

Von Sodenstern, *General der Infanterie* Georg. "To the History of the Times Preceding the Invasion Engagements in France with Special Regard to the South-French Zone." MS # B-276, 13 December 1950. National Archives.

Wiese, *General der Infanterie* Friederich. "The 19th Army in Southern France (1 July to 15 Sept 1944)." MS # B-787, 11 April 1948. National Archives.

———. "The 19th Army in the Belfort Gap, in the Vosges, and in Alsace from the Middle of September until 18 December 1944." MS # B-781, 8 March 1948. National Archives.

Wietersheim, *Generalleutnant* Wend von. "The 11th Panzer Division in Southern France (15

August–14 September 1944).” MS # A-880, 4 June 1946. National Archives.

Wilutzky, *Oberst (I.G.)* Horst. “The Attack of Army Group G in Northern Elsass in January 1945.” MS # B-095, 8 September 1950. National Archives. Wilutzky was the army group operations officer.

———. “The Fighting of Heeresgruppe 'G' in the West: The Final Battle in Central and Southern Germany Until the Surrender (22 Mar 45–6 May 45).” MS # B-703, nd.

Witek, *Generalinttendent* Otto. “The Department of the Oberquartiermeister of the 19 Army.” MS # A-950, 16 June 1950. National Archives.

NOTES

Chapter 1: An Uneasy Alliance

1. Report on Operation Dragoon, Mediterranean Allied Tactical Air Force, 1 November 1944.

2. Joseph Heller, *Now and Then: From Coney Island to Here* (New York: Alfred A. Knopf, 1998), 181–182.

3. Arthur Layton Funk, *Hidden Ally: The French Resistance, Special Operations, and the Landings in Southern France, 1944* (New York: Greenwood Press, 1992), 77–79. (Hereafter Funk.)

4. Henri Faure, "Etais-je un terroriste? . . .", Tome II, http://war.megabaze.com/page html/012-Resistance-Parachuting, downloaded 22 May 2005.

5. *Generaloberst* Johannes Blaskowitz, "Fighting By Armeegruppe 'G' in Southern France until the middle of September 1944," MS # B-800, 16 May 1947, National Archives, 11. (Hereafter Blaskowitz, "Fighting By Armeegruppe 'G' in Southern France until the middle of September 1944.")

6. Jeffrey J. Clarke and Robert Ross Smith. *Riviera to the Rhine: United States Army in World War II, The European Theater of Operations* (Washington, DC: Office of the Chief of Military History, Department of the Army, 1993), 6ff. (Hereafter Clarke and Smith.)

7. "Seventh Army–The Invasion of Southern France (Draft Copy–Supreme Allied Command–Wilson)," August 1944, G-3 records, Seventh Army. Field Marshal Lord Alan Brooke, *War Diaries: 1939–1945* (London: Phoenix Press, 2002), passim. (Hereafter Brooke.) Dwight D. Eisenhower, *Crusade in Europe* (Garden City, NY: Doubleday and Company, Inc., 1948), 282.

(Hereafter Eisenhower.)

8. Eisenhower, 282–283. "Seventh Army–The Invasion of Southern France (Draft Copy–Supreme Allied Command–Wilson)," August 1944, G-3 records, Seventh Army.

9. Brooke, 556, 565.

10. Lt. Gen. Lucian K. Truscott, *Command Missions* (New York: E. P. Dutton and Company, Inc., 1954), 408. (Hereafter Truscott.)

11. "Seventh Army–The Invasion of Southern France (Draft Copy–Supreme Allied Command–Wilson)," August 1944, G-3 records, Seventh Army. Clarke and Smith, 27ff. Truscott, 386.

12. "Seventh Army–The Invasion of Southern France (Draft Copy–Supreme Allied Command–Wilson)," August 1944, G-3 records, Seventh Army.

13. Sixth Army Group history.

14. Michael A. Markey, *Jake: The General From West York Avenue* (York, PA: Historical Society of York County, 1998), passim.

15. Jacob L. Devers, "Operation Dragoon: The Invasion of Southern France," *Military Affairs*, Summer 1946, 11–16. (Hereafter Devers.)

16. Truscott, 383.

17. R. Manning Ancell, with Christine M. Miller, *The Biographical Dictionary of World War II Generals and Flag Officers* (Westport, CT: Greenwood Press, 1996), 336. (Hereafter Ancell and Miller.) Truscott, 382, 532–533. *The 45th* (Paris: Stars and Stripes, 1945). (Hereafter *The 45th*.)

18. Ancell and Miller, 242. Truscott, 548.

19. Breuer, 55.

20. Donald G. Taggert, ed., *History of the Third Infantry Division in World War II* (Washington, DC: Infantry Journal Press,

1947), 192. (Hereafter Taggert.)

21. Andrew Rawson, dissertation research provided to author.

22. Franz Steidl, *Lost Battalions* (Novato, CA: Presidio Press, 2000), 24. (Hereafter Steidl.)

23. Truscott, 548.

24. The Historical Board, 45th Infantry Division, *The Fighting Forty-Fifth: The Combat Report of an Infantry Division* (Baton Rouge, LA: The 45th Infantry Division, 1946), 4ff. (Hereafter *The Fighting Forty-Fifth.*)

25. Truscott, 397.

26. *Southern France*, CMH Pub 72-31 (Washington, DC: U.S. Army Center of Military History, not dated), 7. (Hereafter *Southern France.*)

27. Clifford Peek, Jr., ed., *Five Years—Five Countries, Five Campaigns, An Account of the One-Hundred-Forty-First Infantry in World War II* (Munich: 141st Infantry Regiment Association, 1945), 54–55. (Hereafter Peek.)

28. Truscott, 401–407.

29. Ibid., 407. G-3 journal, VI Corps. Brig. Gen. Frederic Butler, "Butler Task Force," *Armored Cavalry Journal*, published in two parts, January–February 1948 and March–April 1948, 13. (Hereafter Butler.) Ancell and Miller, 43.

30. Funk, 32–34, 38–39.

31. See Seventh Army G-2 files on French resistance activities, RG 407, NARA. Arthur Brown, "The Jedburghs: A Short History," www.freespace.virgin.net/Arthur.brown2/index.htm (as of May 2004). Art Frizzell, et al., "Office of Strategic Services Operational Groups," www.ossog.org, as of May 2004.

32. Clarke and Smith, 39.

33. Breuer, 56–57. Clarke and Smith, 39.

34. Breuer, 37.

35. Allied Forces Headquarters, "Report on Airborne Operations in 'Dragoon,'" 16 September 1944, Seventh Army records. Michel de Trez, *First Airborne Task Force* (Wezembeek-Oppem, Belgium: D-Day Publishing, 1998), 29. (Hereafter de Trez.)

36. Muelle, 125–126. "Seventh Army–The Invasion of Southern France (Draft Copy–Supreme Allied Command–Wilson)," August 1944, G-3 records, Seventh Army.

37. Anthony Clayton, *France, Soldiers and Africa*, London: Brassey's Defence Publishers, 1988, 6–7. (Hereafter Clayton.)

38. Jacques Fremeaux, "*Les Contingents Africain et le Débarquement de Provence (Août 1944)*, www.stratisc.org/partenaires/ihcc/ihcc_44prov_Fremeaux.html (downloaded 24 June 2004). (Hereafter Fremeaux.)

39. Ibid. Clayton, 264–265, 425 fn53.

40. Fremeaux.

41. Edward L. Bimberg, *The Moroccan Goums: Tribal Warriors in a Modern War* (Westport, CT: Greenwood Press, 1999), xi–xiv, 77. (Hereafter Bimberg.) Clayton, 300.

42. Bimberg, 76–78. De Lattre de Tassigny, Jean, *The History of the French First Army*, London: Allen and Unwin, 1952, 55–56. (Hereafter de Lattre.)

43. Bimberg, xi–xiv, 76–78. Clayton, 300. Letter from de Lattre to de Gaulle, 18 July 1944, cited in Jean de Lattre de Tassigny, *Reconquérir: 1944–1945*. Paris: Plon, 1985, 32–33. (Hereafter *Réconquerir.*)

44. Pierre Debray, "Souvenirs de Pierre Debray," www.marechal-lecler.fr.st/ (downloaded 9 January 2004, 31). (Hereafter Debray.)

45. Jacob L. Devers, "Operation Dragoon: The Invasion of Southern France," *Military Affairs*, Summer 1946, 31. (Hereafter Devers.)

46. Colonel Paul Paillole, *Fighting the Nazis: French Military Intelligence and Counterintelligence 1935–1945* (Enigma Books, 2003), 444. (Hereafter Paillole.)

47. "Bolling Haxall Personal Account, August 11, 1987," www.acu.edu/academics/history/12ad/Museum.html (downloaded 31 May 2004). (Hereafter Bolling Haxall.)

48. De Lattre 201 File, RG 331, NARA.

49. De Lattre, 28.

50. "Seventh Army–The Invasion of Southern France (Draft Copy–Supreme Allied Command–Wilson)," August 1944, G-3 records, Seventh Army. See also Seventh Army G-2 files on French resistance activities, RG 407, NARA.

51. Truscott, 393.

52. Allied Forces Headquarters, "Report on Airborne Operations in 'Dragoon,'" 16 September 1944, Seventh Army records.

53. Truscott, 356, 400.

54. Ibid., 388–397.

55. *Major* Percy Ernst Schramm, "OKW War Diary (1 Apr–18 Dec 1944)," MS # B-034, not dated, National Archives, 103. (Hereafter Schramm.) G-2 Report of operations, Seventh Army, Operations in Europe. Seventh Army G-2 report, 20 August 1944.

56. *General der Infanterie* Friedrich Wiese, "The 19th Army in Southern France (1 July to 15 Sept 1944)," MS # B-787, 11 April 1948, National Archives, 2. (Hereafter Wiese.) *Generalleutnant* Wend von Wietersheim, "The 11th Panzer Division in Southern France (15 August–14 September 1944)," MS # A-880, 4 June 1946, National Archives, 1. (Hereafter Von Wietersheim.)

57. Bennett, 124–127.

58. Samuel J. Newland, *Cossacks in the German Army: 1941–1945* (London: Frank Cass, 1991), 56–63, 104. See also George H. Stein, *The Waffen SS: Hitler's Elite Guard at War 1939–1945* (Ithaca, NY: Cornell University Press, 1966), 179–189.

59. Army B intelligence report, No. 297/RG, "Traitors Among the 'Volksdeutschen' [*sic*] of the Wehrmacht." "Source: SR from secret document. Reliability A/1." 13 September 1944, RG 407, Folder "French Army G-2 Periodic + Isums ML-1088, #2."

60. *Generalinttendent* Otto Witek, "The Department of the Oberquartiermeister of the 19 Army," MS # A-950, 16 June 1950, National Archives, passim. (Hereafter Witek.)

61. *General der Infanterie* Georg Von Sodenstern, "To the History of the Times Preceding the Invasion Engagements in France with Special Regard to the South-French Zone," MS # B-276, 13 December 1950, National Archives, passim.

62. Wiese, 4.

63. Blaskowitz, "Fighting By Armeegruppe 'G' in Southern France until the middle of September 1944," 8ff.

64. Wiese, 4.

65. Except as otherwise noted, this entire section on deception is based on Michael Howard, *Strategic Deception in the Second World War* (London: Pimlico, 1992), particularly 32–33 and 147–159.

66. Paillole, 401.

67. Ibid., 402.

68. Schramm, 99ff.

69. Ibid., 81.

70. Report on Operation Dragoon, Mediterranean Allied Tactical Air Force, 1 November 1944.

71. See Seventh Army G-2 files on French resistance activities, RG 407, NARA. Arthur Brown, "The Jedburghs: A Short History," www.freespace.virgin.net/Arthur.brown2/index.htm (as of May 2004). Art Frizzell, et al., "Office of Strategic Services Operational Groups," www.ossog.org (as of May 2004).

72. Schramm, 102ff. Oberkommando. Armeegruppe G: "Kriegstagebuch Nr. 2 (Führungsabteilung)" 1.7.–30.9.1944.

73. Wiese, 11–12. Von Wietersheim, 3. *Oberstleutnant* Werner Drews, "Remarks Regarding the War History of the Seventh U.S. Army (15 Aug–14 Sep 1944)," MS # A-881, 15 January 1950, National Archives, 2. (Hereafter Drews.)

74. Seventh Army G-2 report, 16 August 1944.

75. Ibid., 20 August 1944.

76. Press conference, 14 August 1944, *Réconquerir*, 36–37.

Chapter 2: Invasion

1. Seventh Army report recorded in G-3 journal, VI Corps, for 18 August 1944. S-3 journal, 141st Infantry Regiment. Breuer, 91–98. Clarke and Smith, 99–101. John Frayn Turner and Robert Jackson, *Destination Berchtesgaden: The Story of the United States Seventh Army in World War II* (New York: Charles Scribner's Sons, 1975), 36. (Hereafter Turner and Jackson.)

2. S-3 journal, 141st Infantry Regiment.

3. De Trez, 5.

4. Ibid., 5. Breuer, 83ff. Clarke and Smith, 98–99.

5. Breuer, 148–149. Muelle, 127. Major General Julian Thompson, *Ready for Anything: The Parachute Regiment at War* (London, UK: Fontana, 1990), 267–269.

6. Clarke and Smith, 102.

7. Allied Forces Headquarters, "Report on Airborne Operations in 'Dragoon,' " 16 September 1944, Seventh Army records. Funk, 102. De Trez, passim.

8. Peek, 56–57.

9. Truscott, 409–412. William B. Breuer, *Operation Dragoon: The Invasion of Southern France* (Novato, CA: Presidio Press, 1987), 168. (Hereafter Breuer.) Clarke and Smith, 83, 97. Winston S. Churchill, *Triumph and Tragedy* (Boston: Houghton-Mifflin, 1953), 94–95.

10. Taggert, 202.

11. Clarke and Smith, 113.

12. Peek, 57–58.

13. S-3 journal, 141st Infantry Regiment.

14. Peek, 59–60. S-3 journal, 141st Infantry Regiment.

15. AAR, 143d Infantry Regiment.

16. AAR, 191st Tank Battalion. S-3 journal, 143d Infantry Regiment. Vincent M. Lockhart, *T-Patch to Victory: The 36th Infantry Division from the Landing in Southern France to the End of World War II* (Canyon, TX: Staked Plains Press, 1981), 13. (Hereafter Lockhart.)

17. AAR, 191st Tank Battalion. S-3 journal, 143d Infantry Regiment.

18. Truscott, 413–414. *The Story of the 36th Infantry Division* (Germany: 36th Infantry Division, 1945), 13. (Hereafter *The Story of the 36th Infantry Division*.) AAR, 142d Infantry Regiment. Breuer, 172–173.

19. Truscott, 413–414. *The Story of the 36th Infantry Division*, 13. AAR, 142d Infantry Regiment. *The 45th*.

20. Clarke and Smith, 108.

21. Taggert, 202, 206–208.

22. Audie Murphy, July 1945, Audie Murphy Research Foundation newsletter, Vol. 4, Spring 1998.

23. John Shirley, *I Remember* (Livermore, CA: Self-published, 2003), 28. (Hereafter Shirley.)

24. G-3 journal, VI Corps. Taggert, 208–209.

25. AAR, 191st Tank Battalion. *The Fighting Forty-Fifth*, 95.

26. G-3 journal, VI Corps. *The Fighting Forty-Fifth*, 95–96.

27. Devers, 29.

28. Truscott, 414ff.

29. Blaskowitz, "Fighting By Armeegruppe 'G' in Southern France until the middle of September 1944," 12. Obkdo. Armeegruppe G: "Kriegstagebuch Nr. 2 (Führungsabteilung)" 1.7.–30.9.1944.

30. Wiese, 14. Clarke and Smith, 106–107.

31. Von Wietersheim, 4. Ralph Bennett, *Ultra in the West: The Normandy Campaign of 1944–45* (New York: Scribner's, 1979), 159. (Hereafter Bennett.)

32. Blaskowitz, "Fighting By Armeegruppe 'G' in Southern France until the middle of September 1944," 13.

33. G-3 journal, VI Corps. Breuer, 206ff.

34. Allied Forces Headquarters, "Report on Airborne Operations in 'Dragoon,' " 16 September 1944, Seventh Army records. De Trez, 67ff.

35. De Trez, 235–236.

36. Muelle, 128–130.

37. Truscott, 418. Taggert, 211. Report of operations, Seventh Army.

38. G-3 journal, VI Corps. Truscott, 418ff.

39. Taggert, 211–212.

40. Clarke and Smith, 119.

41. G-3 journal, VI Corps. *The Fighting Forty-Fifth*, 97.

42. AAR, 142d Infantry Regiment. AAR, Company B, 753d Tank Battalion.

43. AAR, 191st Tank Battalion.

44. G-3 journal, VI Corps. S-3 journal, 141st Infantry Regiment.

45. Clarke and Smith, 122.

46. Wiese, 15.

47. Schramm, 84ff, 104. Obkdo. Armeegruppe G: "Kriegstagebuch Nr. 2 (Führungsabteilung)" 1.7.-30.9.1944. Bennett, 159.

48. Blaskowitz, "Fighting By Armeegruppe 'G' in Southern France until the middle of

September 1944," 14ff. Wiese, 19. Bennett, 159.

49. Wiese, 18–19.

50. Report of operations, Seventh Army.

51. G-3 journal, VI Corps. Taggert, 214.

52. *The Fighting Forty-Fifth*, 97.

53. Seventh Army G-2 reports, 17–18 August 1944.

54. Ibid. G-3 journal, VI Corps. Peek, 60–61.

55. Allied Forces Headquarters, "Report on Airborne Operations in 'Dragoon,'" 16 September 1944, Seventh Army records. AARs, First Airborne Task Force. G-3 journal, VI Corps.

56. De Trez, 108. Message, SHAEF Main to 6th Army Group, 19 October 1944, records of the 6th Army Group, NARA.

57. G-3 journal, VI Corps. Truscott, 422.

58. AAR, CC1, contained in G-3 journal, VI Corps.

59. Truscott, 421.

60. G-3 journal, VI Corps.

61. Seventh Army G-3 daily report, 21 August 1944.

62. Ibid. Truscott, 422–423. De Lattre, 74–75.

63. G-3 journal, VI Corps.

64. Taggert, 215–216.

65. Seventh Army G-2 report, 19 August 1944.

66. *The Fighting Forty-Fifth*, 97–99.

Chapter 3: Breakout and the Battle at Montélimar

1. Unless otherwise noted, the story of Butler Task Force is derived from the following sources: Butler; combat interviews, 36th Infantry Division, Major Samsel, executive officer, 117th Cavalry Reconnaissance Squadron, NARA (Hereafter Samsel); G-3 journal, VI Corps; and Lockhart, 19ff.

2. Obkdo. Armeegruppe G: "Kriegstagebuch Nr. 2 (Führungsabteilung)" 1.7.-30.9.1944.

3. James L. Gilbert and John P. Finnegan, eds., *U.S. Army Signals Intelligence in World War II: A Documentary History* (Washington, DC: Center of Military History, U.S. Army, 1993), 153–154. (Hereafter Gilbert and

Finnegan.)

4. G-3 journal, VI Corps. "Field Order #2 (Dragoon)," Seventh Army G-3 records.

5. Ibid.

6. Ibid.

7. Truscott, 424. Devers, 30.

8. G-3 journal, VI Corps.

9. Obkdo. Armeegruppe G: "Kriegstagebuch Nr. 2 (Führungsabteilung)" 1.7.–30.9.1944. "The Invasion of Southern France," interview with *Rittmeister* Wilhelm Scheidt, ETHINT-19, 17 September 1945, National Archives, 4. G-2 daily report, French Army B, 25 August 1944.

10. Obkdo. Armeegruppe G: "Kriegstagebuch Nr. 2 (Führungsabteilung)" 1.7.–30.9.1944.

11. Report of operations, Seventh Army.

12. Von Wietersheim, 4. Taggert, 216. Report of operations, Seventh Army.

13. Truscott, 424–425.

14. Taggert, 196.

15. G-3 journal, VI Corps.

16. Von Wietersheim, 7.

17. G-3 journal, VI Corps. Taggert, 216.

18. Seventh Army G-2 report, 21 August 1944.

19. Truscott, 426.

20. Taggert, 217.

21. Report of operations, Seventh Army.

22. Truscott, 426.

23. Report of operations, Seventh Army.

24. AAR, 753d Tank Battalion. Samsel.

25. Peek, 61–62.

26. G-3 journal, VI Corps. Lockhart, 17.

27. G-3 journal, VI Corps.

28. AAR, 753d Tank Battalion.

29. Butler, 36.

30. AAR, 753d Tank Battalion. Butler, 36. Combined G-2 and G-3 journal, Task Force Butler.

31. AAR, 141st Infantry Regiment.

32. Truscott, 426–427.

33. G-3 journal, VI Corps.

34. Von Wietersheim, 7.

35. Clarke and Smith, 153.

36. Blaskowitz, "Fighting By Armeegruppe 'G' in Southern France until the middle of September 1944," 15–16.

37. G-3 journal, VI Corps.
38. AAR, 753d Tank Battalion.
39. G-3 journal, VI Corps.
40. AAR, 753d Tank Battalion. Butler, 37.
41. G-3 journal, VI Corps. Truscott, 437.
42. AAR, 141st Infantry Regiment.
43. Ibid. "1st Bn 141st Infantry: Montelimar," contained in combat interviews, 36th Infantry Division, NARA. (Hereafter "1st Bn 141st Infantry: Montelimar.")
44. *The Story of the 36th Infantry Division*, 15.
45. AAR, 753d Tank Battalion.
46. AAR, 141st Infantry Regiment.
47. Ibid.
48. S-3 journal, 141st Infantry Regiment. Butler, 37. "2d Bn 141st Infantry: Montelimar," contained in combat interviews, 36th Infantry Division, NARA. (Hereafter "2d Bn 141st Infantry: Montelimar.")
49. AAR, 141st Infantry Regiment.
50. Von Wietersheim, 7.
51. Report of operations, Seventh Army.
52. AAR, S-3 journal, 141st Infantry Regiment.
53. Truscott, 429. Butler, 37–38.
54. G-3 journal, VI Corps.
55. Von Wietersheim, 8.
56. Peek, 63–64.
57. AAR, 141st Infantry Regiment. "1st Bn 141st Infantry: Montelimar."
58. AAR, 141st Infantry Regiment. "2d Bn 141st Infantry: Montelimar." Lockhart, 34.
59. Peek, 64. Lockhart, 36.
60. Wiese, 21. Von Wietersheim, 8.
61. AAR, 142d Infantry Regiment.
62. AAR, S-3 journal, 143d Infantry Regiment. "With the 636th Tank Destroyers at Valence and Montelimar," combat interviews, 36th Infantry Division, NARA. (Hereafter "With the 636th Tank Destroyers at Valence and Montelimar.")
63. AAR, 143d Infantry Regiment.
64. AAR, Task Force Butler.
65. G-3 journal, VI Corps. AAR, 753d Tank Battalion.
66. G-3 journal, VI Corps.
67. Von Wietersheim, 9.
68. AAR, 142d Infantry Regiment.
69. Ibid. Report of operations, Seventh Army. Clarke and Smith, 159.
70. G-3 journal, VI Corps. "Montelimar Road Blocks, a map contained in combat interviews, 36th Infantry Division, NARA. AAR, combined G-2 and G-3 journal, Task Force Butler.
71. G-3 journal, VI Corps. G-3 report, 36th Infantry Division.
72. G-3 journal, VI Corps.
73. Clarke and Smith, 158.
74. AAR, 753d Tank Battalion.
75. AAR, daily unit report, 143d Infantry Regiment. Lockhart, 42.
76. G-3 journal, VI Corps. AAR, 191st Tank Battalion.
77. G-3 journal, VI Corps. Report of operations, Seventh Army.
78. AAR, 141st Infantry Regiment. "1st Bn 141st Infantry: Montelimar." "With the 636th Tank Destroyers at Valence and Montélimar."
79. AAR, 636th Tank Destroyer Battalion. "With the 636th Tank Destroyers at Valence and Montelimar." Sherman, 98–99. AAR, 141st Infantry Regiment. Clarke and Smith, 159–160. Wiese, 22. Von Wietersheim, 9ff.
80. Von Wietersheim, 10. AAR, 141st Infantry Regiment.
81. AAR, S-3 journal, daily unit report, 143d Infantry Regiment. "3d Bn 143d Inf," combat interviews, 36th Infantry Division, NARA. (Hereafter "3d Bn 143d Inf.")
82. AARs, 141st and 142d Infantry regiments.
83. AAR, 191st Tank Battalion. Von Wietersheim, 10.
84. Combined G-2 and G-3 journal, Task Force Butler.
85. Drews, 3.
86. AAR, 753d Tank Battalion. AAR, Task Force Butler.
87. AAR, 753d Tank Battalion. Combat interviews, 36th Infantry Division, various officers, 3d Battalion, 157th Infantry Regiment, National Archives.
88. AAR, Task Force Butler.
89. AAR, 142d Infantry Regiment.
90. Von Wietersheim, 11.

91. AAR, 753d Tank Battalion.

92. AAR, Task Force Butler.

93. Wiese, 23–24.

94. AAR, 142d Infantry Regiment.

95. AAR, Task Force Butler.

96. AAR, 143d Infantry Regiment. Lockhart, 45.

97. Taggert, 220–221.

98. *The Story of the 36th Infantry Division*, 16.

99. AAR, 191st Tank Battalion.

100. Von Wietersheim, 12.

101. Wiese, 24–25.

102. Schramm, 107.

103. F. W. von Mellenthin, *Panzer Battles* (New York: Ballantine Books, 1971), 382. (Hereafter Von Mellenthin.)

104. Oberkommando der Heeresgruppe G: Anlagen zum Kriegstagebuch Nr. 2 (Führungsabteilung) 1.9.–30.9.1944.

105. Witek, 15.

Chapter 4: Battle for the Ports

1. Frédéric Guelton, "*Les Chefs Militaires Francais et la Realité de la Menace Militaire Soviétique, 1946–1950*," in Jean and Jean Kessler Delmas, eds., *Renseignement et Propaganda Pendant la Guerre Froide (1947–1953)* (Éditions Complexe, 1999), 262–263 and 273 n. 28.

2. Clayton, 293–297.

3. Augustin Guillaume, *Homme de Guerre* (Paris: Éditions France-Empire, 1977), 141–143. (Hereafter Guillaume.)

4. Devers, 31.

5. De la Guéronnière. De Lattre, 72. *Les Cahiers de la Liberation de Toulon.*

6. De Lattre, 67, 72.

7. De Lattre note of 16 July 1944. *Réconquerir*, 31–32.

8. *Hidden Ally*, 209–211, 214–215.

9. De Lattre, 68.

10. De Lattre to de Gaulle, nd., *Réconquerir,* 40. De Lattre, 72.

11. Report to General de Gaulle, 19 August 1944, *Reconquérir*, 42.

12. De Lattre, 70–72.

13. General Saint-Hillier, "L'armée Francaise dans le débarquement de Provence," www.france-libre.net/temoignages-documents/1_6_1_20debarquement_provence .htm (downloaded 13 June 2004).

14. De Lattre, 72–73.

15. Clayton, 271, 277–278.

16. "Tarzan, un blindé du 2eme RSAR," www.memoire-net.org/article.php3?id_ article'170 (downloaded 5 February 2005).

17. De Lattre, 37, 73–74.

18. Myron Echenberg, " '*Morts pour la France*': The African Soldier in France During the Second World War," *Journal of African History*, Volume 26, Number 4, 369–371. (Hereafter Echenberg.)

19. *De l'A.O.F. aux Bords du Rhin: Juillet 1943–Janvier 1945, 9e Division d'Infanterie Coloniale* (Strasbourg?: 1945), np. (Hereafter A.O.F.)

20. De Lattre, 73–74.

21. Ibid., 74–75.

22. Ibid., 75.

23. Armee B, HQ, 2d Bureau, "Bulletin de Renseignements No. 2," 19 August 1944, RG 407, Folder "1st French Army G-2 Periodics."

24. De Lattre, 75.

25. Armee B, HQ, 2d Bureau, "Rapport Quotidien," 21 August 1944, RG 407, Folder "1st French Army G-2 Periodics."

26. Report of operations, Seventh Army.

27. De Lattre, 78. Clayton, 321.

28. Report of operations, Seventh Army.

29. Armee B, HQ, 2d Bureau, "Rapport Quotidien," 20 August 1944, RG 407, Folder "1st French Army G-2 Periodics."

30. De Lattre, 82.

31. Report of operations, Seventh Army.

32. *Oberstleutnant* Hasso Grundmann, et al., "The Landings of the American Seventh Army in Southern France August 1944," MS # C-086, National Archives, 1952, 6, 10, 11.

33. Armee B, HQ, 2d Bureau, "Rapport Quotidien," 20 August 1944, RG 407, Folder "1st French Army G-2 Periodics."

34. Report of operations, Seventh Army.

35. *Les Cahiers de la Liberation de Toulon.* Report of operations, Seventh Army.

36. Report of operations, Seventh Army.

37. *Cahiers de la Liberation de Toulon.*

38. De Lattre, 79. Report of operations, Seventh Army.

39. Report of operations, Seventh Army.

40. *Les Cahiers de la Liberation de Toulon.* Report of operations, Seventh Army.

41. Report of operations, Seventh Army.

42. Ibid.

43. De Lattre, 83.

44. Report of operations, Seventh Army.

45. De Lattre, 84–86.

46. Report of operations, Seventh Army.

47. De Lattre, 94.

48. Ibid., 86–88.

49. Report of operations, Seventh Army.

50. De Lattre, 90. *Les Cahiers de la Liberation de Toulon.*

51. De Lattre, 90–91.

52. Report of operations, Seventh Army.

53. Ibid.

54. Armee B, HQ, 2d Bureau, "Rapport Quotidien," 25 August 1944, RG 407, Folder "1st French Army G-2 Periodics."

55. Report of operations, Seventh Army.

56. *Les Cahiers de la Liberation de Toulon.*

57. Report of operations, Seventh Army.

58. *Les Cahiers de la Liberation de Toulon. A.O.F.*

59. *Les Cahiers de la Liberation de Toulon.*

60. Report of operations, Seventh Army.

61. Ibid.

62. De Lattre, 95.

63. Ibid., 96–97.

64. Report of operations, Seventh Army. De Lattre, 96–97.

65. De Lattre, 96–97. *Generalmajor* Schaefer, "244th Infantry Division, Marseille, 19–28 August 1944." MS # A-884. National Archives, 10–12. (Hereafter Schaefer.)

66. Schaefer, 13–14.

67. Ibid., 21.

68. De Lattre, 95–96.

69. Ibid., 95–97.

70. Clayton, 293.

71. De Lattre, 97.

72. Clayton, 300.

73. De Lattre, 97. Guillaume, 147. Report of operations, Seventh Army.

74. Schaefer, 21–22.

75. De Lattre, 98. Guillaume, 147.

76. Ibid. Schaefer, 24–25.

77. Guillaume, 148.

78. De Lattre, 98. Report of operations, Seventh Army.

79. Report of operations, Seventh Army. Guillaume, 148.

80. Guillaume, 148. Schaefer, 17–18, 31–32. De Lattre, 110.

81. Schaefer, 14.

82. Ibid., 14, 20–24.

83. De Lattre, 102–103.

84. Ibid., 99–100.

85. Ibid., 98–99.

86. De Lattre, 101. Schaefer, 29.

87. De Lattre, 101–102.

88. Ibid., 102–103.

89. Report of operations, Seventh Army. Schaefer, 27–28. De Lattre, 103.

90. Guillaume, 149. Report of operations, Seventh Army.

91. Report of operations, Seventh Army.

92. Guillaume, 149.

93. Alexandre Kaminski, *Les Batailles de la Liberation et de la Revanche 1944–1945 Avec le 2eme Cuirassiers,* www.chars-francais.net /archives/jmo/jmo_2cuir.htm (downloaded 15 August 2005). (Hereafter Kaminski.)

94. Report of operations, Seventh Army. Kaminski. De Lattre, 104–105.

95. Kaminski.

96. De Lattre, 105. Kaminski.

97. Kaminski. Report of operations, Seventh Army.

98. Report of operations, Seventh Army.

99. De Lattre to de Gaulle, 28 August 1944, *Réconquerir,* 47. *Hidden Ally,* 214–215.

100. Report of operations, Seventh Army. Guillaume, 150.

Chapter 5: French Pursuit up the Rhône

1. Nancy Ellen Lawler, *Soldiers of Misfortune: Ivoirien Tirailleurs of World War II* (Athens: Ohio University Press, 1992), 177.

2. Armee B, HQ, 2d Bureau, "Rapport Quotidien," 27 August 1944, RG 407, Folder

"1st French Army G-2 Periodics."

3. De Lattre, 117–121.

4. Ibid., 121.

5. Ibid., 121–122.

6. Ibid., 122. "Field Order #4," Seventh Army G-3 records.

7. De Lattre, 122–123.

8. Ibid., 123, 130.

9. Ibid., 131–132. Général Béthouart, *Cinq Années d'Espérance: Mémoires de Guerre 1939–1945*, Librairie Plon, 1968, 275–276. (Hereafter Béthouart.)

10. De Lattre, 123.

11. Winston S. Churchill, *The Hinge of Fate* (New York: Houghton Mifflin, 1950), 616–617.

12. Ibid., 124–125.

13. Report of operations, Seventh Army.

14. De Lattre, 125–126.

15. Report of operations, Seventh Army.

16. G-3 journal, VI Corps. Report of operations, Seventh Army. Truscott, 434.

17. Report of operations, Seventh Army. De Lattre, 128.

18. Ibid. Carnet du S/Lieutenant de la Roche, *Journal de Marche du 8e Regiment de Chasseurs d'Afrique, 1ère partie,* www.chars-francais.net/archives/jmo/jmo 8rca.htm, downloaded 19 August 2005.

19. Report of operations, Seventh Army.

20. Ibid.

21. Ibid. Army B, Etat Major, "Operation Report No. 20," 7 September 1944, RG 407, Folder "French Army G-2 Periodic + Isums ML-1088, #2."

22. Report of operations, Seventh Army.

23. Except as otherwise noted, the account of the battle of Beaune is taken from Kaminski.

24. De Lattre, 145.

25. HQ Army B, "G-3 Report from 071200B to 081200B," 8 September 1944, RG 407, Folder "French Army G-2 Periodic + Isums ML-1088, #2." Army B situation report to Seventh Army.

26. Report of operations, Seventh Army.

27. De Lattre, 144.

28. Except as otherwise indicated, the account of the battle of Autun is taken from de Lattre,

146–151.

29. *"Le Corps Franc Pommiès—49 R.I.,"* www.gers.pref.gouv.fr/acvg/documents/regiment3.htm. This website, which is the website of Department of Gers, indicates that the material in this document comes from the book *L'Epopée du Corps-France Pommiès*, written by Dominique Lormier.

30. "De Neucheze Rober Jean-Marie," www.gers.pref.gouv.fr/acvg/documents/regiment3.htm.

31. HQ Army B, "G-3 Report for 9 Sept," 10 Sept 1944, RG 407, Folder "French Army G-2 Periodic + Isums ML-1088, #2."

32. Second Army Corps Headquarters, 2d Bureau, "General Operations Order No. 6," 9 September 1944, 2330 hours, RG 407, Folder "French Army G-2 Periodic + Isums ML-1088, #2." Steidl, 10.

33. Ibid., 151–153.

34. Report of operations, Seventh Army.

35. Clarke and Smith, 223.

36. French Army, II Corps Headquarters, "Resume de Renseignements No. 10," 12 September 1944, RG 407, Folder "French Army G-2 Periodic + Isums ML-1088, #2."

37. De Lattre, 154.

38. Ibid., 203.

Chapter 6: End of the Race

1. Report of operations, Seventh Army.

2. AAR, VI Corps.

3. Report of operations, Seventh Army.

4. Ibid.

5. Clarke and Smith, 175.

6. Blaskowitz, "Fighting By Armeegruppe 'G' in Southern France until the middle of September 1944," 20. Oberkommando der Heeresgruppe G: Anlagen zum Kriegstagebuch Nr. 2 (Führungsabteilung) 1.9.-30.9.1944.

7. Schramm, 151–152.

8. G-3 journal, VI Corps.

9. Drews, 4. Report of operations, Seventh Army.

10. "Description of action of Company A, 179th Infantry, in the eastern and southeast-

ern sectors of the town of Meximieux, France, on 1 Sept. 1944," combat interviews, 45th Infantry Division, NARA. "Description of the actions of Co. D, 179th Infantry, in the eastern and southeastern sectors of the town of Meximieux, France, on 1 September 1944," combat interviews, 45th Infantry Division, NARA. AAR, 645th Tank Destroyer Battalion. AAR, VI Corps. Report of operations, Seventh Army. Clarke and Smith, 177.

11. AAR, VI Corps.

12. Ibid. Von Wietersheim, 14.

13. AAR, VI Corps. Taggert, 223.

14. G-3 journal, VI Corps. Report of operations, Seventh Army. Truscott, 434.

15. G-3 journal, VI Corps.

16. G-3 journal, AAR, VI Corps. Von Wietersheim, 14–15. *The Fighting Forty-Fifth*, 101.

17. G-3 journal, VI Corps. Medcos 183, 3 September 1944, Wilson to Air Ministry for British Chiefs of Staff, records of 6th Army Group, NARA. Report of operations, Seventh Army. Truscott, 435–437.

18. G-3 journal, VI Corps. Drews, 4. Report of operations, Seventh Army.

19. Von Wietersheim, 19.

20. G-3 journal, VI Corps.

21. De Lattre, 132–133.

22. Ronald B. Sorobey, "Ukrainians Fight for France," *World War II*, September 2004, 44, 46. (Hereafter Sorobey.) Waller B. Booth, *Mission Marcel-Proust: The Story of an Unusual OSS Undertaking* (Philadelphia: Dorrance, 1972), 84. (Hereafter Booth.)

23. Booth, 33. Sorobey, 43–45.

24. Annex I to "Rapport Quotidian du 2eme Bureau," Armee B, 15 Sept 1944, RG 407, Folder "French Army G-2 Periodic + Isums ML-1088, #1."

25. Booth, 27, 31. Report from 1st DB, reported in the "Rapport Quotidian du 2eme Bureau," Armee B, 19 Sept 1944, RG 407, Folder "French Army G-2 Periodic + Isums ML-1088, #1."

26. De Lattre, 131–132. Béthouart, 275–276. Armee B, Etat-Major, Operations Report No. 17, 2 September 1944, RG 407, Folder

"French Army G-2 Periodic + Isums ML-1088, #2."

27. Truscott, 434–437.

28. De Lattre, 134. Béthouart, 277.

29. Béthouart. De Lattre, 136.

30. De Lattre, 137. Sorobey, 47.

31. Clarke and Smith, 183–184.

32. Blaskowitz, "Fighting By Armeegruppe 'G' in Southern France until the middle of September 1944," 23ff.

33. History, Seventh Army.

34. Taggert, 225. Von Wietersheim, 16.

35. Wiese, 29–30.

36. Untitled draft report, combat interviews, 3d Infantry Division, NARA.

37. Ibid.

38. Taggert, 225–228. AAR and G-3 journal, VI Corps.

39. Report of operations, Seventh Army. AAR, VI Corps.

40. Wiese, 29–30.

41. Sixth Army Group history.

42. Truscott, 439–440.

43. Ibid., 440.

44. The account of the ambush at Glainans is from "L'embuscade de Glainans, 7 Septembre 1944," http://perso.wanadoo.fr/clerval/histoire/embusca.htm (downloaded 10 April 2005). This website is quoting *Les Panaches Rouges: Historique du 3e régiment Algériens de Reconnaissance,*" 1947.

45. Report of operations, Seventh Army. Béthouart, 278–279. Truscott, 438.

46. *Generalmajor* Friedrich von Mellenthin and others, "Army Group G in the period of September to the beginning of December 1944," MS # A-999, 11 July 1950, National Archives, 6. (Hereafter Von Mellenthin and others.)

47. *Führerbefehl*, 17 September 1944.

48. Truscott, 439–440.

49. Von Mellenthin and others, 7.

50. Medcos 181, 2 September 1944, Wilson to Air Ministry for British Chiefs of Staff, records of 6th Army Group, NARA.

51. Sixth Army Group history. Report of operations, Seventh Army. "Seventh Army—The Invasion of Southern France (Draft

Copy—Supreme Allied Command—
Wilson)," August 1944, G-3 records,
Seventh Army.

52. Truscott, 441–444.

53. AAR, VI Corps.

54. De Lattre, 155.

55. Béthouart, 280.

56. De Lattre, 160. Report of operations,
Seventh Army.

57. De Lattre, 161.

58. AAR, 191st Tank Battalion.

59. AARs and S-3 journal, 753d Tank
Battalion.

60. AAR, 645th Tank Destroyer Battalion.
Southern France, 29.

61. Sixth Army Group history. Report of
operations, Seventh Army.

62. *Réconquerir*, 62–63.

63. De Lattre, 171.

64. De Gaulle to de Lattre, 7 October 1944,
Réconquerir, 67–68.

65. Lawler, 178.

66. De Lattre, 166–167, 171. Joseph Issoufou
Conombo, *Souvenirs de Guerre d'un
'Tirailleur Senegalais'* (Paris: L'Harmattan,
1989), 66.

67. De Lattre, 176–178.

68. Letter from de Lattre to Diéthelm, 9
November 1944, *Réconquerir*, 75. Clayton,
264–265, 355.

69. *Réconquerir*, 57–58. De Lattre, 161.

70. De Lattre, 30–31.

71. Ibid., 169.

72. Ibid., 169–172.

73. *Réconquerir*, 58.

74. Ibid., 62–63.

75. De Gaulle to de Lattre, 7 October 1944,
Réconquerir, 67–68.

76. *Réconquerir*, 57.

77. Debray, 31–32. "Paraphrase of State
Department Cable," Paris 59, 19 October
1944. (Hereafter Paris 59.) "Paraphrase of
State Department Cable," Paris 175, 6
October 1944. Both cables are in NARA, RG
319, Entry 58, Box 11, Folder "1. Fr & To
France SD 10-6-44 thru 12-31-45."

78. De Lattre, 176. Paris 59.

79. De Lattre, 176.

80. Brosset memo, 3 November 1944,
Réconquerir, 68–71.

81. De Lattre, 178.

82. Ibid., 179. Raoul Salan, *Mémoires: Fin
d'Un Empire* (Paris: Presses de la Cité, 1970),
138–139, 145. (Hereafter Salan.)

83. De Lattre to Diéthelm, 3 October 1944,
Réconquerir, 67.

84. De Lattre, 179.

Chapter 7: Into the Vosges

1. Report of operations, Seventh Army. AAR,
G-3 journal, VI Corps.

2. Clarke and Smith, 235. G-2 Report of
operations, Seventh Army. *General der
Infanterie* Friederich Wiese, "The 19th Army
in the Belfort Gap, in the Vosges, and in
Alsace from the Middle of September until
18 December 1944," MS # B-781, 8 March
1948, National Archives, 3. (Hereafter Wiese,
"The 19th Army in the Belfort Gap, in the
Vosges, and in Alsace from the Middle of
September until 18 December 1944.")
Generalmajor Joachim Degener, "189th
Infantry Division (Kampfgruppe Degener)
(15 Sep–16 Nov 1944)," MS # B-253, not
dated, National Archives, 1ff. (Hereafter
Degener.) Oberkommando der Heeresgruppe
G: Anlagen zum Kriegstagebuch Nr. 2
(Führungsabteilung) 1.9.–30.9.1944.

3. Wiese, "The 19th Army in the Belfort Gap,
in the Vosges, and in Alsace from the Middle
of September until 18 December 1944," 5.
Degener, 11.

4. *Generalmajor* Hans Taeglichsbeck, "LXIV
Corps Defensive Construction (16 Sep
1944–25 Feb 1945)," MS # B-504), not dated,
National Archives. (Hereafter Taeglichsbeck.)

5. Schramm, 187, 192.

6. AAR, G-3 journal, VI Corps. AAR, 36th
Infantry Division. Report of operations,
Seventh Army.

7. AAR, G-3 journal, VI Corps. Report of
operations, Seventh Army. *The Fighting
Forty-Fifth*, 106–107.

8. AAR, G-3 journal, VI Corps. Report of
operations, Seventh Army.

9. Clarke and Smith, 250–251.

10. Wiese, "The 19th Army in the Belfort Gap, in the Vosges, and in Alsace from the Middle of September until 18 December 1944," 6. Oberkommando der Heeresgruppe G: Anlagen zum Kriegstagebuch Nr. 2 (Führungsabteilung) 1.9.–30.9.1944.

11. G-2 Report of operations, Seventh Army.

12. Report of operations, Seventh Army. AAR and G-3 journal, VI Corps.

13. AAR and G-3 journal, VI Corps. AAR, 36th Infantry Division.

14. AAR and G-3 journal, VI Corps.

15. Steidl, 24.

16. The 45th.

17. AAR, 36th Infantry Division.

18. G-3 journal, VI Corps.

19. Schramm, 194.

20. Clarke and Smith, 248. Oberkommando der Heeresgruppe G: Anlagen zum Kriegstagebuch Nr. 2 (Führungsabteilung) 1.9.–30.9.1944.

21. The Fighting Forty-Fifth, 110.

22. Report of operations, Seventh Army. AAR, 36th Infantry Division.

23. Lockhart, 132.

24. Sixth Army Group history.

25. Truscott, 445.

26. Sixth Army Group history.

27. Ralph Bennet, Ultra in the West: The Normandy Campaign of 1944–45 (New York: Scribners, 1980), 174.

28. Charles B. MacDonald, The Battle of the Bulge (London: Guild Publishing, 1984), 21ff.

29. Von Mellenthin, 372.

30. Von Mellenthin and others, 16–17. Grossjohann, 136–137.

31. Von Mellenthin and others, 16–17.

32. Von Mellenthin, 384.

33. Von Mellenthin and others, 17–22.

34. Report of operations, Seventh Army.

35. G-3 journal, VI Corps. Report of operations, Seventh Army.

36. Sixth Army Group history.

37. Letter from Devers to de Lattre, 2 October 1944, Reconquérir, 89. Report of operations, Seventh Army.

38. De Lattre, 195.

39. Sixth Army Group history. Message from 6th Army Group to SHAEF Main, 23 October 1944, records of the 6th Army Group, NARA.

40. Report of operations, Seventh Army.

41. G-3 journal, VI Corps.

42. Report of operations, Seventh Army.

43. Wiese, 7–8.

44. G-3 journal, VI Corps.

45. Clarke and Smith, 272.

46. Schramm, 202.

47. Generalleutnant Edgar Feuchtinger, "21st Panzer Division in Combat Against American Troops in France and Germany," MS # A-871, 17 December 1949, National Archives, 19ff. (Hereafter Feuchtinger.)

48. Taeglichsbeck.

49. Schramm, 205.

50. Report of operations, Seventh Army.

51. Ancell and Miller, 128.

52. Report of operations, Seventh Army.

53. Ancell and Miller, 354.

54. Clarke and Smith, 255–256. Martin Blumenson, "Politics and the Military in the Liberation of Paris," Parameters, Summer 1998, 4–14, reproduced at the U.S. Army War College online, http://carlisle-www.army.mil/usawc/Parameters/98summer/blumenso.htm. John Keegan, Six Armies in Normandy: From D-Day to the Liberation of Paris (New York: Penguin, 1982), 303.

55. Report of operations, Seventh Army.

56. G-3 journal, VI Corps, 1 October 1944.

57. G-3 journal, VI Corps.

58. G-2 Intsum 143, VI Corps, 1 October 1944. G-3 journal, VI Corps. "Notes from OB Team, 79th Inf Div—Action Foret de Parroy 28 Sept–1 Oct," memo contained in combat interviews, 79th Infantry Division, NARA. Oberkommando der Heeresgruppe G: Anlagen zum Kriegstagebuch Nr. 2 (Führungsabteilung) 1.9.-30.9.1944.

59. Combat interviews, Major Gooding, 79th Infantry Division, NARA.

60. Report of operations, Seventh Army. Combat interviews, 79th Infantry Division, NARA. Clarke and Smith, 270. Bennett, 175.

61. Report of operations, Seventh Army. G-3 journal, VI Corps. Clarke and Smith,

290–291. De Lattre, 192–193.

62. Truscott, 446.

63. Ancell and Miller, 34.

64. Report of operations, Seventh Army. G-3 journal, VI Corps.

65. AAR, 45th Infantry Division. *The Fighting Forty-Fifth*, 116–119.

66. Report of operations, Seventh Army. G-3 journal, VI Corps.

67. Ibid.

68. Steidl, 60. Clarke and Smith, 325.

69. Report of operations, Seventh Army. G-3 journal, VI Corps.

70. Report of operations, Seventh Army. Sixth Army Group history.

71. Report of operations, Seventh Army.

72. Keith E. Bonn, *When the Odds Were Even* (Novato, CA: Presidio Press, 1994), 96–97. (Hereafter Bonn.) Clarke and Smith, 327.

73. Report of operations, Seventh Army.

74. Feuchtinger, 23. Clarke and Smith, 271 fn, 334–336.

75. "Operations of the Second French Armored Division From D-Day Through the Liberation of Strasbourg," undated operations report contained in French First Army G-3 operations reports, National Archives. (Hereafter "Operations of the French Second Armored Division.") Report of operations, Seventh Army.

76. De Lattre, 182–185.

77. Ibid., 187. Charles de Gaulle, *The War Memoirs of Charles de Gaulle: Salvation 1944–1946* (New York: Simon and Schuster, 1960), 162. (Hereafter *War Memoirs, Vol. III.*)

78. De Lattre, 187–193.

79. Ibid., 194. *Reconquérir*, 88.

80. Letter from de Lattre to Diéthelm, 3 October 1944 *Reconquérir*, 67.

81. De Lattre, 195–197.

82. Guillaume, 155.

83. De Lattre, 197–198.

84. Guillaume, 157–158. De Lattre, 198–199. Wiese, "The 19th Army in the Belfort Gap, in the Vosges, and in Alsace from the middle of September until 13 December 1944," Foreign Military Study B-781, 3.

85. De Lattre, 197. First French Army, "Account of Operations," 8 October 1944, RG 407, Folder "Fr Army (Outgoing Messages)."

86. Guillaume, 157–158. First French Army, "Operations Summary," 6 October 1944, RG 407, Folder "Fr Army (Outgoing Messages)."

87. *Face aux Marocains*, 151–152.

88. First French Army, "Account of Operations," 9 October 1944, RG 407, Entry 427, Box 24219, Folder "Fr Army (Outgoing Messages)."

89. Guillaume, 158.

90. Ibid., 158–159. First French Army, "G-3 Report from 161200A to 171200A." 17 October 1944, RG 407, Folder "Fr Army (Outgoing Messages)." Debray, 30–31.

91. First French Army, "Summary of Operations on Day 17 October 1944," 17 October 1944, RG 407, Folder "Fr Army (Outgoing Messages)." Guy Deltell, "La bataille du Faing-Béret (Haut du Faing)," http://mapage.noos.fr/4edmm/la_bataille_du_faing-beret.htm (downloaded 17 June 2005). (Hereafter Deltell.) De Lattre, 202.

92. Deltell. Guillaume, 158–159.

93. First French Army, "Summary of Operations on Day 17 October 1944," 17 October 1944, RG 407, Folder "Fr Army (Outgoing Messages)." De Lattre, 202.

94. De Lattre, 202–203.

95. "General Operations Order No. 43," II Corps, 22 October 1944, RG 407, Folder "Armee B (FR) Intell Rpts. Nov 44 ML-1099." De Lattre, 207.

96. Guillaume, 159–160.

97. De Lattre, 203–205.

98. Sixth Army Group history. Sixth Army Group G-2 summary, 28 October 1944.

99. Sixth Army Group history.

100. Von Mellenthin and others, 28–29.

101. Schramm, 207.

102. Report of operations, Seventh Army.

Chapter 8: First to the Rhine

1. Sixth Army Group history.

2. Von Mellenthin, 385.

3. Von Mellenthin and others, 38–39.

4. Report of operations, Seventh Army.

5. *Face aux Marocains*, 158–159.
6. Ibid.
7. Sixth Army Group history. Clark and Smith, 368ff. Von Mellenthin and others, 60–61.
8. Ibid., 63, 72–73. Obkdo. Heeresgruppe G: "Anlagen (Chefsachen) zum Kriegstagebuch Nr. 3 der Führungsabteilung v. 1.10.–31.12.44."
9. AAR, 813th Tank Destroyer Battalion.
10. De Lattre, 1952, 214.
11. Béthouart, 290. *Face aux Marocains*, 160.
12. Guillaume, 159.
13. De Lattre, 1952, 215.
14. Ibid., 223. Béthouart, 288–289.
15. De Lattre, 1952, 216–217, 224.
16. Ibid., 1952, 224. Béthouart, 291.
17. First French Army, "Account of Operations," 17 November 1944, RG 407, Folder "Fr Army (Outgoing Messages)."
18. De Lattre, 1952, 220–222.
19. Paillole, 402–403. De Lattre, 1952, 217–219.
20. Raymond Lescastreyres, "Souvenirs de Guerre d'un Jeune Francais," www.duhamel.bz/souvenir/ (downloaded 20 August 2005).
21. De Lattre, 1952, 225–226. Béthouart, 292. Salan, 134.
22. De Lattre, 1952, 226–227.
23. Béthouart, 292.
24. De Lattre, 228. 6th Army Group History, 48.
25. Béthouart, 294–295. De Lattre, 1952, 229.
26. *Face aux Marocains*, 161–162. Béthouart, 294–295. De Lattre, 1952, 229–230.
27. De Lattre, 231. *A.O.F.*
28. Except as otherwise noted, the account of the battle of Écot is from Salan, 134–136.
29. *A.O.F.*
30. Salan, 136–137.
31. Béthouart, 295. Paillole, 402–403. De Lattre, 218, 231.
32. De Lattre, 232–233.
33. De Lattre, 1952, 233–234. *Face aux Marocains*, 164–167. First French Army, "G-3 Report" 17 November 1944, RG 407, Folder "Fr Army (Outgoing Messages)." See also

First French Army, "Account of Operations," 16 November 1944, RG 407, Folder "Fr Army (Outgoing Messages)."
34. De Lattre, 234–235.
35. The battle of Héricourt is recounted in de Lattre, 1952, 235–237, and *Face aux Marocains*, 168–171. See also First French Army, "Account of Operations," 17 November 1944, RG 407, Folder "Fr Army (Outgoing Messages)."
36. De Lattre, 1952, 237. "Journal de Marche du 1er Regiment de Chasseurs d'Afrique," www.chars-francais.net/archives/jmo/jmo_1rca.htm (downloaded 19 August 2005).
37. De Lattre, 1952, 237.
38. Ibid., 1952, 238–239.
39. Béthouart, 296–297. De Lattre, 1952, 247.
40. De Lattre, 1952, 248–249. 1st French Army, HQ, 2eme Bureau, "Rapport Quotidien du 2eme Bureau," 19 November 1944, RG 407, Folder "First French Army G-2 Periodic Reports."
41. The charge to the Rhine is described in de Lattre, 1952, 248–249.
42. Photograph "Terre 10035 L05" available at www.ecpad.fr.
43. De Lattre, 1952, 249–250.
44. Clarke and Smith, 371.
45. AAR, G-2 daily reports, Seventh Army.
46. "Operations of the French Second Armored Division." Report of operations, Seventh Army.
47. *La 2e DB Général Leclerc Combattant et Combats en France* (Paris: Arts et Métiers Graphique), 1945, 247–253. (Hereafter *2e DB*.)
48. G-2 daily report, Seventh Army.
49. AAR, 45th Infantry Division.
50. G-2 periodic report, French 2d Armored Division, 26 November 1944. Report of operations, Seventh Army.
51. Debray, 35. "Operations of the French Second Armored Division." Report of operations, Seventh Army.
52. "Operations of the French Second Armored Division." Report of operations, Seventh Army.

53. Ibid.
54. Report of operations, Seventh Army.
55. G-2 daily reports, Seventh Army.
56. Report of operations, Seventh Army. G-3 journal, VI Corps.
57. Report of operations, Seventh Army.
58. Schramm, 235–238.
59. Obkdo. Heeresgruppe G: "Anlagen (Chefsachen) zum Kriegstagebuch Nr. 3 der Führungsabteilung v. 1.10.–31.12.44."
60. Report of operations, Seventh Army. AAR, 45th Infantry Division.
61. Helmut Ritgen, *West-Front 1944* (Stuttgart: Motorbuch Verlag, 2001), 194ff.
62. De Lattre, 1952, 252–255.
63. Ibid., 1952, 242–247.
64. Ibid., 1952, 259–262. *Face aux Marocains*, 180.
65. Ibid., 1952, 262–264. Von Mellenthin and others, 74. Grossjohann, 149. 1st French Army, HQ, 2eme Bureau, "Rapport Quotidien du 2eme Bureau," 23 November 1944, RG 407, Folder "First French Army G-2 Periodic Reports."
66. De Lattre, 1952, 264.
67. Grossjohann, 149–150.
68. *Face aux Marocains*, 180.
69. De Lattre, 1952, 271–278. *30th Waffen SS Division*, 28, 36, 38.
70. De Lattre, 1952, 279.
71. Ibid., 281–284. De Lattre to Diéthelm, 28 November 1944, *Réconquerir*, 112.
72. Report of operations, Seventh Army.
73. G-2 periodic report, French 2d Armored Division, 26 November 1944.
74. Ibid.
75. AAR, G-2 daily reports, Seventh Army.
76. Schramm, 239.
77. Report of operations, Seventh Army. Capt. Joseph Carter, *The History of the 14th Armored Division* (The Division: np. [1945]). (Hereafter Carter.)
78. Clarke and Smith, 458–459.
79. Sixth Army Group history. Report of operations, Seventh Army. Clarke and Smith, 440.
80. Report of operations, Seventh Army.
81. AAR, 45th Infantry Division.
82. Sixth Army Group history.

Chapter 9: Stopped Again

1. Report of operations, Seventh Army.
2. Ibid. Clarke and Smith, 467–468.
3. Ibid.
4. Report of operations, Seventh Army. H. K. Brown, "H. K. Brown's WW II 1944–1945 Diary," www.eastmill.com/103rd/compos/410/hk/index.htm.
5. Ibid. *The Fighting Forty-Fifth*, 126.
6. Report of operations, Seventh Army.
7. Carter.
8. *The Fighting Forty-Fifth*, 127.
9. Ibid., 126–127. Report of operations, Seventh Army.
10. Report of operations, Seventh Army.
11. *The Fighting Forty-Fifth*, 127.
12. Report of operations, Seventh Army.
13. Obkdo. Heeresgruppe G: "Anlagen (Chefsachen) zum Kriegstagebuch Nr. 3 der Führungsabteilung v. 1.10.–31.12.44."
14. Report of operations, Seventh Army.
15. G-3 journal, VI Corps.
16. Report of operations, Seventh Army.
17. Ibid.
18. Ibid. Combat interviews, 100th Infantry Division, NARA.
19. De Lattre, 285–286.
20. Ibid., 285–295.
21. "Rapport Quotidien," 1st French Army, G-2, 11 February 1945, Annex IV, RG 407, Folder "G-2 Periodic Reports 1st French Army."
22. De Lattre, 296–299.
23. Sixth Army Group history.
24. Report of operations, Seventh Army.

Chapter 10: Operation *Nordwind*

1. Obkdo. Heeresgruppe G: "Anlagen (Chefsachen) zum Kriegstagebuch Nr. 3 der Führungsabteilung v. 1.10.–31.12.44." *Oberst (I.G.)* Horst Wilutzky, "The Attack of Army Group G in Northern Elsass in January 1945," MS # B-095, 8 September 1950, National Archives. (Hereafter Wilutzky, "The

Attack of Army Group G.") Report of operations, Seventh Army.

2. Gilbert and Finnegan, 154. G-2 estimate, Seventh Army, 29 December 1944.

3. "Rapport Quotidien," 1st French Army, G-2, 25 December 1944, RG 407, Folder "Folder #1 First French Army G-2 Periodic Reports."

4. Report of operations, Seventh Army.

5. Sixth Army Group history.

6. Report of operations, Seventh Army. Sixth Army Group history.

7. Clarke and Smith, 497.

8. Sixth Army Group history.

9. Report of operations, Seventh Army.

10. Ibid. Sixth Army Group history.

11. Forces Francaise Libre, 1ère Division, Etat-Major, "Operations Order No. 1," 1 January 1945, NARA, RG 407, Folder "G-2 Reports, First French Army."

12. Report of operations, Seventh Army.

13. G-3 journal, VI Corps.

14. Obkdo. Heeresgruppe G: "Anlagen (Chefsachen) zum Kriegstagebuch Nr. 3 der Führungsabteilung v. 1.10.–31.12.44." Wilutzky, "The Attack of Army Group G." Report of operations, Seventh Army. Clarke and Smith, 498.

15. Report of operations, Seventh Army.

16. Combat interviews, 44th Infantry Division, NARA. *Generalleutnant* of the Waffen SS Max Simon, "Comment on the Report of 20 Nov 47 on Operation 'Nordwind' ('Sylvester Offensive') by Oberst Einem," MS # C-039, November 1948, National Archives. (Hereafter Simon.) *Oberst* Kurt Von Einem, "Bericht Über die Kämpfe des XIII. S.S. A.K. in Lothringen in der Zeit vom 8. November 1944–12. January 45," MS # B-780, 20 November 1947, National Archives.

17. Report of operations, Seventh Army.

18. Ibid.

19. Combat interviews, Seventh Army, NARA.

20. Report of operations, Seventh Army. *Generalmajor* Alfred Philippi, "361st Volksgrenadier Division (24 Dec 1944–12 Jan 1945," MS # B-428, 22 February 1947,

National Archives. (Hereafter Philippi.)

21. Combat interviews, 14th Armored Division, NARA. Carter. S-3 journal, 117th Cavalry Reconnaissance Squadron.

22. Combat interviews, Seventh Army, NARA.

23. Report of operations, Seventh Army.

24. AAR, 45th Infantry Division.

25. Ibid. Report of operations, Seventh Army. Philippi.

26. AAR, 45th Infantry Division.

27. Report of operations, Seventh Army. Sixth Army Group history.

28. Clarke and Smith, 497.

29. Report of operations, Seventh Army.

30. Eisenhower, 362–363. *War Memoirs, Vol. III*, 169.

31. Charles Whiting, *The Other Battle of the Bulge: Operation Northwind* (Chelsea, MI: Scarborough House, 1990), 44. (Hereafter Whiting, *The Other Battle of the Bulge.*)

32. De Lattre, 307.

33. Report of operations, Seventh Army.

34. Simon.

35. AAR, 45th Infantry Division.

36. AARs, 45th and 70th Infantry divisions. Phillipi.

37. AAR, 45th Infantry Division.

38. Wilutzky, "The Attack of Army Group G."

39. AARs, 45th and 70th Infantry divisions.

40. Ibid., 45th Infantry Division.

41. Ibid., 70th Infantry Division.

42. Ibid., 45th Infantry Division.

43. *Trailblazers* (Paris: *Stars and Stripes*, 1945). AAR, 70th Infantry Division.

44. AARs, 45th and 70th Infantry divisions.

45. Ibid., 70th Infantry Division.

46. Feuchtinger, 50. Wilutzky, "The Attack of Army Group G."

47. Obkdo. Heeresgruppe G: "Anlagen (Chefsachen) zum Kriegstagebuch Nr. 3 der Führungsabteilung v. 1.10.-31.12.44." *General der Waffen SS* Erich von dem Bach-Zelewski, "The XIV. SS Corps in November–December 1944," MS # B-252, 7 December 1946, National Archives. (Hereafter Von dem Bach-Zelewski.) *Generalmajor* Gerhard Hüther, "Commitment of 553d Volksgrenadier

Division, December 1944 to March 1945," MS # B-177, 6 October 1950, National Archives. Operations report and G-2 history, Seventh Army.

48. Report of operations, Seventh Army. Combat interviews, 42d Infantry Division, NARA.

49. Report of operations, Seventh Army.

50. Feuchtinger, 48, 50. Von dem Bach-Zelewski. Wilutzky, "The Attack of Army Group G."

51. Report of operations, Seventh Army.

52. Ibid. "Initial Assault on Herrlisheim by the 56th Armored Infantry Battalion and the 714th Tank Battalion," Seventh Army, available at www.12tharmoredmuseum.org. (Hereafter "Initial Assault on Herrlisheim.")

53. Report of operations, Seventh Army.

54. Combat interviews, 79th Infantry Division, NARA.

55. Ibid., 42d Infantry Division, NARA.

56. Corson, William. "Captured in Hatten, Part 3: Captain William Corson's speech," www.tankbooks.com/stories/schmidt3.htm. (Hereafter Corson.)

57. Combat interviews, 42d Infantry Division, NARA.

58. Carter.

59. Report of operations, Seventh Army. Combat interviews, 79th Infantry Division, NARA. Combat interviews, 14th Armored Division, NARA. Corson. Carter.

60. Ibid. Combat interviews, 14th Armored Division, NARA.

61. "Initial Assault on Herrlisheim."

62. Wilutzky, "The Attack of Army Group G." Report of operations, Seventh Army. Combat interviews, 79th Infantry Division, NARA. Combat interviews, 14th Armored Division, NARA. Carter.

63. "Initial Assault on Herrlisheim."

64. Report of operations, Seventh Army. Combat interviews, 79th Infantry Division, NARA. Corson.

65. G-2 history, Seventh Army.

66. Clarke and Smith, 522.

67. Report of operations, Seventh Army. Combat interviews, 79th Infantry Division, NARA. Combat interviews, 14th Armored Division, NARA.

68. Carter.

69. Report of operations, Seventh Army.

70. Combat interviews, 79th Infantry Division, NARA.

71. Report of operations, Seventh Army. Combat interviews, 79th Infantry Division, NARA. Combat interviews, 14th Armored Division, NARA.

72. Wilutzky, "The Attack of Army Group G."

73. Combat interviews, 79th Infantry Division, NARA.

74. Ibid., 14th Armored Division, NARA.

75. Report of operations, Seventh Army. Combat interviews, 79th Infantry Division, NARA. Combat interviews, 14th Armored Division, NARA.

76. Report of operations, Seventh Army. Combat interviews, 14th Armored Division, NARA.

77. Combat interviews, 14th Armored Division, NARA.

78. Report of operations, Seventh Army.

79. Ibid. Combat interviews, 12th Armored Division, NARA

80. Report of operations, Seventh Army. AAR, 12th Armored Division. Combat interviews, 12th Armored Division, NARA. Accounts of Carl Helton, James Lynch, Carl Lyons, Nicholas Novosel, and Robert Wilken, The 12th Armored Division Memorial Museum, www.acu.edu/academics/history/12ad/Museum.html.

81. Report of operations, Seventh Army. Combat interviews, 12th Armored Division, NARA

82. Report of operations, Seventh Army.

83. Ibid.

84. Ibid.

85. Ibid.

86. Willam L. Shirer, *The Rise and Fall of the Third Reich* (New York: Fawcett Crest, 1983), 1424–1425. Chester Wilmot, *The Struggle for Europe* (Ware, England: Wordsworth Editions Limited, 1997), 622–623, 663–664.

87. Report of operations, Seventh Army.

Chapter 11: Crushing the Colmar Pocket

1. *Face aux Marocains*, 219 (photo).
2. Clarke and Smith, 537.
3. Report of operations, Seventh Army.
4. Yves Gras, *La 1ère DFL, Les Francais Libres au Combat* (Paris: Presses de la Cité, 1983), 401–402.
5. Clarke and Smith, 508, 537–538.
6. Ibid., 538. De Lattre, 338.
7. Béthouart, 310–311.
8. Ibid., 311. De Lattre, 335.
9. De Lattre, 335. Report of operations, Seventh Army. De Lattre to Béthouart, 11 January 1945, *Réconquerir*, 156–157.
10. De Lattre, 335. Report of operations, Seventh Army.
11. Clarke and Smith, 538–539. Report of operations, Seventh Army. De Lattre, 336.
12. Report of operations, Seventh Army. De Lattre, 336.
13. De Lattre, 338–339. Béthouart, 311–312. *Réconquerir*, 171.
14. De Lattre, 1952, 343.
15. Béthouart, 312. Clarke and Smith, 539. 1st French Army, HQ, 2eme Bureau, "Rapport Quotidien du 2eme Bureau," 21 January 1945, RG 407, Folder "First French Army G-2 Periodic Reports Part II."
16. 1st French Army, HQ, 2eme Bureau, "Rapport Quotidien du 2eme Bureau," 22 January 1945, RG 407, Folder "First French Army G-2 Periodic Reports Part II." Clarke and Smith, 539.
17. Clarke and Smith, 539. De Lattre, 347.
18. French Army, HQ, 2eme Bureau, "Rapport Quotidien du 2eme Bureau," 22 January 1945, RG 407, Folder "First French Army G-2 Periodic Reports Part II."
19. Béthouart, 313–314.
20. Ibid., 314.
21. De Lattre, 350.
22. Clarke and Smith, 539–541. De Lattre, 351. Béthouart, 314. Sixth Army Group History.
23. Report of operations, Seventh Army.
24. De Lattre, 355–356. Clarke and Smith, 536. Report of operations, Seventh Army.
25. Clarke and Smith, 541. Report of operations, Seventh Army.
26. Report of operations, Seventh Army.
27. Combat Interviews, 3d Infantry Divivision, "La Maison Rouge—The Colmar Pocket 22 Jan–8 Feb," NARA.
28. Report of operations, Seventh Army. Gras, 403–404.
29. Unless otherwise noted, this account is drawn from combat interviews, 3d Infantry Division, "La Maison Rouge—The Colmar Pocket 22 Jan–8 Feb," NARA.
30. Report of operations, Seventh Army.
31. Combat interviews, 3d Infantry Divivision, "La Maison Rouge—The Colmar Pocket 22 Jan–8 Feb," NARA. Report of operations, Seventh Army.
32. Report of operations, Seventh Army. "Bulletin de Renseignements Nr. 124," 25 January 1945, 2d DB, RG 407, Folder "G-2 Reports, First French Army." "One-Man Stand at Holzwihr," www.tankdestroyersociety.com/audie_murphys_one.htm (as of June 2005). Audie Murphy, *To Hell and Back* (New York: Henry Holt and Company, 2002), 232ff.
33. The account of the battle for the Chateau de Schoppenwihr is from combat interviews, 3d Infantry Divivision, "Colmar Pocket," NARA.
34. Report of operations, Seventh Army.
35. Ibid. Sixth Army Group History, Ch. 6, 77–83. Gras, 410–411.
36. Report of operations, Seventh Army.
37. Ibid.
38. Ibid.
39. Unless otherwise noted, this account is drawn from combat interviews, 3d Infantry Divivision, "Colmar Pocket," NARA.
40. Report of operations, Seventh Army.
41. "Rapport Quotidien," 1st French Army, G-2, 3 February 1945, RG 407, Folder "G-2 Periodic Reports 1st French Army."
42. Report of operations, Seventh Army.
43. Ibid.
44. Ibid.
45. Ibid.

Chapter 12: Across the Rhine

1. De Lattre, 1952, 405–406. Béthouart, 318.

2. De Lattre, 1952, 407–408. *War Memoirs, Vol. III*, 174–175.

3. De Lattre, 1952, 407.

4. Report of operations, Seventh Army.

5. De Lattre, 1952, 409–410, 419–420. Guillaume, 170.

6. Report of operations, Seventh Army.

7. Ibid.

8. Ibid.

9. Ibid.

10. Ibid.

11. Charles B. MacDonald, *The Last Offensive: United States Army in World War II, The European Theater of Operations* (Washington, DC: Center of Military History, U.S. Army, 1990), 258–259.

12. Report of operations, Seventh Army.

13. *Oberst (I.G.)* Horst Wilutzky, "The Fighting of Heeresgruppe 'G' in the West: The Final Battle in Central and Southern Germany Until the Surrender (22 Mar 45–6 May 45)," MS # B-703, not dated, National Archives. (Hereafter Wilutzky, "The Final Battle.")

14. Report of operations, Seventh Army.

15. AAR, 45th Infantry Division.

16. Report of operations, Seventh Army.

17. Wilutzky, "The Final Battle."

18. Sixth Army Group history.

19. Wilutzky, "The Final Battle."

20. AAR, 45th Infantry Division. Report of operations, Seventh Army.

21. *The Fighting Forty-Fifth*, 157. Wilutzky, "The Final Battle."

22. *The Fighting Forty-Fifth*, 157.

23. Report of operations, Seventh Army. Wilutzky, "The Final Battle."

24. Report of operations, Seventh Army.

25. Wilutzky, "The Final Battle."

26. AAR, 45th Infantry Division.

27. G-3 journal, VI Corps.

28. AAR, 45th Infantry Division. *The Fighting Forty-Fifth*, 162ff.

29. G-2 history, Seventh Army.

30. Wilutzky, "The Final Battle."

31. De Lattre, 1952, 419–420.

32. Béthouart, 319. *War Memoirs, Vol. III*, 177–178.

33. De Lattre, 1952, 422–427.

34. *Face aux Marocains*, 230–232.

35. De Lattre, 1952, 428.

36. Ibid., 428–29. Béthouart, 319.

37. De Lattre, 438–441. *Face aux Marocains*, 238.

38. *Face aux Marocains*, 234. De Lattre, 435.

39. Yves Salmon, "Campagne d'Allemagne," March 2001, http://papymac.free.fr/Allemagne_campagne.html (downloaded 15 July 2005).

40. Ibid.

41. Operations report and G-2 history, Seventh Army.

42. Report of operations, Seventh Army. Battalion history, 781st Tank Battalion; *Up From Marseille*, 22; Whiting, *America's Forgotten Army*, 193ff. G-3 journal, VI Corps. Wilutzky, "The Final Battle." *Terrify and Destroy: The Story of the 10th Armored Division* (Paris: Stars and Stripes, 1945). *Generalmajor* Wolf-Rüdiger Hauser, "Report on the Combat Engagements Within the Framework of the First Army During the Period From 24 March to 2 May 1945," MS # B-348, 12 September 1946, National Archives. (Hereafter Hauser.)

43. Search for "warcrimes," Axis History Forum, www.axishistory.com.

44. AAR, 45th Infantry Division.

45. Wilutzky, "The Final Battle."

46. Report of operations, Seventh Army.

47. AAR, 45th Infantry Division. Wilutzky, "The Final Battle." Hauser.

48. G-3 periodic report for 20 April 1944, XV Corps.

49. De Lattre, 252–253.

50. *General der Panzertruppen* Erich Brandenberger, "Seventh Army from 16 December 1944 to 16 January 1945. Nineteenth Army from 28 March to 5 May 1945," MS # A-934, 15 May 1950, National Archives. (Hereafter Brandenberger.)

51. De Lattre, 252–253. Jean-Christophe Notin, *Les Vaincus Seront les Vainqueurs: La France en Allemagne 1945* (Paris: Perrin,

2004), 170. (Hereafter Notin.)

52. Brandenberger.

53. De Lattre, 448–457, 467–481. Béthouart, 325–326.

54. De Lattre, 458.

55. Ibid., 459.

56. Béthouart, 322.

57. De Lattre, 471, 482.

58. G-3 journal, VI Corps.

59. Béthouart, 324–325. De Lattre, 485–486.

60. Sixth Army Group history. Béthouart, 324–325. De Lattre, 485–486.

61. De Lattre, 482–483.

62. Sixth Army Group history.

63. Eisenhower, 412–413.

64. De Lattre, 460–465.

65. Ibid., 490. Eisenhower, 412–413.

66. Eisenhower, 412–413. De Lattre, 491. Yves Salmon, "Campagne d'Allemagne," March 2001, papymac.free.fr/Allemagne_cam-pagne.html (downloaded 15 July 2005). Notin, 267–268.

67. Yves Salmon, "Campagne d'Allemagne," March 2001, http://papymac.free.fr/ Allemagne_campagne.html (downloaded 15 July 2005).

68. Telegram Devers to De Lattre, 26 April 1945, *Reconquérir*, 252.

69. Notin, 263. Letter from Guillaume to Monsabert, 27 April 1945, *Reconquérir*, 255.

70. *Reconquérir*, 252–253.

71. De Lattre, 491–492.

72. Eisenhower, 412–413.

73. Report of operations, Seventh Army.

74. Sixth Army Group history.

75. Debray, 50.

76. Ibid., 50–51.

77. Notin, 359.

78. Ibid.

79. G-3 journal, VI Corps.

80. Brandenberger.

81. G-3 journal, VI Corps. Sixth Army Group history.

82. G-3 journal, VI Corps.

83. Sixth Army Group history.

84. De Lattre, 520.

85. Sixth Army Group history.

INDEX

8/08